PRAISE THE LORD FOR TAX EXEMPTION

OTHER BOOKS BY THE AUTHORS

by C. Stanley Lowell

PROTESTANT-CATHOLIC MARRIAGE
THE EMBATTLED WALL
THE ECUMENICAL MIRAGE

by Martin A. Larson

MILTON AND SERVETUS
THE THEORY OF LOGICAL EXPRESSION
THE MODERNITY OF MILTON
THE PLASTER SAINT
THE RELIGION OF THE OCCIDENT
CHURCH WEALTH AND BUSINESS INCOME
THE ESSENE HERITAGE
THE GREAT TAX FRAUD

PRAISE THE LORD

FOR

TAX EXEMPTION

HOW THE CHURCHES GROW RICH—
WHILE THE CITIES AND *YOU* GROW POOR

Martin A. Larson

C. Stanley Lowell

ROBERT B. LUCE, INC.

WASHINGTON-NEW YORK

This work is dedicated to the principle of church-state separation and to all those who, in ages past or in the present time, have worked and fought to maintain it.

THE FIRST AMENDMENT:

"Congress shall make no law respecting an establishment of religion, or prohibiting the free exercise thereof. . . . ."

THOMAS JEFFERSON:

". . . . to compel a man to furnish contributions of money for the propagation of opinions he disbelieves and abhors, is sinful and tyrannical. . . . ."

> The 1779 Virginia Bill for
> Establishing Religious Freedom

ULYSSES S. GRANT:

"Leave the matter of religion to the family, the altar, the church, and the private school, supported entirely by private contributions. Keep the church and state forever separate."

> Speech delivered in Des
> Moines, Iowa, 1875. Reported
> in 22 *Catholic World* 33, 1876

POPE PIUS IX:

Mortal Error # 55 is that "The Church must be separated from the State and the State from the Church."

> *Syllabus of Errors,* promul-
> gated December 8, 1864

FATHER RICHARD GINDER:

"The Catholic Church must be the biggest corporation in the U.S. We have a branch in almost every neighborhood. Our assets and real estate holdings must exceed those of Standard Oil, A.T.&T., and U.S. Steel combined. And our roster of duespaying members must be second only to the tax-rolls of the U.S. government."

> *Our Sunday Visitor,*
> May 22, 1960

EUGENE CARSON BLAKE:

"Twice in the last twelve months, I have been in communist Europe. It is quite clear to me, as it was not before I went, that one of the reasons for what popular support remains for the communist governments is the people's satisfaction that at least one good thing was accomplished—that the wealth and political domination of the church has been broken."

> *The Churchman,*
> December 1, 1956

FOREWORD

A definitive work on the status of religious tax-exemption is past due. Those concerned with the health of the religious enterprise as well as that of the secular community cannot fail to be impressed with the relevance of church tax-exemptions. The long-continued policy of government which requires neither the payment of taxes by churches nor the filing of reports of income and assets, has helped to create a church-financial colossus.

As this is being written, both the Ways and Means Committee of the House and the Finance Committee of the Senate are engaged in intensive study of tax reform. One of the focal points of their concern has been religious exemptions. Witnesses at the public hearings have repeatedly urged that tax loopholes favoring the churches should be closed. Such testimony has come not from the secular community alone, but from prominent churchmen as well. Some of the churchmen have been among the first to see that certain of the present exemptions cannot be prolonged without jeopardy to the churches themselves.

Our contemporary society has come to think of government primarily as a service agency. The kinds and extent of services suggested for the people or demanded by them constantly increase. As demands are multiplied in the personal area, group demands such as national defense and space exploration also escalate. The result is insatiable demands by the state for more and more revenue. As the screws are applied to the tax-paying populace the pain becomes pronounced and vocal. As people are being steadily required to pay more and more, each island of exemption stands out in jutting prominence.

When it became known that we were doing a book on the subject of church wealth and tax exemption, the measure of public interest was beyond anything we had anticipated. We were beseiged for information by the mass media. *Fortune* magazine did an excellent article on the subject with generous use of our material. So did *Reader's Digest.* *The Wall Street Journal, U.S. News and World Report,* United Press International, Associated Press and *Manchester Guardian* were a few of the printed media that quoted copiously from our work. The authors appeared before Congressional committees and offered their testimony on the matter of religious exemption. Both Dr. Larson and I have received far more invitations to appear on television and radio than we could possibly accept. Some of the interviewers have said that they have rarely presented a topic which drew such sharp and extensive public reaction as this one.

The response of the secular community astounded us. The concern of the religious community we found more understandable. But even here we were hardly prepared for the sympathetic recognition of the need for reform. Perhaps the contemporary state of religion itself may account for this. Most of the barometers of religion indicate decline. We are informed by denominational authorities that there are fewer members, fewer in attendance, fewer young people, smaller seminary enrollments, and that the influence of religion is felt to be lessening. Yet amid this pattern of religious decline, the wealth of the churches continues to increase at about the rate of $5 billion a year.

Is there a casual relationship between these two phenomena? Does increasing wealth help to produce decline in more vital categories? Does the wealth of the churches tend to discourage the loyalty and enthusiasm of the people? Certainly, it is time for the churches themselves to appraise their tax exemptions and the wealth which they are amassing.

We have tried to make a helpful contribution to this endeavor. We have tried to make an adequate calculation as to how much wealth and income the churches possess. We have tried to indicate some of the problems which this wealth and the tax exemptions which generate it have created. Finally, we have proposed certain reforms which we believe might contribute to solutions.

In the preparation of this work we have been deeply indebted to Americans United for Separation of Church and State and its executive director, Dr. Glenn L. Archer. Americans United financed the study of the tax structure in the fourteen cities. We appreciate also the help of Adele Porter, the managing editor of *Church and State,* my secretary Elaine Bowers and Franklin C. Salisbury, General Counsel of Americans United.

C. Stanley Lowell

PREFACE

During each census from 1850 to 1890, provision was made to obtain partial information concerning the value of church properties in the United States. In 1906, the federal government prepared an elaborate but specialized *Census of Religious Bodies,* published by the Department of Commerce in 2 large volumes, an undertaking which was repeated in 1916, 1926, and, in 3 volumes, in 1936. Although these compilations are extraordinarily detailed, they include only the value of parsonages and sanctuaries; and they are based, not on tax records, but on the voluntary and unverified information furnished in questionaires.

Since 1936, no authority has gathered any data whatever concerning religious bodies in this country. No census has even included a question about the religious affiliation of the people.

When one of the present writers published *Church Wealth and Business Income* in 1965, this represented the first scientific attempt to discover the amount of tax-exempt property in this country, what proportions of it are public and private, and, of the latter, what ratios are secular and ecclesiastical, and, finally, how the latter is apportioned among the principal religious divisions.

Since the tax-rolls of four cities had been used in 1964, a reanalysis of these would now indicate what developments had taken place over a 4-year period; but, since a more elaborate study was now contemplated to achieve a broader base for extrapolation, the search began for additional cities to be included in a new survey.

For our research it was mandatory (1) that all exempt properties be listed; and (2) that they carry valuations or assessments. In addition, however, it was also highly desirable (1) that the latter be realistic—i.e., comparable to those on the taxable; (2) that lists of exempts be segregated and divided under various headings or categories; and (3) that totals be available for all of these.

ix

In 1964, an attempt was made to analyze the tax-rolls of Nashville, Tennessee; but the public properties were not even listed and the private exempts carried no appraisals. Since then, the same situation was found in Savannah, Atlanta, Kansas City, Salt Lake City, El Paso, Tucson, and elsewhere.

In Phoenix, San Diego, and Los Angeles, city and county properties are listed together, but these do not include public facilities. Furthermore, the appraisals on the private exempts are unrealistic and there is no division into categories even when there is a single total. In Seattle, information might have been obtained, but analysis would have been so complicated and difficult as to be inexpedient. In Cincinnati, the latest roster of exempts was dated 1957 and the statistics found there were obviously many years old when compiled.

If our experience is a reliable criterion, less than half of American cities can be analyzed at all for the reason that (1) they do not list public properties; (2) they carry no appraisals for any of their exempts; or (3) their records are such as to render analysis prohibitively costly.

In some instances, as in Pittsburgh, Portland, and St. Paul, analysis was possible, but difficult. Others, like Buffalo, Providence, and St. Louis, provided statistics easily organized, but the exempts were drastically underassessed, as they are to a lesser degree in Baltimore, and, for that matter, almost everywhere. Since they do not yield revenue, their appraisals are seldom kept up to date, and they are almost always below parity in comparison with the taxable.

In Boston, where we found one of the highest tax-rates in the nation in February, 1968, the millage was shortly thereafter increased from 101 to 130; and the levy on a $25,000 to $30,000 house now stands at about $1,500. In Buffalo, the situation is comparable. This should not be surprising, since these cities have the highest percentages of exempt property we have found, with the exception of the District of Columbia.

Every city posed a different challenge, for each is characterized by a total dissimilarity in the manner in which records relating to tax-exempt properties are kept. But certain elements are common to all: (1) each has a large and rapidly growing corpus of tax-free real estate; and (2) the problem occasioned by its rapid growth is of increasing concern among assessors, mayors, councilmen, and thinking men and women in all walks of life, all of whom are asking what can be done about this galloping cancer.

On every hand, we were greeted with pleasure and given the utmost cooperation by auditors, statisticians, and executives in the offices where tax-records are kept. It is to be hoped that legislators and the general public may react with the same interest and enthusiasm to the results of our research.

Martin A. Larson

TABLE OF CONTENTS

CHAPTER 1

THE HISTORIC BACKGROUND

THE CULTURAL IMPERATIVE

No other element is as deeply embedded in our socio-political consciousness or so heavily reinforced by age-old precedents as the privileges and preferences enjoyed by ecclesiastical institutions and personnel. Since these were integral in various major cultures which long antedated Christianity, the flowing stream of history simply carried these onward, and reconstituted them in the religion of the western world. Since we are the creatures of our heritage and since this was drawn from many sources before being synthesized under a waning Graeco-Roman power-structure, the developments which then occurred are still integral in European and American ideology and practice.

EGYPT

The predominant religion of Egypt was the cult of Osiris, whose priests achieved dominance about 3,000 B.C. In their great Amen temples, they were the masters of untold treasure. The pyramids of Cheops and Khafre—built about 2900-2800 B.C.—were constructed primarily so that these divine rulers would be assured of rank in the after life commensurate with what they had enjoyed on earth.

The great mausoleum of Cheops alone, with its causeway, required the labor of 100,000 men for 60 years.

We read in Genesis 47:26 that "Joseph made it a law over the land of Egypt unto this day, that Pharaoh should have the fifth part; except the land of the priests only. . . ."[1] This means simply that 20% of all production was levied as a royal tax, except that nothing could be exacted from the lands, the income, or the treasures of the priests.

In fact, Pharaoh himself paid them tribute; they charged heavy fees for their ministrations; and they themselves were even empowered to levy their own direct taxes upon the people.[2] Their principal revenues, however, were derived from the great ecclesiastical estates, also immune to taxation, worked by armies of slaves. In ancient works of art, we often see the slave-driver and the priest standing side by side. James Henry Breasted, in his *History of Egypt,* describes in detail the unimaginable splendor and luxury of the Amen rituals and sanctuaries,[3] which held title to at least 750,000 acres of the choicest lands in the Nile Valley, or 15% of the total; and the priests exploited not less than 107,000 slaves. Including, therefore, the direct taxes levied by the priests, the contributions of the king and the nobility to them, and the additional compensation for services rendered, their emoluments must have been at least one-third of the national income, entirely tax-free. Furthermore, the royal establishment extorted its 20% from the producers, whose lives must have been little else than perpetual labor at a near-starvation level. And then, of course also, there were always new temples to be built, pyramids to be constructed, monuments to be erected, or wars to be waged, all of which, like Pelion upon Ossa, were piled upon the backs of the serfs and slaves.

After the pyramids of Cheops and Khafre were completed, the people, sullen and exhausted, retired to their villages. It was four or five centuries before the smaller tombs of a subsequent dynasty could be undertaken.

In the 14th century, a heretic king named Akhenaton or Ikhnaton declared that all men are the children of the beneficent sun and that Elysium was a myth; and he established a new cult based on this philosophy. He freed the slaves, liberated the convicts, confiscated the temple lands, and taxed the treasure houses of the Osirian priests, who thereupon aroused their followers to such a pitch of frenzy that they slaughtered the heretics in a sanguinary orgy. Thus, the old

14

priesthood regained its lands, slaves, revenues, and church-state union until it was superseded by an even more powerful theocracy under Constantine the Great.

The great cult of Isis, with its celibate priesthood and magnificent processions, developed from the Osirian and spread all over the ancient world. In the first century of our era, there were 58 large temples in Rome alone dedicated to the worship of this goddess, known as the Queen of Heaven and the Mother of God. Sinners addressed their prayers for help and consolation to her, as the divine Mediatrix with access to the Great Osiris.

THE JEWISH ANTECEDENTS

When western religion incorporated the Hebrew Scriptures into its canon, the practices of ancient Judaea exercised a powerful influence. Levites had been consecrated as religious personnel; and we read in Numbers 35:2–8 and Joshua 21:41 that they were given 48 cities "with their suburbs," together with all necessary cattle and equipment. They received, furthermore, what amounted to a triple tithe: one to maintain them (Numbers 18:21–26); a second, either in kind or in money, to supply them and the priests for their feasts and sacrifices (Deut. 14:22–24); and a third, for distribution among the poor (*ib.* 14:28–29).

Since the tillers of the soil, in addition to all other obligations, were required to support the kings and their establishments, it is unlikely that the peasants or serfs could retain even one-third of their produce. The burdens heaped upon the people by David and Solomon became so intolerable that when the latter died and his son Rehoboam ascended the throne, the representatives of the Ten Tribes pleaded bitterly for relief. The new king, however, declared: "my father hath chastised you with whips, but I will chastise you with scorpions." And so "Israel rebelled against the house of David," and, under the leadership of Jeroboam, established the Northern Kingdom with its capital at Samaria, which soon thereafter fell prey to the Assyrians.

But there was one portion in the Jewish population which did not worry about taxes: the priests and the Levites. Not only was their income far in excess of the average: *it was also immune to every form of taxation.* We read in Ezra 7:24: "Also we certify you, that touching any of the priests and Levites, singers, porters, Nethinims, or ministers of this house of God, it shall not be lawful to impose toll,

15

tribute, or custom upon them." The net result of this was that these ecclesiastics were not only released from productive labor: they also enjoyed a living standard far above that of the farmers who provided their luxuries.

THE PERSIANS

In the 6th century, B.C., the great prophet Zoroaster reconstructed the older sun-worship of the Medes into a virile nationalistic creed which, under Darius the Great, made the worship of Ahura Mazda dominant in 23 nations which bestrode the then civilized world. It also established the priests of this deity in positions of tax-exempt authority: actually, since there was virtually no line of demarcation separating things religious from things temporal, they enjoyed revenues and immunities which often exceeded those of the royal establishment itself. Zoroastrianism therefore represents a perfect example of church-state union in which authority was a double-edged sword, wielded by king and priest as the dichotomous representative of the Supreme God.

THE HERITAGE OF INDIA

About 4,000 years ago, an army of Aryans from the Mesopotamian plateau invaded India, where they established themselves as rulers, and consolidated their supremacy through an effective union of church and state. The priests called themselves Brahmanas, or priest-gods; and, in their scriptures, ostensibly based on their much older Vedas, they proclaimed doctrines which made all other castes subservient to them and which made them the masters of India for centuries on end.

The duties of the Brahmanas were to conduct religious rituals, study the Vedas, and *accept* gifts; of the nobles, or Kshatriyas, to bestow gifts upon the Brahmanas, sacrifice to the gods, repel invasion, maintain domestic order, and administer the laws devised by the priests; of the workers, or Vaisyas, to labor at agriculture or trade, serve in the army, make gifts to the Brahmanas, and pay taxes; of the servants, or Sudras, to obey the other three castes, especially the Brahmanas, in return for maintenance.

The Outcastes, who had no rights whatever, were required to perform the most degrading tasks, in return for starvation subsistence.

The basic elements of this system were (1) that all but themselves must be subject to the laws devised by the Brahmanas; and (2) that they levied taxes or other forms of tribute upon all other classes in society, but were themselves subject to no liability whatever.

An integral element in this religious system was the doctrine of reincarnation, according to which no one was to be punished in this life for what he does now but only for his derelictions in previous existences. Outcastes and Sudras therefore could not complain of injustice: they were simply doing penance for evil acts committed long ago. Brahmanas could not be brought to justice for current crime; they were being rewarded for their saintliness in previous lives.

This was perhaps the most successful device ever invented for perpetuating parasites and exploiters in positions of power, affluence, honor, and security without responsibility. Immune to all taxation, they stood above the law.

After this religio-political tyranny had continued for a dozen centuries, a number of revolutionary movements erupted in the 6th century, B.C. Among these, the Buddhist, founded by Prince Guatama, was the most popular and powerful. Actually, it was a coalition between the nobles and the two lower castes to effectuate a constructive separation of church and state. The nobles, in their desire to throw off the domination of a priest-state, encouraged the revolutionary aspirations of the exploited masses; and, under King Asoka, in 256 B.C., established a secular government.

The Buddhists repudiated the Vedas as well as the Brahmanic Codes; outlawed the caste system; divorced the civil authority from the religious; established male and female celibate communal orders; and outlawed the Brahmanic priesthood. However, they too insisted on exemption from taxation. After several centuries, Brahmanism reconquered India in the reconstituted form known as Hinduism. And so, the age-old union of church and state was reëstablished.

The influence of both Brahmanism and Buddhism have been enormous in the western world. The celibate orders in the Roman Catholic Church, which sprang into prominence early in the 4th century, A.D., were based precisely upon Buddhist originals, including their garb, communal organization, and vows of chastity, obedience, and poverty. The influence of Brahmanism upon the Church Triumphant was even more extensive: the designation of father or pappa for its priests, its veneration of relics, its use of the confessional, its imposition of penances, its pilgrimages, its trials by ordeal, its use of excommunication, its prohibition against communication with heretics, its control over the marriage relationship, its bestowal of unparalleled honors upon ascetics, its claim to sole authority as the interpreter of Scripture, its denial of these writings to the laity, its claims to immunity from taxation or trial in the civil courts, its complete domination over education or indoctrination, and, most of all, its claim to priority over the civil arm of the State—not only were all these appropriated after 325 directly from precedents established by ancient Brahmanism—they are totally without antecedents in New Testament Scripture; in fact, most of them are unknown in the Old as well.

THE GREEK AND ROMAN DOMAIN

The Graeco-Roman Empire was definitely secular in spite of its temples, oracles, and vestal virgins; for there was no ecclesiastical hierarchy supported by taxation or seeking to control the state. In Athens, during the centuries of its creative glory, there was no taxation at all, except in time of war; the incidental expenses of the city-state were met through the operation of silver mines, worked by criminals. Rome levied heavy taxes to maintain its far-flung empire, but none of these revenues were used to maintain a priesthood.

THE CHRISTIAN GOSPEL

We should note that early Christianity, as reflected in the Synoptics and the espistles of Paul, espoused a complete separation of church and state. Jesus gave classic expression to this philosophy when he told a tempter (Matt. 22:21): "Render unto Caesar the things that are Caesar's and to God the things that are God's."

When the early Christian missionaries sallied forth, they were (Mark 6:8) to "take nothing for their journey, save a staff only; no scrip, no bread, no money in their purse." These men had an urgent message; they were not building an ecclesiastical polity, collecting funds for cathedrals, or attempting to infiltrate the government. In the *Didache,* probably the oldest extant Christian document, the missionaries, there called prophets and apostles, are strictly forbidden to accept even the smallest pecuniary recompense.

During the first two centuries, literally scores of separate

18

movements proclaiming the Christ of the Gospels spread throughout the Graeco-Roman world. If there was a single dominating element of similarity, it was their desire to be completely independent of the state. Like Paul, in Romans 13:6–7, they taught that taxes should be paid to the government for the performance of its civic duties; but they remained strictly aloof from politics. Under the tolerant Roman rule, all these cults and movements flourished, free to proselytize so long as they obeyed the civil law.

THE THEOCRATIC CHURCH

However, this was not to continue indefinitely: for in the second century, at first in a few centers, and then in greater numbers, clerics began to appear who called themselves deacons, presbyters, priests, bishops, and pappas and who claimed authority over their congregations. In due course, these men accumulated vast amounts of wealth and aggrandized their power. Late in the third century, they began the construction of great churches; penetrated the government at all levels; and assumed the role and perquisites of powerful princes.

In order to consolidate their ecclesiastical and political position, the bishops began holding synods or councils; their demands for tax-exemptions and other preferences brought them into periodic conflict with the state. The clerical establishment, however, grew apace and penetrated every level of society and government.

In 313, Constantine issued the Edict of Toleration at Milan, which gave Christianity parity with the cult of Isis and other great pagan religions. However, following the Council of Nicaea and the defeat and execution of Licinius, the Emperor entered upon the role which established his permanent place in history. By 325, the Catholic Church had become so powerful that even the Emperor was little more than its pawn and servant; and he issued a long series of repressive rescripts, first, against the pagan cults and then with even greater ferocity against the dozens of dissident forms of Christianity, which were the Separated Brethren of that day. Thus was established the first union of church and state in the western world.

Among the preferences granted the new clericals were generous emoluments from the public treasury; a total exemption from all forms of taxation; immunity from military service; and the provision that Catholics alone be eligible to hold political office. The Church was empowered to receive gifts and legacies; and the wealth of all who died intestate *or without direct heirs* was automatically conferred upon it. Old churches were repaired and new ones built at public expense.[4]

All this, however, was only the beginning. After the pagan temples were razed and their worship proscribed, the many deviationist forms of Christianity were visited with even harsher treatment. "Novatians, Valentinians, Marcionites, Paulians, and Cataphrygians" and other dissident Christians who refused to abandon their faith were denounced as the "haters of Christ and the enemies of truth and life, in league with the devil and destruction" and given short shrift between death and exile.[5]

The fulsome Eusebius proclaimed that "Thus were the lurking places of the heretics broken up . . . . and the one Catholic Church, at unity with itself, shone with full luster, while no heretical or schismatic body anywhere continued to exist." [6]

Scarcely was the ink dry with which these words were inscribed than the Donatist schism split the African churches; and soon the bloody Arian wars began to devastate the entire Christian world. At the beginning of the 4th century, the poison of Manichaean heresy had spread quicksilverlike through all the veins and arteries of society. The wars, the terror, and the persecutions which accompanied these, drained so much blood and vitality that three-quarters of the Christian world fell easy prey to Islam, when it burst upon the Mediterranean world in the 7th century.

Not long thereafter, what remained of Christendom was divided between the Roman Catholic and the Eastern Orthodox churches.

In the patristic literature of the 5th, 6th, and 7th centuries, there are many passages reflecting the growth of the Church as a dominant political and economic power. It gradually gained possession of vast estates throughout Europe, especially before its predictions of the Final Judgment in the year 1,000 failed to materialize; these lands were operated by slaves, then by serfs, and finally by peasants. By conservative estimate, these constituted one-third of the arable land and produced one-third of the national income, all, of course, immune to taxation. In addition, the Church received vast revenues from the nobility and from the gradually emerging business classes, as well as from the peasantry, in return for administering the sacraments and for facilitating the removal of tortured souls from purgatory.

20

THE MEDIEVAL TRAGEDY

Productivity dropped to the lowest conceivable level; universal illiteracy engulfed the continent; whatever energy remained went into the construction of churches, cathedrals, convents, monasteries, rectories, etc.; plagues decimated the population at frequent intervals; moral decency ceased to exist; robbers and murderers roamed the countryside at will; the average life-expectancy dropped to 4 years; the virtual extinction of the human race in much of Europe loomed as a distinct possibility; and the terrors with which life was filled made early death a happy escape.

WAR AND REVOLUTION

Some heretical movements, like the Paulician, lingered underground for centuries; and there were sporadic revolts. In the 12th and 13th cenutries, the Manichaean Albigensians of southern France developed a superior economy on the basis of free enterprise and religious independence; but a holy crusade, instituted by Pope Innocent III and led by Simon de Montfort, drowned the heretics in their own blood. Other revolts appeared in Italy, Hungary, Transylvania, Poland, and elsewhere; and for a time the Huguenots appeared on the road to victory in France, until they were slaughtered by the tens of thousands on St. Bartholomew's Day in 1572.

The wars and revolutions which wracked Europe for 500 years were the inevitable legacy of church-state union. In England, Henry VIII confiscated the great abbey estates and cut off all tribute to Rome about 1530. In Switzerland, Calvin obtained complete control of Geneva by overthrowing the Catholic hierarchy with the support of the developing trading classes. In Germany, Luther nailed his 95 theses to the church door in Wittenberg in 1517 and initiated the Protestant Reformation which quickly swept Scandinavia.

We should realize that this movement was economic and political as well as religious. Its objective was to shatter the feudalism and theocracy which were based upon a serf-economy and to replace both with free enterprise and republican forms of government. To accomplish this end, Papal authority was repudiated in favor of Scriptural, and Christ was proclaimed the sole mediator between God and man. In practice, this meant that the feudal estates of the

21

Church were to be confiscated; that Roman clerics would be banished; that monasteries and nunneries, with their celibate orders, would be abolished; that the doctrine of purgatory would be repudiated; that the confessional and penances would be terminated; that a married ministry would supplant a celibate priesthood; that the energies of men would be directed to manufacture, trade, and economic improvement instead of the construction of churches and cathedrals; that the authority of Scripture would replace Papal edicts; that voluntary would replace compulsory religion; that freedom of conscience would supersede an authoritarian hierarchy; that control over marriage and education would become civil instead of ecclesiastical functions; and that the Church, no longer dominant over the state, would limit its activities to spiritual ministrations.

In a word, the Reformation meant that instead of allowing a hierarchy to take from 50 to 75% of their production from the people, the new church would be content with a single tithe; and even more than that, with shackles broken, men could now double, triple, or even quadruple their productivity and so enjoy a fullness of life previously unknown.

In Sweden, under Gustavus Vasa, every church structure (with a few exceptions) was razed, stone by stone, and clerics who would not renounce their allegiance to Rome were sent into exile.

In Holland and other Low Countries the Calvinists were largely victorious after a series of bloody wars.

In Germany itself, Lutheranism emerged triumphant in the 16th century. However, in 1616, one of the most devastating and brutal wars of all history broke out: the Catholic armies moved up from their bases in Spain and Austria, and the holocaust was on. In 1630, Gustavus the Second Adolphus arrived with an army of 35,000; he defeated Wallenstein, Tilly, and other generals in a series of crucial battles, but was himself slain at the battle of Lutzen in 1632. When the war was concluded by the Treaty of Westphalia in 1648, at least 15 million Germans had perished by violence and their number had been reduced to less than 10 million. Cities which had been great centers of trade and manufacture became the habitations of wolves. It was 200 years before Germany regained the population of 1616. Had not Gustavus Adolphus intervened, the Reformation might well have been obliterated.

The Great Armada which sailed into the English Channel in 1588 was organized specifically to reclaim the British Isles for the Vatican;

the ships were well supplied with instruments of torture designed by the Inquisition; and they contained vast supplies of literature to be used in the ideological reconstruction of the English mind. The destruction of the Armada was a tremendous victory for freedom of religion and church-state separation.

The great revolution of 1789 in France reflects all the classic components of the immemorial struggle between church and state. That country had been ruled for centuries by the Lords Lay and the Lords Ecclesiastical, all tax-exempt, who constituted the two upper and ruling castes in the Estates General. The bishops were a dominant power in a government in which cardinals were sometimes the prime ministers. The Church owned a large portion of the land and enjoyed enormous revenues. The peasants and the rising business classes were taxed beyond all endurance. The Church, of course, controlled every aspect of life.

The Huguenots had been massacred in the 16th century; and in the first half of the 18th, when the Camisards of southeastern France attempted to break the church-state union, the oppression and the slaughter became so frightful that hundreds of thousands who survived literally went mad.

About the middle of the 18th century, Rousseau, Voltaire, and the Encyclopaedists began their monumental and incisive attacks upon the church-state union which finally culminated in the Great Revolution. The estates of the Church and the nobles were confiscated; the king and the queen were beheaded; the Bastille and the Tuilleries Palace were razed; a constitutional republic was established; the revenues of the Church were reduced to voluntary contributions; its controls over education and civil contracts were terminated; in short, the union of church and state, which had existed since the 4th century, came to an abrupt termination. But before all this was accomplished, at least two million persons perished on the guillotine or by other forms of violence.

In Italy, there were strong republican movements led by Cavour, Garibaldi, and Mazzini about the middle of the 19th century. To counteract these, Pope Pius IX proclaimed the encyclical known as the *Syllabus of Errors* in 1864.

King Victor Emmanuel II took a great stride in the direction of church-state separation in 1859 when he abolished the ecclesiastical courts and established other reforms which brought the wrath of the Church upon his head. He seized 16,000 square miles of tax-exempt

Papal Estates, which resulted in his excommunication and his sentence to an additional 1,000 years in purgatory. In 1929, Mussolini reduced the Vatican land-holdings to 109 acres, but paid it $90 million as compensation for previous confiscations and, what was even more important, entered into a concordat which is still in effect and through which the Church is able to exercise control over the civil, religious, educational, and cultural activities of every citizen. Even to this day, there is no such thing as divorce in Italy and millions choose permanent adulterous relationships rather than celibate renunciation.

CONFISCATION IN THE NEW WORLD

Central and South America had larger Indian populations than the United States when they were conquered and colonized by the Spaniards, accompanied by their clerical colleagues. The murals of Rivera and Orozco, found in the Palace of Chapultepec and other public buildings, depict the sufferings inflicted by church-state rule upon the Mexicans and their bitter hatred toward this tyranny.

Under the leadership of Juarez, a full-blooded Indian, the Mexicans overthrew the Catholic dominated government in 1857 and confiscated all church lands. However, during the American Civil War, the Papacy and Napoleon III installed Archduke Maximilian of Austria as Emperor, and he promptly restored the wealth, power, and prerogatives of the Church. His reign was short; as soon as the war ended, the American government served an ultimatum upon Napoleon ordering him to remove his 30,000 soldiers from Mexico. When they were withdrawn, the puppet ruler was executed.

However, the church-state union was not abrogated; and the clericals were so successful that by 1926, the Church was reputed to have owned two-thirds of the real estate in Mexico City, all tax-free, and most of it obtained by rituals promising to effect a prompt release of souls from purgatory. Under the leadership of Calles and Obregon —who was assassinated on July 17, 1928, by a Catholic fanatic—the Mexican Congress nationalized (i.e., confiscated) all Church lands. To this day, no church may own a square foot of land in Mexico; nor may it conduct a school, or train anyone for the priesthood within the country, or import other nationals to perform sacramental functions. The religious are forbidden to wear their garb in public or to solicit any money beyond the confines of their 8,000 churches—erected between 1530 and 1926—which they are permitted to retain and operate under severe restrictions and under the privilege of tolerance.

Thinking that the people would rise in revolt, the hierarchy withdrew its sacerdotal ministrations on July 31, 1926. When nothing happened, the Church finally decided after 20 years to make the best of the situation, and reopened its sanctuaries to the public. Mexican boys are now prepared for the priesthood in Jesuit seminaries established in the United States; and what are substantially parochial schools are operated under ingenious disguises. However, the wrath of the Mexican people is evident in the dozens of unfinished churches still to be seen, standing exactly as they were in 1926—some with partial roofs, others with half-built walls. Yet in one small city, we still find 365 costly and ornate Roman Catholic churches. And the Church of the Lady of Guadalupe, with its huge doors of solid gold, its gem-encrusted statue pendant from the ceiling, its opulent treasures, and its thousands of vermin-invested Indians moving slowly on their knees from the rear to the altar, still offers conclusive testimony concerning the potency of the Roman Church.

THE PROLETARIAN REVOLUTION

In a very real sense, the Russian Revolution was a repetition of the French, except that in the former there was no well-developed business community to seize and hold the power; the Kerensky regime therefore gave way to the Bolshevik movement, whose base consisted of some workers in factories owned by foreigners but, much more, of the peasants who hungered to own the land on which they had labored for the benefit of the aristocracy and the Orthodox Church. As in France, all these estates were confiscated, the church-state union which had existed for centuries was abrogated, and a secular state was erected. What we must understand is that this was an upheaval against the theocracy as much as it was against the Czarist-feudal regime.

THE SPANISH DOMAIN

Like the countries of South America, neither Spain nor Portugal has ever had a revolution—which consists of the transfer of the public power from one economic class to another. The people of Spain, which spawned the Inquisition and the Jesuit Order, have suffered persecutions in which literally millions have perished; the auto-de-fés of bitter memory were the public entertainments of the 17th century in which the shrieks of burning heretics mingled with the applause of relatives and neighbors who retained their faith and subservience.

However, even Spain has had its reactions against a church-state union under which, by its concordat, the hierarchy enjoys tax-immunity and exercises complete control over education, the media of communication, and all civil contracts, especially marriage. Every village, town, and city is filled with churches, cathedrals, rectories, nunneries, monasteries, and other visible manifestations of the Church, which also owns vast estates and controls virtually every business monopoly in the nation, such as banks and utilities.

In 1931, the people of Spain elected a Cortez committed to the disestablishment of church-state union. It outlawed the Jesuit Order, abrogated the concordat, confiscated the Church estates, divided the land among the downtrodden peasants, and levied taxes on the enormous unrelated business income of the Church. Sometimes such holdings were simply "nationalized."

However, with the hysterical support of the Catholic hierarchy in the United States and throughout the world, General Francisco Franco gathered an army in Morocco and invaded his country in 1936. The ensuing civil war raged for three years, cost the lives of more than a million Catholics, reëstablished the church-state union, and restored the ecclesiastical properties and tax-immunities which have been the curse of Spain for hundreds of years.

THE EMERALD ISLE

Ireland exemplifies a unique development. When a Cromwellian force captured Drogheda in 1649, more than 40,000 of the inhabitants were put to the sword; and the Protector announced that if Papism could be eradicated only by slaughtering the entire population, he was prepared to employ such drastic measures.

Northern Ireland, which obtained a separate government in 1920, is predominantly Protestant; and while it has less than one-sixth of the territory, it has more than one-third of the population and a much larger share of industry and prosperity. The remainder of Ireland has always been and remains overwhelmingly Catholic, with a government to which the people have reacted by refusing to generate the children demanded by the clergy. In 1841, the population was 8,175,124; in 1914, 4,400,000. In 1968, Catholic Ireland had about 2,880,000 and Northern Ireland 1,480,000.

The potato famine following 1841 sent hundreds of thousands of starving Irish to the United States, where they became a powerful influence in such cities as Boston, and gradually assumed virtual control of the Roman Catholic Church in America.

A LAND OF FREEDOM

When the Founding Fathers established this nation, it was against the backdrop of that almost universal calamity which had constituted European history for centuries and which consisted principally of the strife, bloodshed, violence, and general desolation inevitably consequent upon a church-state union controlled by an authoritarian theocracy. And let it not be assumed that the American colonies were exempt from the poison of religious bigotry, intolerance, and oppression. Early in his career, Thomas Jefferson became a powerful champion of complete religious freedom and church-state separation, which was being outrageously violated by the Anglican Church in Virginia. A law written by him declares "that all men shall be free to profess, and by argument to maintain, their opinions in matters of religion, and that the same shall in no wise diminish, enlarge, or affect their civil capacities." [7]

Jefferson often discussed the horrors which flow from the union of the state with an established church. He explained that when the Anglicans early in the 17th century settled in Virginia and seized "the powers of making, administering, and executing the laws, they showed equal intolerance in this country with their Presbyterian brethren, who had emigrated to the northern government. . . . Several acts of the Virginia Assembly of 1659, 1662, and 1693, had made it penal in parents to refuse to have their children baptized; had prohibited the unlawful assembly of Quakers; . . . . had ordered those already here . . . . to be imprisoned till they should abjure the country; provided a milder punishment for their first or second return, but death for their third. . . . The Anglicans retained full possession about a century. Other opinions then began to creep in, and the great care of the government to support their own clergy, having begotten an equal degree of indolence in its clergy, two-thirds of the people had become dissenters. . . . ." [8]

27

In 1705, the Virginia Assembly had enacted a law under which any person who denied the existence of God or the Trinity, asserted that there are more gods than one, or denied the truth of the Christian religion or the divine authority of the Scriptures could be imprisoned for 3 years without bail. Jefferson declared that all attempts to enforce religious conformity had resulted in failure; and that millions of innocent men, women, and children had been fined, imprisoned, tortured, and burnt without accomplishing this objective. And he remarked ironically: "it does me no injury for my neighbor to say that there are twenty gods, or no god." (Notes on Virginia, Query XVII.) [9]

In 1786, the Virginia Assembly enacted Jefferson's Bill for Establishing Religious Freedom, which, next to the Declaration of Independence, he considered his crowning achievement.[10]

When Jefferson and others of like mind, such as Madison, Washington, and Franklin, hammered out our Constitution, they were well aware that one of their principal objectives was to create a secular state, in which the civil power would be completely independent of any or all churches; in which every man would possess the inalienable right to worship as his conscience dictated, or not at all; and in which no one would ever be required, *or even permitted,* to contribute directly or indirectly to any church through the government. Religion, they realized, to be free, must be completely voluntary.

Such a polity was possible here because none of the Protestant denominations was, by the year 1792, large or powerful enough to enforce its will upon the remainder. Furthermore, all of them had recently fled from religious tyrannies engendered by church-state unions. And thus was created for the first time in the western world, since the abdication of Diocletian, a major commonwealth completely and thoroughly dedicated to the principle of church-state separation.

The First Amendment declares: "Congress shall make no law respecting an establishment of religion, or prohibiting the free exercise thereof. . . . ." This means simply and finally that no law may legally be enacted which has any relevance to the existence, status, activities, or financial operation of any group professing a religious purpose or ideology.

The colonists who debarked at Plymouth Rock in 1620 were Calvinists who sought religious freedom; those who landed at Jamestown in 1607 were secularists, in search of fortune. These were

28

soon followed by Quakers, Baptists, Dutch Reformed, Lutherans, and Presbyterians. By 1750, there were 250 societies of Friends, exceeded in number only by the Anglicans and the Congregationalists. It is therefore obvious that the colonies were settled and consolidated by Protestants and secularists.

CATHOLICS IN AMERICA

The first Roman Catholics outside New Mexico and Florida arrived on these shores in 1634, when Lord Baltimore, a converted Episcopalian, established a Catholic settlement in Maryland. In 1696, there were still only 7 families of that faith in New York City; 80 years later, their descendants were compelled to journey to Philadelphia to receive their sacraments. Even in 1785, there were still only 18,200—of whom 15,000 lived in Maryland—among a population of 3,600,000.

Since the Continental Congress excluded from citizenship any one who gave allegiance to any foreign religious or political authority, Catholics found it necessary to devise a plan by which ecclesiastical primates might be appointed "in such a way as to retain absolutely the spiritual jurisdiction of the Holy See and at the same time remove all ground for objecting to us as though we held anything hostile to the national independence." [11]

In 1785, a group of Catholic communicants in New York organized themselves as an independent congregation, purchased a site for a church in the name of their trustees, and set out to hire a pastor of their own choice. The Jesuit Bishop John Carroll (a refugee from Papal exile in Europe) denounced these rebels in the harshest terms, concluding that their course of action "would result in the formation of distinct and independent societies in nearly the same manner as Congregational Presbyterians." [12]

Several churches, we read, "firmly resisted the authority of the bishops"; [13] and decades elapsed before this kind of mutiny was finally extirpated, and all church properties were firmly titled to the bishop, or perhaps we should say to the Vatican.

The long and bitter conflict between the hierarchy and its lay congregations is detailed in Father Patrick J. Dignan's *History of the Legal Incorporation of Catholic Church Property in the United States,* published in 1935 by P. J. Kenedy and Sons. In countless instances, lay memberships insisted on their rights as Americans to own, and to operate, their own churches, control their finances, and select or dismiss their pastors. The hierarchy, led by Bishop Carroll, realized that the implementation of any such policy would mean the dissolution of the authoritarian Church. Over and over, Dignan emphasized that "in the Catholic Church all jurisdiction and rights flow from above downwards" (p. 51) and that its government must never under any circumstances or any degree be entrusted to laymen (p. 68).

Actually the mortal sin committed by the Know-Nothing Party consisted in demanding trustee-ownership for all church property and aiding lay Catholics in obtaining legislation to make this mandatory.[14]

It was more than a century before the last revolt among lay-Catholics was put down through the establishment of various types of incorporation wholly controlled by the bishop; of these, the "corporation sole" had been established in 21 states by 1935.[15]

Another important issue which appears frequently in Dignan's book was the drive of the Church to obtain and operate tax-free revenue-producing commercial property.[16]

At this point, we should call attention to one of the most important reasons why the Colonies fought with such determination to win their independence. On June 22, 1774, the British government promulgated the Quebec Act,[17] in order to enlist the military support of this province, or at least to prevent it from joining the overseas rebellion. This Act provided that as soon as Britain won the war, all the territory north of the Ohio River and east of the Mississippi (now embracing 12 important states) should become part of Quebec with Roman Catholicism as the established religion. Rather than face such a fate, hundreds of thousands of Americans were willing to suffer the agonies of Valley Forge or to die on the field of carnage.

In the 19th century, the heretical Father Chiniquy led some 25,000 French or French-Canadian Catholics centered in Illinois into the Presbyterian denomination.

By 1790, the 13 original colonies had grown to 16 states with a population of 3,929,214, of whom about 20,000 were Catholics; in 1810, this number had grown to 7,239,881, with still no more than 150,000 of that faith. Its parishes increased only from 27 in 1740 to 124 in 1820.

However, the famine in Ireland and the political upheavals in central Europe soon brought a great flood of Catholic immigrants to these shores: 2,467,317 arrived from Germany alone and 1,694,830 from Ireland between 1841 and 1860.[18] Others came from Austria, France, Italy, Poland, Russia, and southeastern Europe.

Following 1845, therefore, the complexion of American society underwent rapid and drastic alteration. Catholic parishes were soon numbered in the hundreds and then the thousands. In 1880, there were 2,550 parishes; in 1900, 10,339, with nearly 10 million communicants.

It is interesting to note that when public schools were first established, Catholics insisted on the complete elimination of religious instruction in them, a position officially proclaimed by the Second Provincial Council of Baltimore, 1840. "Catholics," we read, "objected to conditions which constrained their children to attend, or take part in, non-Catholic services or instruction. The Catholics initiated and developed the parochial school system in order to meet the demands of conscience and the right of the parent to secure the religious instruction he wished for his child." [19]

THE EXPANSION OF CHURCH PROPERTY

However, the Protestant churches also proliferated. In 1660, there were seven denominations with 154 congregations, of which 75 were Congregational, 41 Anglican, 13 Dutch Reformed, 5 Presbyterian, 4 Baptist, 4 Lutheran, and only 12 Catholic. Two centuries later, there were 52,532 congregations, of which 17,883 were Methodist, 12,150 Baptist, 6,406 Presbyterian, 2,145 Anglo-Episcopal, 2,234 Congregational, 2,128 Lutheran, 928 Unitarian or Universalist, 2,100

TABLE I—THE AMERICAN CHURCH TODAY

SUMMARY OF RELIGIOUS ORGANIZATIONS—1968 [21]

Divisions	Denomi- nations	Claimed, Inclusive Membership	Bodies	Churches (or Parishes)
Protestant and Miscellaneous	97	75,670,311	232	302,348
Jewish	1	5,600,000	3	4,445
Roman Catholic	1	47,468,333	1	23,734 (18,064)
TOTALS	99	128,738,644	236	330,527

31

Disciples of Christ, 728 Quaker, 166 Assemblies or Churches of God, and 2,550 Roman Catholic. In 1960, there were 259,613 congregations of which some 240,000 were Protestant or miscellaneous, divided among 80 denominations and 200 bodies.[20]

It should be pertinent to supply more detailed information concerning the Protestant denominations:

TABLE II—PRINCIPAL PROTESTANT AND MISCELLANEOUS BODIES AND CHURCHES—1968 [22]

Denomination	Bodies	Churches	Inclusive Membership
Adventist	4	3,873	427,649
Assemblies of God	1	8,506	576,058
Baptist	27	98,313	25,510,961
Churches of Christ	1	19,000	2,400,000
Churches of God	9	9,995	544,817
Churches of God in Christ	1	4,500	425,000
Disciples of Christ	1	8,066	1,894,927
Eastern Orthodox	20	1,073	4,122,171
Evangelical United Brethren	1	3,970	732,377
Latter-Day Saints (Mormon)	3	4,775	2,480,899
Lutherans	10	17,909	8,794,106
Methodists	19	54,167	12,907,652
Pentecostals	12	5,386	507,627
Presbyterians	9	14,431	4,412,629
Protestant Episcopal	1	7,562	3,429,153
Reformed Churches	6	1,156	527,775
United Church of Christ	1	6,947	2,063,481
TOTALS	126	269,631	71,757,282
80 Others	106	32,717	3,913,029
GRAND TOTAL	232	302,348	75,670,311

The Southern Baptist Convention, with 34,123 churches and 11,140,486 members, is the largest Protestant body (1969 statistics).

According to information published in 1950 by the National Council of Churches, 75% of all Negroes, or 10,892,694, were then members of some Baptist or Methodist church.

The average membership in Protestant and miscellaneous churches is about 250; in the Roman Catholic parishes, 2,600. There is one synagogue for approximately each 1,300–1,500 of reported Jewish

32

population. Protestant congregations in the large cities, however, are more than twice the average size; in this study, we estimate them at 600.

THE CATHOLIC COMPLEX

In 1785, the Catholics comprised one-half of one per cent of the population and 1.5% of the religious community; in 1890, these ratios had grown to 13.25% and 30.45%; today they are 23.8% and 34.9%. In 185 years, they increased from 18,200 to 47,468,333.

In addition to their 18,064 parishes, 23,734 churches, 4,346 missions, 1,404 stations, and 12,694 chapels, they had in 1968, 788 hospitals, 239 orphanages and asylums, 420 homes for the aged, 124 seminaries with 39,838 enrollees, 305 colleges and universities with 433,960 students, and 13,030 elementary and secondary schools with 5,174,776 pupils. They had another 5,356,340 public school pupils under sectarian instruction during released time. Finally, there is also a vast complex of rectories, correctional institutions, publishing facilities, nunneries, convents, monasteries, diocesan headquarters, etc., which the observer can only contemplate with awe. Beyond all this, there are intangible resources and commercial investments which stagger the imagination.[23]

Between 1830 and 1920, 29,675,138 immigrants arrived in this country from Europe, of whom 22,962,194 came from wholly or predominantly Catholic countries.[24] This left only about 7 million from Scandinavia, England, Scotland, Switzerland, Turkey, and Holland. Had all the baptized Catholics, together with their children and grandchildren continued in the faith, this would long since have become a Catholic nation. That millions of these immigrants forsook the creed of their fathers is obvious from the fact that as late as 1916 the Catholic Church *claimed* only 15,721,815 members in the United States.[25]

Immigration virtually ceased in 1924; and the amazing growth of Catholicism came after 1936. In that year, its claimed communicants numbered 19,914,937; and while our national population increased from 128,180,000 to 200,000,000 between 1936 and 1968—56%—the Catholic Church added 27,555,000 members, or 139%.

The vital center of American Catholicism has now shifted from the church to the school. It operates a vast educational system which begins in the kindergarten and goes upward through the college and graduate study; all of this indoctrination is designed to segregate Catholic youth from the mainstream of American culture and thus construct the foundations for a wholly Catholic nation.

In 1840, there were 200 parish schools in the United States; in 1861, there were more than a thousand. The First Provincial Council held in Baltimore in 1849 declared it "absolutely necessary that schools be established in which the young may be taught the principles of faith and morality, while being instructed in letters." The First Plenary Council, 1852, also convened in Baltimore, directed every parish church that did not already have one to establish a parochial school within two years; that priests who failed to accomplish this objective were to be removed; and any parish which failed to do so was to be subjected to extreme censure. "All Catholic parents," declared the Council, "are bound to send their children to the parochial schools . . . unless it be lawful to send them to other schools . . . . . approved by the bishop. . . . ."[26]

The growth of Catholicism and its educational system have been phenomenal during the past 35 years; it is obvious that the previous massive defections ceased with its authoritarian control of church property, the termination of immigration, and the consolidation of the sectarian schools.

We can only estimate the cost of this complex. An article published in the *National Register,* Sept. 6, 1964, stated that $3,231,073,804 represents the annual community value of Catholic elementary and secondary schools in the United States. . . ." Multiply this by 2 or 3 and we gain some idea of what it must cost the average among 9 or 10 million Catholic families to support this church and the Vatican. Should public support be granted for the Catholic schools, these would very quickly expand to absorb all those now under instruction during released time; and we may be certain that almost over night the subsidies necessary would increase to at least $10 billion. Many other private school systems would then surely come into existence, and the public school would be no more than a memory amidst a welter of 15 or 20 parallel systems operated at fantastic cost and with a minimum of achievement.

THE DANGER SIGNALS

In 1875, President Grant declared in a message to the Congress: "In 1850 . . . . Church property in the United States which paid no

34

tax . . . . amounted to about $83,000,000. In 1860, the amount had doubled; in 1875 it is about $1,000,000,000. . . . So vast a sum, receiving all the protection and benefits of government without bearing its proportion of the burdens and expenses of the same, will not be looked upon acquiescently by those who have to pay the taxes . . . . there is scarcely a limit to the wealth that may be acquired by corporations, religious or otherwise, if allowed to retain real estate without taxation. The contemplation of so vast a property as here alluded to without taxation may lead to sequestration, without constitutional authority and through blood.

"I would suggest the taxation of all property, whether church or corporation. . . . ." [27]

THE GROWTH OF CHURCH PROPERTY

The following table, which traces the growth of only one portion of church wealth, excludes schools, hospitals, cemeteries, correctional institutions, the residences of religious, and most educational facilities.

TABLE III   VALUE OF AMERICAN CHURCHES AND PARSONAGES [28]

Year	All	Jewish	Catholic	Protestant
1850	$ 87,328,801	$ 418,600	$ 9,256,758	$ 77,653,443
1870	352,483,581	5,155,234	60,985,566	286,342,781
1890	676,630,139	6,754,275	118,371,366	551,504,498
1906	1,257,575,867	23,198,925	292,638,787	941,738,155
1916	1,895,446,678	31,176,726	435,545,176	1,428,724,776
1936	3,756,437,777	123,695,037	891,435,725	2,741,307,015

We see, therefore, that while the value of houses of worship and clerical residences grew from $87,328,801 to $3,756,437,777, the Catholic ratio increased from 10.54% to 23.73%; however, even as late as 1936, the Protestants still owned 72.98% of such real estate. As late as 1890, the Methodists with 4,589,284 members and property valued at $132,140,179, were the richest denomination. In 1906, however, the Catholics had outstripped all others both in membership and wealth. By that time, the Baptists, Lutherans, etc., had fallen far behind.

Since religiously used Catholic wealth in the United States exceeds $54 billion as of 1968 and since there are 18,064 parishes, the

TABLE IV TAXABLE AND EXEMPT REAL ESTATE [29]
(In Millions of Dollars)

Year	All	Taxable ᵃ	Exempt	Ratio	Churches	Ratio to Ex.	To All	To Taxable
1850		$ 7,136			$ 87			1.2%
1870		30,069			286			.95%
1880	$ 43,642	41,642	$ 2,000	4.6%				
1890	52,538	46,325	6,213	11.8%	551	8.9%	1.05%	1.8%
1904	62,341	55,510	6,831	12.3%				
1906					942	13.8%	1.5%	1.7%
1912	109,237	96,923	12,314	11.3%				
1916					1,429	11.5%	1.3%	1.5%
1922	176,415	155,909	20,506	11.7%				
1961	(Assessed)	280,485	85,461	23.4%				
1961	(Mkt. Value)	969,000	294,740	23.4%				
1964	1,140,000	815,000	325,000	28.5%	79,500	24.5%	6.9%	9.7%
1968	1,748,630	1,179,152	569,479	32.6%	102,413	18.0%	5.9%	8.7%
1966	1,687,241							

(Cf. *Statistical Abstract* of 1968, p. 427)

ᵃ All totals, except the first for 1961, are full market or replacement valuations.

average for each is more than $3 million; since there are 4,445 synagogues to share $7.5 billion, the portion of each is $1,685,000; and since there are 302,348 Protestant and miscellaneous congregations sharing wealth totalling $40.6 billion, the average for each is $134,200. These sums, of course, include the shares of all churches in the schools and hospitals, the cemeteries, the tax-exempt publishing facilities and retirement homes, etc., belonging to their respective denominations.

Let us see how real property has developed in the United States.

Table Four reflects what has been and is happening. Exempt property constituted only 4.6% of the total in 1880, but grew rapidly to around 12% in 1890. No data is available between 1922 and 1961, when the exempts had skyrocketed to 23.4%. In 1964, it had reached 28.5%, and in 1968, 32.6%, according to the official records.

Tax-exempt church property comprised about 1% of the total real estate for 50 years; but by 1906, it had increased to 1.5%. In 1964, this ratio had zoomed to 6.9%. Between 1890 and 1968, it expanded from 8.9% to 18.1% of the exempt and from 1.4% to 8.7% of the taxable.

THE HISTORIC PARALLEL

American developments over the last two hundred years are strikingly similar to those in the Graeco-Roman Empire between 100 and 300. In the 2nd and 3rd centuries, approximately the same number of Christian organizations came into existence as we now find in the United States. But the Catholic Church grew with the same inexorability that has characterized its development here. Early in its ancient career, it adopted the same principles of monolithic organization and ecumenical absorption which it now pursues. It incorporated the doctrines and practices of its principal pagan rivals and was thus able to absorb their communicants; and, when the time was ripe, it seized and employed the apparatus of the state to extirpate all other religious organizations.

The ecumenical movement now being so ardently advanced by high-placed Protestant and Roman Catholic spokesmen is a substantial repetition of what occurred in the 3rd and 4th centuries. If a single religious complex emerges with a hundred million members, a hundred billion dollars or more of untaxed property, and $25 or $30 billion of annual untaxed revenue, most of it from unrelated business

37

and government subsidies, this will create a crisis which could be resolved only in the alembic of revolutionary expropriation.

THE ISSUE

The heavy property tax and the almost confiscatory levies upon wages, salaries, and business income have intensified the avid desire to expand tax-exempt real estate and increase tax-free income. But if this trend is permitted to continue, the result can only be chaos and destruction, for people will not forever submit to the onerous burdens which will inevitably flow from these inequities.

What President Grant foresaw in 1875 was then only a spot above the horizon no bigger than a man's hand; this has now become a great cloud which darkens the earth; and unless something is done to reverse the developments now rolling on apace, there is little possibility of saving our culture from the terrible tragedies that have overtaken others again and again and again over the ages.

The United States is the last great bastion of religious and political liberty. But if a great ecclesiastical hierarchy comes into being as a result of the ecumenical drive now under way, it will demand and obtain even greater preferences, immunities, and subsidies than are now being given the churches. Since no culture can long survive in which unlimited amounts of real estate and income are immune not only from taxation but even to disclosure, it seems obvious that basic reforms are indicated in this country.

Citations

1. This is confirmed by Breasted, *History of Egypt,* Hodder and Stoughton, 1920, p. 574, 492.
2. *Ib.* 509–10.
3. *Ib.* 491–3.
4. For a full discussion of this, see Eusebius, *Life of Constantine,* II xxx–xlvi, *Nicene and Post-Nicene Fathers,* Series Two, Vol. 1, Erdmanns.
5. *Ib.* III lxiv.
6. *Ib.* lxvi.
7. *Basic Writings of Thomas Jefferson,* Wiley Book Co., 1944, p. 49.
8. *Ib.* 156.
9. *Ib.* 158.
10. *Ib.* 48–49.
11. *The Catholic Yearbook of 1928,* p. 111.

12. *Ib.*
13. *Ib.*
14. Dignan's *History*, 293.
15. *Ib.* 245–268.
16. *Ib.* 57.
17. See *ib.* 42 and *Ency. Britannica*, 1914 ed. Vol. 18, 840–41.
18. 1925 *Statistical Abstract*, 85.
19. Catholic *Yearbook of 1928*, p. 113.
20. Cf. Gausted, *Historical Atlas of Religion in America*, 1962, 160–61.
21. These statistics taken from *The World Almanac of 1968*, pp. 175–176, except those for the Catholic Church, which are taken from the 1968 *Official Catholic Directory*. According to the 1968 *Yearbook of American Churches*, there are 241 bodies with an inclusive membership of 125,-776,656, p. 194.
22. *Ib.*
23. Statistics from the 1968 *Official Catholic Directory*.
24. Cf. 1925 *Statistical Abstract*, p. 85.
25. Cf. 1916 *Catholic Directory*.
26. *The Catholic Encyclopaedia*, 1913, XII, pp. 580–1.
27. Cf. *4 Congressional Record* 175, 1875.
28. Data for 1890, from the 1890 *Abstract of the Census*, p. 259. Data for all other dates, from the 1906, 1916, and 1936 *Census of Religious Bodies*, published by the Department of Commerce.
29. Data for taxable and exempt properties, 1850 to 1922, from 1935 *Statistical Abstract*, p. 268. Data for 1961, *ib.* 1967, p. 437. Data for 1964 from *Church Wealth and Business Income*, p. 110. Data for 1968, based on research presented in this study for the first time.

CHAPTER 2

WHAT THE INTERNAL REVENUE CODE DOES

(Since it is important for everyone to know the provisions of our Internal Revenue Code which deal with church-state relations, we summarize these in the following pages; but, since a detailed and technical analysis may also be desirable, we have prepared a full treatment of the subject in APPENDIX II, p. 303.)

(1) The Code lists 17 categories of organizations which may receive various kinds of tax-exempt revenue.

(2) It has been estimated that there are now more than 1,500,000 entities in the United States which qualify for an exemption. Among these, the most important include "any community chest, fund, or foundation organized and operated exclusively for religious, charitable, scientific, . . . literary, or educational purposes. . . ." None of these are to engage in political propaganda, support candidates for public office, or attempt to influence legislation.

(3) Any exempt organization may create a subsidiary feeder corporation, which itself becomes exempt from federal income taxation if (a) it limits its business to the operation of real estate investments; (b) if it is owned entirely by the parent charity; (c) if all revenues accrue to the latter; (d) if no leases exceed 5 years; and (e) if it is free from encumbrances. This provision enables any church to operate a real estate combine, which itself becomes immune to income taxation.

40

(4) The Code states that the exemption of any organization shall be revoked if any "substantial" portion of its income or activity is directed into political channels. However, since no one knows what "substantial" means, federal bureaucrats exercise very wide discretionary powers. And "substantial" has, therefore, come to mean whatever the Internal Revenue Service says it means, no matter how discriminatory its decisions may be.

(5) Although the Code limits freedom of economic action for many exempt groups, it specifically excuses religious entities, non-profit educational institutions, instrumentalities of government (like the TVA), any denominationally controlled organization, and all qualifying medical facilities from such restrictions. This means, in effect, that all these may do whatever they wish with their revenues and accumulations and need make no financial reports to anyone, such as their contributors, clients, or any level of government.

(6) The Code provides that any of the 17 categories of exempt organizations may receive what is known as "passive" income without tax-liability. Such revenue consists of (1) dividends, interest, and annuities; (2) royalties; (3) property rentals; (4) business leases; and (5) capital gains from the sales of property. In other words, all purely investment income is tax-exempt when received by any of these organizations.

Most exempt organizations are required to file an informational form 990 A when they receive "passive" income. The entities listed above, however, are free from this requirement.

(7) Under the Code, churches constitute the only numerous or important corporations which may engage in unrelated business— that is, active, competitive enterprise—without tax-liability. In addition, the Code also makes such church-activity immune to the necessity of disclosure.

(8) The Internal Revenue Service and/or the Treasury Department have the power to issue Regulations which have the effect of statutory law and which are often as important as the official sections of the Code. Thus it is that the sacerdotal orders of the Roman Catholic Church—such as the Franciscans, the Benedictines, and the Jesuits—have been granted all the immunities conferred upon churches. However, such preferences do not extend, at least in theory, to non-sacerdotal groups like the Christian Brothers and the hundreds of female orders, since none of these are ordained to administer the 7 sacraments of the Roman Catholic Church.

(9) We should also note that tariff schedules permit the importation without duty of vast quantities of merchandise used by the Eastern Orthodox and Roman Catholic churches. These goods are manufactured by cheap labor in foreign countries at a cost much lower than would be possible by American labor.

(10) The Code enables any rabbi or minister of the gospel, if he takes full advantage of the possibilities, to receive the equivalent of a $20,000 or $30,000 salary year after year without tax-liability by the extraordinary provisions and regulations which permit him to receive unreportable income not only to pay all costs involved in the operation of a home but also to pay off the principal of a mortgage at frequent intervals.

(11) No income withholding tax or Social Security contributions may be withheld by any employer from the wages or salary of a rabbi, minister, priest, or member of a religious order.

(12) Formerly, ministers of the gospel were excused from the Social Security program. Under the revised statute, however, ministers, rabbis, and secular priests are required to enroll, unless they make a conscientious objection. However, no contributions to Social Security are made by or required from members of religious orders in the Roman Catholic Church or from priests who have taken the vow of poverty.

(13) Because of the interpretations and regulations issued by the Treasury Department, it is possible even for a secular Catholic priest (one who has not taken the vow of poverty) to live entirely tax-free in a million-dollar mansion, operated by many church-servants and equipped with a fleet of high-priced automobiles. In this case, the living-standards of a multi-millionaire can be enjoyed without the assessment of any tax against personal living costs.

(14) As a *Corporation Sole* or *Aggregate,* a bishop may own, in his own name, unlimited amounts of real estate, cash, stocks, bonds, and other property, and handle all these at his discretion as if they were his personal wealth, without tax-liability or disclosure, under the theory that he is acting as an agent of the church. In this case, all this wealth passes automatically to his successor without the necessity of any instruments to accomplish the legal transferral of the property.

(15) Extremely important also are the provisions of the Code which confer tax-reductions upon those who make gifts to tax-exempt organizations. Of particular significance are the 30% deduction, the

5-year carry-over, the Unlimited Charitable Deduction, and the provision which allows appreciated assets to be transferred at full market value and without tax on capital gains.

It is a demonstrable fact that multi-millionaires can leave larger estates to their private heirs than would otherwise be possible by giving millions to churches or church-related colleges or hospitals. Hundreds of wealthy people pay no income tax whatever on huge incomes by giving a comparatively small portion of their incomes to "charity." What happens, in effect, is that when the tycoon prepares his tax-return, he simply avoids his liability to government by giving what he would otherwise owe as a tax to his private and favorite charity or—in some cases—even to his own controlled, personal foundation.

(16) Among the favorite businesses in which churches are now deeply involved, we may mention (a) the Purchase-and-Leaseback; (b) the Business Front; (c) the "Clay-Brown" operation; and (d) the outright ownership and operation of competitive business enterprise.

In the purchase-and-leaseback, the church uses borrowed money to acquire ownership of, for example, a hotel or shopping center. It then pays off the encumbrance, largely with money which would be used to pay taxes by an ordinary individual or corporation. At the end of a given period, the church can sell the facility back to the former owner for a huge untaxed capital gain.

A business front may be created by a church by lending some money to a partnership, which thereafter pays heavy interest and a 30% deductible contribution to the religious entity. Meanwhile, the business prospers, in part because the members of the church are urged to patronize the front.

In the Clay-Brown operation, a church purchases a going business at an inflated price without investing any money whatever, or at least very little, and pays off the notes out of current income. The former owner is now the manager, and the money he receives is transformed from heavily taxed earned income to lightly taxed capital gains. In addition, he has no Social Security to pay, and can build an estate rapidly from his untaxed capital gains.

In countless instances, churches or sacerdotal orders operate wineries, radio stations, publishing houses, newspapers, nursing homes, retirement centers, luxury housing projects, etc., etc., ad infinitum.

43

Let us repeat that they own and operate such enterprises directly; yet they pay no taxes on the profits, and they are not required to make any disclosure concerning such activities to anyone.

Many and various are the tax-advantages which churches can extend under the Code as a tax-umbrella to private business corporations and to wealthy individuals.

We suggest that the reader study carefully the material presented in APPENDIX II: "Churches and the Internal Revenue Code." Here will be found voluminous documentation, all pertinent citations from the Internal Revenue Code, and numerous examples which illustrate every form of advantage given the churches under federal law.

We have also added to Appendix II a brief summary and comment on the reforms contemplated in the proposed new Tax Bill of 1969 passed by the House of Representatives on August 7, 1969.

CHAPTER 3

THE SWELLING CHORUS

THE PROBLEM POSED

Since it is quite possible that within the foreseeable future half the land in our major cities will be exempt from taxation, thoughtful and knowledgeable people are beginning to express themselves in no uncertain terms concerning the resulting problems. This of course includes the holdings of federal, state, and municipal governments; but the burgeoning domain of the churches is scarcely less imposing. Since tax-exempt wealth is increasing far more rapidly than any other, it is obvious that fewer taxpayers must bear the cost of all public services.

Some tend to think of the problem posed by religious exemptions as highly remote. England, indeed, as well as France, Germany, and Mexico may once have had such difficulties—but not the United States; for we possess a great land-mass in which the areas dedicated to religious use must appear relatively insignificant. But the church never dies and therefore never redistributes; it continues to accumulate and expand across the centuries. Before many generations, this can lead to the condition of "religious inflation" in which there is more church than the people can reasonably sustain. When this happens, social disruptions and political explosions become inevitable.

45

There are those who say that the religious domain could continue to expand for another century or two here without serious repercussions. There is, however, a fatal flaw in such logic; for we are not dealing primarily with prairies, deserts, and mountains, but with the restricted areas of our urban centers. Fire and police protection, water and sanitation service, education, recreation, and countless other services must be financed largely through local taxes derived from real estate. In this shrinking area, every new exemption hurts more than its predecessor. Local use, sales, income, excise, personal property, gross earnings, and various other taxes have become commonplace to replace the revenues lost through the erosion of the tax-base.

In the preceding chapter, we described the advantages enjoyed by churches under the Internal Revenue Code. As a result of their various immunities under the tax laws established by city, state, and federal authorities, many churches are becoming extremely wealthy corporations. They now conduct an enterprise possessing more than $100 billion in physical assets used for religious purposes alone; and theirs is an operation which now collects and disburses more than $22 billion a year and is, therefore, surpassed in magnitude only by the federal government. Among all private "charities," churches collectively are by far the wealthiest. This situation is leading to a reassessment of religious exemptions and perhaps a reappraisal of the entire ecclesiastical structure. Anticlericalism is the normal reaction against a too-wealthy and powerful church; and this is the historic seedbed in which revolution and expropriation find their violent habitat.

LEADING CHURCHES AND CHURCHMEN SPEAK OUT

A surprising array of religious leaders in the United States have exhibited a remarkable candor in discussing church-taxation. A decade ago, Dr. Eugene Carson Blake, then Stated Clerk of the United Presbyterian Church, U.S.A., and now Executive Secretary of the World Council of Churches, declared grimly: "I suggest that 100 years from now the present pattern of religious tax exemption by Federal, State and municipal authorities, if continued, may present the state with problems of such magnitude that their only solution will be the revolutionary expropriation of church property." [1]

46

Elsewhere, Dr. Blake offered the following analysis: "Revolutionary expropriation of church properties was the solution resorted to in 16th century England, 18th century France, 19th century Italy, and 20th century Russia. Mexico still suffers convulsions from such seizure.

"Hard pressed governments sooner or later will turn on wealthy churches and a wave of anti-clericalism and atheism always precedes the clash. Such a feeling already is apparent in the United States." [2]

In an earlier, formal statement he declared: "Consider the new threat that I see, fortunately quite far away yet, but still an increasing threat. I mean the very subject of taxes on churches and their institutions . . . generation by generation more . . . untaxable wealth falls into the hands of the churches. . . . Religious people, for their own good, and for the protection of the commonwealth, must re-examine the tax-free status which, when we were weak and poor, seemed a fully proper encouragement of religious institutions. . . . ." [3]

A Southern Baptist Study Paper adopted in 1960 warned against the wiles of the federal income tax exemption for churches. The Study said that such exemption tends to "(1) encourage promotion of or participation in secular business to the detriment of the principal mission of the church; (2) encourage morally unjustifiable arrangements with businessmen or companies to reduce their income taxes; (3) discourage financial support of church activities by voluntary contributions of all members." [4]

The American Lutheran Church, with 2,400,000 members, at its national convention in Columbus, Ohio, Oct. 26, 1964, passed a policy statement which asserted that churches should be willing to accept "equitable taxation" of parsonages and other related dwellings. Concerned over the question of finances, the Convention observed that "the church faces a constant temptation to turn to commercial and quasi-commercial sources for raising funds." Significantly, it noted also that "to levy upon churches charges for municipal services such as water, sewage, police, and fire protection is consistent with sound public policy." [4]

Dr. Emerson Abendroth of the Christian Board of Education, United Presbyterian Church, declared that "This is a matter that the church should think through very, very seriously. We simply have gone along with the tax exemption policy without thinking about its implications. This policy of the church [to make payments to the municipality for services] is a stepping stone for the church to give greater consideration to its responsibilities to the community in which it lives." [5]

The same denomination made related recommendations to Rep. Mills' Committee on Ways and Means, which published its *Hearings on General Revenue Revision* in 1958. George W. McKeag, appearing on behalf of the General Assembly of the Presbyterian Church, U.S.A., advocated "that the exemption allowed to churches . . . . on unrelated business income be removed from the Internal Revenue Code. . . . ." [6]

Dr. Frederick Schiotz, President of the American Lutheran Church, declared: "With the acquisition by churches of property not directly related to the church, we should re-examine the need for more income (in taxes) to go to the state." Dr. Schiotz explained that he was thinking particularly of church retirement homes, many of which have been granted real estate tax exemption as the property of a church. [7]

Actions of considerable significance were recommended by the United Methodist Church at its June, 1968, General Conference in Dallas, Texas. They called for discontinuance of the "special treatment accorded to churches or associations of churches with respect to exclusion of their unrelated business income from income taxation." The Methodists also called for the abolition "of all special privileges to members of the clergy in American tax laws and regulations."

A Methodist study prepared by the Board of Christian Social Concerns made additional significant recommendations. It urged that churches be required to provide full disclosure of their income in the same manner as other charitable groups. The report also insisted that churches assume "responsibility to make appropriate contributions, in lieu of taxes, for essential services provided by government."

In 1960, the Council of Congregational-Christian Churches (now United Church of Christ) declared that local churches and other related organizations should pay taxes on property they own if such real estate is not used exclusively for religious, educational, or welfare programs. [8]

One of the present authors told the House Ways and Means Committee on Feb. 24, 1969: "while the Founder of Christianity had not where to lay His head and his disciples sallied forth without purse or scrip, some of those who speak in His name have been able to create corporations which make Croesus seem like a pauper."

The Minnesota Council of Churches did not exactly advocate a tax on church bodies of that state, but, in a brochure entitled *Justice for All Minnesotans,* it declared: "If all church bodies in Minnesota paid property taxes . . . $26.8 million could be released for such things as schools, jails, hospitals, cleansing our lakes and rivers. Assuming there would be no cut in present church programs, the average cost per adult church member would be $14.90 per year.

"If all church bodies in Minnesota voluntarily paid only ten per cent of their income (the Biblical tithe), at least $15.5 million more could be released for securing justice for all Minnesotans. Assuming there would be no cut in present church programs, the average cost per adult would be $8.60 per year."

One of the most interesting suggestions for change in the matter of church tax-exemption was advanced by Dr. Eugene Carson Blake when he was serving as Stated Clerk of the United Presbyterian Church. He encouraged the churches to make a definite contribution to their communities in lieu of taxes. He said that this contribution might begin at one per cent of a normal levy and be increased until at least 10 per cent of the usual tax would be paid.[9]

A careful study prepared by the Baptist Joint Committee on Public Affairs in 1960 declared that only property used for religious purposes and programs should receive exemption, and that church-owned business and commercial real estate should be taxed.[10]

Key Christian Scientist leaders have frequently emphasized their position that tax-exemption should not be granted to unrelated business income or commercial activities, merely because they are church-owned.[11] This Church pays property taxes on its great publishing complex near the Mother Church in Boston.

The National Association of Evangelicals, serving a constituency of more than 2 million members, has declared officially that tax-exempt profit-making by churches and their related organizations results in an unlawful subsidy which is forbidden by the First Amendment.

A joint statement of the National Council of Churches and the United States Catholic Conference issued May 2, 1969, favored certain reforms in regard to the tax-exemptions of churches. Specifically, these groups recommended that the section 511 exemption of churches from tax on income from unrelated commercial business be removed; also that revenues from "leasebacks" financed with borrowed money be subjected to taxation. The statement declared that the exemption on profits of unrelated business "makes available to churches a potential advantage over tax-paying organizations engaged in commercial business activities. The National Council of Churches and the United States Catholic Conference favor elimination of the specific exemption of churches from taxation on income from *regularly* conducted business activities, which are unrelated to their exempt functions." However, the statement emphasized that income from investments, such as stocks, bonds, mortgages, bank accounts, etc., should continue in its present tax-exempt status—a position which we regard as unfortunate and unjustifiable.

The Episcopal Guild of St. Ives in New York City has urged that all churches pay some taxes. The group's report [12] showed that church property in New York City exceeded $700 million and that, if taxed, it would produce revenue in the neighborhood of $35 million. The Guild specifically suggested that income taxes be levied against revenues derived from real estate and other church-owned properties unrelated to religious use, and also that "passive income" from stocks and bonds as well as other investments be taxed. The report noted that "the total wealth of organized religion is growing while the needs of government, particularly at the local level, are increasing." The Guild is convinced that churches have a moral and financial obligation to give up their privileged status.

A 1963 study by the Protestant Council of New York City revealed that while its membership was only 250,000, its churches own real estate worth $250 million in Manhattan alone.[13]

Although Dr. Franklin Fry (deceased), formerly president of the mammoth Lutheran Church of America, stated that he favored a continuation of tax-exemption for church sanctuaries, he nevertheless urged that parishes make contributions to their communities for services rendered, such as fire and police protection.[14]

Statements like the preceding, issued by responsible Protestant leaders, could be multiplied *ad infinitum*.

On the other hand, suggestions that church property be taxed or charged uniformly in some manner for services have not been forthcoming to any such extent from the Roman Catholic leadership. Bishop Fulton J. Sheen suggested that his church contribute 5 per cent of its annual income to anti-poverty programs.[15] This, however, would in effect give the Church credit for its own private philanthropy and would not appreciably ease the tax-burden of the community.

50

A CONFRONTATION

A call for action in language which brought the problem into sharp focus was sounded by Dr. Paul A. Reynolds, professor of philosophy at Wesleyan University, Middletown, Connecticut. Addressing the Twentieth National Conference on Church and State in Cincinnati, February 5, 1968, he urged that the property of churches be taxed on exactly the same terms as any other real estate. The government, he contended, should tax the churches in order to keep them private and avoid establishment. He continued: "If anyone says I am thereby taxing religion, my answer is, no, not at all. Not taxing religion, but taxing property. The state looks only at the property, not at the religion. As in the case of color and race and national origin, the state looks *through, not at,* any of these things. . . . .

"The point is that separation of church and state should be restricted to separation of church and state, and should not be extended to separation of property and the state. . . . Only when the church is as disestablished as other private institutions—no more and no less—can its separation from the state be bona fide and clear."

We should note, however, that a panel of clergy and laymen representing religious groups was unanimously in opposition. Dr. Roy Nichols, now Methodist Bishop of Pittsburgh, argued that tax-exemption for churches "represents equal opportunity for all religious groups without discrimination." William R. Schumacher, representing the Cincinnati Roman Catholic Archdiocese, advocated not only tax-exemption but also public subsidies, especially for church schools. Rabbi Stanley C. Chyet of Hebrew Union College, Cincinnati, and Dr. Woodrow Perry, president of Cincinnati Bible Seminary, both favored tax-exemption for churches because of the importance of religion to the morality and culture of the community. "To deny churches a property tax exemption," declared the former, "would be to deny religion a certain legitimacy. . . ." It "does not force a great burden on non-church people" and can be compared to those who, though they have no children, "are taxed for public school support." Dr. Perry argued that, since tax-exemptions are made available to secular education, such benefits to churches provide "a counterbalance in at least this minimal degree."

THE OFFICIAL LAMENT

Assessors and others who know best the plight of their cities are raising their voices everywhere in what is becoming an almost universal and unanimous chorus. In Los Angeles County, California, according to Assessor Phillip W. Watson, at least $25 of a typical tax bill of $350 [a] paid by the owner of a $16,000 home represents taxes paid for somebody else's private exemptions.[16] Of all non-federal land in Colorado, 42% is tax-exempt; and the value of this, according to a legislative committee headed by state senator Ruth S. Stockton, is estimated at $816 million.[17] Although much of the exempt area is in public parks, church camps and recreation centers owned by many denominations account for a substantial share. Senator Stockton's committee recommended that a state fee for services be charged to all exempt institutions.

In St. Louis, the Missouri Collector of Revenue, John K. Travers, suggested that all church property not used for charitable or religious purposes be taxed. Although he felt that property with exclusively religious use should remain exempt, he declared that "all income-producing property owned by [religious] organizations should certainly bear their fair share. They are competing with private enterprise and certainly need the same services that are provided for everyone else." [18]

County Solicitor Maurice Louik of Allegheny County, Pittsburgh, has called for a study of laws which grant tax-exemption, so that abuses and inequities may be corrected. "It is interesting to note," he declares, "that assessed valuations in the city increased from 1966 to 1967 by $46 million but of this amount $37.5 million—or about 80%—[b] was tax-exempt." [19]

Julian R. Garzon, tax-assessor of Minneapolis, Minnesota, stated in 1963 that the rapid increase in religious and other exempt property was threatening the city tax-base. He complained pointedly that national headquarters of certain churches enjoyed local tax-exemptions. "What this means," he declared, "is that we, as Minneapolis taxpayers, support the world-wide work of a particular church, and maybe we don't want to." [20] When Garzon was thwarted in imposing a tax on a bowling alley located in the basement of the Holy Cross Roman Catholic Church, he billed it for personal property taxes on

[a] This amount is obviously very low. Since more than 30% of all real estate is off the tax-rolls and since nearly half of this consists of private exempts, the correct amount should have been $50 or $60.

[b] It is even more interesting to note that between 1967 and 1968 taxable property *decreased* in Pittsburgh by nearly $12 million while the exempt *increased* by more than $55 million (cf. Ch. 6).

52

the equipment. The priest in charge, Msgr. Joseph Siegienski, refused to accept the assessment and appealed to the courts.[21]

The Minnesota House Tax Subcommittee reported recently that the market value of exempt property in that state exceeded $5 billion.[22] The Milwaukee *Journal* stated that between 1950 and 1961 the assessed valuation of tax-exempt property in the city increased from $307 to $625 million, or 104%, while the taxable rose from $1,214,000,000 to $1,974,300,000, or 62.6%.[23] Officials complained bitterly that the tax-base was eroding.

John F. Tarrant, research director for Connecticut's tax department, estimated that tax-exemptions cost the state's municipalities $86 million annually.[24] The Roman Catholic Church owns more real estate in the 81-town archdiocese of Hartford than does the State and its holdings represent 30 per cent of non-government tax-exempt property.[25] In the capital city of Hartford, State properties are assessed at $31,587,230 and Roman Catholic at $36,829,940.

In Rochester, New York, the valuations on tax-exempt property, including churches, parsonages, cemeteries, clubs, "character-building agencies," government buildings, etc., stood at $209 million 1968–1969 and occasioned a tax-loss of $13 million.[26]

David Cooper, writing in the Detroit *Free Press,* Feb. 23, 1969, stated that 21 per cent of the land in the city is exempt and carries an assessed valuation of $981,608,000; and that 43 per cent of all personal property, assessed at $1,030,350,000 is in the same category. If both were taxed, revenues of $43 million would accrue to the treasury.

In Denver, Colorado, Councilman Houston Gibson registered an emphatic "No" when Regis College (Roman Catholic) sought a permit to build a $1.5 million shopping center.[27] He noted that the tax-status of the proposed project had not been clarified (cf. Chapter 5).

Tax authorities in Baltimore, Maryland, have computed the loss through real estate exemptions at $20 million [a] annually.[28] Montgomery County, Ohio, released a report which indicated an annual re-

---

[a] Our research (cf. Ch. 5) demonstrates that property exemptions in Baltimore cost the taxpayers $28,750,000 on present assessments, which stand at 30% less than parity. The real cost, therefore, exceeds $40 million, of which 40%, or $16 million, is occasioned by private ownership; of this, about 65% is religious, which, therefore, costs the taxpayers of Baltimore more than $10 million annually.

venue loss because of real estate exemptions for churches alone at $2,055,513.[29]

A *Citizens Budget Commission Report* has disclosed that if only half the tax-exempt property in New York City could be put back on the rolls, the city could absorb its $400 million annual deficit.[30] The Commission showed that tax-exempt property was increasing far more rapidly than taxable and that the former doubled during the 10 years following 1957. Revenues thus lost amounted to $777 million a year, as against $1.57 billion collected. The *Report* recommended further that the City be given the power to make its own determinations concerning tax-exemptions; and Budget Director Frederick O'Hayes declared that his department would seek such power and would recommend that all tax-exempt institutions and corporations be billed for direct services rendered by the city.[31]

In West Virginia, an opinion issued by Attorney General C. Donald Robertson on Sept. 25, 1962, has had the effect of sharpening tax procedures in that state. He held that "mere ownership of property by church trustees does not assure such property of tax-exemption: the property to be considered tax-exempt must be used exclusively for divine worship." [32] The ruling came as a result of questions that had been raised concerning a 1,500-acre site on which is located the Conference Center of the Episcopal Diocese of West Virginia. It was disclosed that timber and pulpwood were sold, with the revenue going to the Conference Center. The attorney-general said he believed that none of the acreage in question, save possibly the area occupied by a chapel, met the test of having primary use exclusively for divine worship.

When City Manager Gilbert Chavenelle of Dubuque, Iowa, was faced by a prospective deficit of $275,000 for the city due to special expenditures caused by floods, he urged that all properties, without exception, be required to make a proportionate contribution. He noted that 40 per cent of Dubuque's developed land was tax-exempt and that some of its finest buildings were located thereon,—also tax-exempt. Yet, as he pointed out, these structures required the same services as taxable property.[33]

Short of revenue, the city of Anchorage, Alaska, added $20,000 to its annual tax-yield by tightening up taxes on church property not used exclusively for religious purposes.[34] Both Harrisburg and Philadelphia have begun to tax church parking lots.[35] Flathead County, Montana, imposed a real estate tax on its Immanuel Lutheran Home in Kalispell—an institution of the American Lutheran Church. W. H.

Knapton, chairman of County Commissioners, pointed out that the home charged for care and under Montana law did not,* therefore, qualify for tax-exemption.[36] Northwestern University of Evanston, Illinois, originally a Methodist school, submitted its routine annual request for tax-exemption in 1965, only to be confronted by a determined challenge from the state attorney's office.[37] Russell E. Johnson, Director of Appraisals for the County, said that he objected particularly to exemption for certain commercial properties, such as a Pepsi Cola plant, two warehouses, and the Illinois Bell Telephone Company garage. Mr. Johnson observed that in his opinion so long as these commercial properties received city and county services, the University should pay taxes on them.

THE VOICE OF THE PEOPLE AND THE PRESS

Letters to the editor appearing almost daily in hundreds of American newspapers cry out for tax relief in ways which frequently challenge the exempt status of the churches. The following is a typical expression: "I think most people would oppose any taxing of church sanctuaries. But when more and more land is taken, it seems to me their leaders might want to pay taxes in the interest of public spirit. God's business ought to pay its way, too. Who needs the enormous and expensive cathedrals and temples? Not God. The best sermons were preached under the open sky—by Jesus." [38]

The press itself is calling for significant tax reform. An editorial in the New York *Times,* Jan. 31, 1969, cautiously favored a proposal which would transfer from the state to the local community the right to pass upon individual exemptions. "It should be the community's province," the *Times* declared, "to decide which activities it will subsidize by excusing them from property tax."

In a telling article on "Tax Exemptions" the Bradenton, Florida, *Herald* pointed out, Feb. 23, 1969, that whereas the property valuations for Manatee County stood at $481,638,963, exemptions totalled $149,959,140. The article, written by Sally Remaley, goes on to say that if the current increase in exempts continues, it "will eventually deprive states, counties, and cities, even the federal government, of much-needed funds for operation . . . funds which the 'rest of us'

---

* The Montana constitution (which is often flagrantly violated by county assessors) provides specifically in Art. XII, Sec. 2, that no church properties except sanctuaries, schools, hospitals, and nonprofit cemeteries shall be exempt from property taxation.

will be forced to assume or the United States could conceivably go bankrupt."

The Los Angeles *Times* urged passage of a bill pending in the legislature which would limit tax-exemption to property actually used for the qualifying purpose; and it called for a review of the policy which exempts from taxes what it called "luxury life-care homes for the aged." [39]

LEGISLATIVE AND CONSTITUTIONAL PROPOSALS

Perhaps the most impressive evidence of the trend to reduce religious tax-exemptions is reflected in the efforts of various state legislatures, public officials, or constitutional conventions. Fearing the wrath of the churches and not wishing to be branded as irreligious, legislators are understandably reluctant to express themselves openly on this highly sensitive issue. Yet, in spite of this, virtually all the legislators will acknowledge off the record that the problem of religious exemptions is growing more serious every year and that some corrective measures are definitely in order.

An interesting effort to impose taxes on church holdings was undertaken by a member of the Maine legislature, Representative Ernest D. Smith, himself a minister in the Nazarene Church. He described religious tax-exemptions as "one of the greatest problems we have in the state today." Pointing to the large property holdings by exempt groups, including many commercial operations, he added: "No longer can churches be classified as charitable. They own money-making property, rent buildings. . . . The churches have come to the point where they should be willing to pay if they are going to accept services from the state." [40]

Percy L. Smith, Jr., Office Manager for the Assessor in Richmond, wrote us under date of April 18, 1969: "We are looking forward to hearing of your findings regarding non-taxable properties, as this is a big subject in Richmond and Virginia at the present time. . . . The General Assembly of Virginia is now in session studying a revision of the Constitution, and considering the authorization to permit the City to levy a service charge against tax exempt property."

We have no doubt that such developments will become common in other areas of the country during the years ahead.

Representative Francis H. Sherman of Coventry, Rhode Island, has gone on record for curbing religious exemptions. On a recent occasion, he expressed the view that real estate tax-exemptions for churches should be limited to property actually used for religious purposes. He estimated that real estate worth "millions of dollars" was held by churches for investment purposes. He explained that a study of tax-exemptions in the state is now being conducted by a legisaltive commission and added: "It is my hope it will not neglect consideration of this now exempt wealth as a potential source of much needed tax revenue"; and he expressed surprise that the governor, confronted with the task of finding more money, did not seek to tap "this tremendous revenue source before going all out in demanding a highly unpopular income tax." [41]

In Florida, a Commission for Tax Reform uncovered serious abuses in the matter of tax-exemptions. Its chairman, Representative James Sweeny, commented: [42] "We can do a lot of good in ad valorem, particularly tax exemptions." He was highly critical of a Miami church that had been successful in evading tax, as a result of court decree, on a parking lot which it rented for $2,000 a week for commercial use, and he declared: "I'm going to try to get around that decision."

State senate majority leader W. Russell Arrington called upon the Illinois legislature to re-examine the tax-exempt status of real estate owned by churches.

Representative Ernest Lindstrom of Minnesota, Chairman of the Subcommittee on Tax-Exempt Property, held extensive hearings in St. Paul during the summer of 1968 with the objective of preparing legislation intended to reduce the amount of tax-exempt real estate. His work has now resulted in a proposal to amend the State constitution for the purpose of giving the legislature wide and final authority to set all standards, limits, and definitions governing property exemptions. Although church sanctuaries and private sectarian schools would continue tax-exempt, many other categories of property, now tax-free, would be placed under taxation, including retirement homes, parsonages, rectories, church-owned business enterprises, and every facility not used specifically or exclusively for a religious purpose. Even the University of Minnesota and some other state agencies would be required to pay certain taxes, under the proposals advanced by Mr. Lindstrom and his Committee.[43]

In Vermont, a bill was introduced in the legislature which would impose a tax on church-owned property. This proposal, which received the approval of the House Ways and Means Committee, would permit towns to tax all property except that owned by the federal government and highway rights-of-way. The Committee explained that the purpose of the bill was to follow a recommendation of the State Tax Department which urged elimination of many kinds of exemptions, of which the religious was one.[44] The bill, however, was caught in the legislative log-jam at the close of the session and did not get to the floor. Sponsors plan on reintroducing it at the earliest opportunity.

One of the most determined efforts to curb religious tax-exemptions has been made in Pennsylvania. This is remarkable in view of the fact that only a decade ago the legislature passed a bill which would have exempted all church parsonages from real estate tax. The bill was promptly vetoed by Governor David L. Lawrence, a Roman Catholic, who pointed out that provisions of the state constitution and various court decisions bearing on the question made it clear that parsonages are not exempt from taxation in Pennsylvania.

When that state undertook a revision of its constitution, an impressive array of witnesses turned up to urge abolition of the church tax-exemption. Milton W. DeLancey, Secretary of the Pennsylvania State Association of Township Supervisors, told a convention committee that "all property owners should pay their fair share for local services." He urged elimination of all exemptions, including both religious and governmental. Taking the same position was Richard C. Marden, Executive Director of the Pennsylvania League of Cities. Harry Boyer, state president of the AFL-CIO, declared succinctly: "The . . . AFL-CIO believes that the exemption now accorded to religious and other non-profit organizations and institutions is not only unwarranted but unfair to the citizens as a whole. The entire scope of such exemptions should be re-examined and evaluated by the constitutional convention."

The convention sought to compromise the issue with a proposal that churches be required to make payments in lieu of taxes for such services as police and fire protection and garbage and sewage disposal. Even this, however, encountered determined opposition from the Roman Catholic Conference representing the state's 8 dioceses. Their argument was that such charges would add to the costs of the Catholic parochial schools which were already in financial difficulty. The proposed charges were eventually eliminated from the constitution.[45]

The state of New Jersey has encountered revenue problems similar to those of its neighbor, Pennsylvania. The state seeks to finance its growing services, while myriad tax-exemptions choke off its revenues. Russell T. Wilson, head of the New Jersey League of Municipalities, and city tax-assessor for the City of Hackensack, called for a legislative study of tax-exempt property, including that of churches. Assemblyman Webster B. Todd, Jr., of Somerset, said that he was in favor of it and indicated that a bill would be introduced on the subject.[46]

The Arizona *Republic* recently [47] carried the news that Assessor Kenneth R. Kunes of Phoenix had already ordered more than $5 million of exempt real estate in that city to be placed on the tax rolls. He indicated that his work of assessing properties which had been escaping tax illegally was less than half complete. One category of previously exempt properties was that of church parsonages and rectories, but there were others. One important object of his attention was a 248-acre tract almost in the heart of the city owned and leased out by the Church of Jesus Christ of Latter-Day Saints (Mormon) as a revenue-producing farm-operation which paid no taxes.[*]

In a number of sessions of the Oregon legislature in recent years, bills have been introduced which would make possible the taxing of church property. The principal opponent has been Roman Catholic Archbishop Edward D. Howard of Portland, who declared: "The state should not be put in the position of taxing efforts of any citizen to offer worship to the Deity." Confronted with the suggestion that churches might voluntarily pay fees for fire and police protection, the prelate replied: "The members of the churches are already paying [for these services] through their personal contributions." [48]

Nevertheless, a powerful sentiment for drastic reform has persisted in the State legislature. On April 10, 1969, the Oregon House of Representatives voted to tax houses of worship. Such properties, along with lodges, hospitals, and other exempts, would be required to pay 25 per cent of a normal tax levy. Sponsors of the legislation said that it would provide an additional $3.5 million in revenue but, more than that, it would contribute to equity among taxpayers. The bill was eventually defeated. Had it become law, Oregon would have been the pioneer in levying a direct tax upon church sanctuaries.

THE ONTARIO STUDY

The most recent comprehensive study in this area has been made by the Ontario, Canada, Committee on Taxation, which published its

---

[*] On Sept. 18, 1969, the Roman Catholic and Mormon churches sued the assessor of Maricopa Co. for a refund of more than $35,000 paid in taxes on rectories and welfare operations.

findings in three volumes in 1967.[49] Chapter XII (pp. 125–202) is devoted to all facets of tax-exemption and there is a copious treatment of the impact of religious exemptions. The problems arising from tax-exemption for churches in Ontario are the same as in the States. Because of its exhaustive nature and because of its sweeping recommendations for change in the religious exemption, the Ontario *Study* is worth our careful examination.

It asserts that "the merits of tax exemption for churches are increasingly being questioned." And it continues: "We find little to justify burdening all property owners with the cost of the relief given to places of worship in recognition of the indirect benefits they confer upon society generally. If we accept as a fact that there is little prospect of public acceptance for direct subsidy [to churches], the problem we face is that the continued full exemption of places of worship unfairly saddles local property owners with the full burden of the tax relief given to churches."

"It is well to recognize," the *Study* bluntly remarks, "that exemption from normal assessments and taxation constitutes a privilege that can be made available in only one way: at the expense of the remaining taxpayers."

The general arguments against exemption are thus summarized:

"(1) Exemptions narrow the tax base, thereby increasing the tax load on owners of taxable property.

"(2) A tax exemption is an indirect subsidy, the cost of which is not generally apparent, and is subject to less control than a grant, which ordinarily is renewable annually.

"(3) Tax exemption may not distribute a government subsidy in the most equitable or desirable manner.

"(4) The proportion of all properties in the community that are exempt varies from one municipality to another, thereby creating disproportionate burdens among local communities.

"(5) Exemptions are for the most part legislated by the Province but their burden falls on municipalities and local school boards.

"(6) Exemptions, once established, are not readily terminated. Thus, they tend to perpetuate community wishes of an earlier day. In addition, the range and extent of exemptions can grow well beyond justifiable limits."

The authors of the *Study,* however, declare: "We nevertheless hold the view that the indirect benefits to society that flow from places of worship justify some measure of relief from local taxation. We do not believe that there should be full exemption because, in our view,

60

church members who directly benefit from local government services, should contribute to their costs. What this contribution should be is essentially a matter of judgment and we think it should be perhaps one-half the normal tax. We realize, however, that a sudden change from complete exemption of places of worship to 50 per cent taxation, would impose tremendous hardship on churches with limited financial resources. We therefore propose that the change be made in stages over several years . . . We therefore recommend that places of worship and land used therewith, and religious seminaries not classed as institutions of higher learning or as private schools, be reassessed at actual value and taxed on a taxable assessment of 5 per cent of actual value the first year and 10 per cent the second year with increases of 5 percentage points each succeeding year until a level of 35 per cent, or such other maximum percentage as a review of the tax position of places of worship made after five years may indicate to be appropriate."

When the Metro Executive Committee of Toronto backed the findings of the Ontario Committee and urged that churches be assessed 35 per cent of normal municipal taxes, a spokesman of the United Church of Canada spoke out in opposition. Very Reverend Ernest N. Howse, former moderator of the United Church, protested that "it would simply mean that a lot of churches would have to close down." He went on to say: "The downtown churches would be hit the hardest, of course, but even in smaller communities taxes would be on the average about $6,000 or $7,000 a year and many parishes just couldn't afford it. And to make it worse, they'd all close down at one fell swoop." [50]

Such statements, however, at least insofar as they could apply to American sanctuaries, smack more of hysteria than calm reasoning. For we have found literally thousands of churches assessed at less than $50,000; and on such buildings a normal tax on a 35%-assessment would not exceed $450. A tax of $7,000 would apply only to churches with a multi-million dollar replacement value; it would seem that memberships who can afford such magnificence could easily pay a few thousand dollars to their communities.

THE FINAL COURT

Perhaps the ultimate decision on tax-exemption for churches lies in the realm of public opinion. What do the people think? A poll was conducted by CBS in connection with its documentary presentation of

June 18, 1968, "The Business of Religion." In this, three groups described as the public, the Congress, and the clergy were interrogated. The first question asked was whether churches should be required to make financial statements disclosing their wealth, income, and disbursements. The majority said *Yes* (public, 66 per cent; Congress, 66 per cent; and clergy, 53 per cent). The second question was whether churches should be required to disclose their commercial holdings and revenue only. The great majority said *Yes:* (public, 77 per cent; Congress, 89 per cent; and clergy, 84 per cent). The third question was whether church sanctuaries should be taxed. The majority said *No:* (public, 60 per cent; Congress, 89 per cent; and clergy, 79 per cent). The fourth question was whether churches should be taxed on their profits from commercial ventures. The reply was an overwhelming affirmative: (public, 84 per cent; Congress, 96 per cent; and clergy, 93 per cent). The fifth and final question was whether churches should make voluntary contributions to help ease the burdens of property owners who, under present conditions, must pay the entire bill for community services. The response was again affirmative: (public, 59 per cent; Congress, 63 per cent; and clergy, 62 per cent).

We believe that the reactions recorded in the CBS documentary are of the highest importance. The overwhelming conviction among all classes of the population to the effect that churches should make full disclosure of their commercial holdings and revenues and pay taxes on all profits deriving from them, certainly indicate a new departure in American thinking. Although with a smaller majority, the respondents were also convinced that all churches should supply at least their members and contributors with a complete and detailed financial report. This too is a startling innovation. And let us note that while 60 per cent of the general public are still willing to grant tax-exemption to sanctuaries only, a powerful minority of 40% are saying that even these should be subjected to the full ad valorem tax—a thing unheard of twenty years ago. Furthermore, all groups interviewed agreed by substantial margins that all churches should reimburse their communities for the necessary services without which they could not operate. We made this proposal in our *Church Wealth and Business Income* in 1965. These two last reactions are, we believe, the most extraordinary facts revealed in the CBS poll; and we would suggest that leading churchmen consider most carefully the implications of these reactions, on pain of the greatest peril to their immunities in the future.

We have also concluded that developments such as these, and many others of a related nature, are one result of two decades of intensive exposure and effective education promoted by Americans United for Separation of Church and State.

Not integrally related, but not irrelevant either, is another inquiry by Dr. Gallup which indicates a declining influence of religion in American life. A poll taken May 5, 1969, was the most recent of several which posed the question: "At the present time, do you think that religion as a whole is increasing its influence in American life or losing its influence?" The dates and answers follow:

	1957	1962	1965	1967	1969
Increasing	69%	45%	33%	23%	14%
Losing	14%	31%	45%	57%	70%
No Difference	10%	17%	13%	14%	11%
No Opinion	7%	7%	9%	6%	5%

While it would be premature to say that we are approaching the end of tax-exemptions for churches in the United States, there is certainly widespread and deepening interest in the matter on the part of the state, the church, and the general public, as well as among various law-making bodies. It appears, too, that changes in regard to the taxation of church revenue from active and even from passive business income are in sight. No one can be sure what precise direction these will take, or how far they will go. We may assume, however, that in the foreseeable future, religious organizations may be required to pay, if not all, at least a portion of the levies now contributed by secular corporations for the support of the communities which serve and protect them.

Citations

1. *Christianity Today,* Aug. 3, 1969.
2. Detroit *Free Press,* March 14, 1962.
3. *The Churchman,* Dec. 1, 1956.
4. *Religious News Service,* Sept. 15, 1960.
5. Kansas City *Times,* July 8, 1964.
6. *Hearings,* p. 2110.
7. Cleveland *Plain Dealer,* Aug. 25, 1967.
8. Grand Rapids, Michigan, *Press,* July 17, 1960.
9. *Christianity Today,* Aug. 3, 1959.
10. *Religious News Service,* Sept. 13, 1960.
11. *Tax Exemption of Churches and Churchmen,* by Carl Olsen, a Columbia University master's thesis, dated May 8, 1968, p. 41.

12. The New York *Times,* May 20, 1967.
13. *Signs of the Times,* Aug. 1963.
14. *Time,* July 1, 1966.
15. The New York *Times,* Nov. 8, 1966.
16. *The Wall Street Journal,* Aug. 2, 1964.
17. *Religious News Service,* April 6, 1966.
18. *Church & State,* June, 1968.
19. The Pittsburgh *Post-Gazette,* July 17, 1967.
20. The Minneapolis *Morning Tribune,* Feb. 18, 1963.
21. *Ib.*
22. Cf. The Minneapolis *Tribune,* Jan. 17, 1969.
23. The Milwaukee *Journal,* Feb. 11, 1962.
24. *The Wall Street Journal,* Aug. 18, 1964.
25. The Hartford *Times,* Nov. 14, 1967.
26. The Rochester *Democrat-Chronicle,* July 28, 1968.
27. *Church & State,* May, 1965.
28. *The Wall Street Journal,* Aug. 18, 1964.
29. *Study of Exempted Real Estate Property,* Montgomery Co., Ohio.
30. *Christian Science Monitor,* March 29, 1967.
31. *Ib.*
32. The Charleston *Gazette,* Sept. 26, 1962.
33. The Saginaw, Michigan, *News,* July 2, 1968.
34. *Ib.*
35. *Ib.*
36. The Kalispell, Montana, *Daily Inter Lake,* April 14, 1963.
37. Chicago *Daily News,* Aug. 26, 1965.
38. Written by Mrs. Walter Ferguson and published in the Washington *Daily News,* June 13, 1960.
39. The Los Angeles *Times,* May 6, 1968.
40. *Religious News Service,* Feb. 6, 1961, and April 25, 1961.
41. Providence *Journal,* March 13, 1968.
42. St. Petersburg *Times,* Dec. 4, 1968.
43. Cf. The Minneapolis *Tribune,* Jan. 17, 1969, and the Minneapolis *Star,* Jan. 22, 1969.
44. The Buffalo Evening *News,* Feb. 9, 1968.
45. The Philadelphia *Evening Bulletin,* July 28, 1967.
46. The Elizabeth, New Jersey, *Daily Journal,* March 28, 1968.
47. April 7, 1969.
48. *Religious News Service,* June 21, 1966.
49. *The Ontario Committee on Taxation Study* (3 vols.), published by Frank Fogg, Toronto, 1967.
50. *Church & State,* Sept., 1968.

CHAPTER 4

IN THE COURTS

During the Fifties and the Sixties, the tax-exemption of churches has come under challenge in a number of lawsuits. This chapter is a survey of typical cases selected from state and federal records which appear to have a significant bearing on the question.

THE RHODE ISLAND CASE

One suit decided by the Supreme Court of Rhode Island, Dec. 3, 1961, challenged the religious exemption directly.[1] This was brought by General Finance Corporation, a taxpayer of Cranston, which contended that its bill of $82 for city taxes would have been $30 less were it not for the various exemptions, including those granted church properties. It was charged specifically that church-exemption constituted an act respecting establishment of religion and was therefore in violation of the First Amendment.

The Rhode Island Supreme Court held that the granting of tax-exemption is a matter within the exclusive authority of the State legislature. The case was appealed to the United States Supreme Court, which refused to hear it on the ground that "no substantial federal question" was involved.

65

THE MADALYN MURRAY CASE

A widely publicized lawsuit challenging the exempt status of church sanctuaries was brought by Madalyn Murray O'Hair, the well-known atheist, and others, in the court of Maryland.[2] The case got nowhere. The plaintiffs contended that the immunity of churches was an act respecting an establishment of religion and therefore in violation of the First Amendment. The suit was dismissed by Circuit Court Judge Wilson Barnes in Baltimore. He did rule, however, that the plaintiffs had "standing" to bring the suit, a victory of some dimensions in itself.

Counsel for the plaintiffs argued that exemption of church-owned real estate in the city of Baltimore reduced its revenues by $7.5 million annually.[a] He charged that such exemption violated both Maryland and federal law; that it breached Article 36 of the Maryland Declaration of Human Rights, which prohibits the State from compelling any person to contribute to the maintenance of any place of worship; and that it violated Article 15 of the Declaration requiring uniformity of taxation, as well as Article 23, which prohibits the State from depriving a citizen of life, liberty, or property without due process of law.

The plaintiffs asserted further that the religious exemption violates the 14th Amendment to the Federal Constitution because the State of Maryland was depriving citizens without due process; and that it violated the First Amendment because it was an act respecting an establishment of religion.

The Maryland court denied all the plaintiff's allegations. In regard to "standing," however, the court held that "while the impact upon the taxes of the individual plaintiffs is probably not large, the impact on all taxpayers is sufficiently substantial to maintain the suit. . . ."

This meant that the plaintiffs had at least cleared the first big barrier to any taxpayer's suit. Challenges to the constitutionality of government expenditures are often thrown out of court summarily on the ground that the person bringing the suit has not suffered any substantial pecuniary damage. Even if all his allegations are admittedly correct, his own personal loss is in this manner declared to be so

---

[a] Since religious exempts are assessed at about 30% less than parity in Baltimore, the true amount would be at least $10 million. Churches own about 10% of the property in Baltimore, and the total ad valorem tax in 1968 was about $96 million.

unsubstantial as to preclude any cause for action or relief. In this case, however, the court granted "standing" to the plaintiffs, though it eventually held against them.

As to the basic issue, the court held that churches have been continuously tax-exempt in Maryland for 165 years, that such exemptions had been uniformly applied, and had never previously come under substantial attack. The court also justified the Maryland exemption because it is similar to that granted by all other states in the Union.

The same court also cited an opinion of Justice Benjamin Cardozo of the United States Supreme Court that the crucial point in exemption is the presence of a relation between the good of the individual and that of the community. The court denied that the religious exemption violated the No-Establishment Clause and declared that the exemption applied without favoritism or discrimination to all religious groups, whether popular or unpopular, and "represents government neutrality not prohibited by the First Amendment." The court included in its opinion a comprehensive and impressive array of decisions upholding tax-exemption for churches.

When the Murray case reached the Maryland Court of Appeals, this tribunal pointed to Justice Brennan's concurrence in School District of Abington vs. Schempp, June 17, 1962, in which he called specific attention to the fact that the tax-exemption of churches was then in no way under question.[3] The court also cited state and 4 federal cases, in all of which tax-exemption for church property had been upheld.

A NEW YORK COURT REINFORCES THE
MURRAY DECISION

The most recent attempt to upset the tax-exemption for religiously-used real estate was defeated in a decision of the New York Court of Appeals, Walz vs. Tax Commission of New York City, No. 362, Feb. 20, 1969. The plaintiff, Frederick Walz of New York City, charged that such exemption constituted official subsidy of religion and was therefore in violation of the First Amendment. He maintained that he was forced to contribute against his will to the support of religion. But the Court of Appeals held that real property owned by a religious corporation and used exclusively for religious purposes is exempt from taxation; and, furthermore, that this practice is "firmly embedded in the law of this State." However, much to the surprise of the present authors, the Supreme Court has now reversed itself on positions previously held, and has agreed to accept and adjudicate the Walz case.

IS CHURCH REAL ESTATE TAXABLE?

One interesting point raised in an *amicus curiae* brief in the Murray case by Temple Emanuel of Baltimore drew the attention of the Maryland court. In this, it was contended that the State had no power to impose real estate taxes on houses of worship as this would interfere with the free exercise of religion guaranteed by the First Amendment. The Court, however, refused to concede this argument, insisting, instead, that Maryland had the power either to tax or to exempt houses of worship. Nevertheless, the Court conceded that it did see indications of the Temple Emanuel doctrine in Murdock vs. Pennsylvania, a 1943 case in which the U.S. Supreme Court struck down a statute of the city of Jeanette, Pennsylvania, under which Jehovah's Witnesses had been required to buy a license to distribute religious books and tracts.[4] The Maryland Court held that it did not need to explore this issue; that it would not do so in the Murray case; and that if the free-exercise clause of the First Amendment were to be interpreted as forbidding any tax on church property, then no such tax could ever be imposed without a constitutional amendment.

In the Murray case, the Maryland Court simply declared that the religious exemption does not violate federal or Maryland law. Thus, the decision gave approval to tax-exemption for property in religious use, but it did assert that the State has the power at any time to terminate such exemptions, and to impose a tax.

The Murray case was appealed to the Supreme Court, but that body refused a hearing on Oct. 10, 1966. It is therefore of the greatest significance that it has now accepted the Walz case, which is virtually identical to the Murray case.

THE SALE OF AN ACTIVE BUSINESS

One issue which the Supreme Court did adjudicate arose in the famous Clay B. Brown case decided April 17, 1965.[5] This legalized the technique, now becoming so popular among "charities" and churches, by which they become "owners" and "operators" of going businesses without investment, and in which the former owner becomes a manager whose income is transformed from heavily taxed earned income into lightly taxed capital gains. The process by which this is accomplished is described fully in Appendix II.

Here is what happened. The Clay B. Brown Lumber Mill "sold itself" to a cancer research group for $1.3 million—$5,000 down, the rest payable in 10 years. Clay B. Brown then reconstituted itself as Fortuna Mills and leased back the facility. It agreed to pay 80 per cent of its operating profits, exclusive of depreciation and taxes, to the cancer group, which, in turn, agreed to pay 90 per cent of what it realized from Fortuna to Clay B. Brown stockholders in payment for the mill. The Supreme Court declared that Fortuna Mills did not have to pay corporation taxes and that it could treat all profits from the sale as capital gains, taxable at a low rate. We should note that this complicated procedure, necessary for a secular charity, would not be required of a church, which can buy and operate anything outright, without either tax or disclosure.

The Supreme Court decision was obviously a bonanza for religious and other non-profit groups, for it solidified them in a tax-sheltered haven. In fact, the churches are in a much better position than the purchaser of Clay-Brown, for they are empowered to engage in any kind of business with total immunity. The Court urged legislative remedy, pointing out that the opinion "will surely result in large-scale ownership of private businesses by tax-exempt organizations." One justice commented: "I should think that charities would soon own a considerable number of closed corporations . . . which will see no good reason to continue to pay taxes at ordinary income rates."

ARE CHURCH PROFITS DERIVED FROM LIQUOR TAXABLE?

The federal government succeeded in taxing the unrelated business revenue from wine- and brandy-making in the famous Christian Brothers case.[6] This order of the Roman Catholic Church, whose corporate name is the De La Salle Institute, is the largest brandy producer in the United States and possibly the largest manufacturer of domestic wines as well. For years the Order paid no tax on the profits of this lucrative business, claiming exemption as a church. Nothing would ever have been done about this situation (for the Internal Revenue Service never moved of its own accord) had it not been for the merciless publicity to which it was subjected by Americans United for Separation of Church and State. This organization made the Christian Brothers wineries the symbol of the struggle to have the federal Treasury impose taxes on all unrelated business income of churches.

Alarmed by the widespread publicity the disclosure of Americans United had received, the Christian Brothers began to pay taxes in 1959. Then, having protected themselves, they quietly filed suit in federal court to recover the money ($490,000), on the ground that they had been illegally assessed and taxed. The suit created great interest, and for various reasons. For one thing, it disclosed the substantial profits the Christian Brothers were making from their wine and brandy business. In three years alone—1952, 1953, and 1956—net profits were $3,250,000. But this was only part of the story. The figure did not reflect the years 1957–1960, years in which the Brothers had greatly expanded, as a result of a national advertising campaign. The total net revenues must have been above $7 million.

The Christian Brothers pleaded that "plaintiff is exempt as a church." The Order submitted that it had chapel services at its wineries and that all its property was "subject to the control of the Pope." Judge Sherrill Halbert's decision was for the government. He not only held that the Order had been properly assessed in the matter of the $490,000, but that it must pay up all the back taxes which the government in its countersuit had alleged to be due—a total of nearly $4 million.

On the face, this appeared to be a decisive victory for the cause of taxing the unrelated business of churches. Actually, the determination rested on a narrow, technical basis. Judge Halbert found that the Christian Brothers Order was not "sacerdotal" under the Regulations of the Internal Revenue Service. That is, they were not authorized to marry, bury, or administer any of the other Roman Catholic sacraments and, hence, did not technically qualify as a "church." Having rendered his decision on this point, Judge Halbert went on to attack the Regulation itself, describing it as obviously contrary to the will of Congress and therefore really "invalid." He observed that "it would be impractical to accord an exemption to every corporation which asserted itself to be a church. Obviously, Congress did not intend to do this . . . If the doctrine of the Catholic Church were such, work in a winery might be a church function. . . . This however could not transform an incorporated winery into an exempt church; under any reasonable interpretation of the statute . . . . plaintiff is not a church."

Possibly under direction from their superiors, the Brothers did not appeal the case. The Church was said to fear that if the Supreme Court took the case, the entire exemption on unrelated business profits might well be lost. Americans United for Separation of Church and State appealed for a new regulation that would drop the "sacerdotal" definition of a church and define it, rather, in terms of the nature of its work. Such a regulation would have eliminated tax-exemption for all unrelated business of churches. The exemption would then have applied only to income realized from such definitive concerns of the church as worship, evangelism, and missions. The Internal Revenue Service stood pat, however, and made no change. Actually, "sacerdotal" liquor makers, such as the Jesuits, who have a large winery at Los Gatos, California, continue to enjoy tax-exemption even though "non-sacerdotals" like the Christian Brothers at least theoretically are required to pay.

Looking back over the years since the Halbert decision, one can only marvel at how little has been accomplished. The Christian Brothers were forced to disgorge some tax-money. Apparently, there were no other results even in respect to other non-sacerdotal religious orders, which continue to engage in all manner of unrelated commercial activity without taxation. The Internal Revenue Service simply refuses to make any effort to collect on such taxable revenue. Consider, for example, the many women's orders in the Roman Catholic Church. All of these organizations, without exception, are non-sacerdotal, since the Catholic Church does not extend holy orders to any of their members. Yet none of these groups has been affected by the litigation involving the De La Salle Institute vs. United States. In the awesome deference which the government continues to show the religious bodies, it has never moved to tax even those groups which have, in fact, been held to be taxable. The burgeoning of the commercial business of church organizations is the logical outcome of this reluctance.

FURTHER CHALLENGE

The Maryland case of Seversmith vs. Machiz now poses a direct challenge to the exemption of the unrelated business income of churches.[7] The plaintiffs set forth that by virtue of section 511 of the

Internal Revenue Code "there is granted . . . to churches or conventions or associations of churches, an exemption from taxation on *business* income, which is granted to no other federal income taxpayers, individual or corporate; and . . . . there is granted by the Defendant to certain corporations organized and operated exclusively for religious purposes, an exemption from the payment of income taxes on *business* from *investment* income. . . ." and that "consequently many millions of dollars of tax payments are avoided by said exempt taxpayers, and the tax burden of the Plaintiffs and all others similarly situated, is increased so that the Plaintiffs and said others thereby have property taken from them other than by due process of law, in violation of the Fifth Amendment to the Constitution of the United States, and they are thereby denied the equal protection of the laws, in violation of the Ninth Amendment . . . . and the said law relating to said exemption constitutes the making by Congress of a law respecting an Establishment of Religion . . . . in violation of the First Amendment. . . ."

The complaint then set forth a number of church businesses which were allegedly being operated on a tax-exempt basis. The complaint charged that the Società Generale Immobiliare of Rome, a church-holding corporation, made gross tax-exempt sales of nearly $8 million in 1964.[a] In the city of Baltimore an association of churches operated the Virginia Dare Restaurant; the Methodist Church operated the Cokesbury Book Store; the Roman Catholic archdiocese operated a number of commercial businesses, all for profit and tax-exempt.

The case of Seversmith vs. Machiz has not yet gone to trial.

THE STRATFORD RETREAT HOUSE

With headquarters in White Plains, New York, a Protestant entity calling itself the Stratford Retreat House has been purchasing a variety of businesses with little or no investment—a church practice possible without, but encouraged by, the Clay B. Brown decision. The annual active unrelated business income of this church is now said to exceed $15 million. In Civil Action No. 289, dated January 24, 1969, Americans United, Glenn L. Archer, C. Stanley Lowell, and C. David Young have filed a complaint in the United States District Court for

---

[a] Such immunity is specifically provided under Sec. 892 of the Internal Revenue Code.

72

the Southern District of New York against the Stratford Retreat House and Edward J. Fitzgerald, Jr., District Director of Internal Revenue, setting forth that normal corporation income taxes should be levied and collected from this church. The Plaintiffs allege that the church-immunity provided in section 511 (a) (2) (A) of the Internal Revenue Code constitutes a discrimination against all federal taxpayers and against other non-profit corporations like Americans United and that it violates the First Amendment. The Plaintiffs allege, further, that the profits made by the church "greatly exceed $10,000 annually" and that the businesses operated are in such non-religious fields as industrial hardware, ship repairing, and the manufacture and distribution of electrical equipment.

This case will likely go to the Supreme Court. If the Plaintiffs finally prevail, section 511 (a) (2) (A) will be deleted from the Internal Revenue Code, at least insofar as it deals with churches and associations of churches. It is, however, possible that this provision will be outlawed by Congress before this case can reach the highest court.

PARTIAL PAYMENTS

The denominational headquarters complex offers a problem to the tax base of any city in which it is located. Church leaders argue that such buildings constitute simply an extension of their local sanctuaries and should, therefore, likewise be exempt from taxation, no matter what equipment, how many acres, or what spacious facilities are involved. In Nashville, Tenn., where vast Baptist and Methodist enterprises are located, the city has long sought some tax revenue from them. Eventually, it assessed these two large publishing houses, but the Tennessee Supreme Court granted only a small levy on a cafeteria, a parking lot, and the vending machines used by employees.[8] News releases of May, 1969, however, indicate that renewed efforts are under way to place these huge properties under local taxation.

In a 1963-case in Pennsylvania, the American Baptist Convention was required to pay a partial assessment on its national headquarters located at Valley Forge. Judge David E. Groshens ruled that the Convention must pay $18,000 annually on 28.5 acres of land unoccupied by buildings and on 1,500 square feet used as a bookstore.[9] The municipality had sought $130,000 in taxes on an assessment of the entire site, which, of course, is much larger. The court found that the Convention itself was a church under the law and that its buildings were exempt.

SUMMER CAMPS

A sensitive church-state problem has been posed by tax-exemption for the summer camp sites of churches. In a typical instance, a church acquires a large acreage and claims tax-exemption for it as a place of worship. The state may contend that only a small part of the site— perhaps a chapel or auditorium—is used for worship, and the rest should be subject to tax. The issue was fought out in Polson, Montana, in 1964. The verdict, which favored the church,[*] was eventually upheld by the Supreme Court of the state.[10] The county had sought to tax a 22-acre Methodist camp. It argued that the land on which the buildings were located and a reasonable surrounding area should be exempt, but that the balance should be taxed. Judge E. Gardner Brownless ruled against Lake County, stating that "Surely, it is not for the state to limit the methods of teaching or the area used for actual religious worship. . . . No more land than is necessary for the purpose [of worship] is exempt. This clause must be construed with the term 'actual use' and where there is actual use, the amount of land cannot be restricted." This meant simply that "actual use" was whatever the church said it was. Under such an interpretation, there could be no effective limit by the state on the exempt summer camp acreage owned by churches.

SETTING LIMITS

The courts have, however, shown some disposition to set limits to church tax-exemptions. Assessors exhibit similar inclinations. In Dallas, Texas, church properties are exempt only if used for religious purposes. Tax Director Norman Register refused an exemption to a church on pasture land it had acquired as a prospective location for a new church. When Register found cows grazing there, he ruled that the land was being used for commercial purposes and did not merit exemption.

In York County, Maine, the county commissioner rejected an appeal for tax-exemption by the Brothers of Christian Instruction, a

---

[*] This decision was in direct violation of the Montana State Constitution.

Roman Catholic order.[11] The officials declared that they imposed taxes on real estate and personal property from which the Order was deriving income from public sale of bread, poultry products, milk and supplies.

The Pennsylvania Supreme Court, in a unanimous 1963 decision, ruled that church parking lots are subject to realty levy. The cases involved First Church of Christ, Scientist, of West Philadelphia and Second Church of Christ, Scientist, of Germantown.[12] In upholding the tax the court found that parking is "an adjunctive use of property, not part of regular, stated worship, and not actually used for that purpose." The court so held despite evidence that the parking lots were not commercial ventures and were used only by worshippers.

In the case of Tarshis vs. the City of New York (1965), the plaintiff successfully challenged the constitutionality of a plan by which publicly owned land would be offered for sale to churches on a preferred basis.[13] When it was learned that a church was interested in acquiring a site of public land, the public authority would stipulate that bids would be received only from those who would use the land "solely for religious and educational purposes." The plaintiff contended that such a stipulation violated Article XI, Section 3, of the New York Constitution as well as the First Amendment to the federal Constitution. The court agreed. The brief in the case quoted Justice Black in Torcaso vs. Watkins: "Neither a State nor the Federal Government . . . . can constitutionally pass laws or impose requirements which aid all religions as against non-believers."

PARSONAGES

There have been quite a number of suits concerning parsonages or rectories which are exempt in many states, at least when church-owned. However, efforts to exempt the residences of other members of the church staff have failed. The courts have generally held that only houses occupied by an ordained pastor-in-charge may be entitled to exemption. There is a disposition, also, to limit the parsonages to one for each church. For example, when the South Park Baptist Church in Houston, Texas, contended that the residence of its minister of music owned by the church should be exempt from tax, the Texas Supreme Court upheld a decision of the lower court holding that tax-exemption for a "dwelling place for the ministry" means "one dwelling place," even though the church might have more than

75

one minister.[14] Since the South Park Baptist Church already had one exempt parsonage, that was it.

In the District of Columbia, several of the Roman Catholic parishes have more than one priest and rectory. No matter how many there may be, however, only one is tax-exempt. The diocesan bishop has frequently sought to change this ruling, but without success.

INCOME-PRODUCING PROPERTY

Although the state has sometimes been defeated, a number of suits have been won by its effort to collect real estate taxes on property which is producing income for the church. In 1965, the assessor in Portland, Oregon, levied a tax on the Methodist Book Store.[15] When the case was appealed to the State Supreme Court, the Church argued that the store was wholly owned by the Church and that all profits were used for charitable purposes. The court held that under state law the status of earnings was determined, not by their ultimate use, but by the nature of the taxpayer and that the book store was, in fact, a "competitive commercial" business subject to taxation.

A printing plant, laundry and dairy operated by Harding College (of the Churches of Christ) situated at Searcy, Arkansas, were ruled not tax-exempt in 1960 and the school was ordered to pay taxes for the three enterprises.

In 1964, the Alaska Supreme Court upheld assessors in levying a tax on a radio station which had been leased to the Evangelical Covenant Church of America.[16] The station claimed exemption as a church, but the court ruled that it must pay taxes because it was being operated for profit. In another 1964 case in Maryland, land owned by a church was being used to grow soy beans as a pay crop to supplement the church's building fund.[17] The Maryland Tax Court ruled that neither the ownership of the land nor its use by the Church constituted a valid basis for tax-exemption from realty tax.

In San Antonio, Texas, the Daughters of St. Paul, a Roman Catholic order, sought exemption from the ad valorem tax on a gift and book store.[18] On March 11, 1965, the court ruled against them, holding that a non-profit corporation "which owned a building used exclusively by the corporation for sale of books and for nuns' living quarters was not, under the facts, an 'institution of purely public charity' so as to be exempt from city and school district taxes." A rehearing was denied.

The Texas court held that the exemption for "actual places of religious worship" in that state's statute cannot be stretched to include "religious work." [19] Property used for recording radio broadcasts of religious programs, including 15-minute religious services in the building Monday through Friday, did not constitute an actual place of worship qualifying for exemption.

PRO AND CON

On the other hand, some states have suffered setbacks in the courts on this issue. In Minneapolis, a Hennepin County District Court judge held that the Augsburg Publishing House of the American Lutheran Church need not pay $75,000 annually in real estate taxes.[20] Judge Dana Nicholson found the Augsburg operation to be church property for tax-exemption purposes because it published only religious materials. The Hennepin County Attorney pleaded that Augsburg made a profit and should be taxed the same as any other business. Judge Nicholson agreed that while the profits were "substantial," they were not the primary aim of the enterprise. This, he said, was to serve the purposes of the Church.

In an earlier case (1963) the Evangelical Free Church of America received a similar exemption for its press and book store located in Minneapolis.[21]

The Roman Catholic Church has a commercially run cafeteria in the Shrine of the Immaculate Conception in Washington, D.C. When it was assessed personal property taxes on equipment in the cafeteria, the Shrine went to court in 1962 and won an exemption of $4,079, the amount which had been levied and which the Church had paid.[22] A District Court judge ordered the money refunded, citing a District law exempting from personal property taxes all benevolent organizations "not conducted for private gain." Although the business itself showed a profit, the judge said all that was necessary was that the Shrine itself not be operated for private gain.

A decision of the United States Court of Appeals in an Oklahoma case had the effect of applying a restriction on corporations to churches, under a law of that state.[23] The suit arose from an attempt by a relative to break the will of Mrs. Burdine Fletcher. A patient in the St. Anthony Hospital of Oklahoma City just prior to her death, Mrs. Fletcher made a will leaving 160 acres of rich oil and gas lands to that institution, to St. Francis Hospital of Marysville, to the Sisters of St. Francis, and to Mt. Alverno Convent, all of the Roman Catholic Church.

The United States Court of Appeals upheld the challenge to the will on the ground that provisions of the Oklahoma Constitution and the Business Corporation Act forbid the holding of land outside cities and towns by organizations for purposes other than those for which they were chartered. The court held, specifically, that the Sisters of St. Francis could not legally take and hold land for oil and gas production since the corporation was not created to engage in this business. Despite the tax-exempt status of the Church itself, its immunity from financial disclosure, and other forms of preferential treatment, the court drew the line at this point.

CHURCH HOUSING AND RETIREMENT FACILITIES

It is in the field of housing that the churches have suffered their most serious setbacks in the matter of tax-exemption. This has been a lucrative field for the churches, and is growing more so, particularly in the construction and operation of retirement homes. The fact that churches have been exempt from income taxes and even, in many instances, from real estate levies, on these ventures has been the decisive factor in their success. But the government is making some progress in challenging this exemption.

In a precedent-setting decision in 1966, the Florida Supreme Court ruled that church-operated homes for the elderly must pay real estate tax if they charge fees. In a case appealed from the Manatee Circuit Court to the Supreme Court of the United States, the latter upheld the opinion of the lower tribunal that the home was not operated exclusively for religious or charitable purposes.[24] It was a 4 to 3 decision, with Justice B. K. Roberts registering a dissent. He said that the ruling endangers the tax-exempt status of all church-related colleges, schools, and hospitals which made a service charge.

Yet the resulting impact was far from decisive, as is made obvious by the refusal of the Florida Supreme Court to hear an appeal from tax-assessor Hiram Strickland of Bradenton, who was trying to tax Bradenton Manor, a Presbyterian home. In an indignant editorial, the Bradenton *Herald,* Feb. 23, 1969, challenged the Court's position and went on to indict the tax-exempt status of a welter of church-operated retirement homes in the area. It asserted emphatically that these facilities were in no proper sense to be considered charitable;

78

and pointed out that the church-owners planned to pay off the entire cost in three occupancy "turnovers," after which the generous profits would go into "expansion and improvements." In any case, the editorial continued, in a fine strain of sarcasm, the surplus would divert to such charities as "downtrodden coupon clippers." With a final burst of indignation, the editorial concluded: "For churches to accept—much less claim—the right to operate luxury-class retirement buildings tax-free, leeching upon the poor of the community, is neither charity nor Christianity. It's blasphemy!"

We should note here that in a significant 1968 decision, the Supreme Court of Illinois held that church sponsorship of a home for older people was not of itself sufficient to assure tax-exemption,[25] particularly when it could be demonstrated that the facility made substantial profits deriving from an entry fee of $25,000 and monthly payments ranging up to $375. The Court upheld the assessor in levying a tax.

A similar issue faced the court in Minnesota when the city of Rochester sought to tax the Madonna Towers Retirement Home owned by the Oblate Fathers, a Roman Catholic order. The Fathers went to court and won in Feb., 1968, on their contention that the 12-story apartment building, with its nine adjacent townhouses, infirmary, dining hall, chapel, recreation center, and solarium was a "purely public charity," and therefore entitled to real-estate tax-exemption: this, despite the fact that heavy entrance fees are required and very substantial charges are made. The case was appealed to the Minnesota Supreme Court.[26]

Editorializing on this dispute, the Minneapolis *Star* observed: "The root question in real estate tax-exemption is whether the general body of taxpayers should subsidize a particular institution. In this instance, those who could meet the charges are both donors and beneficiaries, just as though they were in a privately operated luxury retirement home which may pay taxes." [27]

The Minnesota Supreme Court handed down its decision on March 28, 1969, which reversed the lower court. The Supreme Court held that Madonna Towers was not a "purely public charity" and that it was properly subject to real estate taxation. The opinion by Justice William Murphy declared that the Court had "little difficulty in concluding that Madonna Towers does not possess the necessary qualities of an institution which serves a purely charitable purpose."

Whether or not certain church retirement homes are subject to realty levy in Wisconsin came to a decision in the Supreme Court of the State, Feb. 4, 1969.[28] The case involved the Protestant Home for the Aged vs. City of Milwaukee, which alleged that at least the new wing of the institution was taxable and sought to impose tax. A lower court agreed.

The Wisconsin Supreme Court, however, reversed the lower court and ruled that the entire Protestant home was exempt. The Court acknowledged that the institution enjoyed substantial income above operational expenses and that it had not admitted any residents free of charge, but these facts alone were not considered determinative. What the Court found decisive under Wisconsin law was that no portion of income had been diverted to private operators or trustees but were being used to expand the institution. That is, revenues were being used to extend the "benevolence" in which the Protestant Home was engaged. The Court concluded: "Since the addition and its two top floors used as a convalescent center are an extension of the benevolent purposes of the Protestant home and are not being operated for profit . . . . we conclude that the property of the Protestant Home for the Aged, including the Bradford Terrace addition and its convalescent center, is exempt from property taxation. . . . ."

A comparable court test in Baltimore, Maryland, was avoided by compromise. St. Mary's Roland View Towers, Inc., is an apartment-house project owned by the Episcopal Church. The municipality sought to collect taxes on the project, which sought complete exemption as a church. Judge James K. Cullen ruled in favor of the church and declared the housing tax-exempt. The city appealed the case. Meanwhile, St. Mary's and other church housing developments sought a compromise with city officials. They made an offer to pay taxes based on a rate of 6 per cent of annual rentals. The city accepted the offer, and its appeal was dropped. It was estimated that payments would be about one-fourth the amount that comparable properties under secular ownership would pay. Joseph Allen, municipal solicitor, hailed the agreement as a "net gain for the city." [29]

SUMMARY

From this survey of relevant litigation (which by no means purports to be comprehensive or complete), it appears that while there has been a vigorous challenge to church tax-exemptions in the courts, this has not been attended by any notable success. The reason for this is clear enough. Courts have based and continue to base their decisions on precedents. This inevitably means that the presumption is in favor of the religious exemptions, since we have had them for so long a time. No matter how strong a particular case may seem to be, the presumption is still in favor of immunity. The long-standing traditional consensus of court decisions is too imposing to be set aside.

At most, the various court actions have had the effect of setting some limits upon religious immunities. For any substantial reforms in this field, it is evident that we must look to legislative action or perhaps to constitutional amendment. As we note elsewhere (cf. Appendix II), a number of proposals are now before Congress to rewrite various provisions of the Internal Revenue Code which relate to the taxation of church income. It is certain that some reforms or at least changes will emerge. However, it is equally certain that these will be compromises forged under extreme pressure from certain clerical groups and they will, therefore, fail to grapple forthrightly with the basic problems that confront the American churches and this nation.

Citations

1. General Finance Corporation vs. Archetta, 176A 2nd 73, 76–79 (R.I. 1961 Powers) Appeal denied, 369 U.S. 423 (1961, P.C.)
2. Murray vs. Goldstein, 241 Md. 383, 216A, 2d 897, cert. denied 385 U.S. 816 (Oct. 10, 1966).
3. School District of Abington tp. Pa. vs. Schempp, 374 U.S. 203, 211, 83 S.Ct. 1560, 10 L. ed. 2d, 844 (1963).
4. Murdock vs. Commonwealth of Penna., 319 U.S. 105, 63 S.Ct. 1162 (1965).
5. Commissioner vs. Brown, 380 U.S. 563, 14 L. ed. 2d 75, 85 S.Ct. 1162 (1965).
6. De La Salle Institute vs. United States, Civil Action No. 7499, U.S. District Court for the Northern District of California, Northern Division.
7. Civil No. 15756, United District Court, District of Maryland.
8. *Religious Herald,* Sept. 13, 1962.
9. C. P. Mongomery County, Penna. 62–9653.
10. Flathead Lake Methodist Camp vs. Webb, 399 P. 2d 90 (1965).
11. Portland *Press Herald,* Oct. 2, 1966.
12. Second Church of Christ, Scientist, vs. City of Philadelphia, 157A. 2d 54, 398 Pa. 65, 75 A.L.R. 2d 1103 (1959).
13. Tarshis vs. the City of New York, 24 A.D. 2d 644, 262 N.Y.S. 2d 538, 263 N.Y.S. 2d 307, 266 N.Y.S. 2d 510 (1965).

14. City of Houston vs. South Park Baptist Church of Houston, 393 S.W. 2d 354 (1965).

15. Board of Pub. Methodist Church vs. Tax Com. 239 Ore. 65, 362 P. 2d 212 (1964).

16. Evangelical Covenant Church vs. City of Nome, No. 457, Supreme Court of Alaska.

17. *Wall Street Journal*, Nov. 4, 1964.

18. Daughters of St. Paul, Inc., vs. City of San Antonio, Court of Civil Appeals of Texas, No. 14342, Feb. 10, 1965.

19. Radio Bible Hour, Inc. vs. Hurst-Euless School District (CA), 341 SW 2d 467E.

20. *Religious News Service*, Dec. 24, 1965. State of Minnesota vs. American Lutheran Church, # 600140, Hennepin County District Court.

21. *Ib.* Nov. 4, 1963.

22. District of Columbia vs. National Shrine, 315 F. 2d 40 (1963).

23. Simler vs. Wilson, 10 Cir., 210F (2d) 99, cert. denied 347 U.S. 954, 74 S. Ct. 681, 91 L. ed. 1000, rehearing denied 347 U.S. 973, 74 S. Ct. 786, 98 L. ed. 1113.

24. Palm Beach *Post,* Oct. 6, 1966.

25. *Wall Street Journal*, May 22, 1968.

26. Tax Commissioner Rufus T. Logan made appeal in Madonna Towers vs. Minnesota Commissioner of Taxation, Supreme Court # 41283).

27. Minneapolis *Star*, March 6, 1968.

28. No. 40, Aug. Term, 1968.

29. *Religious News Service,* May 17, 1966.

CHAPTER 5

THE CHURCH DOMAIN: FOUR CITIES

I. BUFFALO

Near the eastern terminus of Lake Erie where its waters converge into the tumultuous Niagara River before thundering over the Falls, lies the city of Buffalo, which for many years served as the focal point whence immigrants, arriving by steam wagon or Erie Canal, cascaded throughout the Middle West. But many remained to build an historic metropolis, long famed for its port, its grain elevators, its metalurgical industry, and a variety of manufactures.

But changing times have brought new problems, particularly a tax-crisis, which the *Courier-Express* emphasized in a cartoon published March 22, 1968, showing Mayor Sedita standing on a melting slab of ice—called the tax-base—and careening down the River toward the Falls. A series of articles published concurrently in the Buffalo *Evening News* bemoaned the intensifying problem.

In the meantime, the mayor of New York City, acutely aware of what lies ahead, proposed that a study in depth be made of all real estate exemptions. The *Courier-Express* declared editorially on March 23, 1968, that "Lindsay's proposal probably is the first solid effort to harvest revenue from real property" such as "land and buildings owned by private, charitable, religious, educational, professional and similar organizations, by public agencies, and by certain cooperatives . . ."

Indeed, there is a case of double jeopardy in Buffalo: the taxable property is deteriorating and not being replaced; meanwhile, more and more of the land is slipping from the tax-rolls entirely. For example, a sports facility, where the Buffalo Bisons perform, assessed at $4,909,650, was recently added to the tax-exempts.

Buffalo is one of various American cities which absorbed large waves of Catholic immigrants from Ireland, Poland, Germany, Italy, Hungary, Roumania, Czecho-Slovakia, and other southeastern European countries between 1840 and 1920. The names of their descendants still dominate the pages of the telephone directory. Until recently, Roman Catholics comprised at least 45% of the population and 65% of the religious affiliates.

Before 1890, there were few Negroes. Even as late as 1920, in a population of 506,775, there were only 4,733 non-whites. The population grew to 580,132 in 1950, but declined to 532,759 in 1960, of whom 73,388 were Negroes. There are today at least 100,000 fewer whites than 40 years ago.

Catholics, with their 72 parishes, have 90 elementary and secondary schools with 37,996 pupils; also 1 seminary and 6 colleges with 7,917 students. We therefore estimate their number at 200,000, or 37.5% of the population. However, for the entire diocese, the 1968 *Official Catholic Directory* claims a membership of 937,567 among 1,868,291 people, a ratio of 50.2%, down slightly from 1963–64, when it was 53.5%, and more than 75% of the religious affiliates.

Since there are 10 synagogues, we estimate the Jewish community at 15,000, or 3% of the population.

In spite of the Catholic preponderance, there are 260 Protestant and miscellaneous congregations, which comprise a vigorous minority with 158,000 communicants, or 29% of the population. There are, accordingly, 368,000 religious affiliates in Buffalo.

Mr. Luke Pauly, Assessor, who is deeply concerned over the vanishing tax-base, was most helpful in supplying all pertinent records.

Among the largest items of exempt property, we find the city-federal housing projects, assessed at $52,161,840. There is a very complex system of exemptions for railroads (which, until 1954, had no reductions at all) depending on their profit-margins; by 1967–68, this had removed $39,657,180 of assessed valuations from the tax-rolls.

Under the Mitchell-Lama Act, any private individual or corporation may erect what is called limited-profit housing which, after approval

REAL ESTATE ASSESSMENTS IN BUFFALO

Category	1954	1964	1968
TOTAL	$1,314,136,058	$1,494,494,670	$1,522,765,217
Taxable	1,020,347,140	1,036,123,658	1,023,718,576
Ratio	77.6%	69.1%	67.2%
Exempt	293,788,940	458,371,012	499,026,660
Ratio	22.4%	30.8%	32.7%
Increase after 1964		8.9%	
United States	35,065,190	30,827,630	29,131,820
New York State	15,502,710	30,469,100	68,512,340
Erie County	7,017,390	8,376,580	17,475,600
City of Buffalo	77,376,280	79,603,660	87,677,670
Public Schools	40,332,670	51,056,330	55,229,610
Religious	32,535,270	42,787,460	44,119,800
Charitable	5,852,950	9,475,970	10,028,700
Libraries	1,154,510	5,151,960	203,030
Hospitals	12,611,290	25,981,220	27,881,970
Veterans Exemptions	10,566,720	18,737,360	19,130,320
Municipal Housing	21,248,490	51,765,810	52,161,840
Cemeteries	6,528,660	6,455,310	6,455,310
Private Schools	25,361,120	42,817,070	25,624,550
Paraplegics			20,000
Patriotic Associations			3,671,680
Specially Assessed Housing			1,069,430
Railroads		45,642,962	39,657,180
Miscellaneous *	2,635,690	9,222,590	
Bridge Authority			3,016,530
Port Authority			4,628,860
Fall-Out Shelters			600
State Retirement System			2,275,770
Mitchell-Lama Act Housing			1,054,050

* This item was abolished for 1968, when the items comprised there were placed under several new headings. Most of those now classified under Patriotic or Morale Associations, were classified previously as Charitable or Religious.

by the city, enjoys a permanent 50% reduction in assessment.

Mr. Pauly hoped that we would note the problem created by the generosity of his city to veterans, of whom 10,470 in 1968 qualified for reductions in their assessments—under a complicated formula—which range from $300 to $5,000 and make up a combined total of $19,150,320.

In 1930, the taxable property—then assessed at $1,065,500,000—exceeded the present dollar appraisals; and the exempt, then only $195,400,000, comprised 15.4% of the total. Today the railroads, the housing projects, the veterans exemptions, and the sports stadium alone have removed almost 10% of all real estate from the tax-rolls.

And so we see that in spite of the continuing inflation, the tax-base actually *decreased* by 1.2% between 1964 and 1968; and between 1954 and 1968, the taxable sector declined from 77.6% to 67.2% of the total, while the exempt increased by 70%—from 22.4% to 32.7%, of the total.

We note some realignment. For example, assessments on private schools fell between 1964 and 1968 from $42,718,070 to $25,624,550, because the University of Buffalo was absorbed into the State educational system; largely because of this, State properties increased from $30,469,100 to $68,512,340. We also note a sharp decrease under Libraries, from $5,151,960 to $203,030, because the formerly private Buffalo facility was taken over by Erie County, whose assets grew from $8,376,550 to $17,475,600.

Many taxable properties seem to be assessed well above the legal rate of 51%; and, conversely, exempt properties well below it. The Statler-Hilton (1,100 rooms), for example, located on Niagara Circle, was assessed before 1964 at $4,926,290, or $4,470 per room, when the State Supreme Court forced a reduction to $4,067,090. In 1967, this was further reduced to $3,892,550. Meanwhile, the Lafayette (380 rooms) was lowered from $1,151,930 to $798,340. Both, however, are still probably overassessed.

On the other hand, most exempt properties, particularly those belonging to religious organizations, are drastically undervalued, perhaps to minimize the apparent wealth of the owners. For example, the Mount St. Joseph Academy, with acreage and buildings possibly worth $8 million, is assessed at $1,543,050. Canisius College, with 2,730 students and a plant worth at least $15 million, now carries an assessment of $4,512,370, compared to one of $3,242,440 in 1964. The official book value is $12,630,295.

We believe, therefore, that if appraisals on exempts in Buffalo were at parity, they would comprise nearly 50% of the roll.

Since this was one of the 4 cities we analyzed in 1964, we demonstrate in the following what has happened in a short period of time.

EXEMPT PROPERTY IN BUFFALO

CATEGORY	1964	1968	Increase
ALL	$458,371,012	$499,026,660	8.9%
The Public	349,757,772	381,244,650	9.0%
Ratio	76.3%	76.4%	
The Private	108,613,240	117,782,010	8.5%
Ratio	23.7%	23.6%	

THE PRIVATE, EXEMPT PROPERTIES

	The Secular		The Religious	
	1964	1968	1964	1968
Churches, Etc.			$42,787,460	$44,110,800
Benevolences	$ 6,836,270	$ 5,032,200	2,639,700	8,677,180
Hospitals	13,119,030	13,231,670	12,862,090	14,650,200
Cemeteries	6,332,680	6,332,680	122,730	122,730
Schools	1,360,710	1,344,110	22,552,570	24,280,440
TOTALS	$27,648,690	$25,940,660	$80,964,550	$91,841,350
Ratio	25.5%	22.1%	74.5%	77.9%
Change	MINUS	6.8%	PLUS	13.4%

We note that denominational wealth is preponderant in the private sector. In 1954, this constituted 74.5% and grew to 77.9% in 1968. Religious real estate increased in 4 years by almost $11 million, or 13.4%, in a city which is certainly deteriorating and from which people are fleeing by the thousands to construct new houses of worship and more modern religious schools in the suburbs.

After the State absorbed the University of Buffalo, no private secular schools of consequence remained except the Nichols, assessed at $1,037,730. We should note that under cemeteries we have a large secular facility assessed at $6,332,580, which, although private, offers special provisions for sectarian burials. Among secular exempts classified as cultural, charitable, scientific, or patriotic, etc., we find the American Legion, the VFW, etc., with combined assessments of $597,800; the Boys Club, $363,040; the Childrens Aid Society, $195,320; the Rehabilitation Center, $119,030; the Joint Charities, $67,440; the Red Cross, $206,420; the Blind Association, $258,830; the Crippled Childrens Aid, $255,750; the Goodwill Industries, $355,670; the Childrens Society, $371,270; the Ys, $2,479,310; and a number of others. The largest secular exempts are the Buffalo General Hospital, $6,649,050; and the Fillmore Hospital, $5,765,850.

The following reveals further the developments of the last 4 years.

THE DIVISION OF RELIGIOUS PROPERTY IN
BUFFALO IN 1968
($91,841,350)

CATEGORY	Protestant	Catholic	Jewish
Churches and Parochial Schools	$14,770,400	$26,206,080	$ 913,950
Parsonages and Rectories	901,720	1,300,500	27,150
Charities and Benevolences	2,436,160	4,860,740	1,371,280
Hospitals	4,127,240	10,522,960	
Cemeteries	67,730	51,090	3,910
Private Schools	9,420	24,259,900	11,120
TOTALS	$22,312,670	$67,201,270	$2,327,410
Ratios	24.3%	73.2%	2.5%

GROWTH OF RELIGIOUS PROPERTY

	1964	1968
Protestant and Miscellaneous	$23,632,220	$22,312,670
Decrease		5.6%
Catholic	53,948,600	67,201,270
Increase		24.7%
Jewish	2,383,730	2,327,410
Decrease		2.3%

We see, therefore, that while Jewish properties declined by 2.3% [a] and Protestant by 5.6%, the Catholic increased by almost 25%. It is indeed remarkable that religious exempts should have expanded by almost 20%, or $11 million, in a rapidly deteriorating community. In addition to their synagogues, the only substantial Jewish exempts consisted of a Community Center and a couple of retirement homes.

Protestant Charities consist largely of Salvation Army facilities and 4 retirement homes,—Methodist, Presbyterian, Lutheran, and German Evangelical.

Dozens of Protestant churches have assessments ranging from $4,000 to $20,000, or up to $50,000. On the other hand, here as elsewhere, we find that the established denominations have many large and costly sanctuaries. There is the Unitarian-Universalist, $180,950; a People's Community, $121,470; a Nazarene, $139,550; a Reformed, $148,490; a Christian Scientist, $216,680; four Protestant Episcopal, ranging from $104,780 to $358,900; four Baptist, from $115,010 to $281,300; five Presbyterian, from $108,630 to $542,630; seven Lutheran, from $100,550 to $368,490; and eight Methodist, from $111,510 to $360,240.

Since these valuations probably represent about one-third of actual value, several of them must be million-dollar sanctuaries.

Many of the Catholic properties cannot be identified from the tax-rolls since they are titled only to the diocese. However, we know that a dazzling array of 72 churches, headed by the ornate St. Joseph's Cathedral, together with their rectories and 68 parochial schools, are assessed at $27,506,580.

Four Catholic hospitals, with valuations totalling $10,522,960, are identified on the rolls, of which the Mercy, $3,035,880, and the Sisters of Bon Secour, $4,564,050, are the largest. [b]

Catholic Benevolences consist of convents, monasteries, orphanages, and correctional institutions. Most of these are simply residences for male and female religious orders.

---

[a] It should be noted, however, that the new Temple Beth Zion will appear on the next tax-roll with an assessment of $2,509,690, which will more than double the previous total of Jewish exempts.

[b] In 1964, the assessment on the Bon Secour hospital was $3,464,050. During 1964 and 1965, an expansion program costing $6,500,000 was completed, after which the assessment was increased by exactly $1,100,000—about 17% of the new expenditure, instead of 51%.

Schools operated under direct diocesan control constitute the largest item of Catholic wealth. Here we find 6 colleges, 1 seminary, and 22 elementary and secondary schools. The largest diocesan high schools—the Carroll, McMahon, Ryan, Timon, Fallon, Colton, and Daugherty—are not identified on the rolls. The following, however, are listed: Canisius College, $4,512,370; Canisius High School, $1,268,520; D'Youville College, $3,696,080; the Institute of St. Joseph, $1,821,770; and St. Mary's School for the Deaf, $1,404,940.

New York State has established an equalized assessment-rate of 51%; and, since the 1967–68 millage was 75.66 in Buffalo, a $20,000 house should pay a tax of $771. A friend we visited, however, paid $1,250 on a 6-room house which we appraised at $22 to $24,000 and which therefore must have been quite heavily overassessed. The tax on a $20,000 home would not be less than $900. If all exempt property were to be taxed at parity, this home-owner's load would drop to about $500; if the private exempts alone were to be taxed, it would be reduced to about $700.

Since the property tax was $77,555,922.32 in 1967–68, the per capita levy was $148 and that on a family of 5, $740.

Although average assessments on religious properties probably do not exceed one-third of true value, we assume, in the following, that they, as well as all others, stand at 40%.

TRUE VALUATIONS ON BUFFALO REAL ESTATE [a]

	Assessments	True Value
ALL	$1,522,765,217	$3,810,000,000
The Taxable	1,023,718,576	2,560,000,000
The Exempt	499,026,660	1,250,000,000
The Public	381,244,650	955,000,000
The Private	117,782,101	295,000,000
The Secular	25,940,660	65,000,000
The Religious	91,891,350	230,000,000
The Protestant	22,312,670	55,700,000
The Catholic	67,201,270	168,500,000
The Jewish	2,327,410	5,800,000

[a] The total here given reflects per capita wealth of less than $7,200. However, as in St. Louis, Baltimore, and Providence, this results largely from the drastic undervaluation of exempt real estate. If the appraisals were on a parity in the two sectors, we would have per capita wealth of

Since these religious appraisals are undoubtedly too low, for our own information we compute Jewish religiously used real estate at about $10 million; the Protestant, at about $85 million; and the Catholic at not less than $250 million, a total of $345 million, or nearly 15% of all taxable real estate in Buffalo.

II. WASHINGTON, D.C.

The capital of our nation, originally planned by Major Pierre C. L'Enfant under the personal direction of President Washington, was and remains of unique civic design. With its principal arteries running diagonally and named after various states or national symbols, it is in many ways the epitome and microcosm of America. Virtually without industry, it has, nevertheless, as our political center, developed enormously since the vast proliferation of federalism began with the Roosevelt administration in the Thirties. On all sides of the great governmental complex, anchored at the East by the Capitol and by the Lincoln Memorial at the West, we find many outstanding examples of architecture and an endless array of structures in which one of the most elaborate bureaucracies on earth performs its multifarious functions.

However, countless private organizations—many of them tax-exempt—have also built their national centers here in bewildering profusion. Since land is so limited and the demand for it so pressing, its price has skyrocketed several hundred per cent in a few years.

Construction continues at a tremendous pace both in the public and the private sector, especially by the federal government and by such organizations as the National Geographic Society, which have grown fabulously wealthy through tax-exempt income and real estate. Because of this, but even more because of the enormous increase in the price of land, assessments have risen sharply in recent years. Theoretically, these stand at 55% on land and 65% on improvements; however, we have found that these have not kept pace with the continuing inflation. For example, one parcel which recently sold for $60 a square foot is assessed at less than $20; and another, which sold for $378,000 in 1964 and for which $600,000 has now been

---

at least $9,000, which would also be very nearly accurate. We believe that exempt property comprises nearly 50% of all real estate in Buffalo and should be assessed at about $1 billion.

offered, is on the rolls at $140,000. In areas where 9-story buildings are being erected, land is selling for $2 million or more an acre.

The capital was once a beautiful and commodious residential city; but with the influx of Negroes and the vast proliferation of federal agencies and private corporations, the enormous work-force in the city has fled to the suburbs for residence. In the morning, therefore, a vast stream of traffic converges upon the central area, and about 4 P.M., it flows outward in maddening torrents. But on the weekends the city assumes a strange somnolence.

Such is the District of Columbia.

Since the assessor reappraises one-third of all real estate each year, we have a three-year cycle of realistic reassessment.

Between 1950 and 1960, the population of the District dropped from 802,178 to 763,956, which is probably near the present level. The most significant development has been the rapid growth of the Negro community, which increased from 132,068 in 1930 (27%) to 280,803 in 1950 (40%) and 418,693, or 54.8%, in 1960, a proportion which continues to rise and which, so far as we know, is the highest for any major community in the United States.

As the white people, including, of course, the Catholics, have moved to the suburbs, the city has become more and more secularist-Protestant. This is true because the inroads of Roman Catholicism among the colored people have been quite limited.

This situation has created a crucial problem for the Catholic Church. As its more affluent members have removed to Virginia and Maryland, its District schools have lost thousands of registrants and millions in revenue. The communicants who have moved are now, therefore, called upon (1) to build new schools and churches in the suburbs; (2) to staff these largely with costly lay teachers; and (3) to subsidize the institutions they have abandoned.

The Protestant upheaval is only less drastic. The elegant sanctuaries once frequented by them are now often found in the midst of Negro neighborhoods, which cannot or will not maintain such edifices in their former splendor. Some have attempted to integrate, with little future promise. We find, therefore, that the sectarian school system is declining; that the public schools have become almost totally black; that once prosperous white congregations have been replaced by a variety of colored evangelicals; and that the total number of churches has declined sharply.

In 1964, 45.7% of all property in the District was exempt; by 1968, this had increased to 48.3%. Although 71% of this was federally owned, and even though 10% of the religious was concentrated in two great national shrines, it is nevertheless a fact that the true ratio of exempt property is not appreciably greater than in a number of other cities, such as Boston, Buffalo, St. Louis, and Providence.

No item of real estate in Washington can, at least theoretically, qualify for exemption unless it is classifiable in one of 8 categories. Nor are the assessors as lenient as those in many other communities: there are no exemptions for the blind, for veterans, for widows, for residences owned by ministers or professors, or for commercial property operated by non-profit or charitable entities. Exemption was once denied even to the Ethical Society on the ground that it does not believe in a personal deity; the Supreme Court, however, overruled the District Assessor on this point.

The following indicates the developments which have taken place over a 4-year period.

REAL ESTATE ASSESSMENTS IN THE DISTRICT OF COLUMBIA

CATEGORY	1964	%	1968	%	Increase
Total	$4,653,591,031		$6,520,330,649		40.1%
Taxable	2,525,485,494	54.3	3,369,209,432	51.7	25.0
Exempt	2,128,105,537	45.7	3,151,124,217	48.3	48.3
Public	1,723,400,024		2,573,526,868		
Federal	1,491,881,236	70.1	2,250,756,163	71.4	51.1
District	231,518,788	10.9	322,770,705	10.3	39.4
Private	404,705,513	19.0	577,597,349	18.3	42.7
Ratio to Exempt	19.0%		22.4%		

DIVISION OF PRIVATE EXEMPT

	1964	%	1968	%	Increase
Religious	131,551,270	32.5	175,312,761	30.3	33.3
Educational	102,306,795	25.3	151,268,337	26.2	47.8
Foreign	33,198,153	8.2	45,128,552	7.8	36.1
Charitable	20,531,448	5.1	29,105,008	5.0	41.8
Hospitals	49,205,669	12.2	64,393,500	11.1	30.6
Cemeteries	7,497,535	1.8	15,087,362	2.6	101.2
Libraries	3,136,078	.8	3,134,181	.6	.0
Miscellaneous	57,278,565	14.1	94,167,648	16.3	64.4
Ratio to All	8.5%		8.8%		

PRIVATE EXEMPT PROPERTY IN THE D. OF C.
($577,597,349)

CATEGORY	Secular	Protestant	Catholic	Jewish
Churches, Etc.		$ 92,652,902	$ 76,405,347	$ 5,954,508
Educational	$ 59,965,923	19,500,211	71,694,021	408,182
Charitable	14,544,201	6,959,206	5,789,942	1,811,659
Hospitals	43,614,276	3,580,034	17,199,194	
Libraries	3,134,181			
Foreign	44,383,435		745,117	
Cemeteries	5,403,659	3,965,611	4,982,457	735,635
Miscellaneous	92,941,355	15,360		1,210,933
TOTALS	$263,987,090	$126,673,324	$176,816,078	$10,120,917
Ratio to All	45.6%	21.9%	30.7%	1.8%

TOTAL RELIGIOUS PROPERTY $313,610,319

Ratio to Private Exempt	54.3%
Protestant Ratio	40.3%
Catholic Ratio	56.3%
Jewish Ratio	3.3%

We see, therefore, that while taxable property increased by 25% in this 4-year period, the exempt rose by 48.3%. We note also that in spite of the huge aggregations of federal property, private entities increased their assets from 8.5% to 8.8% of the total; and that the ratio of the private sector to all exempts increased from 19% to 22.4% in 4 years. Whereas the federal corpus increased by 51.1%, the properties of Miscellaneous exempts, largely wealthy secular organizations with vast tax-free revenues, grew 64.4%. The dramatic increase in land values is reflected in the fact that assessments on cemeteries increased by 101.2%. The Daughters of the American Revolution has a property on which the land-assessment is $237,000 and that on the building $16,000.

Note carefully the preceding breakdown of secular and denominational exempt real estate in the District.

Secular properties thus constitute the largest sector among private exempts. Among educational institutions, we have George Washington University, with an assessment of $22,068,886, and a comparable sum for Howard University—a Negro institution subsidized by the federal government. We have also branches of Johns Hopkins and Harvard.

There are many secular charities, including the Goodwill Industries, the Boy Scouts, the City Orphan Asylum, the Planned Parenthood, the Red Cross, the Womens Christian Temperance Union, the Home for Incurables, the Boys Club, the Florence Crittenden Home, the Society for Crippled Children, the Home for the Blind, the Animal Rescue League, the National Association for the Relief of Destitute Colored Women, the United Community Service, and many others.

Among secular hospitals and health services, we have Freedman's, the Southeast Center, the Hadley Memorial, the Columbia Womens, the George Washington, the Childrens Casualty, and the Hospital Center, with combined assessments of about $40 million.

Foreign embassies are assessed at $45,128,552.

Under Miscellaneous, we have a unique array of magnificent facilities owned by a variety of organizations, classified as historical, artistic, patriotic, scientific, cultural, professional, or benevolent, with combined assessments approximating $94 million, among which the following are the largest.

95

The National Geographic Society	$13,440,453
The Carnegie Institution	7,069,060
The National Academy of Science	3,768,455
The International Bank of Reconstruction and	
Development	22,674,750
The Corcoran Gallery of Art	2,084,272
The Army Distaff Foundation	2,600,000
The Ys	5,926,190 [a]
The D. A. R.	2,411,825
The Pan-American Health Organization	3,802,752
The National Education Association	7,208,650
The American Pharmaceutical Association	1,809,362
The Brookings Institute	3,302,362
Total	$76,098,131

[a] Note that here, as in Buffalo, we classify the Ys as secular rather than as Protestant-religious.

In addition, we have the Masons, the Oddfellows, the L.O.O.M., etc.; the American Institute of Architects, the Forestry Association, the American Chemical Society and the Medical Society; the National Council of Negro Women, the National Association of Colored Women, the General Federation of Women's Clubs, the American Association of University Women, the National Women's Party, and the National Society of Colonial Dames; the Veterans of Foreign Wars, the American Legion, the Association of Soldiers, Sailors, and Marines, the AMVETS, and the Disabled War Veterans; the Columbia and the American Historical Association, the National Trust for the Preservation of Historic Sites, the Textile Museum, the Meridian House Foundation, the Ford Theatre, and the House Where Lincoln Died.

There are many, many more.

Protestant wealth is concentrated principally in houses of worship, reduced in number from 410 in 1936 and 328 to 1964 to 315 in 1968. Of their total valuations ($92,952,905), more than 20% is comprised in a single church—the Protestant Episcopal Washington Cathedral, assessed at $19,425,621, with a probable replacement cost exceeding $45 million.

Protestant educational property consists almost entirely of the Methodist-owned American University ($16,300,675) and the Sidwell Friends School, $2,005,163.

96

Facilities classified as Protestant Charities include a few missions and rescue societies, but consist largely of orphanages, asylums, and retirement homes belonging to Baptists, Episcopalians, Lutherans, Quakers, Methodists, Presbyterians, and the Salvation Army. Protestant hospitals are assessed at $3,580,030.

There are 13 synagogues assessed at $5,954,508; there is a Hebrew Academy, valued at $408,152; the Charities, $1,811,659, include the Jewish Welfare Board, the Jewish Community Center, a Hebrew Home for the Aged, and a Foundation for Retarded Jewish Children. Under Miscellaneous, we find the B'Nai B'rith Foundation, $1,126,680, and a building housing the Jewish War Veterans, $84,253.

The most extraordinary development in the District is the rapid growth of wealth in a single denomination, even in the face of a declining membership. In 1890, there were 94,203 religious affiliates, of whom 37,502 were Roman Catholics, who therefore comprised 16.35% in a population of 230,392 and who totalled 39.9% of all church communicants in the city. Even as late as 1906, however, they still possessed only 12.5% of the religious property, while the Protestant ratio was 85.4%. Since then the proportion of Catholics has dropped steadily, so that today they probably do not exceed 10 or at most 11%; nevertheless, they own almost 60% of all religious property used by Christian denominations.

Since 17,035 pupils were enrolled in 1964 in 43 elementary and secondary schools (of which 31 were parochial), we then estimated Catholic communicants at 85,000. In 1968, there were 40 elementary and secondary schools with 16,082 pupils, which would indicate a total of 80,000 members. Assuming that each Protestant congregation has an average of 600 members and that each synagogue represents 1,500 persons, we have 22,900 Jews (3%) and 189,000 Protestants (24.9%). This leaves almost 465,000, or 60%, without religious affiliation.

Including the National Shrine of the Immaculate Conception ($12,376,310), Catholic churches and their attached schools carry assessments totalling $76,405,347.

However, in addition to these, the Church owns a dozen private and diocesan elementary and secondary schools, a vast complex of colleges, universities, academies, seminaries, convents, monasteries, retreats, and other properties, many of which are centered in the area of 4th Street and Michigan Avenue. Among these, the most important are:

Georgetown University (7,140 Students)	$22,798,339
Catholic University of America (5,603)	24,513,079
St. Johns College	2,070,259
Trinity College	7,032,087
Catholic Sisters College	1,244,629
Gonzaga College	1,051,154
Sisters of Visitation	2,212,124
Sisters of Providence	1,971,375
Dumbarton College	2,882,952
Total	$65,775,998

There are two important Catholic hospitals: Georgetown, assessed at $11,880,312; and Providence, $5,338,981.

Catholic Charities, $5,789,942, consist, as usual, for the most part of nunneries, monasteries, and correctional institutions. Included, however, is the headquarters of the National Catholic Welfare Conference, the political center of Catholic activity, located at 1312 Massachusetts Ave., N.W., and assessed at $1,086,478. At 3339 Massachusets Ave., N.W. stands the magnificent residence of the Papal Apostolic Delegate, assessed at $745,117 and granted exemption as a foreign embassy.

GROWTH OF EXEMPT PROPERTY IN THE D. OF C.

Category	1964	1968	% Increase
ALL	$404,705,513	$577,597,349	42.7
Secular	182,782,105	263,987,030	44.7
Ratio	45.1%	45.7%	
Religious	221,923,408	313,610,319	41.3
Ratio	54.9%	54.3%	
Protestant	90,747,315	126,673,324	37.4
Catholic	123,809,080	176,816,078	42.8
Jewish	7,367,013	10,120,917	37.4

Between 1964 and 1968, Protestant and Miscellaneous religious property increased by 37.4% but dropped from 40.9% to 40.3% of all such holdings. In the meantime, the Catholic increased by 42.8% and expanded from 55.7% to 56.3% of the total.

We should note that not all religiously owned or even used real estate is on the exempt rolls. For example, since only one rectory for any one parish is exempt, the city is dotted with residences of auxiliary priests on which taxes are levied. An agency of the Catholic Church built a large apartment complex known as the Potomac Plaza; the Watergate Project, costing more than $70 million and standing in the very shadow of the Lincoln Memorial, is a development of the Vatican-controlled and Italian-based international real estate cartel known as the Società Generale Immobiliare. This occupies a ten-acre site on the east bank of the Potomac; it includes five huge structures, with restaurants, a shopping center, and some 1,300 luxury apartments which sell anywhere from about $22,500 to $250,000.

The intangible wealth of the churches in the District of Columbia, although unknown, must be enormous.

If it were not for other income the burden on real estate would be crushing indeed. For example, in 1968, the federal government is making a grant of $70 million and a loan of $33.3 million to the District, which exceed the total real property tax of $101,076,272.96. This money is not considered a payment in lieu of taxes; nevertheless, it equals $44.50 for every thousand dollars of assessed valuation of federal property, compared to the ad valorem rate which is just under 30 mills. Total District revenues in 1968 were the following:

The Real Estate and Personal Property Tax	$109,900,000
Sales, Gross Receipts, and Earnings Tax	91,450,000
Income Taxes	69,200,000
Miscellaneous Taxes	11,750,000
Total	$282,300,000
Non-Tax Fees, Etc.	25,750,000
Federal Grant and Loan	103,300,000
Hoped-for Federal Addition	44,800,000
GRAND TOTAL	$456,150,000

Since we assume that assessments are 50%, the tax on a $20,000 house would be about $300. However, should all District revenues be levied against real estate, the tax on a $20,000 house would be 132 mills, or $1,320—$3,000 for every 5 persons in the District.

We find, finally, that the actual taxes collected total $370 per capita, or $1,850 for a family of 5.

Based on the preceding analysis, the following statistics emerge:

	Assessment	Actual Value
ALL	$6,520,330,649	$13,040,000,000
Taxable	3,369,209,432	6,740,000,000
Exempt	3,151,124,217	6,300,000,000
Public	2,750,526,868	5,145,000,000
Private	577,597,349	1,155,000,000
Secular	263,987,090	528,000,000
Religious	313,610,319	627,000,000
Protestant	126,673,324	254,000,000
Catholic	176,816,078	353,000,000
Jewish	10,120,917	20,000,000

Since assessments certainly do not exceed 50% of value, the Catholic parishes have wealth averaging at least $9.56 million; the 13 Jewish congregations, $1.56 million; and the 315 Protestant and miscellaneous churches, $804,000. These sums, considerably higher than in the country as a whole, result in part from the presence of the national shrines, but much more from the high price of land. However, if we also take into account the overwhelming secularity of the city, its per capita religious wealth does not much exceed that in many other large cities, at least insofar as the buildings are concerned.

III. BALTIMORE

Baltimore, the most populous city included in our survey (939,024 in 1960), has a romantic and colorful history. Founded in 1632 by George Calvert, Lord Baltimore—an Anglican converted to the Catholic faith in 1625—the city was for many years the center of American Catholicism. The first American Catholic episcopate was established here in 1789, and in 1858 was granted priority over all others.

However, in due course, Protestants of various kinds arrived in force and built strong communions. Jews came also, and they soon established themselves in the commercial life of the city.

Because of its semi-southern background, Baltimore has long had a large Negro community which numbered 67,000 in 1890, grew to 167,000 in 1936 and to 329,000, or 35%, in 1960. According to statistics published by the Maryland State Department of Health in

1968, the population was then 913,000, of whom 382,400 (42%) were Negroes. During 1966, there were 9,188 white and 9,866 Negro births.

Before the Civil War, Baltimore was the great trading center for the Virginia planters. In the Eighteen-Fifties, political conflict merged with religious issues when the Know-Nothing Party, a battering ram intended to demolish Catholic power, established its headquarters in Baltimore. Riots and political disorders verging upon civil war became so rampant that occupation by federal troops became necessary for 5 years in the Eighteen-Sixties, when every established routine of life and trade were totally disrupted.

After the great fire of 1904, the city was rebuilt on a far greater scale. It now has many handsome buildings; and its port, which opens into Chesapeake Bay, carries heavy tonnage. It is a great center for surety business and has a variety of manufacturing industries.

The religious history of Baltimore presents a strange paradox. Founded and developed by Catholics, the city has now become predominantly Protestant, but with a powerful Jewish community. One perhaps cynical citizen remarked to this writer: "The Jews own it, the Catholics run it, and the Protestants live here and pay taxes."

Since Catholics have 70 parishes and 82 elementary and secondary schools serving 41,714 pupils, we estimate their membership at 185,000, or 20% of the population. Four colleges have an enrollment of 4,814. In the diocese, with a population of 2,233,500, the *Official Catholic Directory* claims 475,745 communicants, or 21.3%.

There are 511 Protestant and miscellaneous congregations with an estimated membership of 306,000, or 33% of the population. With 41 synagogues, we estimate the Jewish community at 62,000.

The religious affiliates therefore total about 550,000, or 60% of the population; this leaves some 360,000 without denominational ties.

Baltimore has an imposing central area with many new and handsome structures. What strikes the visitor most forcibly, however, is the extraordinary number and variety of religious edifices—many very modest, others commodious and even magnificent. The Cathedral of Mary Our Queen probably cost at least $12 million.

Mr. George M. Downs, of the Statistical Division of the Department of Assessments, offered cooperation without which this analysis would have been impossible, since he placed his own private ledger at our disposal. In this, every item of exempt property is numbered according to its classsification among the 17 categories.

Assessments are uniform on all classes of property, and stand, theoretically, at 67%; but, since assessments on all real estate total only $2,681,624,158, we know that appraisals are probably less than 50%; for, at 67%, we have per capita wealth of only $4,960, compared to $6,000 in Richmond, $9,000 in Denver, $8,300 in Minneapolis, etc.

Mr. Downs stated that valuations on exempts may be 30% lower

PROPERTY ASSESSMENTS IN BALTIMORE, 1964 AND 1968

	1964	1968	Increase
ALL	$2,585,206,168	$2,681,024,158	3.7%
Taxable	2,006,208,768	2,051,684,738	2.2
Exempt	578,997,400	629,339,420	8.6
Ratio to All	22.4%	23.5%	
CATEGORY			
1 Federal	22,667,510	22,064,850	
2 State	25,671,990	27,799,220	
3 City (Inc. Pub. Schools)	249,266,000	276,084,250	
4 Churches, Schools	89,430,950	97,219,410	
5 Colleges, Etc.	33,142,610	40,375,870	
6 Cemeteries	4,577,530	4,676,920	
7 Lodges, Benevolences	7,858,110	8,120,180	
8 Hospitals	43,216,020	43,519,710	
9 Wholesale Market	552,400	552,280	
10 Railroads (B & O)	16,539,770	14,370,530	
11 Housing Authority	39,284,940	40,102,120	
12 Homes and Asylums	17,393,720	16,796,300	
13 Miscellaneous	8,060,970	8,876,130	
14 Market Authority	4,212,260	4,272,200	
15 Blind Persons	1,124,780	1,408,530	
16 Maryland Fort	15,997,840	20,673,220	
17 Non-Profit Housing, Elderly		2,427,700	
Public Exempt	357,652,930	391,548,140	9.1
Ratio	61.8%	62.2%	
Private Exempt	221,344,470	237,791,280	2.5
Ratio	38.2%	37.8%	

than on taxables. However, we use the official records for our projections.

Baltimore has a separate category for the Baltimore and Ohio R.R. —whose holdings, assessed at $14,370,530, reduce the municipal revenues by more than $650,000.

Public housing projects are assessed at $40,102,120.

Blind persons and paraplegics enjoy exemptions on their homes totalling $1,408,532; these may rise to $6,000 for any individual; but if the disability is service-connected, there is no limitation.

Ministers and rabbis enjoy 100% exemptions on residences they own and occupy.

Since Baltimore was one of the 4 cities analyzed in 1964, we have prepared a table reflecting the changes which have occurred.

We note that while valuations on taxable property rose by only 2.2%, those on exempt increased by 8.6%. The following shows the development among private exempts during a 4-year period. (We omit categories 1, 2, 3, 9, 11, 14, and 16, since these are publicly owned.)

PRIVATE EXEMPT PROPERTY IN BALTIMORE

	1964	1968
Secular	$ 77,125,180	$ 78,813,890
Religious	144,219,290	158,977,390
Religious Ratio	65.2%	66.8%

	The Secular		The Religious	
CATEGORY	1964	1968	1964	1968
4 Churches			$ 89,430,960	$ 97,219,410
5 Colleges	$23,589,740	$25,178,840	9,552,870	15,197,030
6 Cemeteries	2,547,970	2,860,470	2,039,560	1,816,450
7 Lodges, Etc.	5,679,920	5,678,440	2,178,190	2,441,740
8 Hospitals	23,567,540	22,770,390	19,638,480	20,749,320
12 Homes, Etc.	1,015,980	1,135,980	16,377,730	15,660,320
13 Miscellaneous	3,059,470	2,983,010	5,001,500	5,893,120
15 Blind	1,124,790	1,408,530		
17 N-P Housing		2,427,700		
10 B & O RR	16,539,770	14,370,530		
TOTALS	$77,125,180	$78,813,890	$144,219,290	$158,977,390
Ratios	34.8%	33.1%	65.2%	66.8%

103

Thus we see that denominational exempts predominate. Actually, the secular would be insignificant were it not for the B & O RR, the Johns Hopkins University, $21,420,620, the Maryland Institute, $2,233,720, the new category of non-profit housing for the elderly, $2,427,700, the Peabody Institute (musical), $1,980,200, the Masonic properties, $1,198,000, and a number of health facilities and nonsectarian hospitals, of which the following are the most important:

The South Baltimore	$ 879,980
The Johns Hopkins	12,240,000
The Maryland	1,104,100
The Union Memorial	2,403,520
The Childrens Industrial School	1,444,560
The Childrens Hospital	1,004,910
Total	$19,077,070

Among secular Homes and Asylums, we have a Home for Incurables, $532,520; the Florence Crittenden Home, $75,000; the Wiessner Orphanage, $18,840; and the German Home for the Aged, $263,020.

Among the secular Miscellaneous—Category 13—we find a great variety, some of which might have been classified under 7 or 12. There are 6 more Legion posts, another S.P.C.A., and several ethnical societies. Among some 45 other organizations, we have the Volunteers of America, $91,140; the Goodwill Industries, $327,060; the

DIVISION OF RELIGIOUS PROPERTY IN BALTIMORE

CATEGORY	Protestant	Catholic	Jewish
4 Churches, Schools	$40,848,410	$49,363,340	$ 7,007,660
5 Colleges, Academies	766,270	13,610,910	819,850
6 Cemeteries	154,370	637,720	1,024,360
7 Lodges, Etc.	1,315,880	959,620	166,240
8 Hospitals	8,060,870	12,629,510	58,940
12 Homes and Asylums	501,120	3,834,640	11,324,560
13 Miscellaneous	1,452,540	597,800	3,842,780
Totals	$53,099,460	$81,633,540	$24,244,390
Ratios	33.4%	51.4%	15.2%

104

Anti-Vivisection Society, $9,080; the Boys Home, $18,380; the Family Welfare Service, $19,760; the Childrens Aid, $26,940; the American Cancer Society, $15,100; the Engineers Club, $141,400; the Planned Parenthood, $32,500; the Tuberculosis Association, $27,020; the Visiting Nurses, $145,000; and the Maryland Workshop, $362,820.

THE GROWTH OF RELIGIOUS PROPERTY

Division	1964	1968	Change
Protestant	$ 45,549,090	$ 53,099,460	Plus 14.2%
Catholic	74,018,640	81,633,540	Plus 10.3%
Jewish	24,651,560	24,244,390	Minus 1.2%
TOTALS	$144,219,290	$158,977,390	Plus 10.1%

The Jewish community, therefore, with about 11.3% of the religious affiliates has 15.2% of the exempt wealth; the Protestants, with 55.3%, 33.4%; the Catholics, with 33.4%, 51.4%.

In 1906, the Jewish community had 2 synagogues and 75 communicants, which increased to 59 and 73,000 in 1936, when they comprised 8.73% of the population and 17% of all communicants. Between 1964 and 1968, the number of synagogues dropped from 42 to 41 and the wealth from $24,651,560, or 17.09%, to $24,244,390, or 15.2%.

During the same period, Catholic wealth increased from $74,018,640 to $81,633,540, or 10.3%.

Protestants in Baltimore present an unusual phenomenon. Whereas in most cities their wealth has been growing much less rapidly than the Catholic, or actually declining, here it increased by 14.2%, from $45,549,090 to $53,099,460, of which $41 million—almost 80%—is concentrated in 511 houses of worship, varying from structures appraised at no more than $4,000 to a dazzling array of churches owned by the leading denominations. The Christian Church has a sanctuary assessed at $221,600; the Christian Scientists one at $224,000; the Seventh-Day Adventists one at $188,640 and another at $212,600; even the Pentecostals have one at $104,000 and the Nazarenes one at $136,980.

The long-established denominations, however, have the greatest wealth and the largest number of churches. The Baptists have 118, of which 6 range from $125,240 to $748,000. The Presbyterians have 37 which carry valuations up to $288,740. The Episcopalians have no less than 41, with 5 ranging from $118,630 to $358,800. The Lutherans have 42 with 15 ranging from $147,790 to $579,200. The Methodists, with 101, have 17 which rise from $132,800 to $568,920.

Under Lodges and Benevolent and Cultural Societies, we classify the following as Protestant:

The YMCA	$120,290
A Methodist Home	230,960
An Episcopal Center	47,450
A Presbyterian Home	253,920
A Church Extension Service	219,560
Total	$872,180

There is a Methodist hospital assessed at $3,943,120 and a Lutheran at $3,309,480. Under Category 12—Homes and Asylums— we find an Episcopal Home, $266,580. Miscellaneous Protestant property consists almost entirely of real estate belonging to the Salvation Army and the Ys.

Opulent as some of the Protestant churches may be, they fade into obscurity when compared to the monuments of the Catholic Church. With the great Cathedral of Mary Our Queen at the head, assessed at $6,903,260, we find dozens of massive churches ranging in valuations from two or three or four hundred thousand dollars into the millions. Often individual properties cannot be identified from the tax-rolls because they are simply titled to the archdiocese; and since the parochial schools are usually not separated from their churches, it is impossible to determine exactly what proportion of the investment consists of educational facilities. At all events, we know that 70 parish churches and their 59 schools, together with some others on the elementary and secondary level, have a combined assessment of $49,363,340, an average of $705,190 for each parish—which probably reflects a true value of at least $1.5 million for these facilities alone. Since the total true value of Catholic real estate in Baltimore cannot be less than $160 million, the average holdings for each parish must be at least $2.4 million.

The principal Catholic properties listed under Academies and Colleges are the following:

St. Mary's Seminary	$ 2,689,750
St. Joseph's College	1,346,980
The Academy of Visitation	342,800
Mt. Saint Agnes College	2,187,960
Loyola College	2,262,100
The College of Notre Dame	3,024,240
Total	$11,853,830

Since Loyola College has 2,982 students, a large campus with a magnificent church, and many academic buildings, an assessment of $2,262,100 seems absurdly low; a realistic 67% appraisal should not be less than $10 million. We know that the assessment is only 33%, for its reported book value is $6,791,262.

The Catholic Church owns and operates the Mercy, the Bon Secours, the St. Agnes, the St. Joseph, and the Jenkins Memorial hospitals, with combined assessments of $12,629,510.

We find also the following under Category 12.

St. Elizabeth's Home	$ 293,800
St. Anthony's Asylum	94,740
The Franciscan Sisters Convent	207,660
The Home of the Good Shepherd	205,360
The Little Sisters of the Poor	340,580
The Seton Psychiatric Institute	857,700
The Sisters of Charity	1,421,900
The Marion Retreat	412,900
Total	$3,834,640

Among Miscellaneous Catholic assets, we have a St. Vincent de Paul orphanage and a few other special services.

Jewish synagogues vary greatly. There is the Chel Yakov, assessed at $43,840 and the Shearith Israel at $45,520; there are others with even less. However, we find the Beth Jacob, assessed at $658,000, the Petach Tikvah at $506,620, the Har Zion Tiffereth at $1,063,500, and the Ahavas Sholom at $1,148,780.

Among educational institutions, we have the Rabbinical College, $355,500, and the Talmudical Academy, $208,000. Jewish cemeteries scattered around the city carry assessments exceeding $1 million. Under Lodges, etc., we find a Jewish Convalescent Home, $156,940.

The heaviest Jewish investments are in Category 12 and 13, where

107

we find a tremendous complex of retirement homes owned by the Associated Jewish Charities, assessed at $14,935,760, of which $11,176,500, is found under Homes and Asylums, and $3,735,300 under Miscellaneous.

Since the millage is 45.9 and assessments theoretically 67%, the tax on a $20,000 home would be $616. Since the total tax in 1967–68 was $94,172,129.47, the per capita burden was $101.

Assuming that assessments are 50% instead of 67% of true value, we arrive at the following totals, which, even so, are certainly very conservative for a city as large and as wealthy as Baltimore.

BALTIMORE REAL ESTATE [a]

	Assessments	True Value
ALL	$2,681,624,158	$5,360,000,000
Taxable	2,051,684,738	4,100,000,000
Exempt	629,339,420	1,260,000,000
Public	357,652,930	784,000,000
Private	221,344,470	476,000,000
Secular	78,813,890	157,000,000
Religious	158,977,390	319,000,000
Protestant	53,099,460	106,200,000
Catholic	81,633,540	164,300,000
Jewish	24,244,390	48,500,000

[a] Under this computation, we have per capita wealth of $6,600, which, in spite of the large Negro minority and the age of many buildings, is probably much too low.

IV. DENVER

At an altitude of 5,000 feet and nestled on the eastern slope of our greatest mountain range, lies Denver, Queen of the Rockies. The city stretches out in all directions from a hill capped by the capitol dome, which is overlaid with shimmering native gold. It is the largest metropolis between Kansas City and San Francisco; to the east stretch endless plains and to the west the highest and most rugged terrain on the continent. Some 65 miles to the south, towers the majestic Pikes Peak, reinforced to the north and northwest by other heaven-reaching crests. Not far distant, rise the Continental Divide and the Rocky Mountain National Park, replete with scenic vistas which reduce Switzerland and its Alps to the dimensions of toys.

The first settlers came to Denver in 1857. In 1864, Governor John Evans, who had founded Northwestern University at Evanston, Illinois, obtained a federal charter to establish the Colorado Seminary, which enjoys the rare privilege of owning unlimited commercial investments immune to local property taxation. The elderly widow Iliff, whose name is borne by the Methodist Seminary adjacent to the University of Denver, has transferred many of her properties to the Colorado Seminary.

There is also a privately owned but publicly operated educational trust known as the Clayton Estate which enjoys the same exemption from the ad valorem tax.

In 1870, the population was only 4,759, but by 1890, when it had reached 106,713, it boasted all the contemporary refinements of a modern city. In the Twenties, when the population had increased to 256,491, the city received considerable publicity because of the unconventional theories of Juvenile Court Judge Ben B. Lindsey.

There are a considerable number of Mexican-Americans in Denver; and although the Negro minority has now risen to about 8% and the Catholic denomination has been growing significantly, it is still predominantly a white Protestant-secularist community. We noted in *Church Wealth* that there were 395 houses of worship in 1964, of which 10 were Jewish, 38 Catholic, and 347 Protestant and miscellaneous. We may say that to a considerable degree it is still similar to what many midwestern cities, now much transformed, were like 50 or 60 years ago.

Denver has many industries and serves as the commercial and distribution center for a vast area. It is also a tourist mecca and vacation paradise. As the oil shale industry, with its allied minerals, develops, its financial importance may well become crucial in the American economy.

Since Denver was one of the 4 cities analyzed in 1964, no difficulty was anticipated. Imagine, then, our disappointment upon discovering that the tax-records had been completely reorganized. As one employee put it confidentially: "A bunch of 'experts' came in here to improve our system, and now we can hardly find our own hands." As if to compound the difficulty, there were three different sets of numbers to designate each category of exempts.

There was, indeed, a separate volume containing a roster of these; but this did not list separate items, and gave only the number of a certain category together with combined valuations in an area designated by a numeral: thus, in area 1,293, there are 6 church properties with a total assessment of $139,980. But there is nothing to indicate whether these are churches, vacant land, parking lots, or whatever; nor is there any clue as to ownership.

In the hundreds of such areas there is no identification by which the seeker can find, for example, the 6 items of church property of #1,293 in the 221 volumes containing over 150,000 cards, where all items, taxable and exempt, are filed in a single sequence.

To find these 6 items, it would therefore be necessary to consult a city plat and proceed thence to the 221 tomes aforementioned. The same procedure would be mandatory for each item of church property (#72, #38, or #92); and then the same routine would be required for every other category of exempts. The analysis completed in 3 days in 1964 would now probably occupy a team for several months.

Our quest, however, was not fruitless; for totals were available for different categories of taxable and exempt property. And these are startling enough; for in Denver, as elsewhere, the ratio of the latter is increasing with every tick of the clock. Since all assessments on existing properties are *reduced* periodically to reflect depreciation, and since little expansion occurred in the taxable sector, total valuations in this area fell from $1,169,942,550 in 1963 to $913,980,280 in 1968, or 22%; at the same time, however, assessments on exempts increased from $215,930,060 to $226,603,370, or 5.1%. The ratio of exempt to taxable was 18.45% in 1963; in 1968, it was 24.8%.

Although the proportion of exempt property in Denver has been far lower than that found in Eastern cities, this did not result from any stringency in the laws. In addition to charitable, cultural, educational, fraternal, and patriotic organizations, virtually all nonprofit entities enjoy exemption: the Masons, Elks, Eagles, Oddfellows; all veterans organizations; the Chamber of Commerce and other civic and business groups; the Bonfils Foundation for the Performing Arts; and many others.

All religious entities, of course, are free from taxation, including the Catholic publishing enterprise at 934–50 Bannock Street, where the *National Register* is published. But this is by no means all: in 1964, there were already 13 large apartment buildings charging full commercial rentals, but nevertheless free from local taxation because they were owned by non-profit organizations, of which 8 were Protestant churches and the others secular groups, such as unions or

110

associations of teachers. All such projects are to be taxed at 6% of the normal rate in 1969 and an equal additional amount each year thereafter until parity is attained.

Since we cannot offer an exact new breakdown of private exempts, we reproduce our statistics for 1964. At that time, the secular exempts were assessed at $25,164,730, and consisted of the following:

The Colorado Seminary	$12,426,200
The Clayton Estate	1,498,030
Hospitals, Sanatoria, Etc.	3,577,840
Other Non-Denominational Charities	6,905,400
Miscellaneous	757,260

THE 1964 DIVISION OF RELIGIOUS PROPERTY
($52,717,740)

CATEGORY	Protestant	Catholic	Jewish
Churches, Etc.	$15,640,010	$ 8,364,590	$1,150,770
Colleges, Etc.	3,202,960	5,247,520	364,960
Hospitals, Etc.	3,910,270	5,098,990	4,918,960
Charities	273,470	1,701,160	486,580
Apartments, Etc.	2,357,500		
TOTALS	$25,384,210	$20,412,260	$6,921,270
Ratios	48.16%	38.72%	13.12%

More than 67% of the private exempt property, therefore, was religious; of this, 38.72% was Catholic, even though such communicants composed less than 17% of the population and 30% of communicants and included a considerable portion of poor Mexican-Americans. Since this denomination has constructed several new parochial schools and has made large additions to its hospitals during the last four or five years, there can be no doubt that its proportionate wealth has increased very substantially.

Since the city now has 11 synagogues, we estimate the Jewish community at 16,000; since there are 39 Catholic parish churches and 34 elementary and secondary schools with 15,038 pupils, we estimate Catholic communicants at 88,000; and since there are 351 Protestant and miscellaneous churches, we estimate their inclusive membership at 210,000. This leaves about 185,000 with no church affiliation.

The following statistics are supplied by the Assessor's office.

111

REAL ESTATE ASSESSMENTS IN DENVER

CATEGORY	1962–63	1964	1967–68
ALL	$1,385,873,210		$1,140,483,610
Taxable	1,169,942,550		913,980,240
The Public	151,258,540		145,120,440
U.S.A.	42,432,500		37,725,710
State of Colorado	17,991,430		19,022,530
City-County of Denver	43,588,040		42,390,170
Housing Authority	9,069,440		9,208,280
Public Schools	38,177,130		36,773,750
The Private Exempt	64,672,120	$77,882,470	81,482,930
87 Clayton Estate	1,584,070	1,498,030	1,038,510
77 Colorado Seminary	8,347,170	12,426,200	13,355,740
91 Parochial Schools	8,479,070		8,905,360
90 Private Schools	3,519,770	3,412,700	4,706,410
92 Churches	19,609,310		18,654,800
93 Hospitals	11,519,350	16,302,080	15,994,080
97 Parsonages	1,252,130		1,366,080
94 Fraternals	2,489,170		4,170,060
95 Other Charities	7,799,100	13,065,580	12,607,750
96 All Others	72,980		584,140
EXEMPT TOTALS	$ 215,930,660		$ 226,603,370
Ratios	15.6%		19.9%

Thus, in 5 or 6 years, the ratio of exempt property increased to about one-fifth of the total; in 1962–3, it was 15.6%; a few years before, it was only 12%.

We noted that real estate appraisals are reduced progressively even with increasing market values. For example, the Clayton Estate, assessed at $1,584,070 in 1962–3, dropped to $1,038,510 in 1968. Meanwhile, the Colorado Seminary, because of new parcels transferred to it, increased from $8,347,170 to $13,355,740, in spite of the fact that valuations on assets previously owned had been sharply reduced. The tax-rolls show 122 separate parcels titled to this corporation in 1968.

Searching through the records by the difficult procedure noted above, we compared the assessments on 18 representative items of exempt property. For 1962–3 the total was $11,786,530 and for 1968 it was $9,413,430. Thus we know that valuations on prime real estate were reduced by more than 20% during this period. It is therefore established that exempt properties must have increased by at least 25 or 30% during these years; and, since assessments stand at 25% of true value, there must have been new construction in this area or acquisition exceeding $200 million.

We note, furthermore, that valuations on public property declined from $151,258,540 in 1962–3 to $145,120,440 in 1967–8. Meanwhile, the private exempts expanded from $64,672,120 in 1962–3 to $81,482,930 in 1967–8—an increase of $16,810,810, or 25.9%, which, because of declining assessments, reflects an actual expansion of at least 45% in five years.

We cannot pinpoint all the owners of this expanding wealth, but we have pertinent clues. We may conclude that the assets of the Clayton Trust remained static, since their appraisals declined by almost $550,000, or 33%. On the other hand, we know that those of the Colorado Seminary must at least have doubled, since their valuations increased from $8,347,170 to $13,355,740.

In 1962–3, parochial schools were assessed at $8,479,070; had there been no new construction, their valuations would have fallen to $5,800,000 in 1968. However, since the total increased to $8,905,360, at least $12 million must have been invested in new construction. And, since nearly 90% of these are Roman Catholic, we believe that this denomination must have expanded its holdings in church-related schools by at least $10 million.

We find also an enormous growth under Private Schools, from $3,519,770 in 1962–3 to $4,706,410 in 1967–8. Since this includes all church schools other than those attached to parish churches, most of these are probably also Roman Catholic. Exactly how the $36,015,760 of assessment allocated to hospitals, parsonages, and other church properties should be divided among the principal religious divisions, we cannot say; but, since the Catholic Church owns three great hospitals—the St. Anthony, the St. Joseph, and the Mercy, as well as the Maria Clinic—it is reasonable to assume that its share in 1968 was considerably larger than in 1962–3.

Properties listed under All Other Charities ($12,607,750) have doubtless undergone a comparable development. We believe that the following estimate for 1967–68 is sufficiently accurate for use in extrapolation. While secular exempts increased from $25,164,730 to

$26,192,930, the following reflects the probable development in the religious sector.

RELIGIOUS PROPERTY IN DENVER

DIVISION	1964		1968	
	Exact Totals	Ratio	Estimated	Ratio
Protestant	$25,384,210	48.16%	$23,500,000	43.1%
Catholic	20,412,260	38.72%	23,500,000	43.1%
Jewish	6,921,270	13.12%	7,500,000	13.7%

The assets of the Catholic Church are, therefore, now fully on a par with those of 350 Protestant and miscellaneous congregations. In 1906, the former owned only 14.34% of the religious wealth, compared to 82.22% belonging to Protestants and 3.44% belonging to Jewish congregations. In 1936, these ratios were 23.23%, 68.41%, and 8.35% respectively.

All assessed valuations stand theoretically at 30% of market or replacement value; but, since these are reduced, as we have pointed out, progressively in spite of inflation, we conclude that they cannot exceed 25% in 1968 and we arrive, therefore, at the following totals.

REAL ESTATE IN DENVER, 1968 [a]

	Assessments	True Value
ALL	$1,140,483,610	$4,500,000,000
Taxable	913,980,240	3,600,000,000
Exempt	226,603,370	900,000,000
The Public	145,120,440	575,000,000
The Private	81,482,930	325,000,000
The Secular	26,192,930	109,000,000
The Religious	54,500,000	216,000,000
The Protestant	23,500,000	93,000,000
The Catholic	23,500,000	93,000,000
The Jewish	7,500,000	30,000,000

[a] From independent evidence (cf. TABLE ELEVEN, Ch. 7), we know that this computation comes very close to precise accuracy.

Colorado has a state sales, use, and rental tax of 3%, to which Denver has added 2%. There is a state income tax, ranging from 3% to 8%, to which is added another 2% for intangibles.

Since the millage is 72.04 and theoretical assessments 30%, we have the following computation:

A Home Worth	$20,000
Will Be Assessed at	6,000
And Pay a Tax of	$430.

With a property levy of $82,623,813.70, the per capita tax in Denver is $161. And we can be sure that, as real estate continues to vanish from the tax rolls, this and other taxes will continue to inch upward, a fate which seems to be progressively universal in these United States of America.

CHAPTER 6

THE CHURCH DOMAIN: THE TEN NEW CITIES

V. RICHMOND

The largest city in Virginia is the Mother of Patriots and, even more than Boston, the fountainhead of American liberty. It was for several years the capital of the Confederacy and is still a distinctively southern metropolis. It is an historic city, where the voice of Thomas Jefferson once reëchoed in legislative chambers, where the Byrds have been prominent for centuries, and where the genius of Edgar Allan Poe spun out his mystical gossamers of poetry and intellectual analyses of crime. It was also the city which Grant shelled into destruction in May, 1864, a catastrophe which heralded the fall of the South and the end of the Civil War.

Richmond, overwhelmingly Protestant, has 92,331 Negroes in a population of 219,958. Since Catholics have 4,183 pupils in their schools, we estimate their communicants at 21,000, or 9.5%. Since there are 256 Protestant and miscellaneous churches, we estimate their membership at 154,000, or 70%. And since there are 5 synagogues representing 7,500 people, we estimate total religious affiliates at 182,000, or 83% of the inhabitants. We found, therefore, that 85% of the communicants are Protestant, 11.5% Catholic, and 4.1% Jewish.

White and colored properties are segregated; the latter make up

42% of the population; but only 6.5% ($1,202,488.85) of the total tax is levied upon real estate owned by them.

In its composite structure, Richmond represents such cities as Savannah, Atlanta, Nashville, Memphis, Mobile, Birmingham, Dallas, Fort Worth, Houston, and others in the South, which probably total some 5 million citizens, or 2.5% of the American population.

Richmond is now an important center of religious education; it has a large port on the James River; and we find within its environs and suburbs, a large variety of commercial and manufacturing enterprise.

We were fortunate in finding an up-to-date volume listing all exempt properties, together with owners and valuations. Total assessments for taxable and exempt property as well as for that owned by the county, state, and federal government were available. Private exempts, however, were not classified in separate categories.

PROPERTY ASSESSMENTS IN RICHMOND

			Ratio
ALL		$1,295,079,360	100%
Taxable		981,163,790	75.7%
Exempt		313,905,570	24.3%
PUBLICLY OWNED		219,311,580	70.0%
City		94,593,990	
Public Schools	$42,023,060		
Recreation and Parks	12,314,210		
Utilities	4,222,870		
General Services	19,068,440		
Police	5,085,160		
Public Works	11,068,640		
Finance, Welfare, Health	811,620		
City-Federal Housing Projects		20,972,580	
Federal Properties		14,979,600	
State of Virginia		88,603,240	
County		522,560	
THE PRIVATE EXEMPT		94,233,600	30.0%

We were also fortunate in the cooperation of the manager of the assessor's office, Mr. Percy L. Smith, who proved a rich source of help and information.

Exempt property, therefore, comprises slightly less than 25% of

117

the total. The largest items in the public sector consist of the federally financed housing projects, the city school system, its recreational facilities, public works, and general services, with combined assessments of $84,474,340. The State owns several educational institutions, of which the Virginia Commonwealth University including its excellent medical division ($33,422,440) is the largest. The State domain includes the capitol, office buildings, a penitentiary, the State Hospital, Game and Inland Fisheries, and a variety of miscellaneous facilities.

Since the tax-rolls make no division among private exempts, we have followed our usual classification.

PRIVATE EXEMPT PROPERTY IN RICHMOND
($94,233,600)

CATEGORY	Secular	Protestant	Catholic	Jewish
Religious Houses			$1,496,760	
Churches, Etc.		$41,372,640	6,412,340	$840,200
Seminaries		3,699,400		87,300
Universities		16,931,000		
Charities	$ 7,473,240	5,682,950		
Cemeteries	369,960		424,310	69,500
Hospitals	9,374,000			
TOTALS	$17,217,200	$67,685,990	$8,333,410	$997,000
Ratios	18.5%	71.8%	8.8%	1.1%

TOTAL RELIGIOUS PROPERTY	$77,016,400
Protestant Ratio	87.9%
Roman Catholic Ratio	10.8%
Jewish Ratio	1.3%

In addition to charitable and benevolent organizations found in the North, we have the Confederate Literary Society, the Poe Foundation, the Sons of the Revolution, the Stonewall Jackson Aerie, the Daughters of the Confederacy, and the Virginia Historical Society.

Among secular health services, we have the Bryan Day Nursery, the Crippled Childrens Hospital, the Retreat for the Sick, and the Richmond Memorial Hospital ($7,131,000).

Whereas in most large northern cities Catholic wealth far exceeds

118

the Protestant, here the former have only 10.8% of religious property while comprising 11.5% of the communicants. The per capita Protestant share is $500, the Catholic only $397.

Protestant congregations exist in profusion; and some of them are housed in magnificent sanctuaries. One Baptist Church is assessed at almost $2 million; and the headquarters of the Foreign Missions of the Southern Baptist Convention is assessed at $1,646,300. There are many Presbyterian, Methodist, Episcopal, Christian, Lutheran, and other Baptist churches which carry valuations ranging from $200,000 to more than $1 million. There are also dozens of modest structures appraised between $6,000 and $25,000.

Nor do Protestant sanctuaries ($41,372,640) comprise all their religious wealth. We find the Southern Baptist University of Richmond ($16,931,000); and the Presbyterian School for Lay Workers and the Union Theological Seminary ($3,699,400). Protestant Charities consist of Methodist retirement and children's homes ($5,682,950).

There are 13 Catholic parishes, 7 elementary parochial schools, 5 high schools, and a number of convents, monasteries, and cemeteries.

Five synagogues are assessed at $840,000, one Jewish school at $87,300, and cemeteries at $69,500.

Assessments are theoretically set at 100%; and the millage at 18.4 is the lowest we have encountered. This means that a $20,000 house will be taxed at not more than $368. Since the total property tax is $18,135,585.48, the per capita levy is $82.88, or $414.40 for a family of 5.

ASSESSMENTS IN RICHMOND AT 100% [a]

ALL	$1,295,069,360
The Taxable	981,163,790
The Exempt	313,905,570
The Public	219,311,580
The Private	94,233,600
The Secular	17,217,200
The Religious	77,016,400
The Protestant	67,685,990
The Catholic	8,333,410
The Jewish	997,000

[a] It is most interesting to note that they are actually 90 or 91%.

119

VI. BOSTON

The capital of Massachusetts was once the stronghold of a rigid Puritanism, later the cradle of the Revolution, and, in the days of its glory, the literary center of America, known as the Hub. Boston, however, has indeed undergone a vast sea-change. Once it was Calvinist, then it became Unitarian in the days of William Ellery Channing, Theodore Parker, and Ralph Waldo Emerson; but, following the great potato famine in Ireland, huge waves of Catholics arrived who, together with others of their faith, transformed this Protestant-liberal citadel into a predominantly Catholic metropolis.

The city grew from 18,300 in 1790 to 670,585 in 1910; but, after rising to 801,444 in 1950, declined to 697,197 in 1960 and to 670,000 in 1968–69. Like several other New England cities, it is preponderantly white, with only 68,493 Negroes—according to the census of 1960.

In the cemeteries of Boston are interred the bones of John Winthrop, John and Cotton Mather, John Hancock, Samuel Adams, and James Otis. Paul Revere is one of its legends and Faneuil Hall is redolent of past glory and present nostalgia. In its teeming harbor occurred the famous Tea Party, which many believe sparked the Revolution. Its area of 47.81 square miles contains a concentration of buildings and public facilities; and when the traveller boards a bus, he quickly emerges into the open countryside.

The city boasts a variety of colleges and universities, as well as a great many church organizations, of which the Roman Catholic is now by far the largest and most opulent. It has libraries, museums, art galleries, and other cultural facilities befitting its historic past. Nevertheless, it is not without trade and commerce also.

There was a time when the publishing industry and American literary celebrities were concentrated within its environs: but the process by which these transferred to New York and elsewhere was long since completed. However, Boston still has its Harvard subsidiaries and a portion of the celebrated Institute of Technology. But it has also a tax-crisis which becomes continually more acute, as real estate continues to vanish from the tax-rolls.

Since the Catholic Church has 72 parishes and 69 elementary and secondary schools with 36,865 pupils, we estimate its communicants at 185,000, who therefore comprise approximately 30% of the white population. There are also 2 Catholic seminaries and 1 college with

1,857 students. Boston College, a major Jesuit institution, with 12,-892 enrollees, is not included in our computation, since it is located in Newton, at the edge of the city: its properties are probably worth $65 million.* The Catholic proportion in the whole diocese is much larger than in the City itself; for, in a population of 3,335,895, the *Official Catholic Directory* claims 1,871,408 communicants, or 56%.

Since there are approximately 210 Protestant and miscellaneous congregations, we estimate their inclusive membership at 125,000; and since there are 19 synagogues, we compute the Jewish community at 35,000. There are, accordingly, about 345,500 religious affiliates, leaving a secularist ratio of nearly 50%, which must view the exemptions and immunities of the churches with increasing cynicism.

The staggering proportion of exempt real estate in Boston cannot be ascribed to its historic past; for as late as 1915, the valuations on taxable property totalled $1,508,707,000, while those on exempt were only $259,182,949, or 14.7%. Yet, in spite of new building permits totalling $1,237,471,000 between 1915 and 1957, taxable real estate carried appraisals of no more than $1,368,025,100 in 1967–68, while those on exempt property had risen to $1,117,719,-200, or 45% of the grand total.

Mr. Emmett Kelley, a District Director in the Assessor's office, greeted us with rejoicing. "I'm glad," he declared, "that some one's going to do something about the vanishing tax-base!" And he produced a study which he himself had prepared some years previously and which showed that taxable property declined in dollar value by $146 million between 1915 and 1957 while the exempt increased by $572,851,251 to $832,034,200. The same development has since continued inexorably and reached $989,719,500 in 1964 enroute to its present level.

What, then, has caused this progressive erosion and escalation? A glance at the chart prepared by Mr. Kelley may furnish a clue: for the drastic increase in exempt property first became apparent in the early Forties with the sharp increase in federal taxation. Since organizations which pay no ad valorem or income taxes can easily retain huge surpluses, they are also able to double or triple their wealth in a single generation.

In Boston, the Assessor uses a long list of categories called Clauses.

---

* The reported book value of plant is $53,479,000.

RECAPITULATION OF EXEMPT PROPERTY, 1967

CLAUSES	ASSESSMENTS
1 U.S.A.	$ 114,330,500
2 Commonwealth of Massachusetts	230,890,400
31 Literary	132,665,900
32 Benevolent	81,397,000
33 Charitable	43,375,400
34 Scientific	3,632,700
35 Temperance Societies, Inc.	6,000
5 Incorporated Organizations of U.S. Veterans	713,500
7 Fraternal Societies	22,000
10 Religious Organizations	30,000
11 Houses of Worship	46,240,400
12 Cemeteries	5,117,900
16,17,18,19,20,21 Special Clauses	3,407,900
22 G. L. Chapter 160, Sec. 87, Railroads	45,200
23 Medical Services	2,500,000
24 Knights of Columbus	235,400
A Public Schools	58,996,200
B-C City Departments	19,664,000
D City Hall and Annex	16,258,000
D-2 City Parking (Commonwealth Lease to City)	5,059,300
F Parks and Playgrounds	90,273,900
I Libraries	5,107,500
J Foreclosures	5,406,900
K Boston Housing Authority	102,496,600
L Health	1,251,600
M Hospitals	12,115,600
N Institutions	10,397,400
O Redevelopment Authority	27,969,200
OO Chapter 121 A, Slum Clearance	68,958,700
P Police	3,790,400
R Printing	360,000
S Public Buildings and Off Street Parking	14,318,600
T Public Works Department	9,653,900
U Welfare	1,031,200
GRAND TOTAL	$1,117,719,200

Percentage of All Property		45
City Property	$ 453,109,000	
Total Publicly Owned	793,329,500	71.4%
Private Exempt	319,389,300	28.6%
Total Assessments in Boston	$2,485,744,300	
Total Taxable	1,368,025,100	55%

One of the largest exempts, then, consists of the city-federal housing projects, $102,496,600, to which we must add the redevelopment and slum-clearance programs, which total $96,927,900. Since these alone total almost $200 million, they comprise 8% of all the property in Boston and add about $150 annually to the tax paid by the average home-owner. It is most interesting to note that the public school system is assessed at a slim $58,996,200, only two-thirds of what is owned by a single denomination.

Here may be the key to why taxes are so onerous in cities with large parochial school systems. We are constantly told that they save the taxpayers great sums of money, since they are privately maintained. But we also find that the same power-structure which promotes a huge sectarian school system also develops extensive "low-cost" housing projects and other tax-free facilities. In some cities, these projects are occupied mostly by Negroes; but in Boston, Providence, and elsewhere the great majority of the tenants are Catholics, who are therefore able to contribute their rental-savings to the Church. Thus it is no accident that Portland, with few parochial schools, no "low-cost" housing, a very small proportion of exempt property, and a magnificent educational complex, also has very low taxes.

In spite of the many Clauses, we find no specific classification for hospitals, or for cultural or educational facilities, as such; often there is little correlation between the nature of a property and the heading under which it is placed. There is a special Clause for fraternal organizations, yet these are scattered under other headings. There is even a separate Clause for the Knights of Columbus and another for the Old South Church, which is valued at $514,000. The telephone directory lists 60 church or religious organizations; and even though there is a specific Clause for this, it contains only a single item, which belongs to the Unitarian-Universalist Church; nevertheless, the headquarters of this denomination is found in another place.

Under Clause 31—Literary—are lumped the Aquarium Corporation, $635,600; the Paul Revere Home, $15,500; the Athenaeum, $460,000; the Horticultural Society, $650,000; the Boston Symphony, $500,000; the Childrens Infirmary, $708,000; the Massachu-

PRIVATE EXEMPT PROPERTY IN BOSTON, 1967
($319,389,300)

CLAUSE	Secular	Protestant	Catholic	Jewish
31 Literary	$ 95,371,200	$ 293,900	$36,092,900	$ 907,900
32 Benevolent	39,782,760	15,807,240	22,644,000	3,163,000
33 Charitable	19,767,800	3,071,600	6,389,600	14,146,400
34 Scientific	3,632,700			
35 Temperance		6,000		
5 Veterans	713,500			
7 Fraternals			22,000	
10 Religious Orgs.		30,000		
11 Houses of Worship		17,500,220	25,334,380	3,405,800
12 Cemeteries	2,866,100	33,700	1,954,500	263,600
13-21 Specials	3,407,900			
22 Railroads	45,200			
23 Medicals	2,500,000			
24 K. of C.			235,400	
TOTALS	$168,087,160	$36,742,660	$92,672,780	$21,886,700
Ratios	52.6%	11.6%	29.0%	6.8%

TOTAL RELIGIOUS PROPERTY	$151,302,140
Ratio of Protestant	24.2%
Ratio of Catholic	61.2%
Ratio of Jewish	14.5%
Ratio of Religious to All Exempt	47.4%

setts Historical Society, $260,000; the Boston Conservatory of Music, $253,000; the Museum of Fine Arts, $3,600,000; the Wentworth Institute, $290,000; the New England Conservatory of Music, $2,302,200; the Junior Achievement, $160,000; the Workers Educational Industrial Union, $393,000; the New England Genealogical and Historical Society, $485,000; the Junior League, $35,000; the School of Optometry, $190,000; etc.

However, the most important properties in this division are

Northeastern University	$12,845,700
Harvard	27,572,200
Boston University	33,586,800
Suffolk Law University	2,793,500
Wheelock College	2,400,100
Simmons College	6,539,000
Total	$85,737,300

There is also a vast accumulation under Benevolences, Clause 32: a Norwegian Old People's Home, the Forty-Niners Club, the Boy Scouts, a Freedom House, a Childrens Center, a Family Service, an Association of American Women, the Boston Day Nursery, the South End Settlement, the Franklin Square House, the Womens Service Club, the Childrens Clinic, the Appalachian Club, the Artists Guild, the Morgan Co-ops, the S.P.C.A., the Masonic Temple, the Shriners Home for Children, the Seamens Aid, the School for Crippled Children, etc.

The largest Clause-32 items are hospitals: the Massachusetts General, $27,054,800; the Medical Center, $5,614,800; and the University, $1,502,600.

Under Charities (Clause 33: $19,767,800), we find civic clubs, ethnical societies, several additional Morgan co-ops, other S.P.C.A.s, the Chinese Merchants Association, the Animal Rescue League, the Colonial Dames, another Family Service, the Girls and Boys Club, the Pipefitters Association, the Dorchester Historical Society, a Home for Aged Women, one for Aged Couples, the United Community Service, the Florence Crittenden Home, and a Home for Little Wanderers.

However, the largest items here also consist of medical facilities, such as the Home for Incurables, $693,000; the Convalescent Home, $485,000; the Osteopathic Hospital, $996,300; the Brigham Hospital, $662,400; the Diabetes Foundation, $497,000; and the Childrens Hospital, $309,200.

Under Literary and Benevolent (Clauses 31 and 32), Protestant wealth would be insignificant except for the Ys ($4,932,000) and the Deaconess Hospital ($9,350,300).

Under Charitable, Clause 33, we find more facilities belonging to the Salvation Army; the headquarters of the Unitarian-Universalist Association at 25 Beacon Street, $265,000; and a Baptist Center, $278,100.

Beyond this, Protestant investments are concentrated in some 210 houses of worship, assessed at $17,500,220, an average of $83,500.

Twenty pages in the 1968 *Official Catholic Directory* are necessary simply to list the properties of the Boston archdiocese. Under Literary—Clause 31—we have schools, academies, seminaries, convents, monasteries, and other institutions assessed at $36,092,000, which means that their replacement value must exceed $100 million. Emmanuel College is assessed at $8,666,000; the Christian Brothers school at $1,202,000; and Boston College High School at $5,348,000, which, with 1,307 pupils, surpasses any public school in the city, at least in opulence. The total valuation for all public schools is less than $60,000,000.

Under Benevolences (Clause 32), the following are identified on the tax-rolls.

The Salesian Society	$ 656,200
The Sons of Divine Providence	536,000
The Daughters of Mary Immaculate	227,600
The Carmelite Sisters	1,009,300
St. Helenas Home	242,900
The Redemptorist Fathers	377,600
The Oblate Fathers	240,000
The Home for Catholic Children	2,685,700
The Bernadine Sisters	750,000
Brothers of Hospitalers	525,000
The Franciscan Missionaries	2,000,000
The St. Elizabeth's Hospital	6,105,500
Carney Hospital	6,575,000
Total	$21,930,800

Under Clause 33, we find many more convents, monasteries, etc. And among these "charities," we have the House of the Archbishop, assessed at $750,000, a $2 million palace.

Intermingled with Catholic houses of worship—Clause 11—we find many rectories, more convents and monasteries, and, of course, the 72 parish churches and their attached schools. Their combined assessment of $23,334,380 seems to be a substantial undervaluation.

Under Clause 31—Literary—we find the Yeshiva Academy, $302,600; three synagogues; and two other schools. Under Clause 32—Benevolences—we have the Jewish Memorial Hospital,

$432,000; the Ladies Bikur Hospital, $1,230,600; the Jewish Women's Health Association, $324,000; the Community Center, $300,000; and the Rabbinical Seminary, $488,000.

It is, however, in Clause 33—Charitable—that Jewish religious investments are concentrated: the Jewish Welfare Association, $600,000; the Ladies Helping Hand, $300,000; the Beth Israel Hospital, $8,483,000; and the Jewish Home for the Aged, $4,406,000.

Under Clause 11—Houses of Worship—we have 16 additional synagogues with a combined valuation of $3,405,800.

Theoretically, assessments in Boston are 30% on residential and 60% on commercial property; and the tax-rate, which was 101 mills in February, 1968, when our analysis was made, was shortly thereafter increased to 130. This means that a commercial facility worth $100,000 will be assessed at $60,000 and pay a tax of $7,800. Since the tax for 1968 totals $198,992,391 (an increase of $46,745,356 over the previous year), the per capita real estate levy is $299, or $1,495 for a family of 5. Boston derives income from a number of levies and excises sufficient to meet a 1968 budget of $300 million. This means that the city government alone costs an average family of five $2,240 a year. If all property were to be taxed equally, the ad valorem tax on a $20,000 house would be reduced from about $860 to $450.

ASSUMING THAT ASSESSMENTS AVERAGE 33%, WE OBTAIN THE FOLLOWING: [a]

CATEGORY	ASSESSMENTS	ACTUAL VALUE
ALL	$2,485,744,300	$7,455,000,000
Taxable	1,368,025,100	4,105,000,000
Exempt	1,117,719,200	3,350,000,000
Public	793,329,300	2,393,000,000
Private	319,389,300	957,000,000
Secular	168,087,160	504,000,000
Religious	151,302,140	453,000,000
Protestant	36,742,660	110,000,000
Catholic	92,672,780	277,500,000
Jewish	21,886,700	65,500,000

[a] Our computation, therefore, places per capita wealth at $11,125, which is probably quite accurate. TABLE ELEVEN, Ch. 7, shows that although assessments are uneven and sometimes quite erratic, they average about 31% of true or reported value.

127

VII. HARTFORD

Lying in the midst of undulating farm lands and watered by the Connecticut River, which carries ships to the ocean, lies the distinctive city of Hartford, capital of its state. In 1920, the population was 138,036, of whom 40,667 were foreign born whites, more than half of them from Russia, Poland, Italy, and Ireland. The population increased to 177,397 in 1950, but declined to 162,178 in 1960, of whom 25,151 (15.5%) were Negroes.

Hartford is graced with handsome public buildings, fine parks, and distinctive religious institutions of higher learning. Its principal business is in the field of insurance. However, it has also considerable manufacture, and serves as the commercial center for almost a million people.

Settled by Dutch pioneers from New Amsterdam and called New Town in 1633, it was renamed Hartford in 1637. During the next century, it became a literary oasis, dominated by such colonial literati as Lemuel Hopkins, John Trumbull, and Joel Barlow. It was the birthplace of John Fiske, and the home of Harriet Beecher Stowe, Charles Warner, Horace Bushnell, and Mark Twain. In 1814, it became the headquarters for the Federalist Party, which advocated greater states rights and a diminution of presidential and Congressional power.

Although the *Official Catholic Directory* claims 812,011 communicants—49.4%—among 1,656,300 people in the archdiocese, the Church has only 15 parishes and 5,983 pupils in its 8 elementary and secondary Hartford schools, which showed a decline of about 15% since 1964. We therefore estimate its membership at 32,000, or 20%. It is interesting to note that of 179,396 receiving religious instruction in the archdiocese, 125,217, or 70%, are enrolled in the public schools.

Since Protestants and miscellaneous groups have 82 churches, we estimate their membership at 50,000. And since the Jewish community with 9 synagogues numbers about 13,500, we conclude that Hartford has an unchurched proportion of 41%, or 66,000.

Mr. Borden V. Mahoney and several of his aides were highly cooperative and supplied us with much supplementary information.

Paraplegics enjoy reductions on home assessments ranging from $1,810 to $13,000. Fifty-eight blind persons have exemptions which begin at $100 and total $136,070; and veterans have been granted

PROPERTY ASSESSMENTS IN HARTFORD

		Ratio
ALL	$1,110,475,751	
Taxable	837,617,301	75.5%
Exempt	272,858,450	24.5%
Public	141,161,130	51.7%
Private	131,697,320	48.3%

PUBLIC PROPERTY

U.S.A.		7,531,320
State of Connecticut		31,587,230
City of Hartford		102,042,580
Board of Education	$28,204,360	
City-Federal Housing	22,481,170	
Parks and Recreation	14,187,570	
Public Works	19,352,430	
Urban Redevelopment	5,279,750	
Other Departments	12,537,300	

CATEGORIES OF PRIVATE EXEMPTS

Hospitals	38,352,960
Colleges and Academies	23,270,990
Parochial Schools	5,457,470
Churches	27,769,100
Convents and Monasteries	1,855,650
Parish Houses	1,752,140
Parsonages	1,848,480
Reformatories	919,130
Educational, Scientific, Literary, Historical, and Charitable	17,923,680
Cemeteries	981,630
Veterans Organizations	62,280
Exempted by Special Act	2,340,040
Exemptions for Specific Classes of Individuals	8,490,770

exemptions totalling $7,689,397. The elderly are eligible to assessment-reductions up to $1,000 through a means test: 644 have qualified for a total of $623,140.

Exempt properties are listed on cards and under separate categories.

The "low-cost" city-federal housing projects and the urban redevelopment program are virtually equal in cost to the entire public school system.

The most important secular exempts consist of the Hartford Hospital, $23,762,750; the University of Hartford, $5,614,580; the Childrens Services, $1,061,810; the Watkinson Private School, $537,680; the Boys Club, $382,600; the Connecticut Historical Society, $466,610; the Red Cross, $249,300; the Institute of

THE DIVISION OF PRIVATE EXEMPTS
($131,697,320)

CATEGORY	Secular	Protestant	Catholic	Jewish
Hospitals	$23,820,990		$12,041,270	$2,490,700
Colleges, Etc.	6,820,220	$15,974,600	476,170	
Parochial Schools		70,400	4,834,200	552,970
Churches		12,231,970	14,276,640	1,260,490
Convents			1,855,650	
Parish Houses		531,280	1,195,030	25,830
Parsonages		661,330	1,143,790	43,360
Reformatories			919,130	
Ed., Sci., Etc.	11,287,810	4,961,190		1,674,680
Cemeteries	738,560	2,810	88,060	162,200
Veterans Orgs.	62,280			
Miscellaneous	673,000			
Individuals	8,490,770			
Special Exempts	2,340,040			
TOTALS	$54,233,670	$34,433,580	$36,829,940	$6,200,230
Ratios	41.1%	26.1%	28.0%	4.7%

TOTAL RELIGIOUS PROPERTY $77,463,750

Protestant Ratio	44.5%
Catholic Ratio	47.5%
Jewish Ratio	7.4%
Ratio to All Exempts	58.7%

130

Accounting, $215,300; the Brotherhood Homes, $222,600; the Athenaeum Art Institute, $4,637,780; the Colt Bequest Foundation, $503,520; the Hartford Medical Society, $331,990; and the Open Heart Association, $120,270.

Protestant and miscellaneous churches, of which many are costly, carry assessments totalling $12,231,970. The Congregationalists have one assessed at $991,500 and four others ranging from $171,460 to $362,680. The Unitarian, $369,290, is one of many outstanding edifices. And there are other beautiful and commodious sanctuaries belonging to Baptist, Presbyterian, Christian, Methodist, Lutheran, and Christian Scientist congregations. The Protestant Episcopal denomination has several handsome structures, including its cathedral, which is assessed at $1,108,200 and is surpassed among religious buildings in Hartford only by the Catholic St. Joseph's Cathedral, assessed at $7,699,210. Several Greek and Eastern Orthodox churches, which we include under Protestant and Miscellaneous, are large and ornate.

There are no Catholic colleges or seminaries in Hartford; and, strangely enough, Protestant wealth listed under Colleges and Academies exceeds that invested in churches; the Episcopal Trinity College and the interdenominational Hartford Seminary have combined assessments of $15,974,600. There are no Protestant hospitals, but there are parish houses and parsonages valued at $1,192,610, and properties classified as educational, scientific, etc., assessed at $4,961,190, among which we find the Ys, $2,254,770; a Congregational Home, $1,196,090; facilities belonging to the Salvation Army, $973,320; and a number of missions and minor charities.

Catholic churches are assessed at $14,077,280; their attached schools, $4,834,200; the St. Francis Hospital, $12,041,270; the La Sallette and 14 other convents and monasteries, $1,855,650; parish houses and rectories, $3,043,510; the House of the Good Shepherd, $919,130; and the Mt. St. Benedict Cemetery, $88,060.

The Jewish community has 9 synagogues, $4,260,490; the Yeshiva and Agudas Achim Schools, $552,870; a Hebrew Home for the Aged, $1,529,630; and 29 cemetery plots, $152,200.

And so we see that the Catholic Church, established in 1843 and made an archdiocese in 1953, has accumulated great wealth in Hartford, but has barely held its own among the communicants of the city. Interestingly enough, even without parochial schools, the Protestant churches own nearly as much real estate as do the Catholic.

131

Assessments, which stand theoretically at 65%, seem realistic. Since the millage in 1967 was 49.9, the property levy was $41,880,855—or $258 per capita, and $1,290 for a family of 5. And since the budget was $49,211,462, this was $303 per capita, or $1,515 for a family of 5.

The tax-liability on a $20,000 house would be $649.

The following estimates the true value of Hartford real estate.

CATEGORY [a]	Assessments	Full or True Value
ALL	$1,110,475,751	$1,665,000,000
Taxable	837,617,301	1,256,000,000
Exempt	272,858,450	409,000,000
Public	141,161,130	211,000,000
Private	131,697,320	198,000,000
Secular	54,233,670	81,500,000
Religious	77,463,750	116,500,000
Protestant	34,433,580	51,700,000
Catholic	36,829,940	55,500,000
Jewish	6,200,230	9,300,000

[a] The theoretical assessment-value in Hartford gives us a per capita wealth of $10,300, which is certainly not far from accuracy. Trinity College (cf. Ch. 7, TABLE ELEVEN) carries an assessment which is 72% of its reported plant value.

VIII. PROVIDENCE

The capital of our smallest state was founded in 1636 by Roger Williams, who was banished from Massachusetts because he rebelled against the Puritan ecclesiastical authorities. A fervent supporter of church-state separation, he founded the first American Baptist church in Providence. For decades, the city was a stronghold of Quaker traders and evangelical Protestants and later the scene of fierce battles during the War of the Revolution. Here was built the first Unitarian church in 1773, the bell for which was cast by Paul Revere. However, when the great immigrant waves reached these shores from Catholic countries after 1840, the complexion of this city, like that of Buffalo and Boston, altered radically; and the Baptist-Quaker citadel of the 18th century fell under the sway of the Vatican.

132

Providence has many treasured memories. During the Revolution, its port on Providence River served as the headquarters for privateers, who preyed on English shipping. The Rhode Island Declaration of Independence was signed on May 4, 1775, exactly two months before the more famous document was inscribed at Philadelphia. Many famous Americans have been born or have resided in Providence.

The city had a population of 252,981 in 1930 and 248,674 in 1950, but dropped to 207,498 in 1960.

Roman Catholics have 28 parish churches, 10,511 pupils in 26 elementary and secondary schools, 3,097 students in 2 colleges, and an estimated membership of 65,000. Since there are 74 Protestant and miscellaneous churches, we compute their communicants at 44,000; and since there are 10 synagogues, the Jewish community is probably about 15,000. The religious affiliates therefore number about 125,000, or 60% of the population. The city is predominantly white; in 1960, Negroes numbered only 11,973, or 5.6%.

Mr. Louis Coté, Assessor, who recently made an analysis of the dwindling tax-base, gave us a complete transcript of the exempt properties.

Wonderful are the number and variety of tax-exemptions in Providence. The blind who live in their own houses qualify; there is a special provision for Gold Star Mothers. Professors at Brown University enjoy exemptions up to $10,000 (totalling $723,730) on residences they own and occupy. The same applies to ministers and rabbis, whose assessments are thus reduced by $511,580. Veterans receive exemptions of $1,000, which Mr. Coté considered discriminatory, since it applies only to home owners and constitutes, in effect, a permanent pension at the expense of other taxpayers and has caused a loss of $10 million in revenue since the end of World War II. By special acts of the legislature, nearly $50 million in assessed valuations have slipped from the tax rolls; this includes all communications utilities, and various other properties, all of which are immune to taxation: in Providence alone, the American Telephone and Telegraph Company enjoys exemption on property assessed at $18,530,000; the Railway Express on $250,000; the Western Union on $40,000; and the Intelex System on $6,500,000. Since the millage is 43, the loss to the city because of these special exemptions is well over $2 million annually.

Furthermore, one hospital and one cemetery enjoy total immunity

133

REAL ESTATE ASSESSMENTS IN PROVIDENCE

ALL		$909,460,170	Ratios
Taxable		607,752,400	66.7%
Exempt		301,707,770	33.3%

Group I

For Blindness	$ 251,950	
Gold Star Mothers	155,580	
Professors at Brown U.	723,130	
Veterans	11,905,820	
Rectories and Parsonages	511,580	
Ch. 15 of Public Law	4,610	
Total	$ 13,552,670	

Group II

Cemeteries	3,359,980
Charitable	4,681,960
Churches	20,946,490
Exempt by Special Charter	3,186,190
Federal Properties	9,089,400
Hospitals	39,757,680
Libraries	4,227,480
Municipal	66,391,690
Schools, Etc.	60,420,610
State Properties	24,871,760
Exempted by Vote	1,940,860
Exempt by Legislature	23,961,000
Acts of Legislature	25,320,000
Total	$288,155,100

from taxation on all commercial properties they may own or acquire. And "This exemption extends," Mr. Coté pointed out, "to any and all property owned by the [Brown] University without regard to its use. This all-inclusive type of exemption is also applicable to property owned by the Roman Catholic bishop of Providence and the Diocese of Rhode Island. . . . regardless of the nature of the real estate owned. . . ." And Mr. Coté even ventured to assert that churches which conduct bingo games on their premises should pay taxes, since this is assuredly not an exercise in religion. And he noted further that "One hospital corporation has built a medical building which it rents

134

THE PRIVATE EXEMPT PROPERTY IN PROVIDENCE
($301,707,770)

			Ratios
THE PUBLIC		$129,638,520	42.9%
THE PRIVATE		172,069,250	57.1%
The Secular		115,465,840	67.7%
Utilities	$25,340,000		
Brown University	30,774,810		
Mary Wheeler School	745,210		
College of Education	442,000		
Bryant Business School	1,900,860		
School of Design	11,469,980		
Butler Health Center	2,263,340		
Lying-in Hospital	2,552,270		
Rhode Island Hospital	21,363,330		
Roger Williams Hospital	4,508,490		
Miscellaneous	14,105,550		
The Religious		56,603,410	32.3%
Protestant Property	10,495,310		18.4%
Catholic Property	38,857,880		68.7%
Jewish Property	7,250,220		12.9%

as doctors' offices" and "as a drug store . . . but enjoys, by virtue of a charter provision, a tax-exempt status."

Thus it is that 142 parcels owned by Brown University, 73 by the Rhode Island Hospital, and scores by the Catholic diocese in addition to its religious facilities appear on the exempt rolls. In addition, certain properties owned by credit unions and national banks are likewise exempt.

Mr. Coté declared also that "Approximately 30% of the land area in Providence is tax-exempt" and that assessments on this "do not reflect present-day values and if I were required to make an estimate, I would place the figure at somewhere nearer to $500 million," (rather than the $301 million shown in the preceding table). The true ratio of exempt property is therefore not 33.3%, but 40 or possibly even 45%. Nevertheless, for purposes of extrapolation in this study, we will here, as elsewhere, use the official statistics.

The nature and use of denominational properties are not specified

135

on the tax-rolls; for this reason, in the following, they are separated only under principal divisions.

We note that the Rhode Island Hospital has grown into an economic colossus because of its tax-exempt status in the ownership of commercial property. We note also that Catholic churches, at least in part for the same reason, own nearly four times as much real estate as the Protestant and that the private exempts have far outdistanced the public, even though the latter include housing projects assessed at $23,961,000.

Among secular exempts, we find the Red Cross, $103,520; the Nursing Association, $98,960; the American Legion, $57,600; the Home for Aged Men and Women, $314,290; the Animal Rescue, $35,580; the Medical Society, $55,880; the Boys Club, $936,280; the Association for the Blind, $80,930; the Boy Scouts, $291,540; the S.P.C.A., $51,690; the Volunteers of America, $68,370; also cemeteries, fraternal organizations, etc.

In addition to their churches, the Protestants have two cemeteries assessed at $1,143,060; a Quaker school, $1,530,360; the Salvation Army, $600,960; and the Ys, $1,231,540.

In addition to the 28 Catholic parish churches and their 24 attached schools, the Rhode Island archdiocese owns a large amount of tax-free commercial property.[*] The Cathedral of Sts. Peter and Paul is assessed at $8,301,650; the St. Pius Church at $2,415,010; and many at sums ranging into several hundred thousand dollars.

Catholic wealth, assessed at almost $39 million, consists in part of the La Salle Academy, $1,392,860; the Friars Minor Monastery, $505,860; St. Elizabeth's Home, $333,860; The Catholic Teachers College, $1,340,600; St. Joseph's Hospital, $4,517,790; and Providence College, $8,064,630. The combined assessments on these are $16,589,720.

We find 10 synagogues assessed about $2,400,000; the Hillel Home, $25,590; the Hebrew Day School, $32,000; a Community Center, $108,600; a Jewish Home for the Aged, $470,890; and the Miriam Hospital, $4,184,520.

In 1967, the net property tax was $34,925,711.08, which comes to

---

[*] According to a news item in the Providence *Sunday Journal,* Dec. 1, 1968, the Roman Catholic diocese will pay $10,000 in lieu of taxes on a new $2.2 million commercial office facility. The normal levy would be $56,760. This was not on the rolls at all when the present survey was made in February, 1968.

$174 per capita. Since the assessments are theoretically 60% of market value and the millage is 43, a $20,000 home pays $510.

Assuming that assessments stand at 50%, we have the following totals:

CATEGORY [a]	Assessments	Full or Market Value
ALL	$909,460,170	$1,818,000,000
Taxable	607,752,400	1,215,000,000
Exempt	301,707,770	603,000,000
Public	129,638,520	259,000,000
Private	172,069,250	344,000,000
Secular	115,465,840	231,000,000
Religious	56,603,410	113,000,000
Protestant	10,495,310	21,000,000
Catholic	38,857,880	77,500,000
Jewish	7,250,220	14,500,000

[a] This computation places per capita wealth at only $9,000 because of the very low assessments on exempt properties.

Since the exempt properties are drastically underassessed in comparison with the taxable, we believe that Protestant assets are about $30 million; Jewish, $21 million; and Roman Catholic, $120 million. In our computation, however, as usual, we use the official statistics.

IX. ST. LOUIS

Just below the point of confluence where the Missouri flows into the Mississippi, lies the Hub of the Prairies, which, including its periphery, is a vast and wealthy conglomerate of trade, finance, transportation, and manufacture. Its core has indeed faded from its pristine splendor, but it is still a throbbing business dynamo.

The city has a variety of colleges, universities, libraries, museums, and recreational facilities. Its Forest Park and zoo are among the finest in the world. The trial of Dred Scott took place in St. Louis. During the Civil War, the State split down the middle in allegiance to the Confederacy and the Union.

The most famous of all American expositions opened here in 1906. Although $42,500,000 was spent in preparation, it showed a profit of

$1 million when it closed after 7 months; and two of its buildings continued in use for decades. In May, 1927, Charles Lindbergh began his historic flight from this city, and thereby etched its name and his own forever in the annals of aviation.

St. Louis had a population of 772,897 in 1920, of whom 9% or 69,854 were Negroes. In 1960, there were 750,026, of whom 28.8% or 216,022 were non-white. According to a recent estimate (*Globe-Democrat,* March 22, 1968) there are now only 693,000; the metro area, however, has grown to 2,395,000.

Founded in 1762 by French trading merchants from New Orleans, the city was named in honor of Louis XV, then king of France. It was ruled intermittently by the French and the Spanish until 1804, when it was incorporated into the United States. Even though a substantial Protestant community has now developed, a majority of the white communicants are still Catholic, who number about 200,000, or 29% of the population; 39% of all white citizens; and probably 65% of the white communicants. In the archdiocese as a whole, the *Official Catholic Directory* claims a membership of 511,669 in a population of 1,928,295, or 26.5%.

Nine synagogues represent a Jewish community of about 14,000.

Since there are approximately 500 Protestant and miscellaneous congregations, of which many are Negro, we estimate their inclusive membership at about 270,000. These are of many faiths: for example, there are 8 Christian Scientist churches and reading rooms in the city and 16 in Greater St. Louis; and no less than 117 practitioners are listed in the telephone directory.

Our analysis was greatly expedited because the Assessor maintains a separate book with all exempt properties arranged under 45 numbered headings, of which only 8 require detailed analysis. Of these, 15 are categories for individual denominations.

Mr. Oliver Dippold, Supervisor of Property Appraisers, was most cooperative and informative. Like many of his counterparts in other cities, he complained that his manpower is insufficient to revise assessments on exempt property, on which valuations are admittedly far below parity with the taxable. While assessments on taxable real estate stand theoretically at 40%, those on exempts are usually less than 20%. We must conclude, therefore, that if both were at parity, nearly one-half the real property in St. Louis would be revealed as exempt from taxation. For example, St. Louis University (Jesuit), with 11,148 students, is assessed at $14,150,960, but its official *book*

PROPERTY ASSESSMENTS IN ST. LOUIS

			Ratio
ALL		$1,770,903,420	
Taxable		1,246,652,510	70.42%
Exempt, 1967		524,250,910	29.58%
In 1966		496,311,240	
Increase in One Year		27,939,670	5.6 %
PUBLICLY OWNED		380,216,690	72.53%
CATEGORY			
Total City Property		225,587,940	
1 Board of Education	$39,620,560		
6 Parks and Playgrounds	67,040,320		
13 City-Federal Housing Auth.	36,323,830		
3, 4, 5, 7, 8, 9, 10, 11, 12, 12a, 44a, and 45: City Departments	82,603,230		
Total U.S.A.		136,781,270	27.47%
15 Buildings, Federal	24,063,570		
16 Ordnance Plant	76,623,600		
17 Veterans Hospital	5,127,000		
17a Urban Redevelopment	30,967,100		
14 State of Missouri		17,847,480	

TOTAL PRIVATELY OWNED EXEMPTS

144,034,220

18 Associations	9,300,350
19 Baptists	6,022,860
20 Catholic Churches	6,785,660
21 Cemeteries	7,532,580
22 Christian Churches	732,760
23 Churches of God	510,690
24 Congregational Churches	368,690
25 Episcopal Churches	787,700
26 Evangelical Churches	2,602,460
27 Evangelical Lutheran	3,148,190
28 Hospitals, Sanatoria, Etc.	25,404,900
29 Institutes	2,300,090

30	Jewish Synagogues	478,260
31	Lutheran Churches	1,597,840
32–33	Methodist Churches	2,667,160
34	Miscellaneous Churches	3,297,650
35	Miscellaneous Organizations	11,641,630
36	Nazarene Churches	98,400
37	Presbyterian Churches	1,772,740
38	Joseph E. Ritter (154 Items)	11,460,520
39	St. Louis University	14,150,960
40	Academies, Schls, Convents	10,435,620
41	Christian Science Churches	827,570
42	Societies	5,128,100
43	Tabernacles	95,420
44	Washington University	14,885,420

value is $72,133,000,[a] and it would require more than $100 million for replacement. Washington University, assessed at $14,885,420, has a plant valued at $78,279,324.

From 1940 through 1950, the tax-rate remained at about 27.4 mills; since 1960, however, largely because of enormous increases in exempt property, it has been rising rapidly and reached $5.11 in 1968. This means that the levy on a $20,000 house has increased from $216 to $410.

Mr. Dippold emphasized that the problem posed by the dwindling tax base is aggravated by various causes.

(1) The 8 large city-federal housing projects, which cause heavy deficits, carry assessments totalling $36,323,830, almost equal to the investment in the public school system. One high-rise apartment, only 6 years old, had been so vandalized internally that it had to be virtually rebuilt at a cost of $1.5 million. Many of the tenants do not pay even their small rents, which average about 25% of what is paid in taxpaying buildings.

(2) Great quantities of property are disappearing from the tax-

---

[a] *American Colleges and Universities,* p. 823.

rolls because of urban renewal and because of private but publicly financed enterprises, like the Busch Stadium.

(3) There are thirteen "charitable" organizations empowered by charters issued under state law to own and operate unlimited amounts of tax-free commercial property. Among these are Washington University, the Sisters of Mary, the German Protestant Orphans Home, St. Vincents School, and the Home of the Friendless. Another of these favored corporations is the Mercantile Library, which occupies space on one floor of a large office building assessed at $980,000 in the downtown area where one of the leading banks of the city is located. The Library continues to amass huge sums of untaxed revenue and pays no tax on its real estate. When the City attempted to revoke the Library's immunity, the latter obtained a permanent injunction forbidding the Assessor from ever again attempting to levy a tax on it.

(4) Some 2,000 acres of prime real estate assessed at $4,760,050 are occupied by the Calvary and Bellefontaine cemeteries, owned by two churches. For commercial development, the land would be worth at least $100 million.

(5) The federal government has a huge factory, assessed at $76,623,600 (double the entire public school system), which manufactures munitions and which is exempt from local taxation, although it bears the same relationship to the community as if it were a private industry. If this and the "low-cost" housing projects were taxed, city revenues would be enhanced by approximately $7.5 million, which would reduce the tax-rate from $5.11 to $4.50 and would save the average home owner $60 on his annual tax bill. If the churches, the chartered exempts, the federal munitions plant, and the "low-cost" housing projects were to be assessed realistically and pay taxes, all tax bills in St. Louis could be reduced by nearly 50%.

(6) In St. Louis, urban renewal and redevelopment projects have removed land assessed at $30,967,100 from the tax-rolls.

(7) Although St. Louis University (Jesuit) is not empowered by charter to operate commercial properties free of taxation, it has been buying hotels, apartment buildings, and other real estate in the area surrounding it; and, by using these facilities as dormitories, residences, etc., all of them have slipped off the tax-rolls.

As Mr. Dippold concluded his dolorous recital, he made a gesture of helplessness, as if to say, "What can we do?"

Assessments on exempt real estate rose by more than $27 million or

5.6% between 1966 and 1967; and this in spite of the fact that the valuations placed on it are the lowest we have encountered. For example, there are 11 Episcopal churches with a combined assessment of $787,700; but among these, the Christ Church Cathedral alone, on downtown Locust Street and assessed at a mere $417,250, certainly represents at least a $3-million investment. The denomination has several churches comparable to structures appraised at more than $500,000 in Richmond and Portland. We would say that Episcopal real estate in St. Louis is worth in excess of $10 million.

However, no one can accuse the Assessor of partiality. The various Baptist bodies have 162 churches assessed at $6,022,860—an average of $37,000. If these are at all comparable to those of other cities, their true value must be at least $35 million.

There are 49 Methodist sanctuaries with a combined valuation of $2,667,160, whereas a 40% appraisal should be at least $6 million.

Busch Stadium, built on land belonging to a municipal corporation, is wholly tax exempt for 10 years, and after that it will be free from half the normal levy for an additional 15. It was financed by the sale of bonds, the revenue from which is non-reportable by recipients on tax-returns. Since this $30-million facility is assessed at only $1,512,290, it appears that the promoters need never worry very much about the ad valorem tax unless the appraisal is drastically increased. A 40% valuation would be not less than $12 million.

Since the appraisals on the property shown in the following table, officially assessed at $144,034,220, would at least have to be doubled to attain parity with the taxable, we compute its true or replacement value at nearly $1 billion. If all religious properties are similarly undervalued, it appears that Protestant religious wealth is about $250 million; Catholic, $330 million; and Jewish, $20 million. The true value of the religiously used real estate in St. Louis is therefore probably not less than $600 million.

In addition to Washington University, the Mercantile Library, and various fraternal organizations, we find among secular exempts the Humane Society, $253,030; the St. Louis Symphony, $430,450; the University of Missouri, $1,330,000; William Jewel College, $664,870; the St. Louis College of Pharmacy, $424,900; the School for Mechanics, $520,540; the Botanical Garden, $1,107,600; a German Home for the Aged, $253,430; the Goodwill Industries, $997,180; a Masonic Home, $887,400; the Boys Club, $304,000; the Red Cross, $764,050; and the Engineers Club, $210,000. Among

PRIVATE EXEMPT PROPERTY IN ST. LOUIS
($144,034,220)

CATEGORY	Secular	Protestant	Catholic	Jewish
18 Associations	$ 3,957,100	$ 4,825,570	$ 535,690	$ 7,850
21 Cemeteries	2,000	4,025,580	3,479,150	2,588,870
28 Hospitals	7,652,520	6,430,190	8,733,380	
29 Institutions		1,802,650	497,440	
35 Miscellaneous	6,177,840	2,088,630	2,678,220	696,940
38 Joseph Ritter			11,460,520	
39 St. Louis Un.			14,150,950	
40 Academies, Etc.	2,981,480		7,454,140	
42 Societies	1,048,450	3,739,910	339,740	
Churches		24,530,120	6,785,660	478,260
44 Washington Un.	14,885,420			
TOTALS	$36,704,810	$47,442,650	$56,114,840	$3,771,920
Ratios	25.48%	32.92%	38.98%	2.62%

TOTAL RELIGIOUS PROPERTY $107,329,410

Ratio of Protestant   44.2%
Ratio of Catholic   52.3%
Ratio of Jewish   3.5%

hospitals, we have the Barnes, $2,277,090; the Park Lane Memorial, $340,830; the Keeney, $1,079,400; the Childrens, $2,701,120; and Washington University, $980,620.

Under Associations, the Protestants have health services and benevolences with assessments totalling $4,738,860. They have also 8 additional hospitals with combined valuations of $6,430,190.

Under Institutes we have Brooke's Bible School for the Deaf, and the Missouri Province Educational Institute: assessments, $1,802,650.

Among Miscellaneous Protestant organizations, the most important are (1) the Home of the Friendless, $407,410—of which some items are commercial—and (2) 23 parcels belonging to the Salvation Army, $1,246,320.

Although the foregoing constitute no mean corpus of property, Protestant wealth in St. Louis, as everywhere, is largely concentrated in its 500 sanctuaries, assessed at a mere $24,530,120. Among these, we find 162 Baptist churches assessed at $6,022,860—an average of only $37,000, as we have already noted. The sanctuaries of other denominations are comparable.

The overwhelming wealth of the Catholic Church is not surprising, since it is the predominant power-structure in St. Louis. It has 79 parish churches and 67 elementary and secondary schools which serve 37,781 pupils. The value of these magnificent churches, together with their attached schools can scarcely be less than $60 million: total assessments, $6,785,660. We believe that the St. Louis Cathedral alone has a replacement value of at least $12 million.

In addition to its magnificent and opulent University, the Roman Catholic Church has 8 hospitals, 2 colleges, 5 seminaries, and 48 other institutions, including convents, monasteries, etc. We found 154 items on the rolls titled to the deceased Cardinal Joseph E. Ritter.

Nine Catholic hospitals carry a combined assessment of $8,733,320: the Alexian Brothers, the Cardinal Glennon, the De Paul, the Franciscans, the Incarnate Word, St. Anthonys, St. Marys, St. Anne, and the St. Louis University.

Under Miscellaneous Organizations, the Catholics have various missions, the Hospice of Alverne, Father Dempsey's Hotels, a Girls Industrial Home, the convent of the Franciscan Sisters, and a monastery of the Augustinian Friars: assessments, $2,678,220.

Under Academies, etc., the Catholic Church has convents, high schools, and the House of the Good Shepherd: $7,390,060.

144

Jewish properties consist principally of an Orthodox Home, $686,180; the Jewish Hospital, $2,588,870; and 9 synagogues, $478,260.

Since the total property tax in 1967 was $63,703,943, the per capita levy was $85 and for a family of 5, $425.

If all private exempts were to pay their fair share of the ad valorem tax; if the federal government did likewise; and if many enterprises, now municipally financed, were once again to assume their former responsibilities, the increased revenue would undoubtedly be sufficient to reduce the millage to what it was for so many years—from 51 to 27. Or, if taxation were to continue at somewhere near the present rate, at least the city would have the funds necessary to meet its plenary needs.

Assuming that all assessments average one-third of true or replacement value, we have the following totals:

ASSESSMENTS AND VALUATIONS FOR ST. LOUIS PROPERTY [a]

	Assessments	Full or True Value
ALL	$1,770,903,420	$5,300,000,000
Taxable	1,246,652,510	3,700,000,000
Exempt	524,250,910	1,600,000,000
Public	380,216,690	1,150,000,000
Private	144,034,220	450,000,000
The Secular	36,704,810	110,000,000
The Religious	107,329,410	340,000,000
The Protestant	47,442,650	143,000,000
The Catholic	56,114,840	185,000,000
The Jewish	3,771,920	12,000,000

[a] The totals here shown place per capita wealth at only $7,900, which is comparatively low; but is explained by the large Negro community and— much more—by the drastic undervaluation of exempt properties. There is no doubt that our computation for taxable real estate is substantially accurate. If the exempt were assessed at $1 billion (as it should be), we would have a per capita wealth of about $10,000, which would be very nearly correct, for a wealthy, but aging and deteriorating city like St. Louis.

145

X. PORTLAND (MULTNOMAH COUNTY)

As the great bird operated by the Western Air Lines begins its afternoon descent in a flight from San Francisco, a window-seat on the right affords a spectacular view of Crater Lake and minutes later of towering, snow-crowned Mt. Hood. A fast ride from the airport soon places the traveller in the highly distinctive city of Portland (385,436), which is the seat of Multnomah County (558,000), and which we think of as the Pearl of the Northwest. Although its downtown is aging, it is well kept and sparkling clean; everything reflects order and prosperity. If any slums exist, they are certainly not in evidence.

Located on the Willamette River at its confluence with the Columbia, Portland has a large port 110 miles from the Pacific. The city is the center of an industrial empire comprised within the Columbia River Basin. It has an equable and delightful climate and perhaps the lowest mortality rate in America. The water supply, from reservoirs in the Cascades, is sufficient for a city of 2 million and so pure that it can be used without distillation for medical prescriptions. A few miles above the city lies the huge Bonneville Dam, which furnishes ample, low-cost power. The area has many parks, bathing beaches, swimming pools, and sports facilities.

Portland is famous for its American Rose Society and its International Rose Test Gardens. It enjoys a brisk foreign commerce and is the center for prosperous lumbering and manufacturing industries.

With only 14.2% of its real estate tax-exempt, the county is, in a real sense, unique among communities covered in this survey; and we include it precisely for that reason, since it represents a dwindling portion of the national scene, more or less duplicated by such centers as Seattle.

Oregonians are obviously highly tax-conscious and democratic. No tax may be augmented by increasing assessments; nor may more than 6% be added to the millage without a popular referendum. No new tax may be imposed except by an affirmative vote in a general election. The State has no sales tax, no intangibles tax, no use tax, no inventory tax, no inheritance tax, no gross earnings tax, no personal property tax on household goods. The flat rate for driving a car is $10. There is a corporation and personal income tax (3 to 9.5%) comparable to those levied in most other states; but these, even when added to the $100 million real estate levy of Multnomah County,

146

perhaps total no more than half of what is drained from communities of similar size in other states through a combination of taxes.

Portland has an excellent central library with branches in various parts of the city which operate under a unique system of private-public ownership. It has a large corpus of property belonging to secular educational, benevolent, charitable, and scientific institutions, such as colleges, universities, hospitals, retirement homes, Boy and Girl Scouts, the Red Cross, the Ys, the Goodwill Industries, fraternal and cultural organizations, ethnical groups, artistic and historical societies, etc., all of which seem to enjoy easy exemption from property taxation.

Multnomah County is one of the few major American communities in which federal housing projects are virtually non-existent. "During World War No. 2," wrote Mr. White, Assessment Roll Supervisor, in reply to our question, "several of these were established." However, practically all of them have since been "replaced and redeveloped, and the last of them is now being phased out."

We note that the citizens of Oregon are, by and large, (1) remarkably self-reliant; (2) highly resentful over unnecessary taxes; and (3) determined not to maintain a wasteful government; permit themselves to be exploited by tax-exempt corporations; or placed under the burden of maintaining able-bodied persons in idleness at public expense.

Oregon is distinctive in that, on one occasion in the Twenties, its electorate voted to outlaw all parochial schools, a popular decision which was invalidated by the Supreme Court of the United States. Oregonians believe in a strict and complete separation of church and state; and, although, for the most part, deeply religious, they insist on pluralistic, independent, voluntary, and self-supporting churches.

It is also obvious that the citizens of this state believe in the public school, for they support it generously; and they demand recreational facilities for all the people, for these are amply provided from public funds.

Portland is still the kind of city of which Americans may be proud. Its crime-rate is low; the streets are safe by day and night—yet the cost of police protection is a minor item in the budget. It has not, like Detroit, New York, Washington, etc., degenerated into a jungle where people live in fear and peril and where the cost of government has risen into the stratophere.

Portland is living evidence of what can be achieved by a self-respecting citizenry, who reject subsidized housing, repudiate sectarian schools, enforce government responsibility, get along without the ministrations of federal bureaucrats, and enjoy an environment where orderly law together with justice prevails.

We might add, incidentally, that pressure groups can present bond issues for approval only at regularly scheduled elections.

In 1960, there were 20,919 non-whites (5.6%) in the city; the Negro proportion, however, was and is only about half of this. In the entire state there were only 18,033 of this race, or 1.04%. The 1968 *Official Catholic Directory* claims 200,509 communicants in the whole diocese, which has a population of 2,008,160—one of the lowest ratios in the United States, outside the South. Portland and its periphery is a predominantly white-Protestant-secularist community.

Mr. Kermit Carson, Deputy Director of the Department of Finance, and his assistant, Mr. Frank P. White, were most gracious and cooperative in making our analysis possible.

The city (88.44 square miles) could not be analyzed separately, since its tax-records are consolidated with those of the County (470 sq. mi.). The work proved laborious; for, even though separate lists of exempt properties with their valuations under 15 categories were available, each item was identified only by a 9-digit number. It therefore became necessary, after transcribing some 2,000 items, to search through 47 volumes of tax-records to discover their individual ownership.

State law requires that assessments reflect actual value. Mr. Carson conceded, however, that since the appraisals on older exempts are not revised quite as rapidly or regularly as those on taxable, there is probably some disparity between the two sectors.

The Church of Jesus Christ of Latter Day Saints (Mormon) owns and operates a large cannery and distribution center known as the General Welfare Corporation, located at 4233–4243 S.E. Belmont Street. This enjoys total tax-immunity on the plea that it is a charity which gives its products without profit to the needy among its own communicants. The properties of this Church, as with the Roman Catholics, are entitled to the presiding bishop, acting in his capacity as *corporation sole*.

The splendid public school system is valued at $152,806,840. Cities and towns have $94,986,320 in real estate dedicated as parks and other recreational facilities, among which are a coliseum and

PROPERTY ASSESSMENTS IN MULTNOMAH COUNTY

CLASS		
	Total Valuations	$4,448,841,144
100	The Taxable	3,815,474,004
110–240	The Exempt	633,367,140

THE PUBLICLY OWNED (71.9%)		455,612,350
110 Federal Government	$124,778,730	
120 State of Oregon	30,086,340	
130 County of Multnomah	17,678,850	
140 Cities and Towns (Parks, Etc.)	93,986,320	
150 School Districts	152,806,840	
160 Water District	2,855,680	
170 Irrigation Districts		
180 Drainage Districts	169,780	
190 Ports	32,767,530	
200 Other Municipal Corporations	482,280	

THE PRIVATELY OWNED (28.1%)		177,754,790
210 Literary, Benevolent, Charitable, and Scientific Organizations	81,939,410	
215 Fraternal Organizations	5,696,660	
220 Church and Religious Organizations	78,941,110	
230 Burial Grounds, Tombs, Etc.	7,487,860	
240 Public Libraries, not Publicly Owned	3,689,750	

stadium used for professional sports. Bonneville Dam, valued at more than $90 million, comprises the bulk of federal holdings, assessed at $124,778,730. Except for the Ports ($32,767,530) there is little additional public property.

In Portland, as elsewhere, the Catholics are experiencing difficulty with their schools. A news item in the Oregon *Journal,* April 8, 1968, stated that "St. Anthony . . . Schools will not open next fall because of a shortage of teaching nuns . . . Father Jack Stige said, 'If we are going to have a Catholic school, it should be Catholic . . .' "

With 10 synagogues, we estimate the Jewish community at 15,000. Since there are 39 Catholic churches and 31 schools with 16,308 pupils, we estimate their membership at 85,000. The 530 Protestant

DIVISION OF PRIVATE EXEMPT PROPERTY
($177,754,790)

CLASS	Secular	Protestant	Catholic	Jewish
210 Benevolences [a]	$19,963,630	$33,411,550	$28,018,810	$ 545,420
215 Fraternals	5,696,660			
220 Churches		49,361,950	25,874,000	3,705,160
230 Cemeteries	7,063,800		232,250	191,810
240 Libraries [b]	3,689,750			
TOTALS	$36,413,840	$82,773,500	$54,125,060	$4,442,390
Ratios	20.5%	46.6%	30.4%	2.5%

TOTAL RELIGIOUS PROPERTY $141,340,950
Ratio to Private Exempt 80.0%
Proportion of Protestant 58.6%
Proportion of Catholic 38.3%
Proportion of Jewish 3.1%

[a] Under classification 210 are included clinics, health centers, hospitals, schools, colleges, universities, clubs, retirement homes, Boy and Girl Scouts, community centers, the Goodwill Industries, historical societies, the Ys, the Red Cross, etc.

[b] Classification 240 covers the main Portland Library and its branches. This is considered a private enterprise, because of its origin and control; but, on the tax-rolls, the land and improvements are titled to the County.

and miscellaneous churches have an estimated membership of 320,000. This leaves only 150,000, or 26%, without church affiliation. It should be noted that although Protestants outnumber Catholics almost 4 to 1, they own only 58.6% of the religiously exempt property.

Tax-rates, which range from 17 to 37.5 mills in the County, average about 27 in 148 taxing districts. Since the 1967 ad valorem tax was $98,202,844.32, the per capita levy was $168. The average house appraised at $20,000, therefore, pays $540; however, since actual assessments are only about 65%, the tax on a $20,000 home will be only $360.

THEORETICAL 100% ASSESSMENTS
IN MULTNOMAH CO. [a]

ALL	$4,448,841,144
Taxable	3,815,474,004
Exempt	633,367,140
Public	455,612,350
Private	177,754,790
Secular	36,413,740
Religious	141,340,950
Protestant	82,773,500
Catholic	54,125,060
Jewish	4,442,390

[a] Since the theoretical 100% assessments show per capita wealth of less than $8,000 in opulent Multnomah Co. and since we know that various properties are assessed at no more than 65% or even less, we believe that all assessments stand very nearly at that level; that per capita wealth is about $12,000; and that total wealth is about $6,500,000,000 instead of $4,448,474,144.

XI. PITTSBURGH

Where the Allegheny and the Monongahela Rivers join to form the Ohio in the midst of a region rich in gas, coal, and petroleum, lies the second city of Pennsylvania, the Steel Capital of the nation. Here the immense Carnegie and Mellon fortunes were amassed; here some of the bitterest conflicts between Labor and Capital were fought to their conclusion; here wealth and poverty, enlightenment and ignorance, bigotry and heroism, have lived side by side down the corridors of time.

In spite of every attempt at reconstruction and renewal, Pittsburgh cannot escape its heritage. It is an empire based on coal and steel, and those who labor in this domain must partake of fire and smoke. This continent knows no second Pittsburgh, although certain smaller centers like Youngstown, Ohio, reek of similar elements.

To Pittsburgh came countless thousands between 1840 and 1920 from Hungary, Poland, Serbia, Roumania, Bulgaria, Russia, Greece, and other lands of eastern and southeastern Europe; and here developed an American empire and social amalgam amidst the dirt, the dust, and the grime of flaming furnaces, unique and unrivalled. During recent decades, there has been a heavy influx of Negroes, who now comprise about 19% in a population of some 600,000.

Its religious complex reflects its ethnical composition. The Roman Catholic Church has 79 parishes and 80 elementary and secondary schools with 43,122 pupils. There are 28 non-Roman but Catholic churches, of which 9 are of the Byzantine Rite, 12 are Eastern Orthodox, 3 Greek Orthodox, 1 Ukrainian Catholic, 1 Orthodox Catholic, 1 Polish National Catholic, and 1 Russian Orthodox.

In addition, there are 27 synagogues and 337 Protestant and miscellaneous churches. We estimate the Jewish community at 40,000; the Protestant and miscellaneous at 200,000; and the Roman Catholic at 210,000, leaving only 150,000 unchurched.

From telephone conversations and correspondence with Mr. Edward Nunlist, Executive Director, Board of Property Assessment, we had learned (1) that although exempt real estate is assessed, there is no division of it into categories; (2) that totals are compiled for each ward; and (3) that there is no separation between the public and the private, much less between the secular and the denominational. Our own analysis of all this in categories would therefore be necessary.

The tax-roll is contained in 79 volumes, covering the 32 wards. Exempt properties, fortunately given in alphabetical sequence, are listed at the back of the final volume for each ward.

Powerful forces have combined to increase the total and the ratio of tax-exempt property. Churches and other private exempts have expanded enormously; and, as if to compound the crisis, railroads and utilities are immune to taxation on all land and facilities necessary for the performance of their services.

152

However, it is the various "Authorities" created by government to by-pass the stringent laws limiting exemptions that have caused the great erosion of the tax-base. Much of downtown Pittsburgh has been razed by the Urban Redevelopment Authority, which still holds title to hundreds of parcels for future expansion. It has sold land to the newly organized Stadium Authority, which will construct a new facility for the Steelers and the Pirates, itself to be immune from taxation, and to be financed by tax-exempt bonds. The Housing Authority has constructed several large projects and has acquired countless parcels of real estate for future use. (Incidentally, the city treasury hoped to obtain $183,000 from the housing projects assessed at $36,293,409 during 1968, but not a penny had been received by midyear.) The Public Parking Authority has expended some $40 or $50 million for tax-free facilities which do not, and may never, yield a cent of revenue, except the use-tax on parking tickets. There is also a tax-exempt Port Authority as well as a General State Authority, which purchases and holds land for potential expansion.

There is a large downtown sports arena, built on public land, exempt from taxation, and financed by tax-free bonds. Forbes Field, formerly the taxpaying property of the Pirates, was sold a few years ago to the University of Pittsburgh, which now derives exempt revenues from a classic sale-and-leaseback operation. The Pittsburgh Steelers perform in the University of Pittsburgh's football stadium, on a similar basis.

Even so, Pennsylvania is less generous in granting exemptions for some purposes than are other states: there are no special immunities for widows, professors, veterans, paraplegics, the blind, for ministers of the Gospel, or even for parsonages and rectories owned by churches. Nor are the properties of fraternal orders exempt. As yet, there is no State income tax, although pressure for one is mounting. The cost of a car license is only $10.

Nevertheless, because of the enormous growth of the "Authorities," onerous taxes are exacted. There is a general state sales, use, rental, and room tax of 6%, which, according to an editorial published in the Pittsburgh *Press,* May 21, 1968, was increased illegally from 5% because several legislators voted "Yes" for absent members who were opposed to the increase. The City levies a full 2% gross earnings tax on all salaries, wages, and net business income, expected to produce $13.2 million in 1968.

What has happened is shown in the following:

153

REAL ESTATE ASSESSMENTS IN PITTSBURGH

Year	Taxable Property	Exempt Property	Ratio
1943	$1,044,010,664	$296,779,953	28.4%
1960	1,201,801,924	401,976,603	33.4%
1967	1,261,944,126	553,235,311	43.8%
1968	1,250,267,148	608,464,034	48.7%

In a few years, therefore, exempt property increased from slightly over one-fourth to very nearly half of the taxable. During the 1967–68 12-month period, while the taxable was actually declining by nearly $12 million, or 1%, the exempt increased by $55 million, or 10%. Should this trend continue, as it certainly bids fair to do, it will be only a few years until one half of the total real estate will be paying the entire tax.

1968–69 ASSESSMENTS ON PITTSBURGH REAL ESTATE

CATEGORY		Valuations	Ratios
ALL		$1,858,731,182	100%
Taxable		1,250,267,148	67.3%
Exempt		608,464,034	32.7%
The Public		322,182,578	52.95%
Board of Education	$ 49,067,258		
City of Pittsburgh	80,411,930		
Allegheny County	31,990,640		
State of Pennsylvania	25,365,164		
Parking Authority	17,676,625		
U.S.A.	37,274,450		
Urban Redevelopment	41,900,317		
Port Authority	2,202,785		
Housing Authority	36,293,409		
The Private Exempt		286,281,456	47.05%
The Secular	160,621,966		26.4%
The Religious	125,659,490		20.6%

We see that Urban Redevelopment still has title to property worth almost as much as the entire public school system; and the Housing Authority is not far behind. It appears that every category of exempt has expanded beyond all reason except that most important one of

PRIVATE EXEMPT PROPERTY IN PITTSBURGH
(Total: $286,281,456)

CATEGORY	Secular	Protestant	Catholic	Jewish
Railroads	$ 57,838,739			
Utilities	22,455,455			
Churches		$23,116,117	$27,581,716	$ 4,147,514
Parochial Schools, Charities, Convents	3,820,162	5,197,815	6,893,058	3,102,620
Other Schools, Universities	53,355,315	1,922,590	16,249,570	579,320
Hospitals	20,530,985	4,934,710	20,159,980	8,007,940
Cemeteries	2,621,310	2,890,600	826,190	49,750
TOTALS	$160,621,966	$38,061,832	$71,710,514	$15,887,144
Ratios	56.1%	13.3%	25.1%	5.5%

TOTAL RELIGIOUS PROPERTY	$125,659,490
Ratio to All Exempt	43.9%
Proportion of Protestant	30.29%
Proportion of Catholic[a]	57.07%
Proportion of Jewish	12.64%

[a] It should be noted that if the 28 Catholic churches of rites other than the Latin were added to the Roman properties, their ratio would not be less than 65% and the Protestant would not exceed 23% of the total.

all: the public school system, assessed at a mere $49,067,258, only two-thirds the assets of a single church.

Railroads and utilities enjoy unique exemptions in Pennsylvania; and their immunity has certainly helped to create the need for other taxation. In Pittsburgh alone they enjoy exemptions totalling $80 million; and since the tax-rate is about 60 mills, this involves a tax-avoidance of nearly $5 million, or about 40% of the revenue obtained from the gross-earnings tax.

Under secular Benevolences ($3,820,162), we have, among others, the Graphic Arts Foundation, the Historical Society of Western Pennsylvania, the Allegheny Widow's Home, and the Mellon Theatre, Gymnasium, and Library, assessed at $551,400.

Assessments on secular schools, colleges, and universities reflect considerable wealth. We should note that a part of the $35,095,905 credited to the University of Pittsburgh consists of a baseball field and football stadium in which the Pirates and the Steelers contend for victory.

The Mellon Institute	$ 4,487,190
Chatham College	4,643,090
The Community College	216,900
The University of Pittsburgh	35,095,905
Carnegie Institute of Technology	7,045,100
Ellis Schools Corporation	718,500
The Institute for the Blind	1,151,630
Total	$53,358,315

There are several private secular cemeteries, among which the Homewood, assessed at $2,216,490, is the largest.

Protestant and miscellaneous congregations have sanctuaries assessed at $23,116,110, of which many are substantial, even magnificent. We find, for example, the First Presbyterian, $1,387,200; the German Evangelical Protestant, $719,250; the Trinity Episcopal Cathedral, $1,487,000; and the East Liberty Presbyterian, $2,862,320. However, there are literally hundreds of extremely modest edifices, assessed between $3,000 and $25,000. We could only pause in wonder at the House of God Which Is the Church of the Living God and the Pillar of Good and Truth: assessment $2,805.

Protestant properties include the Salvation Army, $1,008,740; the Ys, $2,253,700; the Home for Incurables, $164,500; the German

156

Protestant Home for the Aged, $91,060; the Home for Children, $360,710; and the Home for the Friendless, $373,595.

The largest Protestant cemeteries are the Allegheny, $1,823,600; the German Evangelical, $450,000; and the Presbyterian Uniondale, $547,000.

The Presbyterians with 104 churches, a theological seminary, $1,921,590, and a great hospital, $4,934,700, easily constitute the strongest Protestant denomination. There are 74 Methodist congregations, 70 Lutheran, 25 Protestant Episcopal, 17 United of Christ, 16 Christian, and a wonderful variety of apostolic, apocalyptic, miscellaneous, and unclassifiable entities.

Nevertheless, the Roman Catholic Church predominates in wealth, power, and communicants. Many of its churches are million-dollar-plus edifices; and the 79 parishes with their parochial schools have properties with assessments averaging about $350,000, and therefore worth by conservative estimate at least $1 million each.

In addition to its parish holdings, the Church operates a number of higher educational institutions as well as several private and diocesan high schools: among these, are Duquesne University, $12,859,349;[a] the Catholic Institute, $1,257,930; Mt. Mercy College, $1,807,150;[b] and St. Paul Seminary, $325,196. There are also convents, monasteries, and protective institutions, with combined assessments of $6,893,059, as well as Calvary and St. Mary cemeteries assessed at $826,190.

Catholic hospitals ($20,159,980) include the Mercy, St. Joseph's, Pittsburgh, Divine Providence, and Villa de Marillac.

Pittsburgh has 27 synagogues assessed at $4,147,514; of these, the Rodef Shalom, $1,031,320; the Shaare Torah, $236,550; the B'nai Israel, $462,400; and the Beth El, $443,550, are the largest.

The Jewish Community Center, the Jewish Young Mens and Womens Center, and the Jewish Home for the Aged have valuations totalling $3,102,620. Other Jewish assets are the Montifiore Hospital, $8,007,940; the Hillel Academy, $277,390; and the Hebrew Institute, $301,750.

---

[a] The official book value of its plant is $28,863,062. Since this is probably considerably less than its replacement value, we conclude that the assessment cannot exceed one-third of true value, instead of the 50% theoretically established.

[b] The reported plant value of Mt. Mercy College is $8,520,000, or more than 4 times its assessment.

In Pittsburgh, land is taxed at 41 mills and the improvements at 20.5 mills by the city; the school levy is 17 and the county tax 13 mills on the whole: which comes to about 60 mills on all real estate. All properties, of whatever nature, are taxed under the same formula and theoretically assessed at 50% of actual or replacement value.

The following indicates the tax-yield from a $20,000 house.

Assessment on Land	$3,300
Assessment on Improvements	6,700
City Tax on Land	133.35
City Tax on Improvements	137.35
School and County Tax	300.00
Total Ad Valorem Tax	$ 570.70

The 1968 property levy in Pittsburgh was $70,826,581.81, or about $117 per capita. The actual revenue, however, was $102 million, which averages $166 per person, and $830 for a family of 5.

Although assessments are theoretically 50% of true value, our observations indicated that they are much nearer to 33.3%. On this assumption, which gives, even so, a very modest total for a city so large and wealthy as Pittsburgh, we obtain the following estimates:

ASSESSED AND TRUE VALUATIONS FOR PITTSBURGH [a]
REAL ESTATE

CATEGORY	Assessments	Actual or Replacement Value
ALL	$1,858,731,182	$5,550,000,000
Taxable	1,250,267,148	3,750,000,000
Exempt	608,464,034	1,800,000,000
The Public	322,182,578	935,000,000
The Private	286,281,456	855,000,000
The Secular	160,621,966	480,000,000
The Religious	125,659,490	375,000,000
The Protestant	38,061,832	114,000,000
The Catholic	71,710,514	215,000,000
The Jewish	15,887,144	45,000,000

[a] Computing assessments at 33.3 instead of 50% is obviously justified, since a group of colleges and universities (cf. Appendix I, Table X) are assessed at only 28% of reported book value. And the total which we project reflects a per capita wealth of only $9,250, which is certainly conservative for a city as wealthy as Pittsburgh.

XII. CLEVELAND

Situated some 200 miles southwest of Buffalo, also on Lake Erie, stands its largest port, and one of the great manufacturing cities of America. Its polyglot ethnic composition is reflected in the fact that in 1920, when its population was 796,841, of whom 239,535 were foreign born and 310,241 were of foreign parentage. Among these, Poles, Hungarians, Germans, Roumanians, Serbians, and Slovakians were predominant. No wonder, then, that the Roman Catholic Church is great and powerful beyond all others in Cleveland.

The population of the city increased to 914,808 in 1950, but declined to 876,050 in 1960, and is estimated at 813,000 in 1968–69. In the meantime, the growth of the Negro community has been similar to that in other great northern cities; it increased from 30,150, or 3.8%, in 1920, to 253,108, or 29%, in 1960. It is probably 35% or more at the present time. Mayor Stokes is a Negro.

As in St. Louis, the majestic glory of Cleveland, which reached its height in the Twenties, has now faded. The well-kept but modest dwellings of the foreign-born and their descendants have now become the slums, overpopulated by prolific Negroes. As in Washington, New York, and Detroit, fear and peril stalk the streets, especially after dark. Riots, bloodshed, crime, mayhem, and arson have plagued the city, while race-tension has continued to mount.

And so the magnificent library, auditorium, and art gallery stand as the monumental creations of another era. There are many Protestant churches, some of them outstanding; but over all, hover the wings and the power of the Vatican.

Previous communication with Mr. L. B. Mitchell, Chief Deputy, Board of Revision and Tax Assessments, had established that the exempt properties in Cleveland are listed on some 4,200 3 × 5″ cards, each of which carries a description of the item, the name of the owner, and a number indicating the category to which it belongs. Totals in each category for the current and preceding years are available.

As late as 1963–64, the ratio of exempt property was only 17%; this, however, is now 24% and constantly rising.

Since a 24%-exemption ratio seemed low, we suspected that un-taxed properties might be drastically underassessed; and there is no doubt that some disparity exists. When, however, we became aware of the stringent laws governing exemptions in Ohio, we were surprised that even this proportion should be immune. For there are no preferences for railroads, utilities, widows, veterans, ministers, professors, paraplegics, or the blind, or even for parsonages and rectories owned by churches; the properties of fraternal orders and veterans organizations, and the great majority of professional, cultural, and other nonprofit groups are taxed; there is no such thing as wholly or partially tax-free housing for the elderly and the crippled; there are no chartered corporations which may own tax-exempt commercial property.

As the law is written, it is difficult to see how any church, or, in fact, any private organization can qualify for exemption; for we read that only "charities" accessible to the general public on the same terms are eligible. Churches are granted immunity on the theory that they are public institutions because a stranger may drop in and sit through a service; but, since membership is prerequisite for participation in a Masonic or Oddfellow ritual, the real estate belonging to fraternal orders is taxed.

Even church sanctuaries do not escape every obligation; for if a congregation acquires a property before a sidewalk is laid, a street paved, or a sewer installed, it must pay for this.

Under "Rules to be Observed by Applicants and County Auditors" when exemptions are requested or processed, we read:

"5) Ownership by the state or political subdivision is not sufficient, in and of itself, to entitle property to tax exemption—the specific property must be used exclusively for a public purpose."

Since rectories and parsonages are private residences, they are taxed. However, by or under some unexplained procedure, monasteries and "dormitories for sisters" are exempt, as is Madonna Hall, a retirement residence owned and operated by an order of the Catholic Church.

One Catholic rectory was partially exempt because a portion was used to instruct prospective converts in the faith.

However, the great municipal stadium near the waterfront, where the Indians and Browns perform, pays an ad valorem tax: but Mr. Mitchell conceded that its assessment may be at less than parity. The Burke Airport and the huge City Airport ($17,341,000) pay taxes on those portions which are leased or rented for private use.

Ohio has a general 4% tax on transient rooms and retail sales. But there is no use tax nor is there any personal property tax on household goods. Ohio has an inheritance tax, but as yet no income tax—although pressure for one is building. The fee for a car license is only $10, as in Oregon and Pennsylvania; but each county may impose an additional $5 road tax. There is a 5% tax on intangible income and one of 2 mills on investments. On January 1, 1968, the city of Cleveland imposed a gross earnings tax of ½ of 1% on all wages, salaries, and net business income; this was quickly doubled.

However, in spite of the stringent laws governing exemptions, property has been slipping off the rolls at an alarming rate. We can be sure that if all the immunities found in Providence, Pittsburgh, Boston, Buffalo, and St. Louis were in force in Cleveland, one half of its land would already have escaped the tax-collector.

ASSESSMENTS ON CLEVELAND REAL ESTATE

CATEGORY	1954	1963	1967
ALL	$1,760,884,570	$2,185,819,760	$2,171,561,500
Taxable	1,464,248,280	1,804,594,230	1,649,918,320
THE EXEMPT			
The Public	173,976,650	216,134,110	313,736,990
1 U.S.A.	29,467,850	10,329,870	37,895,990
2 State of Ohio	3,522,760	5,203,380	9,350,750
3 Cuyahoga Co.	8,280,090	20,708,190	21,744,510
4 Park Districts	178,210	229,190	569,720
5 Municipality	79,936,240	93,001,240	120,802,360
6 Board of Ed.	52,591,500	66,228,520	82,957,580
13 Metro Housing		13,257,770	32,495,680
15 Public Libraries		7,125,950	7,920,400
The Private	122,659,640	165,091,420	207,906,190
7 Private Schools	18,135,310	29,236,740	36,561,050
8 Churches	51,216,090	57,583,290	75,583,230
9 Charities	48,168,300	66,542,880	92,854,850
10 Charities		1,270,540 [a]	
11,12 Graveyards, Etc.	5,139,940	10,517,910	2,907,060 [b]
TOTALS	$296,636,290	$381,225,530	$521,643,180
Ratios	16.9%	17.4%	24.1%
Parcels of Exempt	3,084	5,082	4,137

[a] This category was for public halls, in effect for 1963 only.
[b] The reason that valuations for Graveyards, Etc., decreased in 1967 is that the items formerly listed there were shifted to Category 5.

161

The salient facts emerging from these statistics are (1) that taxable properties actually declined by 10% between 1963 and 1967; (2) that the exempt increased by nearly 40%; and (3) that church wealth grew by more than 50%. It is also quite certain that present trends will continue or accelerate, because enormous expansion is now taking place in the exempt sector. It should be noted that Category 13 (Metro Housing) with assessments of $32,495,680 in 1967 did not even exist in 1954; and that private schools and "charities" were the only categories which virtually doubled their holdings between 1954 and 1967.

Since only Categories 7, 8, 9, and 11 are private exempts, the following table makes an analysis of these.

PRIVATE EXEMPT REAL ESTATE IN CLEVELAND
($207,906,190)

CATEGORY	Secular	Protestant	Catholic	Jewish
7 Private Schools	$21,324,300	$ 71,270	$15,165,000	
8 Churches		30,829,490	43,216,290	$1,537,450
9 Charities	56,128,080	15,138,000	15,430,730	6,158,520
11 Cemeteries	1,778,620	419,070	617,460	91,910
TOTALS	$79,231,000	$46,457,830	$74,429,480	$7,787,880
Ratios	38.1%	22.3%	35.8%	3.8%

TOTAL RELIGIOUS PROPERTY	$128,675,190
Proportion of Protestant	36.10%
Proportion of Catholic	57.84%
Proportion of Jewish	6.06%

Secular schools—Category 7—consist of the Ohio College of Orthopedy, $172,170; the Cuyahoga County Community College, $1,092,980; and the complex now formed by the union of Case Technological Institute and Western Reserve University, which have property assessed at more than $20 million. However, since WRU is primarily a medical institution, most of its facilities are found in Category 9, where we find hospitals and other health services, with assets assessed at well over $30 million, of which $17,099,160 belong to the University Hospital and the affiliated Benjamin Rose Institute; $6,826,830 to the Cleveland Clinic; $3,323,360 to the Fairview

Hospital; $107,310 to the Babies Dispensary; and $833,230 to the Womens Hospital.

In addition to the secular charities found in most cities, we have here the Cleveland Grays, the Goodrich Social Settlement, the Deutches and the Deutcher Frauen Verein, and the Womens Philanthropic Union. Among the larger cultural or artistic corporations, we have the Musical Art Association, $2,188,250; the Cleveland Institute of Art, $1,111,570; the Horace Kelly Art Foundation, $6,169,380; the Cleveland Museum of Art, $655,940; the Western Reserve Historical Society, $387,010; the Playhouse Foundation, $201,810; and the Western Reserve Dormitories, $3,789,500.

The city boasts a unique "Benevolence" known as the University Circle Development Foundation, which purchases land for future cultural and educational expansion in the area of the Case-Western Reserve complex and the great art museum which belongs to the City. At the time of this analysis, the Circle Development Foundation had title to properties assessed at $3,390,100.

Classified as Protestant "Charities" we have the following:

St. Lukes (Presbyterian) Hospital	$ 4,734,510
The Methodist Episcopal Deaconess Soc.	1,268,410
The Lutheran Hospital	2,479,730
The Salvation Army	1,258,220
The Ys	3,755,520
The Nat'l Benevolent Assn. of Christian Churches	557,090
The Christian Science Nursing Home	59,690
The Baptist Home	20,650
The Presbyterian Home	132,500
Total	$14,266,320

The major Protestant investment is in its 430 churches. There is the Old Stone Presbyterian, located on the City Square, $1,058,320; the Protestant Episcopal Trinity Cathedral, $709,780; the Methodist Episcopal, $814,920; and First Church of Christ, Scientist, $1,120,680. Although there are various Protestant churches valued at from $60,000 to $175,000, there are literally hundreds of modest edifices assessed at from $3,000 to $50,000.

Jewish properties consist of a few small cemeteries; 7 or 8 synagogues, of which the Tiffereth Israel, $1,145,600, is the most outstanding; Mt. Sinai Hospital, $5,072,040; the Jewish Convalescent

163

Home, $456,850; the Hillel Foundation, $33,630; the Jewish Community Center, $524,420; and the Council of Jewish Women, $50,150.

Since the Roman Catholics have 119 parish churches, 112 parochial schools, 4 seminaries, 3 colleges, 17 diocesan or private high schools, 5 elementary or special schools, 7 hospitals, and a vast complex of convents, homes, monasteries, protective institutions, and other facilities, it is no wonder that this denomination is predominant. It has 88,255 pupils, 207 seminarians, and 1,949 college students. Its largest sanctuary is the Cathedral of St. John the Evangelist, located downtown on Cathedral Square, where we find also a rectory, the diocesan center, and St. John's College, with a combined assessment of $4,152,310, which seems extremely low, since the land alone should be worth more than that.* The Cathedral, assessed at $1,922,020, certainly represents an investment 3 or 4 times greater than the Old Stone Presbyterian or First Church of Christ, Scientist. If this disparity is general, we can only conclude that Catholic properties are undervalued in comparison with those of other denominations. Nevertheless, there are dozens of Roman churches assessed at anywhere from $250,000 to $900,000, with cash values certainly triple these amounts. The St. Stanislaus is assessed at $1,038,060; the Holy Name, $1,024,960; the St. Ignatius, $1,254,980.

Since Catholic churches and their parochial schools are assessed at $43,216,290 under Category 8, we conclude that the true combined value of these ranges anywhere from not less than $110,000,000 to a possible $135,000,000.

The additional schools and colleges which comprise the Roman Catholic educational complex carry assessments of $15,165,480 and must, therefore, be worth at least $40 million. Although Ursuline College and the Jesuit John Carroll University, with a combined enrollment of 4,158, are listed in the *Official Catholic Directory* as Cleveland facilities, they are located beyond the city limits and do not enter into our computation: if these were added, they would certainly increase the Catholic totals by at least $15 or $20 million.

There are also 4 hospitals and a number of convents, monasteries, correctional institutions, and retirement homes with combined assessments of $15,149,610. Madonna Hall is assessed at $408,590.

---

* The truth of this statement is confirmed by the fact that one portion of the Square is St. Johns College which, assessed at $2,072,050, reports a book value of almost three times that amount, $5,997,752.

There are several Catholic cemeteries with combined assessments of $617,460, of which the Calvary is the largest.

We estimate Cleveland Catholics at 340,000; the Jewish community at 12,000; and Protestant and miscellaneous membership at about 260,000.

Since the total current tax levy is $90,910,498.43, the per capita ad valorem tax is approximately $106, or $530 for a family of five.

And since the millage is 55.1 and the ratio of appraisals theoretically 40% of true value, the owner of a $20,000-house has a tax-liability of $440, which is comparatively low and should be credited to the stringent Ohio laws governing property exemptions. However, as taxable land continues to fall away from the rolls, the exactions upon remaining real estate will certainly increase.

Assuming that assessments are one-third of replacement value, we obtain the following results:

TOTALS FOR CLEVELAND REAL ESTATE [a]

CATEGORY	Assessments	Actual Value
ALL	$2,171,561,500	$6,500,000,000
Taxable	1,649,918,320	4,940,000,000
Exempt	521,643,180	1,560,000,000
Public	313,736,990	940,000,000
Private	207,906,190	620,000,000
The Secular	79,231,000	235,000,000
The Religious	128,675,190	385,000,000
The Protestant	46,457,830	139,000,000
The Catholic	74,429,480	223,000,000
The Jewish	7,787,880	23,000,000

[a] The computation shown in this table, which reflects per capita wealth of only $8,000, is probably very nearly accurate, because of the very large Negro community, the extensive and spreading slums, the aging residential areas, the deteriorating commercial structures, and the flight of white people and capital to the surrounding suburbs and cities.

XIII. ST. PAUL

The Twin Cities, themselves distinguished by contrasts, represent a considerable segment of the American scene. St. Paul developed on a predominantly Catholic base; Minneapolis, on the other hand, has been and remains the capital of New World Lutheranism; and, like Methodist-Baptist Nashville, presents a great concentration of Protestant power.

These two cities and their environs now constitute a megalopolis of nearly 1,750,000 people, with a burgeoning electronics industry, a variety of smaller manufacturing enterprises, and perhaps the world's greatest milling complex. One of the largest assembly plants operated by the Ford Motor Company is located here. This is also the distribution center for an area comprising several states, including more than half a million square miles, where several million people live amidst fertile plains and prairies.

Each city already covered in this survey except Denver has a port on a river, on inland waters, or on one of our oceans. Nor are the Twin Cities exceptions: for as it flows through them, the Father of the Waters, already several hundred feet wide and of ample depth, carries freight and pleasure craft in abundance downstream even to St. Louis and beyond.

In St. Paul, Mr. Leonard L. Peterson, Principal Clerk in the Office of the Assessor, and Mr. Horace Contini, Chief Clerk in the Office of Records, gave us their utmost cooperation.

During recent years, the federal government has constructed a number of "low-cost" housing projects; and considerable portions of the city have been razed and rebuilt under Urban Redevelopment. Although some of these areas are intended for private ownership, real estate titled to the Authority increased from $2,844,090 in 1962 to $8,119,473 in 1968, which means that it owned land valued at more than $60 million.

Fraternal and veterans organizations enjoy no exemptions; and if a church rents out a parsonage, this is restored to the tax-rolls. There are no exemptions for widows, veterans, ministers, professors, paraplegics, or the blind; nor are immunities extended to secular non-profit housing projects, as in Colorado or under the Mitchell-Lama Act in New York. There is, however, a single corporation, the Methodist-oriented Hamline University, which, because of its special charter obtained long ago, may own and operate commercial properties free from the ad valorem tax. It has title to 68 items of real estate in St. Paul alone, including at least 4 apartment buildings; and the assessments on its holdings increased from $448,550 in 1962 to

166

$1,120,180 in 1968—which reflected a replacement value of at least $10 million.

At least in part because of the increasing ratio of exempt property, a sales and use tax of 3% was instituted by the State in 1967, revenues from which are returned to local taxing units so that substantial reductions may be given to farmers, business men, and those living in their own homes. There is both an income and an inheritance tax; but there is no use or rental tax on apartments, services, or equipment, and household goods are not subject to personal property taxation.

Privately owned and otherwise exempt properties (except cemeteries) are required to pay for tree-trimming and for street and alley oiling.

It was interesting to learn that the First Presbyterian Church of Merriam Park pays the city of St. Paul $100 annually in lieu of taxes.

A unique feature of the Minnesota tax-structure is that all railroads and telephone companies are exempt from local taxation; however, the former pay 5% and the latter 7% of gross earnings to the State.

Our survey includes all of Ramsey county (population at least 425,000), of whom slightly more than 300,000 live in St. Paul. Since exempt items are listed in 6 large volumes without division into categories, it was necessary here, as in Richmond and Pittsburgh, to separate these according to the system used throughout this study.

Protestants now outnumber Catholics in the County; and we should note that the Negro ratio in the Twin Cities does not exceed 3.5% and is probably not over 1% in the State.

New appraisals are made for exempts every 6th year; this was done in 1962 and 1968. Sub-totals were available for St. Paul, but not for Ramsey County during the summer of 1968, when our analysis was completed.

Thus, taxable property increased officially by 7.1% and the exempt by 27.3%; the public by 37.9% and the private exempt by 17.6%. City-County-State property increased from $18,108,740 to $25,764,087 and that belonging to private entities from $42,116,650 to $50,525,592.

Assessments on synagogues declined while those on Protestant churches increased 11.8%. Meanwhile, a most revealing development was under way. Since Catholics control St. Paul politically, they have repeatedly defeated bond issues intended for the construction of new

167

public schools. It is therefore no accident that assessments on their churches and attached schools increased from $6,639,900 to $9,780,900, or 47.3%, while those on public schools actually declined from $6,815,950 to $4,309,800, or 36.8%. It is probably a fact that much more money is invested in sectarian than in public education in St. Paul.

ASSESSMENTS IN ST. PAUL

YEAR	1962	1968
CATEGORY		
ALL	$256,707,780	$289,737,382
Taxable	184,546,880	197,763,750
Ratio	71.9%	68.2%
Rate of Increase	7.1%	
The Exempt	72,260,900	91,973,632
Ratio	28.1%	31.8%
Rate of Increase	27.3%	
TOTAL PUBLIC EXEMPT	30,051,380	41,448,040
Rate of Increase	37.9%	
TOTAL PRIVATE EXEMPTS	42,116,650	50,525,592
Rate of Increase	17.6%	

In Ramsey County outside of St. Paul, however, where the Lutherans are preponderant, we have an entirely different situation. In this area, with a population somewhat less than half of St. Paul's, there are only 10 Catholic parishes; and the Independent Schools, as the public system is called, carry assessments of $14,666,042, which reflect a cash or replacement value of about $120,000,000, a per capita investment 500% higher than in the city. While taxable properties in the County as a whole increased between 1962 and 1968 by 13.5%, the exempts did so by 24.5%, and rose from 32.1% to 33.8% of the total. The greatest proliferation occurred among private exempts, which increased from $34,704,972 to $47,746,184, or 37.6%. In the following analysis of Ramsey County, the sub-totals are our own, drawn from the official records.

It should be pointed out that the federal government has a huge arms plant assessed at $12,858,980, worth at least $100 million. We have also the capitol and the Historical Building in St. Paul, assessed at $4,185,930. City properties include the airport, assessed at $975,700; parks and playgrounds, $2,970,538; and the library and museum, $401,820.

168

ASSESSMENTS IN RAMSEY COUNTY

CATEGORY	1962		1968
ALL PROPERTY	$367,248,210		$435,136,208
The Taxable	249,317,133		288,160,732
Ratio	67.9%		66.1%
Rate of Increase		13.5%	
Residential	136,833,447		154,914,393
Commercial, Etc.	112,483,686		133,246,339
The Exempt	117,931,077		146,875,473
Ratio	32.1%		33.8%
Rate of Increase		24.5%	
The Public Properties	68,559,447		85,084,463
Rate of Increase		24.1%	
Federal	15,060,120		15,973,190
Villages, Schools a	11,499,530		14,666,042
City-County-State b	41,999,797		54,445,231
The Private Exempts	49,371,630		61,791,010
Ratio to All Exempts	41.8%		42.0%
The Specials			
The Railroads	13,807,608		12,643,795
The Telephone Co.	859,650		1,401,030
Rate of Decrease		−4.2%	
Other Private Exempts	34,704,972		47,746,184
Ratio to All Exempts	29.4%		32.5%
Rate of Increase		37.6%	

a This line includes village and township properties for 1962, but the Independent Schools only for 1968.
b This line includes non-school village and township property for 1968.

Secular health services include the Childrens, $181,520, and the Miller Hospital, $852,880; and the Amherst Wilder Foundation, $1,163,750.

In addition to the Summit, under secular schools we have the William Mitchell College of Law, the International Institute, and the Boys Vocational School, all with modest valuations.

Assessed valuations on "Charitable" and religious property increased officially 37.6%, but we are convinced that their true growth was substantially greater. For example, the assessment on the Summit School—a private, secular institution—was reduced from $239,940 in 1962 to $124,340 in 1968; and synagogues, assessed at $574,470 in St. Paul in 1962, were only $451,450 in 1968, even with one magnificent new facility. The railroads were reduced by about $1.2 million. If this policy of reduction has been uniform, private exempts must have increased far more than the records indicate and now probably comprise 40% of all real estate, rather than the 33.8% shown in the statistics.

The following offers a further analysis.

PRIVATE EXEMPT REAL ESTATE (EXCEPT RRS. & THE TELEPHONE COMPANY) IN RAMSEY COUNTY

($47,746,184)

CATEGORY	Secular	Protestant	Catholic	Jewish
Churches		$10,678,344	$11,935,530	$460,750
Benevolences	$ 752,260	3,300,580	1,147,260	401,960
Cemeteries	407,100	11,200		2,760
Colleges, Schools, and Convents	328,640	5,255,030	7,488,010	70,890
Hospitals, Etc.	2,248,710	1,717,080	1,540,080	
TOTALS	$3,736,710	$20,962,234	$22,110,880	$936,360
Ratios	7.8%	43.9%	46.4%	1.9%

TOTAL RELIGIOUS PROPERTY	$44,009,474
Protestant Ratio	47.6%
Catholic Ratio	50.3%
Jewish Ratio	2.1%

Even profit-making cemeteries are exempt in Minnesota.

Under secular benevolences, we have the Hill Reference Library, $170,800; the Community Chest, $60,120; the Red Cross, $68,830; the Goodwill Industries, $79,460; the Alano Society, $19,980; the Boy Scouts, $28,500; and others with smaller assets.

Secular exempts comprise a minor portion of the total in St. Paul: they have only $3,736,710, or 7.8%.

The Jewish ratio, also small, consists of 8 synagogues, of which the Mt. Zion, $173,560, and the Temple of Aaron, $128,200, are the largest. Among Hebrew Benevolences, we have the Community Center, $254,340, and a Home for the Aged, $102,040. There is also a Talmud Torah School, $70,890, and a few small cemeteries. We estimate the Jewish community at 12,000.

Ramsey County has a virile Protestant community estimated at 215,000, with 365 churches, of which 110 are outside St. Paul. The Lutherans with 106 congregations predominate.

There are hundreds of modest Protestant sanctuaries, some assessed at $3,000, or even less. But there are splendid edifices also, such as the Gustavus Adolphus Evangelical, assessed at $200,450, and the Hope Presbyterian, $261,000. With virtually no parochial schools, Protestant wealth is, nevertheless, very nearly on a par with the Catholic.

Among Protestant Benevolences we have

The Presbyterian Central Towers	$ 420,560
The St. Paul Home (Episcopalian)	146,220
The Board of Christian Service (Luth.)	841,890
The Baptist Conference	351,820
The Lutheran Home	108,340
The Redeemer (Lutheran) Arms	280,060
The Presbyterian Homes	132,390
The Ys	870,020
Miscellaneous	49,380
Total	$3,200,680

Among Protestant health services, we have

The Lyngblomston (Luth.) Nursing Home	250,580
The St. John Lutheran Hospital	512,190
The Riverview (Lutheran) Hospital	101,720
The Baptist Hospital	852,590
Total	$1,717,080

There are various Protestant schools, colleges, seminaries, and universities.

Hamline University (Methodist)	$1,120,180
Concordia College (Lutheran)	638,580
American Lutheran Theological Seminary	122,850
St. Pauls Bible College (Christian Missionary)	87,080
Macalester College (Presbyterian)	1,846,310

171

Bethel Baptist Seminary and College	476,500
United Theo. Seminary (United Ch. of Christ)	475,450
Central Lutheran School (Elementary)	61,810
Lutheran High School	227,220
Total	$5,055,980

Catholics, with an estimated 140,000 communicants, have 46 churches, 45 schools with 32,089 pupils, and 4 colleges and seminaries with 3,449 students. The Cathedral of St. Paul, assessed at $853,820, has a dome sometimes mistaken for that on the State House. These churches with their attached schools, together with some other properties, carry a combined assessment of $11,935,530, which means that their value is appraised at not less than $92 million. There are several multi-million-dollar edifices, such as that of St. Gregory, $269,930; St. Leo, $342, 880; the Sacred Heart, $282,850; the Blessed Virgin, $325,040; the Nativity, $348,850; St. Agnes, $349,430; and St. Luke, $532,320.

However, the Catholic Church probably has more wealth in other assets than in parish churches and their subsidiary facilities. Since many of its properties are titled to the diocese, we cannot always determine exactly what they are. The following, however, are clearly identified.

An Orphanage	$ 596,830
The Sisters of Charity	298,010
The House of the Good Shepherd	206,610
St. Joseph's Hospital	1,540,080
St. Joseph's Academy	201,220
Visitation Academy	108,720
The College of St. Thomas	1,420,480
St. Paul's Seminary	603,320
St. Paul's Academy	351,870
Holy Spirit High School	247,640
The College of St. Catherine	992,910
Lady of Peace H. School	336,420
The Derham Hall H. School	247,640
St. Paul's Priory & Sch.	2,093,390
Nazareth Hall Seminary	884,200
Total	$10,129,540

Since the total real estate levy in St. Paul for 1968 was $45,651,595.92, this was about $150 per capita. However, the weight of this tax falls much more heavily on commercial property than on owner-occupied residences.

Full and True appraisals are first entered on the records, which are theoretically 33.3% of cost, market, or replacement value, less depreciation. Assessments, reduced to 40% of F and T, are then inscribed on the rolls.

Those living in their own homes are, however, granted what is called a Homestead Exemption, which provides that the first $4,000 of F and T be reduced to 25% instead of 40%. Finally, after the tax has been computed on this basis, a further reduction of 35% of the general tax-rate is financed with a refund from the State, drawn from the 3% sales tax.

Since the St. Paul millage in 1968 was 262.9, the following tax was imposed on an owner-occupied house appraised at $18,000.

Full and True Appraisal	$6,000	
Homestead Assessed Value		
(25% of $4,000)	1,000	
Total Assessment	1,800	
Debt Rate of 31.91 × 1,800		$ 57.44
General Rate (231.99 × 1,800)	415.78	
Homestead Credit: 35% of the		
General Tax	−145.52	270.26
ACTUAL TAX PAID		$327.70

If the owner should rent his house, he would find quite a different tax-bill:

Full and True Appraisal	$6,000
Assessment at 40%	2,400
ACTUAL TAX DUE	$ 630.96

There can be no doubt that, unless F and T appraisals are well below 33% of the replacement cost, the taxes on commercial properties must be very onerous indeed. For example, a

Warehouse, Valued at	$100,000
With F and T of	33,333
Assessed at	13,333
Would Pay a Tax of	$ 3,586.58.

173

which is at least double what would be exacted in the average community. This inequality is now being tested in the courts.

Based on official computations, the following are the estimated values of real estate in Ramsey County.

CATEGORY	Assessments	Actual Value [a]
ALL	$435,136,208	$3,480,000,000
Taxable	288,160,732	2,305,000,000
Exempt	146,875,473	1,176,000,000
Public	85,084,463	681,000,000
Private	61,791,010	495,000,000
Secular	18,403,968	147,230,000
Omitting Utilities and RRs	3,736,710	30,000,000
Religious	44,009,474	352,000,000
Protestant	20,962,234	167,700,000
Catholic	22,110,880	176,800,000
Jewish	936,360	7,500,000

[a] The official assessments in Ramsey County place per capita wealth at $8200. Since we have found from the reported property assets of colleges that assessments are about 11% instead of 12.5% of true value, we estimate actual per capita wealth at about $9,500.

XIV. MINNEAPOLIS

In 1890, the population of St. Paul was 113,156 and of Minneapolis, 164,738; by 1960, this disparity has grown to 311,340 vs. 521,718. However, the differential in material facilities appears to be even greater; for Minneapolis seems much larger, far more massive and modern, more generously endowed with hotels, factories, office buildings, and shopping centers. In spite of the fact that St. Paul has the capitol-complex, the business area of her sister-city appears almost triple in size and affluence.

St. Paul, however, is preeminent in the magnificence of her Catholic churches and the importance of her sectarian schools. And even though she has several colleges and universities, all these, even when combined, comprise a much smaller educational corpus than the tremendous University of Minnesota, with its 40,000 students, located near the heart of Minneapolis.

Like Portland, Minneapolis is clean and prosperous. Traffic hums through its broad streets and boulevards. Its Negro community, which increased from 1.4% in 1920 to about 3% in 1960, has engaged in some rioting and looting, but not to the extent common elsewhere. In the whole state, its ratio is only 7 tenths of one per cent.

Minneapolis has a large religious community with 376 churches—one for each 1,250 of the population: 37 are Roman Catholic, 8 Jewish, and 311 Protestant and miscellaneous. There are 88 Lutheran congregations, 31 Methodist, 26 Baptist, 13 Protestant Episcopal, and 11 United of Christ. In a present-day population of about 400,000, we have some 290,000 religious affiliates: 80,000 Catholics, 12,000 Jewish, and 200,000 Protestants and miscellaneous.

Mr. Gordon E. Moe, Assessor, Mr. John Taylor, Director of Assessments, and Mr. Orville Dagget, Administration Manager, were all most helpful.

FULL AND TRUE VALUATIONS IN MINNEAPOLIS

CATEGORY	1962	1968
ALL	$1,234,159,750	$1,321,729,950
Taxable	954,798,965	973,212,372
Exempt	312,393,105	348,517,578
Ratio	25.3%	26.4%
1 Public Schools	39,543,235	37,455,874
2 Private and Church Schools	10,498,855	6,358,965
3 Colleges and Universities	36,333,410	51,786,212
4 Public Properties	91,212,370	101,158,836
5 Churches	45,401,870	44,431,031
6 Public Hospitals [a]	33,053,850	45,460,795
7 Charities and Benevolences	14,401,720	14,036,515
8 Cemeteries	8,915,475	12,249,000
9 Railroads	27,075,740	28,060,250
10 Telephone Company	5,956,580	7,520,12

[a] "Public" here means only that they are accessible to the public.

It will be noted, first, that appraisals here, as in St. Paul, must have been reduced radically, since valuations were $2 million less on the public and some $4 million less for private and church schools in 1968 than in 1962. Since we know that new facilities were constructed in both sectors, it is obvious that the actual as well as the comparative growth of exempt property was far greater than indicated in the statistics.

Since 1954, the following exempts alone have removed property with valuations of $115 million from the tax-rolls:

Freeways	$20,609,660
Housing and Redevelopment	11,624,470
Schools	694,460
The University of Minnesota	1,393,900
Total	$37,799,041

Before 1956, there were virtually no city-federal housing projects. Combined with some for redevelopment, these have now removed land valued at $35 million from the tax-rolls; and they account in part for the increase in assessments in the public sector from $91,212,370 to $101,158,836 since 1962. Category 4 includes also real estate belonging to city, state, and federal governments. Since only Categories 4 and 1 (Public Schools and Public Properties) exclude all private property, it was necessary to transcribe every item from cards bearing numbers 2, 3, 5, 6, 7, and 8. Of these, only 2 and 3 are entirely private.

EXEMPT REAL ESTATE IN MINNEAPOLIS

CATEGORY	Public	Private
1 Public Schools	$ 37,455,874	
2 Private and Church Schools		$ 6,358,965
3 Colleges and Universities	48,109,887	3,676,325
4 Government Properties	101,158,836	
5 Churches		44,431,031
6 Hospitals	21,586,276	23,874,520
7 Charities and Benevolences	1,882,920	12,153,595
8 Cemeteries	1,602,150	10,646,850
9 Railroads		28,060,250
10 The Telephone Company		7,520,100
TOTALS	$211,795,943	$136,721,636
Ratios	60.8%	39.2%

The University of Minnesota, listed under Category 3, had literally hundreds of parcels, with F and T appraisals exceeding $48 million.

Private colleges play a minor role, but charitable institutions are overwhelmingly private and largely Protestant. Hospital services are

FULL AND TRUE APPRAISALS ON PRIVATE EXEMPTS[a]
($101,141,286)

CATEGORY	Secular	Protestant	Catholic	Jewish
2 Private Schools	$ 2,214,150	$ 1,401,565	$ 2,609,250	$ 134,000
3 Academies, Etc.	11,300	3,665,025		
5 Churches		28,834,880	14,670,751	925,400
6 Hospitals	777,300	14,062,350	5,918,000	2,216,870
7 Benevolences	5,488,465	7,220,630	300,500	44,000
8 Cemeteries	9,874,750		715,900	56,200
TOTALS	$18,365,965	$55,184,450	$24,214,401	$3,376,470
Ratios	28.16%	54.56%	23.94%	3.34%

TOTAL RELIGIOUS PROPERTY $82,775,321
Protestant Proportion   66.6%
Catholic Proportion   29.2%
Jewish Proportion   4.1%

[a] Note that in this table railroads and the telephone company are omitted.

almost equally divided between public and private, the latter being also predominantly Protestant.

More than half of secular "charities" consist of private cemeteries, exempt from taxation even when operated for profit. Among private secular schools, we note the following:

Hamline University (Sheridan Hotel)	$ 250,000
The Dunwoody Institute	1,400,680
The Phail School of Music	110,000
The Northrup Collegiate	342,770

As in most cities, secular "charities" or "benevolences," Category 7, are of great variety. We have the Art Museum and Gallery, $883,800; the Memorial Blood Bank, $262,500; the Boys Club, $365,100; the Red Cross, $151,450; the Society for the Blind, $177,000; the Goodwill Industries, $83,800; the Jane Harrison Home, $298,000; the Swedish Institute of Arts and Sciences, $125,000; the Institute of Arts, $1,230,000; the Alliance Residence for Aging Men and Women, $165,000; the Sister Kenny Foundation, $1,006,900; etc.

The principal secular medical facilities are the Masonic Hospital, $613,200, and the Franklin Hospital Nursing Home, $94,100.

The Jewish community has the Sheltering Home for Children, $44,000; the Talmud Torah School, $134,000; 8 synagogues, $925,400, of which the Beth El, the Temple Israel, and the Adath Jeshurun are the largest; the Hillel Foundation, $109,300; the Mt. Sinai Hospital, $2,216,870; and some cemeteries.

Among 37 Catholic churches and their attached schools, with F and T appraisals of $11,808,410, the Basilica of St. Marys, $959,000, and the Church of the Annunciation, $871,300, are the most splendid.

St. Marys, $5,918,000, is the only Catholic hospital.

Under Category 2, we find many Catholic schools; however, many of these are listed also under 5, simply as church properties. In addition to the parochial, other schools clearly identified on the taxrolls have appraisals totalling $5,411,230.

Minneapolis is one large American city in which Scandinavian Protestants predominate. It should therefore be no surprise to find a great variety of Protestant—particularly Lutheran—institutions, classified under Category 2 or 3. The largest of these are (1) the Lutheran Augsburg College, $3,307,935; (2) the Protestant Episcopal Brech School, $781,515; and (3) the Covenant Minnehaha Academy, $358,000.

Protestant hospitals abound: the Methodist Asbury and Walker, $927,800; the Presbyterian Abbott, $1,554,150; and 4 Lutheran: the Swedish, $3,191,200; the Deaconess, $1,518,510; the St. Barnabas, $3,846,550; and the Fairview, $1,715,040.

Among large Protestant charities, we have the Salvation Army, $513,300; the Augustana Home, $647,500; St. Olafs Residence, $391,550; the Lutheran Ebenezer Home, $763,000; the Lutheran Childrens Home, $320,400; and the Ys, $2,764,600.

However, the preëminence of Minneapolis Protestantism is reflected most clearly in its hundreds of churches. There are indeed scores of modern but modest sanctuaries with F and T appraisals ranging from $7,000 to $60,000. On the other hand, many are magnificent, such as the Westminster Presbyterian, $690,000; the Trinity Lutheran, $612,500; the Protestant Episcopal Cathedral of St. Mark, $568,000; and the Mt. Olivet Lutheran, $756,000, with a congregation of 10,000, the largest of its denomination in the United States. This church has also a parsonage with a F and T valuation of $50,300, which means that its replacement value probably exceeds $200,000.

In the Protestant orbit, we find the headquarters of the Minnesota Council of Churches, $507,000. We have also the Billy Graham Christian Crusade complex, $697,100, and the Augsburg Publishing House, $1,135,000, which Mr. Dagget considered the two sorest spots on the scene of tax-exempts. According to the *Religious News Service* of May 3, 1968, this corporation did a gross book business of $8,675,682 and had a net income of $664,107 in 1966. It is currently making a contribution in lieu of taxes and would not, we were told by a Lutheran layman, seriously contest full taxation, provided other entities of similar character were placed under the same obligation.

The increasing ratio of exempt property in Minneapolis, and even more in St. Paul, is developing into a crisis. Under extreme pressure from the general electorate, taxes for home owners, farmers, and some business men have been sharply reduced; but the heavy exactions upon most commercial real estate are bringing desperate demands for relief.

Ernest A. Lindstrom, mentioned in Chapter 3, was particularly concerned over such exempts as the Madonna Towers, owned and operated by the Oblate Fathers in Rochester, in which retirees pay initiation fees of $19,900 to $34,000 for the privilege of occupying small apartments, after which they are charged monthly dues ranging upward from $225. As we have already noted, the Supreme Court of the State has now decreed that this facility must pay local taxes.

Since the property tax in Minneapolis totalled $76,978,160.42 in 1968, the per capita levy was about $160. However, we know from reported plant values of colleges and universities, as well as from the very low totals shown below, that appraisals in Minneapolis do not exceed 75% of true value. This means that total replacement value should be about $5,400,000,000 and that per capita wealth is actually about $11,500. This means also that the tax on a $20,000 house is only $235, instead of $330.

The following estimates for Minneapolis real estate are obtained by multiplying the Full and True appraisals by 3, which is the theoretical value set by the taxing authorities.

THE VALUE OF MINNEAPOLIS REAL ESTATE

CATEGORY	Assessments	Replacement Value
ALL	$1,321,749,950	$4,000,000,000
Taxable	973,212,372	2,950,000,000
Exempt	348,517,578	1,050,000,000
The Public	211,795,943	638,000,000
The Private	136,721,636	412,000,000
(Omitting RRs. & Tel. Co.)	101,141,286	305,000,000
The Secular	18,365,965	55,500,000
The Religious	82,775,321	249,500,000
The Protestant	55,184,450	166,500,000
The Catholic	24,214,401	73,000,000
The Jewish	3,376,470	10,000,000

CHAPTER 7

TOTALS AND PROJECTIONS

BASED ON FOUR CITIES

Having analyzed our 14 cities, we may now combine the results and extrapolate projections based on them.

Since 4 of these were surveyed in 1964, we are able to observe precisely what the developments have been over a 4-year period.

TABLE I

GROWTH OF PROPERTY ASSESSMENTS IN 4 CITIES

CITY	All Real Estate	
	1963–64	1968
Washington	$ 4,653,591,031	$ 6,520,330,649
Baltimore	2,585,206,168	2,681,624,158
Buffalo	1,494,494,670	1,522,765,217
Denver	1,385,873,210	1,140,483,610
TOTALS	$10,119,165,079	$11,865,203,634
Increase	17.2%	

We see, therefore, that property values as a whole have increased with inflation and new construction at an average rate of 4.3% annually; but, as demonstrated in the following, the taxable sector has, in certain instances, actually declined.

In the period between 1964 and 1968, the proportion of exempt property expanded from 33.4% to 37.2% of the total and increased by 33.3% while the taxable did so only by 9.8%.

181

TABLE II

CHANGES IN TAXABLE AND EXEMPT ASSESSMENTS
(In Thousands of Dollars)

CITY	Taxable Property		Exempt Property	
	1963–64	1968	1963–64	1968
Washington	$2,525,485	$3,369,209	$2,128,105	$3,151,124
Baltimore	2,006,209	2,051,685	578,997	629,339
Buffalo	1,036,124	1,023,718	458,371	499,027
Denver	1,169,942	913,980	215,931	226,603
TOTALS	$6,737,760	$7,358,592	$3,381,404	$4,506,093
Ratio	66.6%	63.8%	33.4%	37.2%
Increase	9.8%		33.3%	

TABLE III

COMPARATIVE DENOMINATIONAL GROWTH IN 4 CITIES
(In Thousands of Dollars)

CITY	Protestant		Catholic		Jewish	
	1963–64	1968	1963–64	1968	1963–64	1968
Washington	$ 90,747	$126,673	$123,809	$176,816	$ 7,368	$10,121
Baltimore	45,549	53,099	74,019	81,634	24,652	24,244
Buffalo	23,632	22,313	54,049	67,201	2,384	2,328
Denver	25,384	23,500	20,412	23,500	6,921	7,500
TOTALS	$185,312	$225,585	$272,289	$349,151	$41,325	$44,193
Ratios	37.1%	36.4%	54.5%	56.3%	8.3%	7.1%
Rate of Growth	21.2%		28.3%		6.9%	

Here we find a sharp disparity; for while Protestant assets dropped from 37.1% to 36.4% and the Jewish from 8.3% to 7.1%, the Roman Catholic increased from 54.5% to 56.4%. Jewish religious wealth increased by 6.9%, the Protestant by 21.2%, and the Catholic by 28.3%.

In our 1964 study, we multiplied the combined assessments in the 4 cities by 68 in order to compute the total wealth in the United States. By this method, we obtained the following results:

RELIGIOUS PROPERTY IN THE UNITED STATES [a]

Protestant and Miscellaneous	$28,000,000,000
Roman Catholic	44,500,000,000
Jewish	7,000,000,000
TOTAL	$79,500,000,000

* The reader should note that in our 1964 extrapolation, we assumed that all assessments on exempt property in the 4 cities averaged 40% of actual value. Even though there was some variance from this norm, it was demonstrable that the results so obtained could err only by being too conservative, i.e., too low in their totals.

In the following statistics (TABLE FOUR), we use the same yardstick for 1968, even though, again, there is some individual variance.

The reader should note further, however, that in TABLE SEVEN and EIGHT we use only the exact statistics shown in the analysis of the 14 cities,—with results that are almost identical.

We omitted the Washington Cathedral and the National Shrine of the Immaculate Conception from the base on which to extrapolate, since these, with combined 1964 assessments of $27,400,861, are not local churches. Using the same formula for 1968, except that now we multiply by 69 instead of 68—because the population in the 4 cities has not kept pace with the national—we arrive at the following results:

TABLE IV

THE VALUE OF RELIGIOUS PROPERTY IN THE 4 CITIES IN 1968

DIVISION	Assessments	Market or Replacement Value	Times 69
Protestant	$225,585,454		
Less	19,425,612		
Net	206,159,833	$ 515,399,582	$ 35,553,000,000
Roman Catholic	349,150,880		
Less	12,376,310		
Net	336,774,570	841,936,445	58,093,000,000
Jewish	44,192,717	110,481,792	7,623,000,000
TOTALS	$587,127,137	$1,467,817,819	$101,269,000,000

	1964 [a]	1968
Ratios: Protestant	35.22%	35. %
Catholic	55.96%	57.5%
Jewish	8.82%	7.5%

[a] Cf. *Church Wealth and Business Income,* p. 109.

We see that religiously used and exempt property increased by nearly $22 billion, from $79.5 to $101.27 billion, or 27.5%.

183

BASED ON THE FOURTEEN CITIES

Our next table indicates the racial and denominational composition of the 14 cities. Estimates are based on the assumption that there are 1,500 Jews for each synagogue, since some 6 or 7 million share 4,445 of these. We estimate 2,600 Roman Catholics for each parish church, since this is the average claimed in the *Official Catholic Directory*. We estimate 600 members for each Protestant church, for although the average in the nation as a whole is only 250, those in the large cities have memberships substantially more than double in size.

TABLE V

RELIGIOUS AND RACIAL COMPOSITION OF THE 14 CITIES

		Ratio of
Population	7,774,737	Population
Non-White	1,670,669	21.5%
Religious Communicants	4,870,000	62.6%
Protestants	2,666,400	34.3%
Catholics	1,934,000	24.8%
Jewish	270,900	3.5%
Unchurched	2,904,300	37.4%

Note that the Negro proportion in our 14 cities is almost double that of the national, because of their heavy concentration in Washington, Richmond, Baltimore, Cleveland, and St. Louis. However, the Catholic ratio—24.8%, is very near the national, which is 23.8%; and the same is true of the Jewish (3.5%) and the Protestant, 34.3%. Since our computation projects an overall church membership of 62.8%, this gives a total of 125.6 million, which is virtually identical to the 125,778,656, which is given as the inclusive religious membership in the 1968 *Yearbook of American Churches*.[a] This indicates again that our 14 cities do indeed constitute a near-replica of the whole nation.

It should be pointed out that these totals include all children enrolled in Sunday schools, all adults with any kind of affiliation, all persons baptized as Catholics, and all members of the Jewish race. Among these, there are, of course, millions who never attend any church.

In fact, in the *Yearbook*[b] cited above, it is stated that whereas 49% of American adults attended church in 1958, only 44% did so

---

[a] p. 194.   [b] *Ib.* 228.

in 1966; this means that the unchurched have increased by some 11 or 12 million in 10 years and that less than 54 million among all American adults now engage in any denominational activity. The actual number doing so among 125 million above the age of 21 in 1967–68 probably did not exceed 40%, or 50,000,000 individuals.

However, since well over $1 billion is currently being invested in the construction of church sanctuaries alone,[a] in addition to vast sums expended for other religious or related facilities, it is obvious that as attendance declines, the wealth of the churches continues to expand at an even greater inverse ratio.

The following table seems to indicate that among large religious groups, the Roman Catholics are most active. The educational institutions conducted by this denomination have continued to expand on the college and university level. In their elementary and secondary schools, however, which had been growing without interruption until 1964, there was a decline of 5% in the 14 cities and 8% nationally. Concurrently, the number of public school pupils undergoing Catholic instruction during released time is increasing rapidly. And while

TABLE VI

THE CHURCHES IN 1968

CATEGORY	In 14 Cities	Nationally
Protestant Churches	4,444	302,348
Catholic Parishes	747	18,064
Synagogues	260	4,445

CATHOLICS UNDER INSTRUCTION

EDUCATIONAL LEVEL	1964	1968
Collegians and Seminarians		
In 14 Cities	56,321	67,979
In the United States	454,922	473,298
Elementary and Secondary Pupils		
In 14 Cities	414,874	394,736
In the United States	5,625,404	5,174,776
Released Time Pupils in U.S.	4,316,931	5,356,340
Total under Instruction	10,374,336	11,093,024
Claimed Catholics in the U.S.	44,874,371	47,468,333
Ratio to Population	23.6%	23.8%

[a] *Ib.* 215.

TABLE VII [a]

THE TAX LOAD IN RELATION TO EXEMPT RATIOS OF PROPERTY
(Property Valuations in Millions of Dollars)

CITY	FULL VALUE All	Exempt	Ratio	TAXES ON A $20 M HOUSE	SALES TAX ON $8,000	BOTH TAXES
Baltimore	$ 5,300	$ 1,260	23.5%	$616	$240	$ 856
Boston	7,455	3,350	45.0	910	240	1,150
Buffalo	3,810	1,250	32.7	900	160	1,060
Cleveland	6,500	1,560	24.1	440	320	760
Denver	4,500	900	19.9	430	400	830
Hartford	1,665	409	25.5	649	280	929
Pittsburgh	5,550	1,800	32.7	571	480	1,151
Portland	4,450	633	14.2	540		540
Providence	910	302	33.3	516	400	916
Richmond	1,295	314	24.3	368	160	528
St. Louis	5,300	1,600	29.6	410	240	650
St. Paul	3,480	1,175	33.8	327	240	567
Minneapolis	4,000	1,050	26.4	335	240	575
Washington	13,040	6,300	48.3	300	240	540
TOTALS	$67,255	$21,903	32.6%			

[a] We should point out again, and it should be emphasized, that in certain cities, especially Portland and Minneapolis, the actual tax will be considerably less on a house than here indicated.

total Catholics receiving indoctrination increased from 10,374,336 to 11,093,024, or 6.9%, the total number of these who had been baptized by a Catholic rite increased from 44,974,371 to 47,468,333, or 5.8%; and from 23.6% to 23.8% of the entire population.

The following deals with another aspect of our enquiry.

We noted in our analysis of Washington that the federal government contributes more to the District than is obtained from the property tax; and that there are various other levies, including a gross earnings tax and a sharp income tax, which add at least $400 to the levies imposed upon the average family. It should also be noted that the lowest taxes are found in such cities as Minneapolis, Portland, and Richmond, where, as it happens, only small parochial school systems exist.

We should also note that in Pittsburgh a family with a $10,000 income pays a gross earnings tax of $200, which increases the direct levies noted in the above table to $1,351; and that in Cleveland this exaction is $100, creating a comparable obligation there of $860.

We are now ready to project our totals from the 14 cities to the entire nation. Since their population, 7,774,737, comprises 3.85% of the national, we multiply by 26 for extrapolation. And again, since the great religious shrines in Washington are not local churches, we have omitted their valuations from our base.

TABLE VIII

FULL VALUE OF REAL ESTATE IN THE 14 CITIES
AND THE NATION
(In Millions of Dollars)

CATEGORY	In 14 Cities	Ratio	Times 26
ALL	$67,254	100%	$1,748,604
Taxable	45,352	67.4	1,179,156
Exempt	21,903	32.6	569,456
Public	15,328.5	70.0	398,446
The Private	6,574.5	30.0	170,938
The Secular	2,635.5	40.6	68,394
The Religious	3,939	59.4	102,524
The Protestant	1,561.1	39.2	40,588.6
The Catholic	2,087.6	53.4	54,277.6
The Jewish	290.5	7.4	7,547.8

We find, therefore, that in spite of lower assessments on exempts, this sector has now risen officially to 32.6% of the total. Were all

187

valuations at parity, there is no doubt that the ratio would now exceed 35% and might be approaching 40%.

According to the 1967 *Statistical Abstract*,[a] the true or market value of all exempt real estate in 1961 was $294,740,000,000, or 23.4% of the total. In our 1964 study, we computed this at $320 billion, or 28.5%. Since this has now increased to 32.6%, it is obvious that the law of increasing exemptions continues to operate, year after year, with a kind of inexorability.

What will happen if the present trend continues is nothing less than a mathematical certainty. Between 1961 and 1968, exempts have been increasing officially at the rate of 1.17% each year, with, of course, a compensatory decrease in the taxable. If the same tempo continues, the exempts will therefore reach 50.15% and the taxable will drop to 49.85 % of the total in 15 years—in 1984, perhaps a symbolic year to be fraught with inexpressible tragedy.

But remember, these are totals based on official statistics, which are substantially below parity for the exempts.

Our computation shows that the total value of real estate in this country has now reached $1,748,630 million; the taxable, $1,179,150 million; the exempt, $569,456 million; the publicly owned, $398,508 million; and the private exempt, $170,938 millions, of which the secular stands at $68,394 million.

The remarkable accuracy of our projections is confirmed by the *Statistical Abstract*,[b] which placed the market or replacement value of all taxable property at $969 billion in 1961, compared to our 1964 projection of $1,140,000,000,000.[c] The 1968 *Statistical Abstract*[d] places the gross value of all real estate as of 1966 at $1,673,561,-070,000, compared to our projection of $1,748,604,000,000 in 1968.

Our two computations, the first based on the survey of the 4 cities, which were examined in 1964, and the second, drawn from our current analysis of all 14, produce extraordinarily similar results.

THE COST OF EXEMPTIONS TO THE TAXPAYERS

The per capita ad valorem tax in our 14 cities ranges from $83 in Richmond to $258 in Hartford and $299 in Boston; and the following demonstrates the practical effects of property exemptions.

---

[a] P. 437.   [b] *Ib.*

[c] *Church Wealth and Business Income*, p. 110.

[d] P. 427.

TABLE IX

TOTAL VALUE OF ALL RELIGIOUS PROPERTY IN THE U.S.
(In Millions of Dollars)

CATEGORY	BASED ON 4 CITIES		BASED ON 14 CITIES
	1964	1968	1968
Protestant	$28,000	$ 35,550	$ 40,588
Roman Catholic	44,500	58,100	54,277.6
Jewish	7,000	7,620	7,547.8
TOTALS	$79,500	$101,270	$102,413.4

TABLE X

TAX-AVOIDANCE BY EXEMPT PROPERTIES

Total Property Tax Paid in 14 Cities	$ 1,110,047,071
Average, Per Capita	$ 143
For a Family of 5	715
Projected Total Property Tax in United States	28,861,222,000 [a]
Average Millage in 14 Cities Computed on Full Value	21.7
Combined Tax Avoided by Exempts in 14 Cities	$ 475,273,400
(On Property Worth $21,903 Million)	
By Public Exempts	332,605,575
By Private Exempts	142,666,650
By Secular Exempts	57,081,850
By Religious Exempts	85,476,300
Tax Avoided by Exempts in the United States	12,357,098,400
By Public Property	8,647,748,950
By Private Property	3,709,329,900
By Secular Exempts	1,484,128,100
By Religious Exempts	2,222,383,800
Cost on This Basis to Average Family of 5	
For All Exempts	310
For Private Exempts	93
For Religious Exempts and Their Organizations Alone	55.50

[a] According to the 1969 *Statistical Abstract*, p. 428, the total property tax collected in the U.S. was $19,054,000,000 in 1962. By extrapolating from our 4 cities in 1964, the total property tax would then have been about $21 billion. In 6 years, therefore, this increased by nearly $10 billion, or more than 50%, to be paid by an ever-dwindling ratio of taxpayers.

189

TABLE XI [a]

PROPERTY TAX COMPARED TO CITY-COUNTY TAX BUDGETS

Government Complex	Budget	Per Capita	From Real Estate Tax	Per Capita	Ratio of R. E. Tax to Budget
Washington [b]	$456,150,000	$600	$101,000,000	$133	22.1%
Baltimore [c]	327,003,456	360	106,592,670	117	32.6%
Buffalo & its Half of Erie County [d]	211,023,498	398	83,349,389	157	39.5%
Denver [e]	168,253,860	336	69,276,836	138	41.2%
Richmond [f]	66,825,173	304	18,148,600	83	27.2%
Boston (Est) [g]	300,000,000	448	198,992,391	298	66.0%
Hartford [h]	49,211,462	304	40,637,725	251	82.6%
St. Louis [i]	88,981,611	129	16,936,766	24.5	19.0%
Multnomah Co. [j]	138,187,571	246	75,199,239	134	54.5%
Pittsburgh [k]	68,200,000	177	37,000,000	112	54.2%
Cleveland [l]	101,400,000	122	42,800,000	51.5	42.2%
Minneapolis [m]	129,600,617	270	100,855,617	210	77.6%
St. Paul [n]	43,931,273	146	20,824,521	69	47.4%

[a] For a detailed explanation of some of the above budgets, cf. TABLE XI in the Appendix.

It should be pointed out that one reason for the variations found in the above statistics is the fact some include only a fraction of the ad valorem tax collected and others do not cover some of the most important operational costs, such as schools and the cost of county government operating on the same level as the municipal.

The purpose of this table is to show the ratios of various budgets which derive from the real estate tax and from other sources. However, this task proved very difficult, because in many instances the ad valorem taxes collected in a city go also to support the county, the state, independent school districts, and other authorities. Sometimes there are a number of separate and independent budgets, and in some cases all of them receive revenue from different sources. In most cases, the sales tax is collected by the state; sometimes this is returned in part to maintain local schools and governments. It was therefore not possible to compute this factor, either as a cost to taxpayers or as revenue to cities or schools. Furthermore, additional grants were sometimes received from county, state, and federal levels; and these vary from almost nothing in some places to huge allocations in others. Finally, there are many special federal agencies and programs which allocate funds to schools, and of these no computation could be made in the present study.

It is therefore impossible to present a complete or accurate picture. The subject is so complex that a comprehensive treatment would require a vast amount of additional research, or even a separate volume.

However it is quite obvious that as the tax-base has eroded, and the cost of local government has expanded, all cities have been forced to increase their ad valorem taxes or resort to many new levies. We now have local income taxes, franchise taxes, gross earnings and net profits taxes, occupation taxes, merchants and manufacturers taxes, inventory taxes, sales and use taxes, as well as fees, excises, and licenses in profusion.

The above table will convey some concept of the degree to which local taxing units now depend upon grants and subsidiary levies to meet their operational costs. Portland and Minneapolis have so far resisted the trend to a considerable degree; but the former only, among our cities, is still without a sales or use tax; it operates with a very low tax rate and virtually without any grants whatever from any outside source.

[b] Since the District of Columbia is a self-contained unit of government, it was easy to obtain a complete report on expenditures and income.

[c] The Baltimore budget includes all income and covers all expenditures, including those for schools.

[d] Since we have complete data for Eric Co. and for Buffalo, including school costs, we combine the per capita costs for the two by assuming that half of County expenditures are allocated to Buffalo.

[e] We should note that the city and county of Denver operate under a single, joint budget, which includes $62,745,460 for its schools.

[f] In the case of Richmond, all property tax collections go to the city, and the city budget covers all expenditures, including schools.

[g] Since we were not able to obtain up-to-date or complete statistics for Boston, the budget total is an estimate.

[h] For Hartford, we were able only to obtain data for the real estate tax and the budget.

[i] The St. Louis budget does not include any grants from other levels of government, nor is the cost of schools, etc., included. About $46 million of ad valorem real estate tax collected in the city goes to the county, schools, etc., and $72 million of budgeted expenditure comes from additional sources.

[j] Multnomah County (including Portland) retains all the taxes it collects from property and receives virtually nothing from outside sources. There is no sales or use tax to be collected or to be distributed.

[k] The Pittsburgh budget does not include anything for schools or the county government. About $38 million of the ad valorem tax in the city goes for schools and the county.

[l] The budget for Cleveland does not include anything for other levels of government. About $50 million collected from the ad valorem tax is diverted to schools, the county, etc.

[m] The budget given for Minneapolis includes total expenditures for the city and the portion of county government which operates within the city. The cost of schools is also included. This is, therefore, a plenary budget.

[n] The cost of schools and county government is not reflected in the St.

Paul budget. The local ad valorem tax in St. Paul is about $51 million, of which, as the reader will note, less than $21 million is used to operate the municipal government itself.

COMMENTARY AND EVALUATION

We must note again that in the Protestant classification we have usually included the Ys; all non-Roman but Catholic churches; and all such miscellaneous cults and denominations as the Buddhist, Islamic, Swedenborgian, Ethical Culturists, Unitarian-Universalists, Jehovah's Witnesses, the many New Thought groups, the Church of Jesus Christ of Latter Day Saints, and various others which are not really Protestant at all. Had these been excluded, the Protestant ratio, deriving from the 14 cities, could not have exceeded 35%; and had all Catholic denominations been included with the Latin Rite, this classification would have been at least 57% and possibly 60% in the final extrapolation.

Furthermore, there can be no question that our totals are extremely conservative in the exempt sector. Our statistics are indeed taken directly from the records of representative cities; and therefore rigorously used and exempt real estate cannot possibly be less than $102.4 billion. However, since many of the assessments in this area stand at considerably less than parity with the taxable, it is virtually certain that the true value of religious exempts must now be approaching and perhaps surpassing $110 billion.

We may therefore declare as established fact that Protestant and miscellaneous properties used for religious purposes and exempt from taxation are now worth well in excess of $40 billion; Jewish, not less than $8 or $10 billion; and Roman Catholic at least $60 billion.

And all this, of course, does not include a great deal of real estate owned by churches, since some parsonages and rectories are taxed and since most of their commercial investments (including many housing projects and retirement homes) are subject to the ad valorem levy. Nor does it take into account at all the vast reserves of church wealth in the form of cash, stocks, bonds, land contracts, mortgages, and business corporations or ventures of infinite variety, which are discussed in Chapter 8.

We may therefore state without reservation that religiously used real estate alone now equals or exceeds 10% of the taxable in the United States.

192

CHAPTER 8

THE BUSINESS OF RELIGION

TOTALS UNKNOWN

As we have already shown, the religiously used real estate of the churches constitutes a vast domain. To this, however, must be added a huge but less definitely known corpus of intangible and commercial assets. All of this may be more than a tax-burdened citizenry can bear —more than even the mighty resources of this country can tolerate. What, then, is the total of church wealth? A completely satisfactory answer to this question is not available, for churches are not required by law to make financial reports as are other organizations. Hence, there is no official collection of facts on which one may draw.

Many churches indeed keep good records and make these available to their members and the public. But there are serious gaps in such information. For example, the largest and wealthiest denomination in the United States, the Roman Catholic, publishes no general financial records at all. Even its members, who are constantly importuned to contribute, have little or no idea of its assets or revenues; nor are they informed as to how much has been spent or what is done with the money. As a "corporation sole" or "aggregate," the diocesan bishop knows the facts about his own diocese, but beyond that he has no knowledge. A spokesman for the New York archdiocese has even asserted that no record exists as to the total revenues received by the 150 Roman Catholic dioceses in the United States.[1]

193

Several years ago, the Roman Catholic Church ordered a study of its financial operations by an outside agency. In its report, the agency commended the Church for the excellency of its financial operations, but was critical of its practice of never supplying its members with financial statements. The Church, however, has continued in its traditional secrecy. When Archbishop Terence J. Cooke was appointed by the Pope to succeed Cardinal Spellman in the New York see, his priests promptly petitioned for the publication of complete financial reports. Such reports have never been made in the history of the archdiocese and there is no indication that Archbishop (now Cardinal) Cooke intends to change this policy.

SECRET OPERATIONS

The Parish Council of Our Lady of the Rosary Church, Buffalo, N.Y., issued a call in 1960 for an end to "secrecy" in the operation of the Buffalo diocese. A controversy had erupted when Msgr. J. Stanley Ormsby, the pastor, refused to obligate the parish for $120,000 as requested by Bishop James A. McNulty. The church council headed by a layman, Gerald Pavlak, urged that the diocese make public its entire financial situation. Pavlak said: "All we ask is to find out where our money goes and for a little better administration." [2]

The curious anomaly of his church in calling for public subsidy to its schools while refusing to publish its balance sheet impressed a Roman Catholic spokesman, Bishop Joseph L. Bernardin, general secretary of the U.S. Catholic Conference.[3] He urged publication of Catholic school finances to reveal the problem. But when it was pointed out to him that such information would be pointless without a complete disclosure of church revenues, disbursements, and assets, he replied: "Perhaps in the mechanics of the thing it is impossible to reveal school finances without publishing total church financial resources."

The National Federation of Priests' Councils meeting in New Orleans March 26, 1969, called for an "open accounting" of financial assets on the part of all 154 dioceses and archdioceses in the United States.[4] "This is the direction the church must take if it wishes to continue on the road to openness and honesty," said Father Henry Brown, pastor of St. Gregory's Church, New York City.

In the face of definite grass roots sentiment, however, the Church remains adamant. In a statement presented on behalf of the United

194

States bishops of the Roman Catholic Church to the House Ways and Means Committee early in 1969, general counsel William R. Considine of the USCC, pointed out that in the past churches have not been required to make annual income reports to the government, and that "it is desirable to maintain this freedom of the churches from intimate governmental scrutiny." He added: "If Congress decides to abolish the exemption of churches from the tax on unrelated business income, only those churches that engage in unrelated business activities should be required to make reports, and the reports should be limited to the unrelated business activities." [5]

There is another important church which, like the Roman Catholic, has conducted its business in concealment: the Church of Jesus Christ of Latter Day Saints (Mormon) with headquarters in Salt Lake City. This Church, which now claims some 2,500,000 members throughout the world, makes its communicant statistics readily available, but refuses to divulge any financial information whatsoever. A request for certain facts in this area brought the following reply.

"Dear Mr. Larson:

"I have been requested by President Joseph Fielding Smith to answer your letter in which you requested various financial statistics pertaining to our Church. We regret that we do not have in this office such information. That type of information is maintained under the close supervision of the First Presidency and ordinarily is not made available. Even should you write to them, we do not believe that they would be in a position to furnish you the answers to most of your questions.

"In answer to one question where you indicate a rumor of the Church owning and controlling a majority interest in the Union Pacific Railway—according to what we have heard in the past, such a statement is not true. However, we do not know whether or not the Church has any stock in that railroad. We regret that we are not in a position to assist you with answers to these questions.

Sincerely,
Earl E. Olson
ASSISTANT CHURCH HISTORIAN"

However, the Reorganized Church of Jesus Christ of Latter-Day Saints—another Mormon group with headquarters in Independence, Mo., does publish regular financial reports and makes these available on request. Its 1968 statement shows assets of $11,260,183, which, apparently, does not reflect the holdings of any individual congregations.

We could obtain no information whatever for this study from Jewish religious leaders or organizations. They assured us that no central financial records are kept. As matters now stand, it is apparent that each religious organization—Protestant, Catholic, or Jewish —is an actual or potential financial empire, amenable to no one.

The United Church of Christ refused to make its financial report available to us, but the contents of its portfolio are well known.

Most Protestant churches, however, render financial reports to their members and make them available to others upon request. But there are loopholes here also. For instance, some of the reports include only the assets held by the headquarters of the denomination and do not reflect the wealth of the individual churches. Again, virtually autonomous boards may make their own reports to their own trustees, but not to the general denomination. Until government itself requires comprehensive financial statements from the churches, the difficulty in getting complete and accurate information will continue.

SOURCES OF INCOME

Churches have many sources of revenue. These include the collection plate, tithes, and pledges from the faithful, charges for clergy services, contributions from the public, and business income, both passive and active. But there are many other sources of income. Wills and legacies, for example, provide a regular lift to parish or denominational income. Many churches now have tax-exempt foundations whose business it is to solicit systematically for large donations and bequests. A brochure mailed to many thousands of prospects by the Roman Catholic Society for the Propagation of the Faith contains the following interesting and instructive appeal:

"After properties, securities or cash have been transferred to the trust, the securities, or property, may be sold by the trustee and the proceeds reinvested, all without liability for a capital gains tax, regardless of how low the original cost of these properties to you may have been. The proceeds will then be reinvested in securities appearing to offer attractive possibilities for future growth of income. You will enjoy the personal satisfaction attendant to lifetime charitable giving although possession by the Society for the Propagation of the Faith is postponed until after your death."

196

It is a fact that by means of such giving, wealthy people may leave more to their heirs than if they had given nothing at all.

Many churches actively and systematically solicit wills. Catholic groups regularly send letters to lawyers reminding them that a good Catholic is expected to put his church in his will for at least 10% of the corpus. The press regularly notes large bequests made to churches. An Associated Press dispatch reports that Mrs. Ruth T. Wallace of Saratoga Springs, N.Y., who died Jan. 2, 1967, bequeathed $2.5 million to the Pope and another $2.5 million to the Redemptorist Fathers of New York. Thus, the Roman Catholic Church netted $5 million tax free from this one will.

There can be little doubt that wills produce at least $1 billion a year for the churches.

United community funds or chests are another typical source of church revenue. Catholic Charities of Denver, Colorado, a $1,-780,893-operation, receives 57 per cent of its income from the United Fund. When the Sisters of St. Vincent de Paul, a Church order, set out to build a new children's home in Saginaw, Michigan, a principal source of funds was the Saginaw County United Fund. This was a natural development since St. Vincent's had been receiving a large part of its budget from this source for many years. Principal religious groups in many communities share in such funds.

Although bingo is legal in only 11 states, the Catholic Church makes substantial profits from it in all 50. In New Jersey, where it is legal, churches and their related organizations realized a net profit from this source of $25,358,856 in 1967. When New York City police raided the Church of the Most Precious Blood and closed down its roulette wheels, Father Donald D'Ippolito, pastor, complained that the crack-down had cost the parish $25,000. A layman, Philip Vitello, said that gambling had been going on at the churches for 41 years without interference.[*] Many a parish nets $50,000 or more each year from bingo: if this should be the average, the total would be about $1 billion. Even if the New Jersey figure is reduced to one-half for a typical state operation, this would still mean an annual income from this source of $500 million.

Yet another source of income for the churches is government—federal, state, and municipal. Chapter 10 is devoted to an analysis of these subsidies. There is naturally no tax on such income. Chapter 10 shows church income from government sources annually to be an estimated $7,000,000,000.

CONTRIBUTIONS FROM MEMBERS

The American and Protestant Orthodox bodies whose finances are reported in the 1968 *Yearbook of American Churches*[7] had an annual income of $3,266,533,260. There are, however, 172 additional bodies, many of which, to be sure, are small. We should note, however, that they include the nation's largest church, the Roman Catholic, with 47.5 million members, as well as the Church of Jesus Christ of Latter-Day Saints and the Christian Science Church—both powerful denominations.

Since the 60 religious bodies which did report membership contributions totalling $3,266,533,260 in 1967 had 45.5 million members, the per capita giving was $72. If we now add the 73.5 million in the bodies not represented in the *Year Book* tabulation, and the 6 million who comprise the Jewish community, we have a total of 125 million. Assuming that the rate of giving was the same in all denominations, we have membership contributions totalling $9 billion. Mortimer Caplin, former Commissioner of Internal Revenue, estimated itemized and deductible church donations (which would not include all), in a televised interview with CBS-TV, June 18, 1968, at $7.5 to $8 billion. If Protestants, Catholics, and Jews contribute at a similar rate, this would mean that Protestant donations are $5,185,000,000, the Catholic, $3,384,000,000, and the Jewish $432,000,000. These figures are undoubtedly too high for the Protestants and too small for Jews and Catholics. The Catholic elementary and secondary school system alone may cost as much as $3 billion to operate. And how much money flows annually from the American parishes into the coffers of the Vatican? The German magazine, *Der Spiegel,* stated in an article published in 1958 that the New York archdiocese alone ships more money to Rome than it is able to obtain from all the Catholics in Europe combined. It is true that large subsidies for the Catholic schools now come from the federal government; but, since the parents themselves must still pay much of the bill, there can be little doubt that their Church in America costs them at least $5 billion, or an average of from $500 to $600 annually for every family.

WASHINGTON, D.C.—A SYNOPTICON

We believe it will be informative to examine the extent of unrelated business income and investments in the context of a single representative city. While it is obviously impossible, simply by passing down a street, to recognize with certainty which businesses or holdings are owned by churches, some information is available. For this survey, we have chosen the nation's capital, though in its profusion of church business, it is similar to other American cities.

The most conspicuous religious complexes in Washington, D.C., are the Episcopal Cathedral and the Shrine of the Immaculate Conception. The former is assessed at $19,425,612 but cost at least $40 million. The latter carries an assessment of $12,376,310, but must have cost more than $30 million. These vast and ornate structures appear on their face to be purely religious, designed for nothing but worship. Even a cursory inspection, however, reveals a definite commercialization. For example, the Washington Cathedral has long conducted a tax-free souvenir and novelty shop; and, according to an article in *Christianity Today,* Dec. 23, 1966, it operates a Christmas card business which has grossed $6,200,000 since its inception in 1926. Profits are devoted to the maintenance and expansion of the building.

The Shrine of the Immaculate Conception operates a shop and restaurant for tourists. The courts have ruled that despite its large profits, these come under the general umbrella of church exemption. Close by, we find the Catholic University Press, which also produces substantial revenue and which enjoys tax-exemption on income as well as on land and buildings.

A third great shrine is soon to be constructed. Julian Lowe, president of the Potomac Stake of the Church of Jesus Christ of Latter-Day Saints, announced that the Mormon temple soon to be erected would be a major structure comparable in size and splendor to the other great religious edifices in the national capital. This is to be built mainly with funds available from the Mormon headquarters in Salt Lake City. The location is a commanding 57.4-acre site in nearby Kensington, Maryland. The Church spokesman emphasized that this temple, like others of his faith, would be open only to Mormons in good standing but that a visitors' center would be included in the complex. No dollar estimate was mentioned, but a monument of this magnitude will certainly involve an expenditure running into millions.

Proceeding with our survey, we find an enormous and hideous apartment-house and business development, which cost some $75 million, cluttering the area in which some of the noblest national shrines and monuments are located. This complex, called Watergate Towne, was built by an international real estate cartel known as the Società General Immobiliare of Rome, in which the Vatican has controlling interest. Just across the street at 24th and H Street, N.W., the Vatican had previously tested the area with a $4.4 million apartment complex, the Potomac Plaza. The Vatican had a little trouble getting a needed change of zoning for Watergate Towne until its American Apostolic Delegate applied his pressure in the right places. The Vatican also dispatched its ace trouble-shooter, Professor Luigi Moretti of Rome, to the scene. Between them, they managed to charm the protesters and secure official acceptance for the Watergate monstrosity, which has now quite ruined what was once one of the loveliest portions of our capital city.

We note that the Vatican never intended to retain or manage either of these condominiums. The Potomac Plaza has already been sold to individual tenants; and apartments in Watergate are now being filled with notables vieing with each other to purchase the luxury units at prices ranging from $30,000 to $250,000. Tenants will enjoy their own barber and beauty shops, post office, Riggs Bank, men's haberdashery, bakery, grocery, liquor store, drug store, restaurant, swimming pool, gift shop, and garage facilities.

Indicative of Vatican cash reserves was the fact that Immobiliare originally planned to build the Watergate project without borrowing a dime. It was only as opposition developed within the banking community that the cartel finally announced it would borrow some of the funds.

Rivalling Watergate Towne is the proposed $63 million high rise business complex of the Seventh-Day Adventist Church to be built adjacent to Montgomery Mall at Cabin John, near Washington. It, too, will require a change in zoning which residents of the area are vigorously opposing, as they did in the case of Watergate. Opponents of the zoning change describe the proposed project as "a Manhattan skyline in suburbia." The Washington *Star*[8] stated that the complex would straddle Democracy Boulevard and "would include 800,000 square feet of office space, equal to the office space in downtown Bethesda (Maryland)." In addition, there would be 150,000 square feet of retail space and 1,700 apartment units.

Adventist leaders have stated that the Church inherited the site and that they wish only to dispose of the property to the best advantage.

Anyone interested in good eating and drinking with a church flavor need only patronize Martin's Carriage House in Georgetown. This is another Catholic leaseback.

If the need is for housing, churches offer it under almost every denominational brand. Perhaps the latest, although one cannot begin to keep up with them all, is the Fellowship House, a 140-unit apartment at nearby Reston, built with a federal loan of $1.4 million. A visit to the grounds of the old Sibley Hospital brings us to an ecumenical housing program sponsored by both Protestant and Roman Catholic churches and financed with low-cost federal funds.

The new Bethel Baptist Church Housing Corporation is the developer of a one-block area on Rhode Island Avenue between 8th and 9th Streets, N.W. The United Church of Christ is handling a $2 million-apartment and commercial high rise in a half-block area bounded by R Street and by 7th and 8th Streets, N.W. Here we find financing by F.H.A. The Lincoln-Westmoreland Housing Corporation is the church-front promoting this undertaking.

The Mount Airy Baptist Church is the developer of a 298-unit highrise apartment complex at North Capitol St. and New York Avenue. It is to be called Tyler House and will be built by the Church with federal funds to provide residences for low-to-moderate income families. The Gospel Spreading Church was a pioneer in this type of enterprise. Mayfair Mansions and Paradise Manor were early multi-million dollar projects in northeast Washington. They were built under the leadership of the Church pastor, Elder Solomon Lightfoot Michaux.

In the Washington environs, a luxury home real estate development called Parkwood was owned by the Society of the Divine Saviour, a Roman Catholic order of nuns. The project should have been a big money maker, but was unfortunate enough to have a dishonest promoter, who made off with some millions of corporation funds. The fate of Parkwood is described in Chapter 9.

More blessed were the Sisters of Mercy, another celibate order, which also owned extensive acreage in Montgomery County. A routine story in the Washington *Post* [9] noted that the Sisters were seeking a change in zoning for their 290-acre site. A visit revealed that only one small building had been completed, but that the entire site enjoyed tax-exemption as religiously used land, which, originally purchased at a very low price, had appreciated greatly in value. The Sisters were therefore ready to subdivide and sell off residential lots at premium prices, on which there would, of course, be huge capital gains entirely exempt from taxation.

A rather unlikely business for a church is the Newton Asphalt Co. of Alexandria, Virginia, owned by the Roman Catholic archdiocese of Austin, Texas. When the archdiocese used its ample surplus to purchase the business and then leased it back to the owners, it was only one more investment added to many others owned by the same entity. When reporters assumed that some religious use was intended for the property, Father Eugene Walsh explained: "I would think it is a simple matter of investment. No new Catholic facility is planned. . . ."

Cemetery operations seem more appropriate for a church. At any rate, this business has proved highly lucrative for at least one Washington corporation,—St. Paul's Episcopal. While other churches have also entered this field, St. Paul's Rock Creek Park and Ft. Lincoln—both in the District of Columbia—and Mount Comfort in Alexandria, Virginia, have all been extremely successful. Rock Creek Park is owned and managed directly by St. Paul's; the other two by the Capital Cemetery Corporation, which is owned by the Church.

Directly opposite to our national capital and just across the street from the Supreme Court building, at 100 Maryland Ave., N.E., stands a handsome apartment house owned by the Methodist Church. Some of the space is used as a denominational headquarters, but most is rental space, including a restaurant. Title to the project is held by the Methodist Board of Social Concerns, which also owns highly valuable acreage in the neighborhood of Methodist-owned American University.

There are also at least half a dozen church-owned retirement homes in the capital which have qualified as charities and have, consequently, been relieved of property taxation.

The preceding is by no means an exhaustive survey of commercial property owned or developed by church corporations. There is no definite way of discovering the full extent of these holdings, for a great deal of real estate may be titled to church-owned corporations, the names of which offer no clue as to their true ownership or control. Furthermore, leasebacks often cause no alteration in the taxpayer of record, since former owners continue to pay the ad valorem tax.

We know that tax-exempt, religiously owned property in the District was assessed in 1968 at $313,610,319 and was probably worth at least $650,000,000. We believe that the commercial investments of churches in the same area on which local taxes are paid but the revenue from which is immune to disclosure or income taxation, may already be considerably greater. If this is true, we are forced to the conclusion that church property in the District of Columbia is now approaching the fantastic total of $1.5 billion.

THE AMAZING MORMON COMPLEX

Another convenient way of viewing the wealth of the churches is to examine that of a single denomination in some detail. For this purpose we single out the 2.5 million-member Church of Jesus Christ of Latter-Day Saints (Mormon). This denomination, by refusing to provide any financial information whatever, constituted itself a challenge.

Many facets concerning Mormon assets are easily verified. The skyscraper office building to be erected by this Church in New York City has already been noted. Other holdings include the Deseret Publishing Co.; the Orlando Livestock Corporation with over 300,000 acres of cattle land in Georgia and Florida; a number of hotels, including the Hotel Utah and a large motel belonging to the same corporation in Salt Lake City; poultry and dairy farms; a large chain of radio and TV stations, including KSL in Salt Lake City; and 135 welfare farms in Utah and Idaho alone. The Church also owns many industrial buildings, the Utah-Idaho Sugar Company, the leading Salt Lake City department store, insurance and publishing enterprises, and Laje Village, a fashionable tourist resort in Honolulu. In 1960, the Mormons sold Zion's First National Bank of Salt Lake City to a local business group for $9,819,314.[10] In 1967, Zion Securities, a wholly owned subsidiary of the Church, was granted commercial zoning for a three and one-half acre shopping center in Honolulu.[11]

Although the elected State officials would not divulge the slightest information concerning Mormon exempt property in Utah, sometimes officials of the Church itself prove more communicative. According to Harold B. Lee, one of the Twelve Apostles, the Church owns 650 farms, 30 canneries, a soap factory, a coal mine, a flour mill, a rug and clothing plant, and five salvage processing plants.[12] It would indeed be interesting to know how many of the farms are classified as "welfare" institutions and what taxes any of them pay, if indeed, any of them pay anything at all.

The Mormon Church has been offered $100 million for a site comprising 260,000 acres which it owns in Florida, where Governor Kirk hailed the transaction as possibly the largest single sale in land consummated between private interests in American history.[13]

The huge Deseret Farms project was put together by Mormon officials in the early Fifties. The area is strategically located between Cape Kennedy and the rapidly developing Disney World, and has therefore appreciated spectacularly during the past decade. The announcement of the sale was accompanied by the usual and oft-reiterated assertion that the Church of Jesus Christ of Latter Day Saints pays full taxation on its profits from "unrelated" business.

While the Mormon Church steadfastly refuses to disclose its holdings or its income, it is without doubt exceedingly wealthy. It may well be the richest per capita in the United States. Several years ago, J. Bracken Lee, a former governor of Utah and now mayor of Salt Lake City, declared that the income of the Church was $1 million a day.* It would undoubtedly be much greater now. On Jan. 11, 1962, the New York *Times* quoted a Mormon official as saying that the Church was erecting $50 million worth of buildings each year and completing a new chapel every working day. The Church has 185 institutes and 2,000 seminaries, which operate adjacent to colleges and high schools for the purpose of providing denominational instruction during released time.

It is true that Mormons set an example for the nation in thrift and industry. Their large Brigham Young University at Provo, Utah, proclaims that it has never accepted a dollar of federal subsidy. The Mormons have, however, found other ways of using public funds. For example, Dixie College at St. George, Utah, is technically a public institution owned by the State; yet the Mormons have, in effect, transformed it into a sectarian facility. A letter sent to all Mormon Seminaries reads:

"We of Dixie College faculty and staff (which are 100% LDS) think that the environment of the Dixie Campus and the associations

---

* On a recent visit to Salt Lake City, one of the present writers interviewed the Mayor, who confirmed that he had indeed made this statement to a newspaper reporter.

204

your young people would have with the Dixie students (90% of which are LDS) would be excellent.

"Dixie College was originally founded by the Church in 1913. It was operated by the Church until 1933 when they turned it over to the State of Utah. Its church influence, however, has been retained and the LDS Institute, therefore, receives enthusiastic support from the faculty."

The letter is signed by Max B. Welcker, Administrative Assistant. It is worth noting that a completely new and excellent plant has been built with State and federal funds. The institution now enrolls about 1,000 students.

Despite all half-hearted denials and evasions, the impression persists that the Church still owns a large or controlling interest in the Union Pacific (once known as Brigham Young's Railway) and that a number of its directors are Mormons. Various knowledgeable persons in Salt Lake City declared to one of the present writers that there is always a Church Apostle on the Board.

Certainly, many members of the Church believe this to be true. As we have seen, its officials refuse categorically to deny such ownership, and there is certainly ample reason to believe that it does in fact exist, or has, at least, existed in the past.

In a vigorous dissent from a F.C.C. ruling which renewed the license of Salt Lake City's KSL, owned by the Mormon Church, the Washington *Post*,[14] quoted Nicolas Johnson as saying that this church is a "media baron" with its ownership of TV-AM-FM stations in Idaho Falls and Seattle, and radio stations in Kansas City and New York City, and a $20 million investment in the Los Angeles *Times*. The Commissioner added that the Church has major investments in the sugar beet industry, department stores, hotels, a large insurance company, 600 farms, factories, salvage stores, and 40 mills. An inquiry at the F.C.C. disclosed that the Mormon Church owns the Bonneville International Corporation, which owns 98.2 per cent of KSL TV, AM and FM, Salt Lake City; 99 per cent of KIRO TV, AM and FM, Seattle. It also owns KMBZ AM and KMBR FM, Kansas City, Missouri; WRFM AM and WNYW FM, New York City; also 23.3 per cent of KID TV, AM and FM, Idaho Falls, Idaho; and 62 per cent of KBOI TV, AM and FM, Boise, Idaho.

No one except the top officials of the Mormon heirarchy knows the actual wealth and revenues of their church; but these must be reckoned in the billions, and much of this is in the form of commercial investments and unrelated business income.

The Mormon Church declares that its subsidiary corporations pay real and income taxes on all "unrelated" business property and income, and on any property not used specifically for church or church-related purposes. Such statements, however, would be much more convincing if they were accompanied by a complete and independently audited financial statement and report. The Mormon "welfare farms" are certainly exempt from real-estate taxation, for the Utah Tax Commission issued a ruling in 1966 which made them so officially. Attorney General Phil L. Hanson protested the ruling and urged a hearing before the Utah Supreme Court. Officials of the Utah State Tax Commission professed total ignorance when asked by our representative for an estimate concerning the number and the true value of the Mormon "welfare farms" in the state.*

How much credence may be attached to Mormon protestations that

---

* We should note that the troubles which plagued the Mormons from the very beginning were closely related to their economic and political policies and the church-state union which they advocated and practised. As the Saints were driven from Kirtland, Ohio, then from three different counties in Missouri, and finally from Nauvoo, Illinois, usually to the accompaniment of gun fire, every conflict could be traced directly to the ambition of the theocratic Church, which sought the political control, not only of its own people, but also of its non-Mormon neighbors. This created friction, which soon developed into fierce hostility and finally into open warfare. The claim of Church-leaders that they have been persecuted solely for their religious beliefs is controverted by the historic facts. For other sects and cults with even more bizarre doctrines and rituals were allowed to dwell in peace amidst conventional surroundings.

Even after the removal to the Great Salt Lake Basin, the same economic-theocratic prepossessions continued to cause friction and hostility. The Church was brought under partial control by the presence of United States army troops in 1867; but only after the federal government had summarily seized all Church property and was about to execute judgment upon it in 1890, did the Church abandon polygamy—and then only civilly, not theocratically. With this renunciation, Utah was admitted as a state to the Union.

Although Mormonism is vastly different and far more conventional they pay taxes on non-religious property or unrelated business income was recently revealed in Phoenix, Arizona. According to a news item in the Phoenix *Gazette*,[15] the Church bought 248 acres of prime land within the city limits in 1960, from which revenue has since been drawn as cultivated farmland. This acreage, now worth about $5 million, was obtained from the State at a cost of $1,550,000. Although a Church official is reported to have stated: "To my knowledge" this land "was never exempt, and it is not exempt now," the official records prove that not one nickel of taxes was paid on this enormous business investment in at least 8 years, and this in spite of the fact that such exemption is categorically forbidden under State law.

---

today than it was a century ago, it still retains its theocratic structure; its economic demands upon members are very heavy; it operates in complete financial secrecy; its churches are titled to its bishops, as with the Roman Catholics; it has grown into an economic colossus; it penetrates political life wherever possible; it maintains its hold upon its own youth by elaborate and expensive systems of indoctrination; and it retains its iron grip upon the political structure of Utah, and wherever else it can.

In Salt Lake City, other denominations have made some progress, although their holdings, by comparison, seem insignificant. However, in the smaller cities scattered about the State, other religious groups are virtually non-existent. In these lesser towns, the tourist finds a magnificent LDS church, but no other; he will find a public school, probably with an all-Mormon board. A careful questioner learns that non-Mormon businessmen get few customers and when any one applies for work, the first matter usually to be determined concerns the church-affiliation of the applicant.

The Mormons operate a tight community. They glory in the persecution of their forbears and the hardships of their pioneers. The Church is first, last, and always. And this theocratic entity is growing rapidly in wealth, influence, and political power. As for its young people, they worry very little over indefensible matters of doctrine and history: they are members of an organization that has vast financial resources and that can strike deadly blows at enemies.

In Salt Lake City it no longer seeks to destroy members who have become lukewarm or lethargic in the faith; it has declared a kind of truce. If left alone, the Church rarely attacks. But in Utah, an open critic would find it very difficult to survive in any normal occupation or employment. The church-state union is the most pervasive—even if subtly concealed—fact of life.

We have emphasized the curtain of secrecy behind which the Church of Jesus Christ of Latter-Day Saints operates; but now at last some light has begun to appear. In May, 1969, while on a radio call-in program on KSXX in Salt Lake City, one of the present writers learned from a local citizen that definite information existed concerning the extent and ownership of privately owned, exempt property in that area. We learned that Earl Baker, the county assessor, has gradually developed a file-index covering this. The information contained therein is neither complete nor current—in fact, the valuations shown are about 15 years old, probably stand at no more than half of parity, and do not yet include all parcels of exempt land.

We discovered, furthermore, that representative Rex Oberhansley had introduced a bill into the State legislature which would require the proper authorities in all cities and counties to list every item of exempt property, together with realistic valuations, on the tax-rolls. The bill was buried under an avalanche of negative Mormon votes.

In the office of the county assessor, Chief Deputy Don Stott permitted us to examine the file of exempt properties, which were listed on hundreds of cards, each of which carried a description of the real estate, the name of the owner of record, and the valuations for land and improvements.

A team of auditors cooperating with Oberhansley had previously analyzed this file and determined the amount of tax avoided, as follows:

PRIVATELY OWNED EXEMPT REAL ESTATE IN SALT LAKE COUNTY

Category by Ownership	Tax Avoided	Per Cent	Approximate Valuation	Probable Current Value	% of Religious
TOTAL	$3,330,481.95	100	$166,500,000	$333,000,000	
LDS CHURCH	2,921,495.13	87.7	146,000,000	292,000,000	93
Catholics	78,191.53	2.4	3,910,000	7,820,000	2.5
Protestants	143,581.36	4.3	7,190,000	14,360,000	4.5
Non-Sectarian Charities	187,223.93	5.6	9,400,000	18,720,000	
Religious	3,143,268.02	89.4	157,100,000	314,180,000	100

Since assessments are theoretically 20% of true value and the millage about 100, we multiply the amount of tax avoided by 50 to obtain the theoretical valuations. However, since these appraisals are probably no more than half of what we find on taxable property, we double these totals to compute replacement values.

The astounding facts which emerge are (1) that the LDS Church owns exempt property in Salt Lake County alone worth about $292 million; (2) that this constitutes 87.7% of the total of tax-free real estate; and (3) that this comprises no less than 93% of the religiously used wealth. And there can be no doubt that the various corporations and businesses owned outright by the Church have even more property on which local taxes are paid, but the revenues from which are immune to all taxation and disclosure. According to this computation, the LDS Church owns real estate in Salt Lake County worth at least $600 million. Since all real estate in the County is assessed at $739,306,536 and therefore worth about $3.6 billion, we find that the Church owns outright nearly 20% of all the real estate within its borders.

In the smaller communities and the countryside of Utah, we may be certain that the proportion of exempt property owned by the Church is even greater.

Nowhere else have we encountered anything comparable to what is here revealed. In Utah, the Latter-Day Saints constitute a virtually complete monopoly in the fields of religion and tax-exempt property. And we might add that the direct and indirect ownership and control by the Church over every kind of business and commercial investment is scarcely less extensive and monopolistic.

We note finally that the LDS Church has an enormous complex of tax-exempt canneries, storehouses, welfare farms, etc., which produce and distribute immense quantities of food and other merchandise. We know that only tithers in good standing can qualify for such "relief"; and if only the poor receive it, the Mormons must have the largest proportion of indigents ever known. Since this is simply incredible, we suddenly come to a possible understanding of the nature and purpose of the enormous "welfare project." Can it be that it is an elaborate method of conveying tax-free goods worth hundreds of millions of dollars to the loyal members of the Church, no matter what their economic status may be, so that they may be able to contribute more generously to their powerful hierarchy and the purposes of the Church? We can scarcely escape this conclusion; and we might add that we know of no comparable operation anywhere else in the world. It is indeed a marvel and a wonder to contemplate and to behold.

THE BUSINESS INCOME OF CHURCHES

The corporations, boards, agencies and local congregations of the churches place surplus funds in a variety of investments—bonds, mortgages, industrial securities, real estate, or leasebacks. The revenue thus accruing, known as "passive income," is not subject to taxation. The church may also acquire and operate any kind of commercial enterprise. This is sometimes called "active income" because the church actually owns and presumably controls the business; or it may be called "unrelated business" because it bears no relation to the religious concerns for which the church was established and received its generous tax-exemptions. Typically, such a business will pay real estate taxes, though occasionally, as in the case of many retirement homes, it may escape even this levy under the blanket of church immunity. The church is not subject to income tax on the profits from such business.

A fairly good estimate of the tax-exempt investments of some of the churches is possible. Many Protestant churches publish quite acceptable records which are made available upon request. One of the problems with these reports is that one can never be sure that they are complete, for many groups operate through a plethora of semi-autonomous boards and agencies. Each may publish its own reports without any general compilation by the denomination. These agencies may be in a dozen different locations and unless one knows the interior workings of the particular organization, the records are difficult to locate and compile.

The Roman Catholic community is even more difficult to assess. The blanket secrecy which has characterized the general denominational policy of the Church for centuries is accentuated by the fact that its subsidiary orders operate substantially as autonomous organitions. There is such a bewildering maze of Catholic activities and entities that there are probably very few Catholics who have any real comprehension of it. All of these groups balk at full disclosure.

COMMERCIAL INVESTMENTS

It is evident that the "unrelated business" of the churches is growing rapidly. Here, again, records are difficult to obtain. Much of this commercial activity is carried on by off-beat churches. One does not even know their names, much less their business activities. It takes a misstep, a chance accident, a disgruntled competitor, or some local controversy to bring the matter into view. Sometimes a business is purchased and leased back by a local congregation or an association of local churches with some attendant publicity.

Many of the older and well established churches rely heavily on unrelated business, or revenues from securities. For example, the All Souls Unitarian Church of New York City, which has a budget of $227,000, obtains an income exceeding $80,000 from its portfolio-endowment of $2 million. As these investments grow through additional gifts and bequests and the increased value of securities, the church becomes less and less dependent upon the voluntary contributions of its parishioners.

Following are the assets of a few of the Protestant and miscellaneous bodies operating in the United States. These figures reflect only the church investments in stocks, bonds, and commercial real estate, and do not include any exempt or religiously used property.

American Baptist Extension Corporation	$ 7,868,788
American Baptist Pension Reserve	73,696,865
Southern Baptist Annuity Board	169,359,234
Southern Baptist Foundation	9,121,101
Baptist State Convention Foundations	96,476,021
Protestant Episcopal Church	86,766,111
Disciples of Christ	40,400,000
Lutheran Church of America	135,714,969
American Lutheran Church	33,048,639
Methodist Board of Pensions (General)	22,432,217 [a]
Methodist Board of Pensions (Permanent)	81,215,796
Meth. Bd. of Missions (Includes Women's Div.)	93,947,374
Methodist Investment Fund	23,347,716
Presbyterian Church in the United States	6,985,176
Meth. Bd. of Christian Social Concerns (Est.)	10,000,000
Reorganized Church of Jesus Christ of LDS	11,360,183
Unitarian-Universalist Association	26,467,705
United Church of Christ (Estimated)	175,000,000
United Presbyterian Church, U.S.A.	140,931,986
American Bible Society	85,449,384
TOTAL	$1,329,589,265

[a] Does not reflect merger with Evangelical United Brethren Church.

These statistics are admittedly fragmentary. There are, without doubt, numerous agencies and boards in all these denominations which do not appear here. Also, we have here only a partial accounting for no more than 12 bodies out of some 232. While those listed include some of the larger groups, it is reasonable to assume that a total tabulation would multiply the $1.3 billion by several times. The *Wall Street Journal*, observing that the stock investments of the United Church of Christ were $175 million, projected some interesting conclusions.[16] Extrapolating on this base, the writer made the following computation: since the United Church of Christ has 2 million members of median financial status with an average portfolio of $90, all American churches (if their assets of this kind are comparable) would have stock and bond holdings totalling $11 billion.

Actually, since thousands of individual churches have their own independent portfolios and since some of them have grown into financial colossi, we believe that a comprehensive total would exceed $20 billion in such investments.

A close look at the resources of one major denomination—the United Methodist—is provided by Roger Burgess, secretary of its Board of Health and Welfare Ministers. He declared [17] that Methodist agencies employ 50,000 persons, have an annual operating budget of $400 million, and disburse $1 billion for all purposes.

Interdenominational agencies sometimes invest in securities also. Perhaps the wealthiest of these is the American Bible Society, which receives support from most major Protestant denominations. This organization has built up substantial reserves and has an impressive portfolio exceeding $85 million. Since the organization is structurally related to churches, the Society encounters no problem in securing religious tax-exemption.

The extent of stock-holding by churches received dramatic demonstration in 1967 when Eastman Kodak became involved in a labor dispute. The churches intervened with something more than pious protestations; for it developed that they were substantial investors as they began to withhold their proxies from management. The following were some of the church-holdings noted: United Presbyterian Church, U.S.A., 3,628 shares; Reformed Church in America, 2,000; the Protestant Episcopal, 5,000; the United Church of Christ, 11,000; the United Methodist Church, 10,500; and others in lesser amounts. The holdings of the churches listed above therefore totalled $2.7 million in this one corporation. The First National City Bank of

New York lost a $10 million Methodist account when it persisted in doing business with the government in South Africa, contrary to the wishes of the Church's Board of Missions.[18]

How some churches invest their funds is illustrated by an operation of the Lutheran Church of America. In 1967, the body invested $1 million with the Kissell Development Company, an investment guaranteed by mortgages.[19]

An interesting sidelight on the extent of church activity in the stock market may be observed in the *Research Report* of the New York Stock Exchange,[20] which indicates that its member brokers make $50 million in annual commissions handling transactions for non-profit groups, including churches, college endowments, and foundations. Assuming that such organizations keep 50 to 60 per cent of their assets in securities and projecting a growth of about 8 per cent a year, the *Report* projects a portfolio for these groups of $57 billion in 1975.

THE CHURCH PUBLISHING ENTERPRISE

Protestants operate vast publishing interests. Some of the giants are the Methodist Publishing House (Abingdon Press), which does a business of $40 million annually; the Baptist Sunday School Board, with its Broadman Press; the Westminster Press (Presbyterian); the Augsburg Publishing House (Lutheran); the Beacon Press (Unitarian-Universalist); the Concordia (Lutheran). Every such entity comes under the umbrella of total federal income-tax exemption; usually, their large plants are immune also to local property taxation. We have already seen how the Augsburg people won their case in the courts for exemption on the ground that their primary aim was to serve the purpose of the Church, rather than earn their generous profits.

THE BUSINESS OF COMMERCIAL REAL ESTATE

The "unrelated business" of churches spreads over the entire spectrum of commercial enterprises. Sometimes related and unrelated business may be combined in the same operation. When the Mormon Church built its skyscraper complex at W. 58th Street near 5th Avenue in New York City, Gerald G. Smith, president of the Eastern States Mission, reported that "any part of the building that is not specifically church will be taxed." [21] The complex includes a chapel,

213

an auditorium, administrative and missionary offices, an information bureau and library—all of which would presumably be immune to taxation.

Wesley Methodist Church of Minneapolis, First Methodist Church of Chicago, and the Philadelphia Methodist Conference all own substantial office buildings in these cities. The church pays real estate taxes only on those parts of the facilities which are in secular use, but none on income derived from the rentals.

There are probably hundreds of elaborate office buildings in the United States owned by churches.

A mere listing of denominational assets by no means indicates the extent of tax-exempt church wealth in this country. Many individual congregations are wealthy in business and commerce in their own right and this wealth is not usually reflected in the denominational statistics. For example, Trinity Episcopal Church located on Wall Street in New York has commercial assets of more than $50 million. Trinity owns 18 major business buildings in the city. It owns 74 Trinity Place where church offices fill seven of the 25 floors. It owns the 17-story Standard and Poor's Building. Its commercial real estate holdings are assessed at $32 million but are, of course, worth much more. Trinity pays real estate taxes on its commercial properties, but not on any portion engaged in church activity. Land in the Trinity area sells for $400 a square foot. Trinity Church and the graveyard (98,000 square feet) are valued at $40 million.[22]

Another entity in the Croesus class is Christ Episcopal Church of Cleveland which has erected a $676,000 medical building, which carries a mortgage covering 75 per cent of the cost. The parish has declared that it will pay federal income taxes on the rental income proportionate to the mortgage-balance. Thus, at the start, payments would be on 75 per cent of the net income, but would decline to zero with the liquidation of the encumbrance. Christ Church also owns the Shaker Savings Association building on Farnsleigh Road in Cleveland.

St. Paul's Episcopal Church in Richmond, Virginia, operates a 200-car commercial parking garage; the profits run about $2,700 a month, on which no federal income tax is due.

The Muskingum Presbytery of Ohio purchased the multi-million dollar Superlite Block Company of Phoenix, Arizona, in 1964, and sold it a short time later.

The Friends Select School, founded in 1689, owns a square block

214

of highly valuable real estate in Philadelphia. The Friends have built a modest two-story building for their school and now project a 20-story office complex which will cost $20 million. The tax-free rentals from the facility are intended to pay the operating costs of the school.

In 1968, a palatial office-motel-apartment project was announced in Pittsburgh, which, according to the press releases, would become the city's convention center.[23] One of the principal promoters was said to be a "national religious group," included for no other apparent purpose than to spread over the facility the warm blanket of church tax-exemption.

SUMMER CAMPS

Churches carry on active programs geared to the summer vacation period. This leads them to acquire spacious tax-exempt sites in rural areas. These camps may be used for both related and unrelated business. In a popular vacation state such as Colorado, such holdings affect adversely the entire tax-base. La Foret, a 500-acre camp near Colorado Springs, belongs to the United Church of Christ. Then there is the Jewish Community Center, the 160-acre J-B-Double-C Ranch near Ebert. The Episcopal Church owns and operates the spacious Evergreen Conference Grounds. The Roman Catholic diocese has Camp St. Malo near Allens Park; it has also similar facilities known as Santa Maria, the Camp of Catholic Charities, Our Lady of the Rockies, and a camp owned by the Catholic Daughters of America. There is also the El Pornar, a luxurious retreat for women operated by the Sisters of Charity, and the Sacred Retreat House for Men, near Sedalia, operated by the Jesuits.

The United Presbyterian Church has its 20,000-acre Ghost Ranch, which lies outside Colorado's borders near Santa Fe, N.M., and which is open the year round. The Boulder Presbytery has its own 123-acre camp in the University Peaks area and a second camp near Bailey.

The Methodist Church entered the camping and recreation business early, with handsome sites at Pine Crest, near Palmer Lake; at Beaver Creek in the Arkansas Valley, at Camp San Isabel, near Rye; and at the Grand Mesa Camp, where Methodists and Baptists share facilities. Methodists, in addition, own the Diamond Ranch near Chugwater and the Circle J. Ranch near Ten Sleep, both in Wyoming.

The American Baptists have their own camp in the Black Forest; and two individual Baptist congregations—Calvary and First Baptist

—share Foss Camp at Indian Hills. The Lutheran Valley Ranch, an 880-acre facility near Florrisant, Colorado, is owned by the Missouri Synod. Near Canyon City in the Sangre de Cristos, the American Lutheran Church owns Hillsdale Camp, which embraces more than two dozen buildings.

Wyoming and New Mexico, therefore, as well as Colorado, feel the impact of religious exemptions!

THE LEASE-BACK OPERATION

Irresistibly lured by the financial increment which inheres in tax-advantage, churchmen are being drawn progressively into commercial ventures. The usual *modus vivendi* is to acquire title to the business by purchase, which is effected with borrowed money or a very small down payment. The important matter is to accomplish change of ownership on almost any terms. Then the business is leased back to the original owners for their continuous operation. In effect, the church pays off with funds not paid in taxes. The new ownership in no way alters the operation of the business; it simply relieves the owner and the operator of heavy tax-burdens.

Some years ago, *Christianity Today* explained how this kind of operation can work: "Suppose a church buys a one million dollar business that, in view of tax exemptions, shows an annual profit of $120,000. It can borrow $800,000 to purchase the business at the preferred loan rate of four per cent, or $32,000.[*] Hence, on an investment of $200,000, the church will net $88,000 or 44 per cent.

"Suppose, however, that the net were only 25 per cent. Even an investment of 25 per cent doubles in less than three years, quadruples in six, and in 30 years will mutiply itself one thousand times. Starting with a million dollars and encouraged by the present tax exemptions for religious bodies engaged in unrelated business activities, any church by this procedure could own America in 60 years!"[24]

The only thing that has protected this country so far from such a catastrophe is the fact that churches have not, as yet, fully exploited the possibilities. Now, however, as they are acquiring the requisite techniques, commercial enterprises among churches are becoming commonplace. Although totals are unavailable, we can offer some computations concerning the nature and scope of such activity.

---

[*] A higher rate of interest, of course, would now prevail, but the advantage of a church over taxpaying competitors might now be even greater.

The potentialities envisaged by *Christianity Today* are more than mere speculation. In 1954, the First Baptist, Second Presbyterian, and First Christian Church of Bloomington, Illinois, purchased the Biltmore Hotel of Dayton, Ohio, for $3.5 million. They leased it back to the original operators for $250,000 a year, who, of course, assumed all maintenance and operating costs. The churches received a net annual income, without any effort on their part, over and above a large increase in equity. In 1963, the churches sold the property back to the original owners for a tax-free capital gain exceeding $1 million.

The South Georgia Conference of the Methodist Church received as a donation the Ware Hotel of Waycross, Ga., valued at $350,000. The church will operate the hotel through the previous management, with certain floors reserved for retirees. The Peachtree Hotel of Atlanta, Ga., has been donated to the Georgia Baptist Convention and will also be operated as a retirement home. Both operations will be exempt from the local real estate tax and from income-tax levies.

The Southern Baptist Convention owns one of the largest textile mills in the nation—Burlington Mills in North Carolina. This is arranged on the basis of a leaseback deal under which the church will complete payments and own the facility outright in 20 years. Then it can make a tax-free sale at an appreciated figure and pyramid its profits. The Convention owns properties which are leased back to such well-known concerns as Bemis Bags, the Borden Company, Dunlop, Firestone, Fruehauf, Hutrig, Rath, Mack Trucks, and others.

EXAMPLES OF UNRELATED PROTESTANT BUSINESS

Although comprehensive information in this field is unavailable, we can cite numerous specific instances. The Southern Baptist Convention owns and operates a $600,000 radio and TV center at Fort Worth, Texas. The Baptist Commission serves 1,400 TV and radio stations weekly and employs a staff of 70.

The Loma Linda Food Co., whose products are found in thousands of stores, is a tax-exempt business owned by the Seventh-Day Adventist Church. It has plants in California, Oshawa, Ontario, and in Mt. Vernon, Ohio, and has sales offices in all principal American cities.

San Pasquel Academy of San Diego, Calif., a Seventh-Day Adventist School, owns and operates the Golden Rule Bindery, whose slogan is "Bound to Wear." It can easily underbid taxpaying competitors; and was therefore denounced by the Printing Industries Association of San Diego "on evidence that the tax-exempt status of the religious institution operating a bindery gave it a competitive advantage." The Association complained also that "the Golden Rule Bindery operates with student help at pay levels based on the Federal Minimum Wage Law." Said F. W. Whitney, general manager of the Association: "We vigorously oppose any public support of such specially privileged industrial activity." [25]

The Evangelical Brethren United Church (recently merged with the Methodist) has developed a lucrative business in the printing and sale of trading stamps. Its large Otterbein Press in Dayton, Ohio, has engaged in this for years and has turned the large tax-free profits over to the Church.[a]

The Temple Baptist Church of Los Angeles owns a downtown office building and the Philharmonic Auditorium. Old North Church (Episcopal) of Boston derives much of its income from sales of pewter, old-fashioned stick candy, lanterns and antiques—all manufactured in a shop on the premises.

The International Church of the Four-Square Gospel in Los Angeles, also active in the communications field, owns and operates two radio stations valued at more than $3 million.

The Amana Church Society, which has only 754 members, owns 25,000 acres of choice farm land in Iowa and operates an extensive business in the processing and sale of food stuffs. It also does an immense business in the manufacture of electrical appliances, notably refrigerators and related equipment, estimated at several million dollars annually.

MORE ABOUT PROTESTANT CHURCHES

The interdenominational National Council of Churches, with headquarters on Riverside Drive, New York, operates from a $20-million skyscraper, its valuable site being a gift from John D. Rockefeller, Jr.

---

[a] Evidently, however, the Internal Revenue Service discovered some flaw in the Church-affiliation of the Otterbein Press, for in Jan., 1969, it announced revocation of that organization's income tax exemption and moved to collect not only the tax due for 1968 but, presented a cumulative bill going back to 1958. Tax payments for the period would run considerably more than $2 million. The Church has appealed the case.

Trailing the National Council, but by no means to be disdained, is the International Council of Christian Churches founded by Dr. Carl McIntire. This group has substantial real estate holdings in Cape May, N.J. The I.C.C.C. owns the two largest hotels in the community as well as a complex of beachside houses. In all, it owns property in the area assessed at $1,500,000. The group operates a four-year college in Cape May and a seminary at Elkins Park, Penna. Also, it owns at least one radio station (the McIntire broadcasts are heard on 635 stations) and a weekly publication, *The Christian Beacon,* with a circulation of 120,000. Contributions roll in at the rate of $3 million a year.

How a church can take advantage of the religious exemption was illustrated by a deal involving the Mt. Olivet Methodist Church of Arlington, Virginia. A prominent realtor, Joe Brown, announced a gift to the church of $126,000. He could deduct this sum for tax-purposes through the carryover during a 6-year period. The gift represented the value of an apartment house donated to Mt. Olivet Church, which thereupon sold the asset. Now, had Brown himself completed the sale, there would have been a 25 per cent capital gains tax. The Church, however, being exempt, did not have to pay this and was, thus, thousands of dollars to the good while the government was poorer to the same extent.

OIL AS A RELIGIOUS LUBRICANT

One of the present writers, during a conference with the Honorable Wilbur Mills, was told the following story by the Chairman of the House Ways and Means Committee. A colored Protestant church in Arkansas owned some land on which oil was discovered. As the generous royalties flowed in, the members, instead of paying to support the church, began receiving large checks. Suddenly, hundreds of persons saw the light of the Gospel, were converted, and sought to join the church. The board of trustees thereupon met in emergency session and closed the membership rolls. After all, the oil should not be spread too thin!

CATHEDRAL OF TOMORROW

The Cathedral of Tomorrow in Akron, Ohio, has acquired an impressive array of unrelated commercial businesses, including a shopping center and a 13-story apartment house in Akron, the Nassau Plastics and Wire Co. of Brooklyn, the Unity Electronics Co. of Elizabeth, N.J., and the Real Form Girdle Co. of Brooklyn. When questioned about the extensive commercial ventures owned by this church, the pastor, Reverend Tex Humbard, pointed out that in at least one case his organization had "outbid" the Catholic Church. "If the Catholics, the Baptists, and the Episcopalians weren't doing it—we would not do it," he declared. He added that "the Internal Revenue Service has checked and everything is in order." [26]

THE STRATFORD RETREAT HOUSE

Another entity that has done well in tax-exempt business is the Stratford Retreat House of White Plains, N.Y., which proclaims itself a "nonprofit, religious organization (interdenominational-Protestant) exempt from income taxes on its unrelated business income from Section 511 of the Internal Revenue Code." In order to finance its religious program, Stratford Retreat House has acquired four going businesses, to wit, the U.S. Distributors, Inc., Shelby, N.C.; the J.F.D. Electronics Corp., Brooklyn, N.Y.; Pierside Repairs, Inc., Brooklyn, N.Y.; and the inventory together with some machinery of the Brach Mfg. Division of General Bronze Corp., Woodbury, N.Y., with a plant located at Sayreville, N.J.

The first two corporations were acquired under agreements whereby the purchase price was fully covered by a combination of short- and long-term notes given to the sellers. The installment payments on these, which are being met out of current profits, are thus transformed from earned income into capital gains. In both instances, the acquired businesses have shown good operating results and the former managements have been retained.

The other companies were also acquired through purely paper transactions in which the Church pays for the business out of current profits, thus lending its tax-immunity to the managers by transforming high-taxed earned income into low-taxed capital gains. One evaluation presents the following summary: "As assets, Stratford House has three operating divisions . . . The company is owing the major portion of the purchase price of all three represented by notes given to the former owners. However, under the purchase agreements, each division thus has been left with sufficient working capital so that it is able to operate independently and pay its bills within terms. Management states that each division has operated profitably to date.

Dr. John Grew Taylor, pastor of the Retreat House, has actively promoted his objective of acquiring businesses and paying for them out of the amounts saved in taxes. In a letter dated Aug. 22, 1964, he announced it as his purpose "to acquire . . . in 15 years a concern for which the purchase price is $5 million and also a hotel in Boston for something over $1 million. These operations are done with no cash being required on the part of the Retreat House . . . . a church corporation under New York State law."

In a memorandum accompanying his letter of Aug. 22, 1964, Dr. Taylor waxes jubilant:

"What is the effect of the transaction? The church has loaned its tax umbrella to the seller. The seller has more than doubled the normal sales price. He has retained his lucrative salaried managerial position and, in effect, control of the business. The owner has walked off with a capital gain on the whole deal. Here's how: the owner draws a salary and runs the business just as he did before, but he also gets at least 70 per cent of the earnings for 10–15 years. More important, he is not drawing the money as dividends, taxable as ordinary income, but as installments of the purchase price on capital gains."

Wonderful and fearful are the devious means by which all, except the government and the taxpayers, are enriched. Dr. Taylor has made certain that he really has a church, qualifying as such under Section 511 of the Code. Therefore he explains in his memorandum that "the Retreat House is a church corporation with full sacerdotal functions, including the right to ordain to the ministry . . . under the law of New York State, and is composed of clergy and laymen of various Protestant denominations . . . . who conduct spiritual retreats, hold religious services, etc., interdenominational and ecumenical."

Then Dr. Taylor adds this clincher to his dithyramb: "The Retreat House itself puts no cash in any purchase and therefore there is no limit to the number of transactions it may enter. The church offers only its tax shelter . . . . a considerable item, for it will double the company's profits by eliminating its corporation taxes . . . . this feature, fully recognized by Congress in 1954 . . . has been operating since. (The Catholic Church a few weeks ago put together a group of nursing homes in Boston under the 511 plan.)"

The potential of this kind of operation is demonstrated by the recent sale of one of the Stratford enterprises, J-F-D Electronics Corporation, to Riker Video for a reported price of $2 million.

CHURCH RETIREMENT HOMES

Homes for the elderly are especially lucrative to religious groups. As already noted, church homes in this category are frequently exempt from real estate taxation through classification as a church. As recognized charities, they are also exempt from all income taxes. This explains why churches since 1956 have handled 75 per cent of the retirement facilities now being built under the auspices of the F.H.A. and 51 per cent of similar facilities being financed by the Community Facilities Association, a fact reported by the *Wall Street Journal* early in 1966. It should be pointed out, incidentally, that these agencies provide construction funds at much less than the government must pay to provide them through the sale of bonds.

Very few of these church-operated homes for the elderly—already a multi-billion-dollar business—are in any sense charitable enterprises. The church rarely invests any of its own money, since such projects are financed entirely with low-interest federal funds.

Some of them require tax-deductible entry fees up to $45,000 or more and up to $400 a month for service charges. No tax-paying enterprise can possibly compete against such odds. And it should be noted that these enormous entry fees are possible because the payments are tax-deductible as donations to a church-charity.

Although the revenues of these enterprises may not be diverted for personal profit, they can be used for additional appointments or luxuries in the projects or invested in expansion or new facilities. Such income may also be used for the support of the church itself and its various programs, including large salaries for clerics, who, in turn, can avoid all income taxation under Section 107 of the Internal Revenue Code.

Conversion of the New Washington Hotel of Seattle into a Roman Catholic retirement home, the Josephinium, cost King County $18,000 a year in taxes, according to Joe M. Burke, president of the Associated Clubs of the North End.[27] Burke stated that tax-exemption for retirement homes results in a $700,000 annual loss in revenue to the State of Washington. Only 2 per cent of the homes serve the needy, he said, and most are church-related. Burke contended that not only retirement homes but also all property leased to the government as well as public facilities should be taxed.

There are still other advantages available to churches in the housing business. In a Richmond, Va., $900,000-apartment complex with 80 units, something new has been added. Not only will the FHA insure the low-interest mortgage, *it will also pay up to 75 per cent of the rent.* When the project is completed, it will be sold to the Ebenezer Baptist Church.

In West Palm Beach, Florida, the Carmelite Sisters of the Roman Catholic Church operate the 250-room Pennsylvania Hotel. Although this competes with other hotels catering to permanent guests, it has been tax-exempt. The religious order purchased the hotel for $800,000 in 1964 and converted it into a nonprofit retirement home. Free of tax, the hotel was able to operate at a generous profit.

In 1964, the Austin, Texas, diocese of the Catholic Church acquired a chain of 22 Massachusetts nursing homes, ten of them in Boston, for $4.7 million. There was no public mention of the amount of the down payment. The properties were immediately leased back to the original owner, Geriatrics Management, Inc., of Milton, Mass. The change in ownership brought the homes under the umbrella of church-exemption, which enables them to return a much increased profit.

In Hagerstown, Maryland, Rev. James Robinson of the Ebenezer African Methodist Episcopal Church, was engaged in a federal housing program for 75 to 100 low-income families. For the housing, Robinson asked tax-exemption—which the city refused—whereupon he went to the Maryland legislature and secured passage of a bill empowering the city of Hagerstown to grant the immunity he demanded. The Hagerstown *Mail* reported that the properties will not be assessed for regular property rates, and described an additional advantage enjoyed by Rev. Robinson and his congregation; they would not have to abide by the federal guidelines which provide that resident families with excessive income must vacate in favor of those with lower incomes.

Across the continent in San Diego, California, St. Paul's Episcopal Church has broken ground for a federally financed $1.2 million 11-story addition to St. Paul's Manor, a retirement home. The First Congregational Church, also of San Diego, plans to raze its present sanctuary and replace it with a 20-story apartment building that would have a church school, offices, and a chapel on the ground floor

223

and the church sanctuary on the rooftop. Federal financing—of course.

The Roman Catholic archdiocese of Denver is the sponsor of a $3.5 million 300-unit apartment building which will be financed with federal funds and also draw rent supplements from the government.

Pittsburgh may hold the record for church housing projects. It has East Liberty Gardens, sponsored by the opulent East Liberty Presbyterian Church, East Liberty Lutheran Church, and Eastminster Presbyterian Church. The 136-unit townhouse development will be built on a five-acre site in a renewal area and will also include 160 homes in an adjacent area that are to be rehabilitated. The churches will obtain a 3 per cent federal loan for the project. Holy Cross Episcopal Church will manage the Homewood rehabilitation center, also under the federal rent-supplement program. The Episcopal Diocese of Pittsburgh has proposed a 203-unit apartment house for the elderly in the Lawrenceville area, while an 87-unit moderate-income development is sponsored by the American Jewish Congress and a 156-unit apartment for the elderly by the St. Francis Roman Catholic order. The Alleghany Baptist Union and the Pittsburgh Baptist Union have combined in a low-to-moderate income-housing project which will be federally financed. A possible 100 to 150 units have been proposed by the Bethel African Methodist Episcopal Church for the Hill District. An Interfaith Church Council, financed by a $250,000 foundation grant, has been formed, including Protestants and Catholics, to investigate further housing possibilities.

The Alabama-West Florida Conference of the United Methodist Church is planning a 200-unit federally underwritten apartment for the aged to cost $3 million. In Tampa, Florida, Pennsylvania Village has vaulted its owner-church into high finance with a $1.5 million housing complex of 148 units. The sponsor is the United Presbyterian Church, U.S.A.; the financing angel is the federal government.

In Worcester, Mass., the Episcopal Housing Corporation has undertaken a $1.5 million housing project for the elderly. It is to be built with federal funds in conjunction with the U.S. Department of Housing and Urban Renewal. In Toledo, Ohio, the Roman Catholic diocese has launched a $2.5 million housing development to be built entirely with federal funds on the basis of a 40-year mortgage. A $200,000 annual rent-subsidy will guarantee the rents. In Brownsville, Texas, the Roman Catholic diocese will sponsor a $2 million, 200-unit housing project to be financed with federal funds. A diocesan spokesman declared: "It must be emphasized that the diocese . . . is involved only to the extent of sponsorship for the projects, contracting an agency for collecting the rents and selecting the tenants." Rent-subsidies by the government will make up any difference between the tenant's payment and the estimated average monthly cost of $135.

The Beatitudes, a gigantic retirement home in Phoenix, Arizona, is sponsored by the United Church of Christ. It contains 500 units and represents an investment of about $5 million. It was financed by private capital but the entire mortgage has been guaranteed by the federal government. It pays local taxes, but is exempt from income taxation. Once the mortgage is retired, the sponsoring church, known as the Church of the Beatitudes, should be able to operate its entire program opulently from the income of this project.

CLOSEUP OF A CHURCH HOUSING PROJECT

Episcopal Retirement Homes, Inc., of California, offers a splendid example of the church engaged in business. This operation has two substantial projects in retirement housing; St. Paul's Towers and Canterbury Woods, the former being the second highest building in Oakland's East Bay. It has 286 apartments with rentals ranging from $200 to $365 monthly. Even this, however, is not rent, but represents only a service charge, since the tenant pays an entry fee which ranges from $12,500 to $47,000. Yet nothing has been purchased except a life-tenancy, which expires with the occupant, whose interest reverts to Episcopal Homes, which can then resell it. It would seem that with a single turnover, the corporation will easily recover the entire original cost of $11 million and can then construct a new facility with the money.

The Rev. Darby Betts is not only the rector of St. Paul's Episcopal Church; he is also the president of Episcopal Retirement Homes. In addition to his salary from the Church, he enjoys a further emolument of $8,400 from the housing corporation. St. Paul's Church derives also a $25,000 annual income from the apartments in the form of office rental of two floors in its parish house. The commercial use does not disturb the tax-exemption of the parish house and the church. This is true because St. Paul's Towers is listed as a "welfare organization." The project advertises that a widow living alone may sell her private home "on which taxes must be paid" and come into

St. Paul's or Canterbury Woods, using the price for an entry fee, and then live in the church housing tax-exempt for the rest of her life.

Lester Kinsolving of the San Francisco *Chronicle* reports that the only fly in the ointment is a reservation expressed by the Alameda County Grand Jury which in December, 1967, issued a statement noting "extensive indignation about the unfairness of the exemption from property taxation granted to luxury care housing." [28] He also cited a report of the Alameda County Board of Supervisors to the effect that the assessed valuation of California retirement homes climbed from $25 to $42 million between 1964 and 1966.

St. Paul's Towers and Canterbury Woods have by no means exhausted the potential of retirement home construction for the Episcopal diocese of California. The same Mr. Kinsolving reported [29] that it now plans another high-rise to be erected on land owned by it and immediately adjacent to its Grace Cathedral on Nob Hill. The land was originally donated in order to protect it from "mere commercialization." The moving spirit behind this project is the same Rev. Darby W. Betts who envisioned the previous developments. The new facility is to be constructed over the present parking lot and diocesan headquarters.

These are but a few examples chosen virtually at random from thousands of projects which churches are operating in conjunction with the federal government. Since the latter supplies all the money at interest-rates far below the market and even guarantees the rentals, the church makes no actual contribution and runs no risk whatever. The profits are certainly very large, even excessive, particularly in the case of retirement homes for the well-to-do. Tax-exemption is crucial, since it confers a tremendous advantage over secular competitors in the field.

THE ROMAN CATHOLIC CHURCH

We reserve for special analysis the business and wealth of the Roman Catholic Church. The subject is extremely difficult, in part because of the complexity of the Church itself and even more because of the secrecy under which its financial activities are cloaked. It includes many different kinds of organizations, all of which have considerable tax-exempt wealth, property, and business.

We begin with the Vatican, that fabulously wealthy power with headquarters in a tiny 108-acre enclave in Italy. The Vatican's riches are relevant to this study only to the extent that it has investments in the United States or obtains revenues from communicants in this country. Its real estate developments are handled around the world by the Società Generale Immobiliare of Rome, in which it owns the controlling interest. Some vast Vatican projects in the United States have already been noted in this chapter.

Another example of shrewd Vatican investment is offered by the $25-million commercial and residential complex which it has proposed for Fisherman's Wharf in San Francisco, for which the Immobiliare is already on the job. It has plans for a 300-room hotel with 200 luxury apartments, offices and retail shops. The complex is to be called the Italian Center and is to house that country's Counsel General, and import Italian products of all kinds. Although this project will pay real estate levies, the income taxes are another matter. It is a well-known fact that the Vatican has steadfastly refused to pay any tax on its profits to the Italian government. Sec. 892 of the I.R.S. code exempts it from American taxation.

Although it is not strictly relevant to this study, one can scarcely refrain from noting the enormous revenues enjoyed by the Vatican, as a result of its penetration into almost every facet of Italian corporate business. *The Vatican Empire,*[30] by Nino Lo Bello, states that the Vatican is by far the largest owner of shares on the Italian bourse and that it owns one-third of all the real estate in Rome, as well as all the utilities and most of the apartment houses in the city.

PROFITS FROM THE PILL

This same intriguing author, himself a Roman Catholic, has unearthed additional and spicy information. In an article published in the Denver *Post,*[31] he reveals that the Vatican has controlling interest in one large pharmaceutical house and a partial interest and control in another, both of which are doing a multi-million-dollar business in the manufacture and sale of birth-control pills. These corporations are, first, the L'Istituto Farmocologico Serona with its central offices in Milan and its plant in the suburbs; the second is the Lepetit Company of the same city, which sells the pill under the brand name Enovit and is licensed by G. D. Searle of Chicago. Lo Bello reports that sales were tremendously stimulated by the Pope's Encyclical, *Humanae Vitae,* which brought the use of contraceptives dramatically to the attention of the Italian people.

227

THE DENVER POST

THE DENVER POST
14   Tues., March 18, 1969

Vatican Owner, Part Owner of 2 Firm. Making and Selling Birth Control Pill

By NINO LO BELLO

(Editor's Note: The writer is author of a new book published by Simon & Schuster, "The Vatican Empire," which deals with the financial operations of the Vatican.)

ROME—Pope Paul's encyclical condemning contraception has given rise to a birth-pill explosion right on the papal doorstep.

Awkward as this may be for Vatican officials, they will soon be riding on the horns of still another dilemma with the revelation that a Vatican-owned pharmaceutical house has been producing and is marketing oral birth control capsules.

L'Istituto Farmacologico Serona, which has its main offices in Milan and its plant a few miles outside the city, is a thriving drug company with a capitalization of $1.4 million. The Serona firm markets in all of Italy's major cities a pill called Luteolas, selling at 1,200 lire ($1.92) for a box of 20.

To add to the tsk-tsk, another major manufacturer of pharmaceuticals, the Lepetit Company of Milan, sells a similar product under the brand name of Enovit, under license from G. D. Searle of Chicago. The Vatican has a minority participation in Lepetit, which markets a packet of 20 pills at $4.64.

ALTOGETHER there are eight brands of birth-control capsules being offered today in Italy, a nation where 8 out of every 10 persons is a Roman Catholic.

In this country the 1968 in-

"BEING CATHOLIC, I WOULDN'T DREAM OF TAKING THE PILL FOR BIRTH CONTROL, BUT MY PRIEST SAYS IT'S GREAT FOR NERVOUS TENSION."

crease in the sales of contraceptive pills over the preceding year is 45.3 per cent— with the pharmaceutical industry already predicting that sales figures at the end of 1969 will break all records.

Though Italian law prohibits the selling of birth-control pills, the fact is that they are openly available in all drugstores—but only on doctor's prescription. This is possible because the boxes are not marked as "birth-control pills" but as a medicine to regulate the menstrual cycle. The packages state that the contents cannot be used to prevent pregnancies.

However confusing this fuzzy kind of double-talk may

be to some, most Italian doctors have no qualms about prescribing the use of these capsules — "to cure gynecological ailments."

WHAT makes the situation even a bit more farcical is that in most cases the cost of the pills is reimbursed by the state medical aid program.

"It's an Alice in Wonderland situation," explained the woman pharmacist at the corner of Viale Gorizia and Corso Trieste. "The Italian government finds itself paying for supplying birth-control pills which are prohibited under Italian law."

Long before Pope Paul's

pronouncement, Italian pharmacies had the bill on the shelves, but sales were tually nil. Ironically, it the papal decree that u tentionally provided the p with so much publicity tha massive dose of free adv tising (prohibited by Ita laws) gave a shot in the to the sales, which have s skyrocketed into a multin lion dollar business.

ALREADY the effect the birth rate in cer sections of Italy, especia in the industrialized Nort visible. In the Piedmont gion centering around T where sales of the pill been among the heavies the peninsula, even before publication of "Human Vitae," the birth rate h dipped to the lowest of sector or country in Euro

Since scripture neither demns nor commends c traception, many Italian olics prefer to make their decisions about it. In a event, they like to ref the current controversy "the bitter pill of Pope P

THE DENVER POS
Founded Oct. 28, 189
H.H.Tammen and F.G.E

*Dedicated in perpetu
the service of the p
that no good cause sha
a champion and tha
shall not thrive unop*

HELEN G. BONFI
President
PALMER HOYT,
Editor and Publis
DONALD R. SEAW
Secretary-Treasure

According to Lo Bello, druggists and even priests are now advising Italian women that, although the pill is sinful and illegal as a pregnancy-preventative, it may be taken "to reduce nervous tension." Directions on the package containing the drug state that it may be taken to regulate the menstrual cycle according to the "rhythm" method, which is approved by the Church. Now if some use the pill to prevent conception, that is, of course, unfortunate. This rationale does not really seem too convincing, but it does suffice to preserve this particular source of Vatican profit.

CATHOLIC WEALTH AND TAXATION

The Vatican is known to have extensive investments both in the United States and Canada, but no complete picture can be given because of the traditional secrecy characteristic of this organization. Immobiliare itself is reportedly the largest real estate cartel in the world with investments on four continents. Concerning the Vatican's tax-situation, certain facts have been established. Since Watergate Towne is not a church, real estate taxes are levied upon it. This is no problem, however, since the apartments were built not to be operated but to be sold. The profits from such sales are not subject to taxation. It was set forth in Seversmith vs. Machiz that in 1964 the Società Generale Immobiliare had already realized nearly $8 million in gross sales, all exempt from taxation.

At the home base in Italy, it is certain that no tax was paid. But that picture is apparently to be changed. Tax-exemption for the immensely wealthy Vatican has been a sore subject with succeeding Italian governments. In 1965, the Italian weekly *L'Espresso* published the information that the Vatican held about one-fifth of the shares of all companies listed on the Italian stock exchange and declared that the normal tax on this would total between $16 and $24 million. This large exemption has frequently been blamed for the sad plight of Rome's finances, particularly when added to the Vatican immunity from taxation on its income from utilities and apartment houses. The Vatican has consistently refused to pay any tax on its vast income or even to divulge its total. It has been the Pope's position that the Vatican, as an independent state, need not report its business or pay any taxes to another civil government.

In his book, *The Changing Vatican,*[33] Alberto Cavallari notes that reliable sources indicate the Vatican has a gold reserve of $11 billion, three times that of Britain. He observes that it may be dangerous logic for the Vatican to continue to feel that its sacredness is too exalted to be subject to listing its holdings and expenses.

After brave starts and lame halts, the Italian government, headed by Premier Giovanni Leone, has announced that it will not oppose the majority which has gone on record as favoring the end of the Vatican exemption from taxation on dividend-income. The Vatican has hinted that it might, in retaliation, make a massive shift of its investments in order to avoid taxation, a move that would undoubtedly have wide repercussions on the Italian economy.

THE MAGNITUDE OF THE CHURCH

The Vatican business in the United States is only a small portion of that Church's wealth in this country. It might be noted in passing, however, that the Vatican may receive more than $1 billion annually in revenue from the Catholic parishes in the United States. We believe that lay Catholics would like to know precisely how much of their money flows in a golden stream to Rome; and that they would be amazed, should they learn the truth.

The Roman Catholic Church is the largest religious organization in the United States. In common with other churches, it enjoys tax-exemption on its real estate and on both passive and active business income. Some idea of its real estate and other forms of wealth may be gathered from the remark of Thomas J. Gibbons, a lay official of the New York Catholic Conference, that this church probably ranks second only to the United States government in total annual purchases.[33] A remarkable estimate of Catholic wealth was offered by the nationally syndicated priest, Father Richard Ginder, in the diocesan paper, Our Sunday Visitor: "The Catholic Church must be the biggest corporation in the United States. We have a branch office in every neighborhood. Our assets and real estate holdings must exceed those of Standard Oil, A.T. & T. and U.S. Steel combined. And our roster of dues-paying members must be second only to the tax rolls of the United States Government." [34]

There are (in 1968) 28 archdioceses and 122 dioceses of the Roman Catholic Church in the United States. Reports of diocesan wealth are seldom disclosed. In a statement published in connection with a bond prospectus, May 1, 1967, the Boston archdiocese listed its assets at $635,891,004, which are 9.9 times its liabilities. This leaves a net worth of $571,704,953. We might add, that since our research (Chapter 3) demonstrates that the 72 Boston parishes out of 409 in the archdiocese have assets totalling $277.5 million, we conclude that the $635.9 million must be only the book, not the present market value, of its actual wealth; or the total set forth may not include the enormous holdings of the religious orders.

The values of Catholic, Protestant, and Jewish religiously used real estate based on an analysis of the tax-rolls of 14 cities and extrapolations therefrom were noted in Chapter 5, 6, and 7. We estimated Catholic exempt and religiously used real estate to be worth $54,278 million; the Protestant, $10,588 million; and the Jewish, $7,518 million.

THE RELIGIOUS ORDERS

As we have seen, church assets include much more than religiously used real estate. All dioceses and numerous parishes of the Roman Catholic Church engage widely in "unrelated" or commercial business for profit, as do the religious orders. Vast amounts of wealth of the Roman Catholic Church center in the latter. There are 414 women's orders and 125 orders for men, making a total of 539 currently operating in the United States. Much of their wealth is in religiously used real estate and is reflected in the figures presented in previous chapters of this book. The religious orders have, however, gone extensively into unrelated business and real estate speculation, which, together with their stock and bond portfolios and other investments, substantially increase their assets and revenues.

In these orders, tens of thousands of men and women have sworn to give life-service to the Church in return for maintenance. All have taken a vow of poverty, which means that they may have neither personal property nor income. Whatever they earn or receive is turned over without withholding tax to their orders. This labor force is a tremendous asset to the Catholic Church. While other churches have religious orders, in none do they have comparable significance. In the typical case, the nun, brother, or priest may be engaged in a distinctly religious task such as teaching in a church school. But such persons may be and often are engaged in secular work for the state or for a private agency, in which case their salaries go, without tax, to their orders. Or, again, such persons may be assigned to commercial activity within the order itself for the purpose of producing revenue.

How rich, then, are these religious orders? Again, we run into a blanket of silence. No public reports are ever made. All these orders enjoy special immunities. If they are sacerdotal, they are accorded the same tax-exemption as a church. Since the Internal Revenue Code does not specify such immunity, it is established by regulation rather than by statute. Some hints as to the assets of religious orders can be garnered from an occasional bond-prospectus published on their behalf. Assets of a few of the women's orders obtained in this fashion are as follows:

Grey Nuns of Charity	$ 3,084,683
Congregation of the Third Order of St. Dominic of St. Mary	3,652,000
California Institute of the Sisters of the Immaculate Heart	7,299,510
Dominican Sisters of St. Catherine of Sienna of Kenosha	7,763,320
Little Sisters of the Poor	25,000,000
Sisters of Christian Charity, Wilmette	6,376,400
Sisters of Charity	66,533,833
Dominican Sisters	24,316,000
Sisters of Mercy	39,754,132
Sisters of St. Francis, Buffalo	13,171,908
Sisters of St. Joseph of Newark	17,899,384
Sisters of Charity–Grey Nuns	34,950,000
Sisters of St. Joseph	11,800,000
Sisters of Charity of St. Elizabeth	16,028,661
Sisters of Charity of Providence	90,187,000
Sisters of the Holy Cross	110,892,759
Sisters of Mercy, Omaha Province	75,600,000
Sisters of the Sorrowful Mother	93,636,516
Missionary Sisters, Servants of the Holy Spirit	11,400,691
Sisters of St. Francis of Assisi	18,151,523
Sisters of St. Joseph of Concordia	13,284,564
Benedictine Sisters	3,736,000
Sisters of Loretto	11,449,300
TOTAL	$705,968,184

The assets of these 23 orders (of which we have at least some fragmentary knowledge) average $30,695,513. Extrapolating on this basis, the assets of the 414 women's orders would total $12.7 billion.

There are, however, many indications that this is an inadequate estimate. For example, the Little Sisters of the Poor, with three provinces in the United States and a hospital in almost every diocese, probably alone have wealth totalling at least $1 billion.

THE JESUITS

The 125 men's orders of the Catholic Church are for the most part older and better established than the women's. They are also far wealthier. The richest is the Society of Jesus, which qualifies as a power in international finance. The traditional secrecy shrouds the wealth of the Jesuits, but it is known to be awesome. A decade or so ago, the influential German magazine *Der Spiegel* assigned its top reporters to the task of ferreting out the facts on the Vatican's financial empire. The American wing of the Jesuit Order came in for special investigation. How accurate is the *Der Spiegel* material? There is obviously some truth in it. The Jesuits have done some stuttering but have never issued a full-fledged denial of the allegations in *Der Spiegel* regarding their wealth. Nor have they done what would lay the entire issue to rest—make a complete disclosure of their financial resources and revenues, certified by a reliable firm of independent accountants.

Here is a typical paragraph from *Der Spiegel:* [35] "The Jesuits are one of the largest stockholders in the American steel companies, Republic and National; they are also among the most important owners of the four greatest aircraft manufacturing companies in the United States—Boeing, Lockheed, Douglas, and Curtis-Wright. Furthermore, they have a controlling interest in the Phillips Oil Company . . . and in the Creole Petroleum Company, which has a great many oil concessions in Venezuela."

The article in *Der Spiegel* also makes the interesting assertion that A. P. Giannini, founder of the Bank of America (originally the Bank of Italy), was acting as an agent for the Jesuit Order. This, too, has never been denied, to our knowledge. It should be noted that tax-exempt securities may be held under assumed names, or by individual members of the Order.

There are many demonstrable facts about the Jesuit financial empire. They own large interests in TV and radio. Jesuit Loyola University in New Orleans owns and operates tax-free Station WWL-TV and WWL-AM and FM radio stations, whose competitors have com-

233

plained that Loyola's tax-exempt status as a church place them at a great disadvantage in soliciting advertising business. Said Louis Reed, sales manager of the taxpaying WDXU-TV: "We've lost some business because of their rate structure. I don't want to be critical of their rates—but it's been rough competing with them." [86] The Jesuits operate a large tax-free winery at Los Gatos, California.

The Society of Jesus is admittedly the wealthiest of the Catholic men's religious orders with an unreported annual income from investments estimated at $250 million. No tax is paid on this. Among its many ventures, the Society operates 28 universities. Some of these, such as Fordham in New York City, Marquette in Milwaukee, and St. Louis University are vast institutions which have drawn enormous subsidies from the government.

There are 124 additional religious orders for men in the Catholic Church. Most of them have impressive assets and some are known to be very wealthy. Like the churches themselves, the religious orders never die. There is no redistribution of their property and wealth from generation to generation. There is, instead, a steady process of accumulation, powerfully aided and abetted by tax-exemptions. To extrapolate on the resources of the Catholic men's religious orders using a figure three times the average of the women's, appears reasonable. On the basis of a $90 million average, the 125 men's orders would show a total wealth of $11.2 billion, or a grand total for all religious orders of approximately $23 billion. Actually, we believe that this estimate is too low by several billion dollars.

We should note, however, that a considerable portion of this wealth is in the form of religiously or educationally used real estate and is therefore included in the computations in Chapter 5, 6, and 7. But much of it is also in commercial real estate, in unrelated business, and in large portfolios of securities. These items are above and beyond the totals given in preceding chapters. It should be emphasized also that these amounts are very conservative indeed. Actually, we believe that the Jesuits alone possess wealth exceeding $12 billion.

ACTION GROUPS

This account would certainly be inadequate without some mention of groups affiliated with the Roman Catholic Church, of which some are wealthy in their own right. Sometimes their relation to their

Church is not altogether clear. Consider, for example, the Knights of Columbus, whose commercial interests we will discuss later. Let us point out here that this is a completely Catholic organization. It is limited to Catholics; it consistently supports Catholic causes; it spends much of its time and income in activities designed to make Catholic converts. In addition, there are 15 listed Catholic action groups and many others with funds of their own. Some of these have many units or divisions. Like comparable Protestant entities, they carry on business, possess portfolios, and produce substantial profits. Such groups as Opus Dei and the Christophers possess considerable property and business in the United States.

Opus Dei, an international Catholic fellowship, is active in many nations as well as in the United States. Some idea of its financial resources can be gathered from a critical report published in its homeland—Spain—in 1967.[37] This report asserted that 14 banks, 16 construction and real estate companies, 4 chemical makers, 10 publishing companies, and 5 film concerns were owned and operated by Opus Dei. The organization issued a vague denial asserting that it was not "a source of economic directives." But, again, there was no financial statement presented to the public that would have put all doubts at rest. Opus Dei has been active in the United States for 20 years, claiming about 50 projects in 12 cities, including Chicago and Washington.

To single out one other of the many groups in this category, we might mention Father Gregory's Sacred Heart Auto League, which sponsors the Apostolate of Prayerful Driving. Operating from Walls, Miss., this organization invites membership donations for which it agrees to provide prayers for the member's family while they are on vacation trips.

There are 207 associations and societies affiliated with the Catholic Church and these cover almost every conceivable interest and specialty. All possess substantial financial resources. Then there are all the "free lancers"—groups headed by priests and under ecclesiastical control, which operate their own fund-raising programs. One of the best known is the famous Boys Town, Nebraska, whose contributions have for many years far exceeded the needs of the institution itself. Boys Town has an elaborate establishment. According to Dr. George S. Bancroft, writing in *Presbyterian Life,* Dec. 15, 1960, it has a field house superior to that of the University of Nebraska. Surplus funds of the school are said to be used for loans to Catholic parishes.

235

Some mention should be made of the quasi-religious groups which operate commercially but bear some relationship to churches. These are both Protestant and Catholic. For example, churches conduct a considerable insurance business. The giant in this field is the Lutheran Brotherhood, which has over $3 billion of life insurance policies for Lutherans only, but is only one of three operated by the same denomination. It ranks 71st among the nation's 715 companies. The Lutheran Brotherhood reports assets of $410 million. Also among the 15 church-related insurance companies is the 200-year-old Presbyterian Ministers Fund.

Roman Catholics have 8 of the church-related companies. Largest is the Knights of Columbus with well over $1.5 billion of insurance for Catholics only. The Catholic Association of Foresters advertises that it is "chartered by law to serve Catholics only," and that it is "not organized to make profit." Its home offices are in Ft. Lauderdale, Florida, and Hamden, Conn. Its brochure states that it has paid over $62 million in benefits to members. There is also the Polish Roman Catholic Union of America which was one of 6 groups barred in July, 1967, from doing business in Maryland.[38] The Mutual Protective Insurance Company of Omaha, Nebr., advertises that it is "the Catholic Company" and "especially for Catholics." The Massachusetts Catholic Order of Foresters is another which confines its business to Catholic clients.

Ties between the insurance operations and the parent church are close. The Lutheran Brotherhood, for example, is obligated by its charter to "aid the Lutheran Church" and, as noted, its service is confined to Lutherans. Such groups being mutual companies owned and operated by churches, they pay no taxes on corporate income.

Another productive area for the church is in the publishing field. As we have seen, such enterprises often enjoy real estate tax-exemption so long as they are owned by the church and produce materials intended for religious use. Even though they are profit-making enterprises, no tax is levied on their income. There are 94 publishing houses for Catholic books and pamphlets in the United States alone. There are 515 Catholic periodicals claiming a circulation exceeding 29 million.[39] It is true that not all of these show a profit and some require subsidies. On the other hand, some return a handsome margin. The *Catholic Digest,* owned by the St. Paul Diocese, reported in 1961 that it had a paid U.S. circulation above 750,000 and that it grossed $5 million annually. Most religious journals solicit paid advertising. When the publication is owned directly by the denomination, the church-exemption covers it, and there is no tax on the profits.

The Colorado Graphic, a newspaper published in Denver, Colorado, is a subsidiary of Bannock Publications, Inc., a Roman Catholic corporation which also publishes the *National Catholic Register,* one of a chain which includes 26 newspapers in the *Register* system. The Bannock publications declared in the *Graphic* [40] that it is a "sister corporation of the non-profit Catholic Press Society, Inc.," but insists that it is "a fully taxed Colorado Corporation" which prints many Denver area publications and even does typesetting for New York firms. However, Cervi's *Journal,* May 7, 1969, points out that the director of the Bannock organization is none other than Archbishop James V. Casey and adds that it is the "tax-exempt Catholic Press Society, publishing agent for the (tax-exempt) Denver Catholic Register and a number of other tax-exempt weeklies in the national tax-exempt Catholic Register system." We noted in Chapter 5 that the plant in which the Bannock publications are printed and in which the corporation carries on its commercial enterprise is wholly exempt from the Denver property tax.

OTHER CATHOLIC BUSINESS

The Catholic Church, with its various orders and organizations, operates more widely in "unrelated business" than any other church. While no general reports of such activity are made public, a good deal of information is available. When a five-alarm fire in San Francisco destroyed an enormous warehouse, a newspaper reporter found that it belonged to the Catholic archdiocese. The building suffered damage estimated at $500,000. It had been leased to Gibraltar Warehouses.

The holding of tax-exempt real estate for speculative purposes has been a common church-operation. The Catholic archdiocese of Hartford, Conn., for example, purchased 121.5 acres of unused land in New Britain, Conn., for $23,500. To protect itself against high taxes the church "put a body" on the premises and listed it as a cemetery. Over the years, the church was able to avoid about $200,000 in taxes. In 1966, the church removed the body and sold the acreage for $607,-500.[41] No capital gains tax, of course.

A source of steady profit to the Catholic Church is its ownership of denominational cemeteries in many communities. These may be owned and operated by individual parishes or by the diocese. The Chicago archdiocese owns and operates 24 tax-exempt cemeteries, from which it derives substantial tax-free income.

According to the Milwaukee *Sentinel,* June 20, 1969, De Rance, Inc. of that city is a feeder foundation for the Roman Catholic religious orders. Among other assets, De Rance has a 47 per cent interest in Miller Beer. In 1968 Miller had sales totaling $145 million. It is the eighth largest producer of beer in the United States.

In his comments before the Mills Committee (*Testimony,* p. 1465, Part 4) Congressman John W. Byrnes noted that University Hill Foundation, a "feeder" for the Roman Catholic Loyola of Los Angeles, was operating at least 24 separate businesses, including a plastics business, three sand, gravel and concrete businesses, a foundry, three dairies, a hotel, a printing establishment, a business of manufacturing windows, oil burners, rubber treads and locks. All, he said, were operated under arrangements designed to provide tax exemption for their profits.

At least two of Chicago's largest garbage dumps are owned by the Chicago archdiocese of the Catholic Church. The ownership of both came to light as a result of community controversies. The Glenview dump came under fire as a danger to aircraft in the vicinity since birds were attracted by the refuse. The other, a 320-acre facility near Oak Brook, was the object of complaints because of the rats, flies, and other pests drawn to the area. The dumps were leased by the archbishop of Chicago to the John Saxton Sand and Gravel Corp., owned by prominent Catholic laymen.

The New York archdiocese recently sold its one-half interest in sales royalties of Listerine for $25 million. The profits which had been tax-exempt, were used, the diocese said, "for the good causes of the church."

The penchant of the Catholic Church for commercial business has, as we have already noted, occasionally stirred the criticism of competitors. The president of Technology, Inc., Dayton, Ohio, complained that his company had been euchered out of a $500,000 Air Force contract because the winner, the University of Dayton, came under the umbrella of tax-exemption. The university is owned and operated by the Roman Catholic Society of Mary. Since the school enjoyed immunity from income taxation, it was able to take this into consideration when it offered its bid.

From storage and trash disposal, the Catholic commercial activity

238

ranges far. For a long time the Boston archdiocese owned Loew's State Theatre, which was assessed at $1,140,000. In 1966, the same see sold station WIHS-TV for $2,276,513. St. John's University of Collegeville, Minn., an institution of the Benedictine Fathers, operates the most powerful FM radio station in the state, KSJN-FM. In Columbus, Ohio, the Catholic Church of Josephinium owns the building which houses Montgomery Ward. The building was recently refurbished at a cost of $600,000 and rented to the Internal Revenue Service, among others.

One local church, St. Andrews of Chicago, owns two California hotels—the Hollywood Roosevelt and the Sacramento El Rancho. They were purchased for $10 million from Illinois Wesleyan University (Methodist). Parochial schools of the Los Angeles archdiocese derive a $250,000 annual income from a lease on land owned by the arch-diocese in the Wilshire business district on which a $30 million office complex has been erected. When the diocese of Hartford, Conn., purchased the Bond and Vendome Hotels, the Hartford *Times* [42] pointed out that $59,000 would be lost annually in taxes.

THE KNIGHTS OF COLUMBUS

The business investments of the Knights of Columbus, a fraternal group closely related to the Catholic Church, are impressive. They have a vast insurance business and in 1966 reported assets of $281,228,300. The Order owns the land under Yankee Stadium, which it leased back to the Yankee organization in 1961 for 24 years at $182,000 per year. On Dec. 31, 1965, the Knights reported that their portfolio included $55.6 million in securities. They own also the $4.5 million Stix-Baer, the Fuller Dry Goods Co. property in St. Louis, the former New Haven Railway headquarters building, Crucible Steel's Detroit Warehouse, the Brunswick-Balke-Collender Co. building in Chicago, the site of the $5 million Sheraton Hotel in New Haven, and department stores in Camden, N.J., and Philadelphia. The Knights also own the $1.8 million steel tube mill of the Bridgeport Brass Co., the St. Louis Frontenac Apartments, and numerous other real estate investments. They pay no income taxes on the commercial income derived from these properties.

One of the large projects of the Knights was Christopher Homes built with federal funds at Tucson, Arizona, in 1963.[43] The cost was $5,099,820. However, they obtained a construction loan which was

$516,000 more than necessary to complete the project. They collected the rents for four years, but made only one payment on the mortgage. Then the government foreclosed. In the fall of 1967, the University of Arizona purchased the property for $2.4 million, or 43 cents on the dollar. The taxpayers lost $4 million on this transaction.

BUSINESSES, MANY AND VARIOUS

Canned and baked goods and meat products have provided many businesses for churches. Some of the operations are carried on directly by the Church itself, or its religious orders. Others are leased back to operators. In either case, church ownership spreads the blanket of tax-exemption over the business. Trappists of St. Joseph's Abbey, Mass., manufacture 27 flavors of jelly on their 2,300-acre farm, which are sold in all 50 states and Canada. No tax is imposed and the business flourishes. Actually, this immunity is interdicted under the Internal Revenue Code, since the Trappists are non-sacerdotal.

Some 200 monks of Our Lady of Gethsemene Abbey, Bardstown, Ky., another Trappist institution, conduct a prosperous business in cheese, fruit cakes, hams, bacon, and sausage. St. Benedict's Abbey, Aspen, Colorado, has a 3,800-acre ranch and 500 head of cattle herded by cowboy monks. Their beef brings prime prices and the profits are exempt from tax. Another 52 monks of the Abbey of Genesee, near Rochester, N.Y., produce Monk's Bread in a modern, automatic bakery. Trappistine nuns of Wrentham, Mass., produce several kinds of expensive candies which are sold in fancy candy shops throughout the nation.

The Dominican Sisters of Mission San Jose, a Roman Catholic order, specialize in fruit cakes. The order advertises its products widely and carries on an extensive mail-order business. Purchasers must pick up their orders after sending in their check to the central office. Pick up points are at four Dominican convents, two of which are in Los Angeles and others at San Gabriel and Anaheim.

The Cistercian monks, a Catholic order, have a pretentious dairy and beef business in connection with their abbey near Dubuque, Iowa. They have 2,000 acres of tillable land and large herds of dairy and beef cattle. They also operate a sawmill, stone quarry, apple orchard, apiary, and bakery. They have a large alfalfa dehydrating plant to facilitate commercial marketing.

240

St. John's Bread, a product of the monks of St. John's Abbey, Collegeville, Minn., is actually produced by commercial bakeries under a franchise from the monks, who pay no taxes on their profits. Monastery Bread is made by the Trappist monks of Berryville, Virginia, and sold exclusively at Giant Food Stores. St. Leo Junior College and Preparatory School of St. Leo, Florida, are operated on profits from an orange grove owned by the Benedictine Fathers. White Monk Foods are the tax-exempt products of Our Lady of Spring Bank, a Cistercian Monastery of Okauchee, Wisconsin.

The Daughters of St. Paul, an order of Catholic nuns, have a profitable printing business which they have operated since 1932. They have published hundreds of titles and millions of books at Jamaica Plain, near Boston, in a plant which is a part of the Novitiate. One Catholic industry in Walls, Mississippi, assumes a religious tone by producing small plastic statues of saints for automobile and home, under the direction of Father Gregory Bezy.

Nuns of the staff of St. Boniface Parish in Detroit operate a commercial parking lot near Tiger Stadium, home of the Tigers and Lions. The nuns advertise that "we stress courtesy. We never scrape fenders. We've never had any vandalism here."

The St. Labras Indian School, which belongs to the Capuchin priests of St. Joseph, operates a costume jewelry business at Ashland, Montana, with a considerable mail order trade, and a reported income of $894,809 in 1961. The Marist Fathers have a recording business in Hawaii headed by Father John McDonald who specializes in the production of recorded Hawaiian music. Proceeds of the sales are used for St. Catherine's Church and the Marist Seminary. St. Peter's fishing lures are commercially produced by the Franciscan Nuns of the Most Blessed Sacrament at Our Lady of Angels Monastery in Birmingham, Ala.

The Divine Word Missionaries operate the Universal Gift Shop near Chicago. It is called Hwan Chyou and features all sorts of art objects. An advertisement proclaims that many items are "one of a kind."

The commodious 120-acre shrine and retreat center, Our Lady of the Snows, near Belleville, Illinois, offers an example of a commercial activity frequently encountered among Roman Catholic religious orders. Since the ostensible purpose of the Center consists of religious activities and programs, its tax-exemption was easily established on the basis of its religiously rigged "grotto" and its seven stations of the

Cross. Yet this operation of the Oblate Fathers has a pronounced commercial aspect. It has a plush motel called Pilgrim's Inn and a large restaurant and gift shop called St. Joseph's Hall, operated for business income. At the religious shrines, long-burning prayer candles retail for $1 and one may purchase a squirt of holy water for 25 cents. There is also a widely advertised Apartment Community, a retirement home which draws tenants from all over the State. Atop it all, is the tower of WMRY-FM radio, also operated by the Oblate Fathers. While no balance sheet on Our Lady of the Snows is ever published, one can be quite sure that its various enterprises, all untaxed, keep the Shrine well in the black.

Large profits have been made by the Roman Catholic Church in liquor. The Carthusian Order claims that it has a secret formula for the production of Chartreuse, which is described in its advertisements as a "superb liqueur." The Jesuits' Novitiate brand is widely known and sold. Christian Brothers advertises the largest selling brandy in the United States. Save for the Christian Brothers, all these operations are exempt from income taxation. Since the Brothers are "non-sacerdotal," this technicality in the Regulations of the Internal Revenue Service led to their being taxed. See the account of this in Chapter 4.

Some church businesses have paid real estate taxes. Others have not, or have claimed exemption from such liability.

In St. Paul, Minnesota, a second-hand store operated by St. Claver's Catholic Church was taxed by County Assessor Ronald V. Powers. St. Claver's claimed exemption for the business on the ground that its profits—which ran from $3,000 to $4,000 a month—went to the support of its parish school. Actually, the business had been there a long time, paying taxes, before the Church acquired it. The Assessor insisted that it should continue to pay its ad valorem tax. He pointed out that one of St. Paul's largest department stores occupied a site owned by the archdiocese and that it paid real estate taxes. He could see no difference between the two cases. No question was raised regarding the profits of the business, which were automatically exempt from tax because it was church-owned.

Sometimes an unusual bequest may throw a church into an unusual business. The Catholic diocese of Worcester, Massachusetts, received a 400-acre estate in 1967. According to the *Daily Telegram* of that city, Nov. 16, 1968, this acquisition forced a unique problem upon the Church. How could the estate be made productive without a big capital outlay? Finally, the site was converted into a natural area and a demonstration farm, where people could come to enjoy the open spaces. Beef cattle and chickens will be installed, as well as an orchard. Parishioners can come for a religious retreat and enjoy nature at the same time. According to latest reports, business is flourishing.

A SUMMARY AND ESTIMATE

We cannot emphasize too strongly the fact that the known enterprises of churches are comparable to that portion of an iceberg which is visible above the water. And the instances we have discussed in this chapter are but a small fraction of what is known and could be cited.

How much commercial or "unrelated" business is owned by the churches? Again, we run into the blackout in which churches are permitted to operate. We discover certain items of information piecemeal—but usually because there is a fire or an accident, or a controversy of some kind! Taking into account not only the denominations but the activities of local churches as well, a ball-park estimate would be in the neighborhood of $12 billion for the Catholics and perhaps $4 billion for the Protestants.

As we near the end of this portion of our survey covering the business of religion, it is appropriate to offer some estimate of this phase of the untaxed wealth of the churches. To be sure, they have yet another tremendous source of income in addition to those we have discussed—principally government subsidies. This source will be analyzed in Chapter 10, but, in anticipation, we shall include this in the following tabulation.

These computations are largely self-explanatory. It might be stated that income from stocks and bonds and investment real estate (passive income) is reckoned at 5 per cent. This is obviously low, since it does not indicate any increment from capital gains which, in an era such as this, are substantial. The revenue from commercial business is computed at 10 per cent, certainly a reasonable estimate. Voluntary contributions include, of course, support for parochial schools and the Vatican.

The $1,000,000,000 given below as the income of the Jewish religious corporations is simply an estimate, since we have been unable to obtain any specific information on the subject.

The business of religion in America is gigantic, not alone in its

CHURCH WEALTH AND INCOME

	Protestant	Catholic
Annual Voluntary Contributions	$ 4,000,000,000	$ 5,000,000,000
Passive Income	450,000,000	650,000,000
Active Business Income	400,000,000	1,200,000,000

Government	Protestant	Catholic
Federal	$2,250,000,000	$3,750,000,000
State	210,000,000	455,000,000
Municipal	105,000,000	250,000,000
TOTAL	$7,000,000,000	

	Protestant	Catholic
Miscellaneous (Wills, Community Funds, Bingo, Raffles, Etc.)	2,565,000,000	4,435,000,000
	800,000,000	1,500,000,000
TOTALS	$ 8,215,000,000	$12,785,000,000

CHURCH ASSETS

	Protestant	Catholic
Stocks, Bonds, Investment Real Estate	9,000,000,000	13,000,000,000
Commercial Business Property	4,000,000,000	12,000,000,000
Personal Property	500,000,000	900,000,000
Religiously Used Real Estate	40,588,000,000	54,277,600,000
TOTALS	$54,088,000,000	$80,177,600,000

Omitting Jewish Religiously Owned Commercial Investments, We Have:

Protestant Wealth	$ 54,088,000,000
Catholic Wealth	80,177,600,000
Jewish Wealth	7,547,800,000
TOTAL RELIGIOUS ASSETS	$141,813,400,000

ANNUAL CHURCH INCOME IN THE UNITED STATES

Protestant	$ 8,215,000,000
Roman Catholic	12,785,000,000
Jewish	1,000,000,000
TOTAL	$ 22,000,000,000
Combined with Assets	141,813,400,000
TOTAL WEALTH AND INCOME	$163,813,400,000

visible, institutional spread, but also in its portfolio of stocks and bonds, its real estate and business investments. The many tax-exemptions which government provides greatly accelerate this development. If the present trend continues, it is only a matter of a little time before the churches, collectively, will have attained the oppressive status which has inspired drastic corrective action and even violent expropriation in other times. Indeed, this stage may already be much nearer than many of our complacent clerics care to believe.

Citations

1. The New York *Times,* Nov. 8, 1966.
2. The Buffalo *Courier Express,* Sept. 17, 1968.
3. *Religious News Service,* April 9, 1969.
4. The New York *Times,* March 27, 1969.
5. The Pittsburgh *Press,* Feb. 18, 1968.
6. The New York *Times,* Sept. 25, 1968.
7. Published by the Council Press, N.Y., Louis B. Whitman, editor.
8. March 20, 1969.
9. July 8, 1967.
10. The New York *Times,* Oct. 22, 1960.
11. *The Monterey Peninsula Herald,* Feb. 23, 1968.
12. *Religious News Service,* Dec. 10, 1968.
13. *Today,* Broward County, Fla., Dec. 31, 1968; also *Religious News Service,* Jan. 10, 1969.
14. Jan. 23, 1969.
15. Feb. 3, 1969.
16. August 15, 1964.
17. *Religious News Service,* Oct. 17, 1968.
18. New York *Times,* Feb. 10, 1968.
19. *Ib.* Aug. 8, 1967.
20. *The Christian Science Monitor,* Nov. 19, 1968.
21. The New York *Times,* Jan. 11, 1962.
22. *The Investor's Reader,* Oct. 4, 1967.

23. The Pittsburgh *Press,* Feb. 18, 1968.
24. *Christianity Today,* Jan. 19, 1962.
25. The San Diego *Independent,* Jan. 22, 1968.
26. *Church & State,* June, 1967.
27. The Seattle *Times,* Dec. 6, 1966.
28. June 22, 1968.
29. The San Francisco *Chronicle,* Feb. 14, 1969.
30. Published, 1968, by the Trident Press.
31. March 18, 1969.
32. Published by Doubleday, N.Y., 1968. Cf. pp. 109–110.
33. *The Catholic Herald,* Nov. 18, 1965.
34. *Our Sunday Visitor,* May 22, 1960.
35. August 13, 1958.
36. *The Wall Street Journal,* Aug. 18, 1959.
37. The New York *Times,* May 8, 1967.
38. The Washington *Post,* July 8, 1967.
39. *Religious News Serviced,* Sept. 13, 1967.
40. The Washington *Post,* Feb. 19, 1969.
41. *Church & State,* July–August, 1967.
42. June 29, 1965.
43. Arizona *Republic,* Sept. 16, 1967.

CHAPTER 9

ON THE BORDER

The perennial temptation of wealth is that he who has it always develops an insatiable desire for more. The possession by churches of large sums beyond their current needs has often drawn them irresistibly into speculation. In a rapidly expanding economy, there are many "sure things" available, propositions "guaranteed" to produce large and rapid profits for those with the wherewithal to invest. The passion for larger and larger returns has often brought the churches close to the line of the legally illicit and occasionally across it. The story of church-ventures into the realm of speculative finance is a fascinating one.

FRAUDULENT BONDS

The Mid-City Baptist Church of New Orleans with 4,700 members is the largest in the city, is growing rapidly, and ranks second in property assets among all in the Southern Baptist Convention. Its enterprises include a day nursery, kindergarten, elementary school, high school, book shop, printery, cafeteria, and bus company. But when it went into a high-rise apartment and hotel complex, trouble developed.[1] The Church, its pastor, Rev. J. Paul Driscoll, and others were charged by the Securities and Exchange Commission with defrauding the public in the sale of over $12 million in church bonds over a period of 12 months.

The Church used bonds to beget bonds. It "borrowed from Peter to pay Paul" with the result that there eventually developed a mounting spiral of debt. A high-rise building next to the church was financed by the sale of $4 million in bonds to the Peden Corporation of Cleburne, Texas, and World Oil and Gas Corporation of Fort Worth, Texas. These corporations went into receivership without paying for them. The SEC charged that money thus obtained was actually used to pay interest on earlier issues and not for the advertised purpose of building the high-rise, for which little more than excavation was ever completed. Untaxed income from the apartment-hotel was to pay off all previous bond-issues, but the plan went awry. Mid-City Church joined others in filing suit to recover funds in unpaid bonds from the Peden and the World Oil and Gas Corporation. Other churches involved in the debacle included one Assembly of God, 3 Baptist, 3 Christian Scientist, and 14 Church of Christ congregations.

SPECULATION IN REAL ESTATE

The First Christian Church of America ran into difficulty on a real-estate deal near San Francisco.[2] The "church" was allegedly a real-estate investment group which held no services. It paid $2.8 million in Jan., 1966, for 2,140 woodland acres. The operation came to light when the church sought to sell the land to the State of California for $3,367,000. The owners did not want to sell, but there had been a public clamor to take the land from speculative development and add it to the adjoining Mt. Tamalpais State Park.

The State countered with an offer of $3,012,000, which would have meant a profit of $212,000 for the Church. But having borrowed heavily on the property, the owners declared this was not enough. Holders of liens against the land stated that it would take the $3,367,000 to clear the obligations. State Parks Director William Penn Mott, Jr., refused to pay this price and said the State would not file a condemnation suit. As the controversy mounted, the Internal Revenue Service moved in to investigate the First Christian Church of America to see whether it really was a church under the law. The IRS found it to be a church for tax exempt purposes.

Speculative business of the Baptist Church of Fort Walton Beach, Florida, brought that congregation into difficulties with the law in

1966 as a result of a complicated series of financial manipulations.[3] The SEC charged the pastor, Rev. Yancy L. Anthony, the Church secretary, Winifield Lyon, and 10 others with fraud.[4] The Church had about 60 listed members. It was the owner of record of three paint stores in Fort Walton Beach and a number of other businesses including "paper" banks in Panama and the Bahamas.

The Church contracted with Martin Tilden and Aubrey Kahn to issue $6 million in 6 per cent bonds. The security offered as collateral consisted of the "mineral rights" on 640 acres of land in Arizona, for five years, which had been obtained at a total price of $210. The holders assigned the lease to the Church. Rev. Anthony then produced a geologist's appraisal which stated that the mineral rights on the 640 acres were actually worth $12 million. It developed, however, that the geologist was none other than an employee of a company owned by the men who got bonds issued by the Collegiate Baptist Church.

At this point, Martin Tilden and Aubrey Kahn, the individuals who obtained the Church bonds, used them to acquire properties for themselves and for the Collegiate Baptist Church. The Church was reported to have received 20 per cent of all the properties or monies acquired by them with the use of the bonds as security. Messrs. Tilden and Kahn were reported to have disposed of $200,000 of the bonds to one Owen Meddles, who, in turn, disposed of them to William M. Netterville, who, in his turn, pledged half of them as collateral for a $41,000 bank loan in New Orleans. In obtaining the loan, Mr. Netterville presented a balance sheet of the Church and a letter printed on the stationery of a New York Stock Exchange firm. Netterville was also named a defendant in the charges brought by the SEC.

This federal agency eventually obtained a permanent injunction in federal court against the defendants which enjoined the Church, its pastor, and others from selling any unregistered bonds or other securities, and from making false and misleading statements in regard to such offerings.

The penchant for unregistered bonds of dubious value has entrapped church organizations on other occasions. In April, 1969, the Securities and Exchange Commission filed a complaint in Federal District Court, New York City, against the Baptist Foundation of America and Church Aid Foundation, Inc. The former is a California group and the latter is incorporated in Washington, D.C. These organizations, and 42 others, were charged with selling $2.5 million of unregistered shares of the Dumont Corporation of Fort Lee, N.J., a computer service, as well as a food and financial concern. The complaint alleged that "false and misleading" information concerning Dumont sales and earnings had been disseminated. Detailed stories appeared in the press.[5]

JUST WHAT AND WHEN IS A CHURCH?

The Puritan Church of Peoria, Illinois, was the object of a lawsuit brought by the government in 1959.[6] The United States Circuit Court of Appeals denied tax-exemption to the organization, and the Supreme Court refused to review the case.

At stake were incomes of $201,000 and $259,000 in two years of operation. The Internal Revenue Service challenged the claim of the Church to a religious exemption on the ground that it was not really a church, that its principal function was not religious, but rather that of disseminating political propaganda. The court held that the Puritan Church was not exempt and that its income from contributions should be subject to taxation.

ORDAINING EVERYBODY

There may be more than meets the eye in the operation of the Rev. Kirby J. Hensley, pastor of the Universal Life Church, Inc., of Modesto, California. This organization was succinctly described in two articles by Charles McCabe.[7] Rev. Hensley's specialty is ordaining anybody to the ministry who so desires. This is, of course, a private matter which each church handles in its own way. If a church should decide, as this one has, to confer ordination upon anyone who requests it, who is to say that it is wrong? Are not Rev. Hensley's reverends as good as any others? It can be argued that this is the way the Universal Church has chosen to operate and that this is the free exercise of religion.

But when one considers the profit-potential, it appears that more than free exercise of religion is involved. Each "minister" who is "ordained" by Rev. Hensley is thereby empowerd to set up "churches" which are just as tax-exempt as the largest, and can easily become fronts for tax-exempt business. With this possibility in mind, reporter

250

McCabe insisted that the State must "police the clergy and charge them proper taxes on earned income. . . ."

According to late news reports, "Reverend" Hensley has been sentenced to a year in prison for fraud by a California court.

UNREGISTERED BOND ISSUES

A unique advantage enjoyed by churches is exemption from the requirement of registering bonds with the SEC. This has permitted them to indulge in unsound practices which are forbidden to all other groups, who must register, and come under the supervision and regulation of the Commission. Ridge Lutheran Home, Inc., of Burnsville, Minn., failed to make interest payments on $1.5 million of unregistered bonds, which it had sold to finance the home.[8] The only visible undertaking of the corporation as of December, 1967, was a partially built home owned by Carl R. Anderson, president of Lutheran Home, Inc. Anderson resigned. Construction was halted late in 1967 when the interest payments became delinquent.

At a hearing before the SEC, Eugene W. Linse, Jr., secretary of the Home, testified that two checks totalling $85,000 had been drawn on the bank account of Ridge Lutheran Home, Inc., and paid to Anderson. Mr. Linse said this had been done without board authorization and that at the time he did not know about them. Ridge Lutheran Home, Inc., was under investigation by the Post Office Department and the Minnesota attorney general.

CASH BURNING IN POCKETS

Large cash reserves in church treasuries have proved an almost irresistible temptation to indulge in speculative investments. In an expanding economy, cash cleverly invested can increase rapidly. Churches, like individuals, have been quick to seize such opportunities. After all, churches are composed of individuals easily enticed by hopes of rapid temporal gain.

In 1966, the Baptist Convention of Texas was involved in a controversy over such an investment—this one involving $2 million used to purchase California real estate.[9] No wrong-doing was proved or even alleged in the transactions, but there was considerable criticism because of the speculative nature of the investment. Involved

251

was a 100-acre site to be developed as part of a marina near San Diego. But there were other properties also. A committee of the Convention headed by Dr. E. H. Westmoreland was appointed to investigate. Dr. A. B. White, executive vice president of Church Loan Corporation, said that 27 acres at the site had been leased for $100,000 annually. Near Anaheim, according to Dr. White, 600 acres were purchased for $682,000, for which the agency later refused an offer of $2 million. Dr. Westmoreland stated that in his view the Church should avoid speculative investments of this kind and concentrate on loans to local churches.

RELIGIOUS ORDERS

Evidence of the great wealth of the Catholic orders is to be seen in the large amounts of cash some of them have available for highly speculative investments. The Poor Sisters of St. Francis Seraph of the Perpetual Adoration provide a ready example. This group received nation-wide notoriety in 1967 because of dealings with Ernest Medders, a supposed Texas millionaire tycoon.[10] The Poor Sisters, it turned out, had been providing him with $40,000 a month from 1962 up into 1967—nearly $2 million in all. The grants to Mr. Medders were "loans" provided in the hope of a big return to the Order when this man came into the vast oil fortune of over $500 million that he was supposed to inherit. But the payoff never came; instead, there came the sad disclosure that there were no oil wells and, indeed, no fortune of any kind. The funds which the Poor Sisters had advanced to Mr. Medders so that he could "prove his claim" had all gone down the drain.

Where did the Poor Sisters get the money to finance Mr. Medders in his life of affluence? They got it from bond issues and from government grants. Shortly after their problems with Mr. Medders were revealed, the Poor Sisters sought support from the public in the form of a bond issue of $4.5 million. They noted on the prospectus a net worth of $86 million. The new money was being sought to provide partial financing of the $46.8 million expansion of seven hospitals which belonged to the Order.

Another source of money for the Poor Sisters was the federal government which made a long series of grants. The hospitals owned and operated by the Poor Sisters and the cumulative federal grants under Hill-Burton made to the institutions below are listed herewith.[11]

252

FEDERAL FUNDS FOR THE POOR SISTERS

Hospital	Location	Number Sisters	Number Beds	Hill-Burton Funds
St. James	Chicago Hts., Ill.	16	250	$ 1,593,000
St. Francis	Evanston, Ill.	30	401	197,259
St. Francis	Beech Grove, Ind.	12	291	
St. Margaret	Hammond, Ind.	23	393	2,339,268
St. Elizabeth	Lafayette, Ind.	28	448	850,640
St. Joseph's	Logansport, Ind.	18	132	400,000
St. Anthony's	Michigan City, Ind.	13	100	2,163,332
St. Anthony's	Terre Haute, Ind.	16	285	841,952
St. Anthony's	Louisville, Ky.	19	244	2,554,481
St. Joseph's	Memphis, Tenn.	16	400	
St. Alexis	Cleveland, Ohio	15	335	
St. Jude	Memphis, Tenn.	?	?	697,102
TOTALS		206	3279	$11,667,634

These statistics reveal that 9 hospitals belonging to a single province of one religious order in the Catholic Church obtained $11.6 million from the federal government, which may very well have provided the funds for such a speculation as the Medders deal. It should also be noted that the same Poor Sisters have 7 schools for nursing, a college and several secondary schools, for which they have drawn additional federal grants. Thus, by the accident of a bad investment, the large tax-exempt resources of one religious order came to light.

We should note that if all of the 788 Catholic hospitals have been subsidized to the same extent, they must have received grants totalling more than $1 billion.

Another incident occurred in 1968 which resulted in a complaint by the SEC and a criminal indictment of a man accused of bilking another Catholic religious order, the Society of the Divine Savior.[12] Again, it was a story of large amounts of ready cash turned over to a speculator in the hope of a quick and large tax-free profit. Victor J. Orsinger, a Washington attorney and realtor, became the confidant of the Order and received millions from the Sisters for investment. They had raised their money in fund-raising drives for a seminary in Rome and for missionary work in Africa. They obtained $3 million in this manner, but the money actually went, via Orsinger, into Parkwood, a plush real-estate development near Washington, D.C. Eventually, the Society, which owned Parkwood from 1956 to 1961, sank an additional $4.1 million of its funds, also obtained for religious purposes, into this housing project. Parkwood, however, did not come through as expected. It was plagued with mounting deficits, and nobody seemed to know where all the money had gone. In 1966, the Securities and Exchange Commission charged that Orsinger had diverted some of the funds to his own use. The report stated that he and his associates "have been and are now employing devices, schemes and artifices to defraud, and engaging in transactions, practices and a course of business which would and did operate as a fraud upon certain persons."

The matter was eventually referred to the grand jury, which promptly handed down an indictment against Orsinger. It is to be noted that because of the status accorded by federal authority to the Society of the Divine Saviour under the Internal Revenue Code, the bonds were not registered. Eventually, Orsinger was found guilty of stealing at least $1.5 million from the Sisters of the Divine Saviour. One bizarre detail revealed during the trial was the disclosure that this man had once spent $40,000 of the Sister's money for the purchase of gems and jewelry. Had Orsinger been honest and had Parkwood been the success which the Sisters anticipated, it would have returned them a handsome tax-free profit. It was only when their speculation, financed with government grants and bond issues, failed, to the accompaniment of malodorous publicity, that some of the facts involved were revealed. This incident does, however, bring into sharp focus the substantial sums which some church groups have available for highly questionable adventures.

A CASE OF OPULENT POVERTY

Let us now turn the spotlight on Christ's Church of the Golden Rule in northern California.[13] The key to its policy is its insistence that every member surrender all his property and wealth to the Church. This provides initial capital for a tax-exempt domain which now includes an ultra-modern motel, restaurant, and gift shop; it has also a new garage and service station, as well as a sawmill and a large cattle operation near Willits, California. No one is quite sure what other properties and businesses are owned by this tax-free corporation. Another source of capital was the $2 million in cash which the

254

Church received when it sold its previous headquarters, a 3,000-acre site at Point Reyes, California. If someone becomes disenchanted and wants to leave, he may do so—but he cannot take anything with him. "We don't have to give them anything back, and we don't," declared Harold Von Norris, one of the founders.

As in the Catholic orders, all members of Christ's Church of the Golden Rule take a vow of poverty. This is highly useful in their relations with government. Because they own nothing and have no income, one-third of the members are actually able to draw regular monthly welfare checks. Furthermore, they can receive unlimited unrelated passive business income without reporting it to the IRS. It is therefore, a simple matter to live in homes valued at $100,000, as some of them do.

Another delightful element in the situation is that the Church pays no salaries. Every member works at some job, but is paid nothing. No income means no tax and no social security. All the worker receives in cash is a small monthly allowance of about $10 for spending. Welfare payments totalling some $63,000 a year have aroused the ire of the taxpaying citizens. In every instance the check is signed over by the recipient to Christ's Church of the Golden Rule and adds to the income of that already affluent institution. Charles Hillinger of the Los Angeles *Times* reports county assistant district attorney, Gerald Sperry, as saying: "I don't object to their socialist experiment *per se*, but I don't believe taxpayers up here should have to pay for it."

It should be stressed that the independent Christ's Church of the Golden Rule has not been charged with any violation of the law. From all indications, the Church has kept its operations strictly within the technicalities of a law which serves the Roman Catholic Church and its religious orders so well. The point is that it has exploited every possible angle of the church-exemption to its advantage. In so doing, it has again demonstrated the deficiencies of the laws which make possible such exemptions for churches and clergy.

A UNIVERSITY SCANDAL

It happens that the president of Arizona State University,* in Tempe, and his Director of Physical Plant Planning, John Ellingson, are Mormons. Two or three years ago, the University, with taxpayers'

---

* He has resigned to accept a position in the educational system of Utah.

money, purchased three homes located next to the Mormon Institute of Religion and simply turned them over to this entity, which has since collected the rents from them for its own use. As if to compound insult, the Institute has rented the houses at low rates to two of its own teachers and to a Mormon relative of a University official. Kenneth Kunes, Maricopa County Assessor, complained bitterly that there is nothing he can do to place the property on the tax-rolls since they are titled to the State; but he added that "the deal stinks to high heaven." [14]

All of this became public knowledge by sheer accident because terrific pressure was brought against the owner of a 4th home, Charles Schisler, to sell this, presumably for the same ultimate fate. When he refused, the University sued in Superior Court, to force him to sell under condemnation proceedings. And so Mr. Kunes became aware of the situation.

THE CRYING NEED FOR REFORM

Such instances as are recorded in this chapter are only a few of many; but they certainly demonstrate not only the need of protecting the public from the effects of church tax-exemption, but, further, of protecting the churches from unscrupulous operators. There may also be need to protect the churches from themselves. The laws as they now stand are a constant lure to unscrupulous manipulators to use the church as a tax-exempt front for transactions and diversions in themselves highly unethical or even illicit. These laws also tempt the clergy from their duly appointed spiritual tasks into the commercial arena, for which they were assuredly never intended. After all, it is hard to resist the temptation to enter a field where one has at least twice as much chance of success as a competitor. The problems which may have been purely theoretical at one time are now very real and practical as the churches utilize, more and more extensively, the commercial advantages conferred on them by existing law.

We do not, of course, know how many illegal or semi-licit situations like the preceding exist in the United States. They are rarely discovered, except by accident. Their name is probably already legion, and they must be increasing by leaps and bounds.

Citations

1. *National Observer,* Nov. 20, 1967; *Religious News Service,* Dec. 20, 1967; the *Wall Street Journal,* Dec. 13, 1967; and *Christianity Today,* Oct. 11, 1968.
2. The San Francisco *Sunday Examiner & Chronicle,* Dec. 3, 1967.
3. The New York *Times,* March 11, 1966.
4. S.E.C. vs. Collegiate Baptist Church, Civil Action No. 66–416—Civ. U.S. Dist. Court, So. District of Fla.
5. The *Wall Street Journal* and the *New York Times* of April 9, 1969.
6. *Religious News Service,* Jan. 13, 1959.
7. The San Francisco *Chronicle,* March 31 and April 1, 1969.
8. *Religious News Service,* Dec. 14, 1967.
9. *Ib.* Sept. 25, 1967.
10. Cf. e.g., *Life,* April 7, 1967.
11. *Church & State,* June, 1967.
12. *Ib.* May, 1968; cf. the Washington *Post,* May 11, 1968; and *Religious News Service,* March 1, 1966.
13. Cf. article by Charles Hillinger in the Los Angeles *Times,* July 21, 1968. Cf. also the San Francisco *Chronicle,* Nov. 2, 1961.
14. Cf. articles in the Arizona *Republic,* March 26, 27, and 28, 1969.

CHAPTER 10

MANNA FROM GOVERNMENT

There is another very important source of church revenue which certainly demands detailed attention: tax-subsidies for religion. In what many believe to be a complete violation of the federal First Amendment as well as of numerous and explicit state constitutional provisions, government at all levels is now providing many kinds of front- and back-door subsidies for the construction and operation of churches and their related organizations. Several years ago, Senator Sam J. Ervin of North Carolina sought to have his Committee on Constitutional Rights make a study of all federal aid to churches. His staff gave up in despair. They found that there was such a diversity of programs, such overlapping and interlocking, and such a bewildering assortment of overt and covert sources of government aid to religion, that it was simply impossible to bring them all together in a single, complete, and accurate tabulation. There are, for instance, more than 250 federal aid-to-education programs alone, and church schools are participating in most of them. Since one division usually is not aware of what others are doing, King Confusion reigns supreme.

Fred P. Graham writing in the New York *Times* asserts that "each year the Office of Economic Opportunity funnels about $90 million into programs run by churches; another $60 million in federal money is being spent to aid students in non-public elementary and high schools, and nobody knows how much U.S. money is being spent to construct science labs, dormitories and other facilities in church colleges." [1]

BALANCING THE BUDGET

Adele Porter, researcher for *Church and State* magazine, estimated that "at least $6.5 billion flows to church-related institutions and groups in the various categories." [2] She said that by cancelling the sectarian benefits, the highly unpopular surtax established in 1968 might not have been necessary. She stated that an estimated total of $5.5 billion in federal church-grants was conservative, to which another $1 billion given churches by state and municipal authorities must be added. This stupendous sum should be compared with the $9 billion voluntarily contributed by their members to Protestant, Catholic, and Jewish religious institutions. The principal sources of federal aid to church organizations are the Hill-Burton Act, the National Defense Education Act of 1958 (often renewed and expanded), the Higher Education Act of 1963, the Economic Opportunity Act of 1964, and the Elementary and Secondary Education Act of 1965. In addition, however, churches cut in on many other federal-aid benefactions.

The Hill-Burton Act, which provides construction funds for private, including sectarian, hospitals, was passed originally in 1946. It has been renewed and extended many times since. During its history, billions of dollars of federal money have been channeled into such institutions. Most of the leading religious denominations have sought and obtained these funds for their hospitals. Indeed, there are few communities of any size where one does not observe handsome edifices belonging to churches, and erected with federal funds.

Various judicial determinations have underscored official approval for such subsidies. But the issue of a sectarian medical code governing a hospital built with public funds has never been squarely brought before the Supreme Court. The issue is real enough, for many church related hospitals operate under a sectarian medical code which bars certain therapies and procedures that are commonly available in other hospitals. It seems unreasonable to believe that public funds for such a hospital could be constitutional. No doubt, some day, we shall see an adjudication of this issue. In the meanwhile, funds of the federal government pour into sectarian hospitals in golden streams.

259

The distribution of funds to churches for the performance of antipoverty programs has become so notable that reports from the Office of Economic Opportunity are sometimes referred to as "the parish list." In some communities the distribution of antipoverty funds is simply a routine business in which the churches get together and divide up the federal melon. When R. Sargent Shriver, long-time head of the OEO, spoke at the Diamond Jubilee Banquet of the Sisters of the Blessed Sacrament, he presented a government check of $7 million to the Natchez-Hattiesburg Roman Catholic Diocese for anti-poverty programs and declared: "Three or four years ago it was practically impossible for a federal agency to give a direct grant to a religious group. Today we are giving hundreds of grants without violating the principle of separation of church and state." [3] To us, this seems like saying that you can cut a man's throat without doing him the slightest injury.

How important these government antipoverty funds can be to church budgets is illustrated by the "parish list" of grants for church programs in Chicago during fiscal 1967:

Roman Catholic	$1,040,377
Episcopal Diocese	34,285
First Presbyterian Church	63,785
Greater M.E. Church	48,710
Greater St. John A.M.E. Church	59,789
Ecumenical Council	130,000
Chicago Council on Religion and Race	201,803
Total	$1,578,749

And so, while the Protestant churches sell their inheritance for a bowl of pottage, the feast goes to the Roman Catholics. Only 4 out of 97 Protestant denominations got so much as a penny.

In Denver, Colorado, the chapter of Americans United for Separation of Church and State made an effort to compute the amount of government subsidies provided for church-related institutions there during 1967. It found four principal categories of church aid: (1) church-related administration of federal money; (2) instructional aid to church schools; (3) construction of church-related academic facilities; and (4) church-related hospital construction. It traced allocation in these categories as follows:

I. Grants to students, loans to students, payments to students for part-time work, fellowships, etc.

The Iliff School of Theology (Meth.) $	37,752	
Loretto Heights College (Catholic)	86,488	
Regis College (Catholic)	128,106	$ 252,346

II. It was impossible to pinpoint the amounts of instructional aid given to church schools without an audit of all individual school districts, including their activities and funds, though it was evident that substantial aid was being provided. For example, funds were advanced at public expense for parochial schools, sufficient to provide one half-time instructor and 7 full-time teachers. Minimal Cost.

	60,000	60,000

III. The construction of academic facilities:

Regis College (grant) $	580,973	
Regis College (3% loan)	580,973	1,161,945

IV. For hospital construction, cumulative totals:

Catholic	10,339,731	
Protestant and Jewish	2,584,186	12,923,517

V. Miscellaneous federal aid:

Regis College	11,817	
Loretto Heights College	81,325	93,142
GRAND TOTAL		$14,490,950

Thus we see that of nearly $14.5 million poured into the sectarian institutions of one community, more than 90% went to the Catholic Church, although its communicants there constitute less than 18% of the population and fewer than one-third of the religious communicants in the city. Of the total grants, about $3.5 million was simply an annual allocation. If all Catholic parishes in the country were subsidized at the same rate, they would be receiving annually a total of almost $2 billion from two or three federal agencies alone.

261

The Philadelphia publication, *Catholic Standard and Times,* an organ of the archdiocese, contains in its July 5, 1968, issue a summary of all its programs financed by the federal government, of which 11 are listed: Operation Discovery, Operation Overbrook, Operation Outbound, Newman Camperships, Contact, Ravenhill Day Camp, S.A.I.L., Pope John Centers, R.S.V.P., Operation Manna, and the S.H.A.L.O.M. Day Camp. Grants for these projects totalled at least $505,080. For a comparable set of church programs, the Pittsburgh diocese received $435,690. Equally impressive was the grant of $819,748 awarded by OEO to the New Mexico Council of Churches for antipoverty programs. It is safe to surmise that the latter grant may well have topped by a considerable margin the entire previous budget of the New Mexico Council.

It is further interesting to note that the New Mexico Council of Churches, which includes both Protestant and Catholic Churches, had received earlier grants for its migrant projects totalling $2,577,043, thus making a total from this one government source of $3,396,791 in a three-year period: private charity at public cost. In the neighboring state of Arizona the Protestant Council of Churches received an allocation for 1969 of $679,548 for its migrant work-projects. Grants to this same group over the previous two years brought the total to $2,326,817.

THE CHURCH-RELATED COLLEGE

If a small church-affiliated college has an expert with a grasp of the federal labyrinth, it can obtain a substantial portion of its annual budget from the government. It can maintain several faculty members through various grants, subsidize many students, and erect most of its buildings with monies so obtained. What a federal grant can mean to a minor church-related institution was illustrated in the case of Anderson College, which is owned by the Church of God and located in Anderson, Indiana. It received a government grant of $1,076,251 for a new academic building, the beginning of a $20 million campus expansion. Additional grants are clearly indicated as the construction proceeds. The story of Anderson College is being duplicated all over the United States.

Another example of federal subsidies is offered in the aid-program for students with exceptional needs. This is only one of a considerable number of similar projects, but it brought 5 small church-related

colleges in Erie, Crawford, and Mercer Counties of Pennsylvania a
total of $435,300 in a single year.

Allegheny College (Methodist)	$ 40,750
Cannon College (Catholic)	218,150
Mercyhurst College (Catholic)	31,300
Thiel College (Lutheran)	101,600
Villa Maria College (Catholic)	43,500
Total	$435,300

MORE AID FOR CHURCH SCHOOLS

Under the Elementary and Secondary Education Act of 1965, a
portion of the funds is mandated to church schools. These are allocated for libraries and various forms of instructional equipment and
service. The law was intended to provide for students in these schools
from a central, publicly controlled location where students of all
faiths and races could be served. But in practice the books, funds,
teaching service and equipment are often channeled directly into the
church schools. Occasionally, as in the case of a parochial elementary
"experimental school" operated by Ursuline College of Louisville, an
entire church school is financed by the government. In Philadelphia,
New York, and Denver—to name but three instances—teachers in
church schools are being paid directly from federal-aid funds.

A number of states such as Michigan and Ohio have now set up
comparable programs to channel their funds into church schools. The
Toledo, Ohio, school system reports that in 1967 a total of $260,147
was set aside for church and other private schools there. Of this total,
$246,742 was provided for 37 Roman Catholic schools and the
remainder for four Lutheran schools and one non-sectarian, private
institution. In 1968, this amount had risen to $523,027.

The Dayton, Ohio, school board reports approval of applications
for $121,349 for 20 church schools, Protestant and Catholic. The
Youngstown, Ohio, Roman Catholic diocese reported that it had
received $550,000 in state funds for equipment and materials for the
first six months of 1968, and that it would receive one and one-half
million dollars for such purposes by the completion of the 1969
school year. In Pennsylvania, $4.5 million was allocated to parochial
schools.

There are many additional federal-aid programs for church institutions. Free meals are provided by the government for parochial schools and even for church summer camps. United States food distribution abroad and at home has been handled by Protestant and Roman Catholic agencies. Also, there have been extensive federal grants to churches and missionary agencies abroad under the banner of war claims and damages; allocations in the millions for overseas church schools under the Agency for International Development; and vital assistance to churches under Urban Redevelopment programs of the federal government in cooperation with local municipalities.

Duquesne University of Pittsburgh, Marquette University of Milwaukee, King's College of Wilkes Barre, Penna., Fordham University of New York City, and St. Louis University—all Roman Catholic—are a few examples among many church-owned and operated institutions of higher learning which have profited enormously by Urban Redevelopment programs. For example, Duquesne paid $1 million for land which cost the government $11 million to acquire, then erected buildings on the site with government grants and loans. In such programs, the government has used its eminent domain to oust people from their homes and businesses and acquire their land. Then it clears the site of buildings and sells the land at an enormous loss to the church schools. Finally, the government provides the funds for construction and may even pay for the teaching later done in the completed buildings. In many cities, clergymen sit on Urban Renewal Boards and make sure that their own private institutions profit handsomely in a wild scramble for the loot.

STUDENT AID

One of the innumerable student-aid programs is called "Upward Bound." This provided $28,161,285 for the 1967–68 school year. One of the recipient schools was the Catholic Marist College of Poughkeepsie, New York, which was given $176,918 to assist 130 students. Church-related institutions drew about half of the total grants for "Upward Bound."

The utility of federal aid to a church institution is demonstrated in the case of Catholic Providence College. Having received a grant of $1 million for its library, the school was able to invest $600,000 in land to be held for speculative profit. Webster College, also Roman Catholic, near St. Louis, received an annual grant of $350,000 from

264

the federal government in a single category, although its enrollment is less than a thousand. Holy Name Hospital (Catholic) Teaneck, N.J., received a federal grant of $203,534 to expand its school of nursing which then increased its enrollment from 173 to 215, and was consequently able to qualify for an additional $10,000 in student grants.

Marymount College (Catholic) in Boca Raton, Florida, with a student body of 350, obtained two one-million-dollar housing grants for dormitories, a $55,000 antipoverty grant to study migrant children, an $81,115 grant to train migrant workers, and a $10,000 educational grant to promote women's education—all since its founding in 1963.

Many new denominational colleges are virtually being created with federal funds. Oral Roberts University, whose founder has now joined the Methodist Church, is an excellent case in point. This is already a multi-million-dollar facility which runs large ads in *Life* magazine to entice students to its campus. Thus Christianity has been wedded to the federal government and to commercialism.

STATE AID CHALLENGED

State subsidies to church institutions came under fire in the case known as Horace Mann vs. Maryland Board of Public Works.[4] The plaintiffs challenged the constitutionality of four State of Maryland construction grants ranging from $500,000 to $750,000 to church-related colleges. These allocations were identical to those which the Federal Office of Education was making every day under the Higher Education Facilities Act. The professed object of the suit was to reach the Supreme Court with the constitutional issue of public grants to church-related colleges.

The plaintiffs prevailed by a split decision in the Maryland Court of Appeals which held that the state's grant to Western Maryland (Methodist) and to St. Joseph and Notre Dame of Maryland (Catholic) were, in fact, acts respecting an establishment of religion and therefore unconstitutional. It was a straight First Amendment case since Maryland law contains no specific disclaimer on the subject. The Maryland attorney general appealed the case, but the Supreme Court refused a hearing. This meant that the Maryland decision was left standing as a just and proper decision. Thereupon, the four colleges simply went to the Federal Office of Education and got the money from this agency. Initial grants of $1,719,667 to Notre Dame of Maryland, $278,738 to Western Maryland, and $248,474 to St. Joseph have since been followed by additional grants. In 1968, for example, St. Joseph alone received nearly $100,000 under a variety of federal programs, all possible because at that time there was no way for taxpayers to challenge them in federal court due to lack off "standing to sue."

The net result of the Maryland case was, therefore, the granting of far greater government funds to the colleges than they had been denied by the State courts. How these State grants, declared unconstitutional even by Maryland's highest court, could be replaced by larger ones from the federal government, remains a deep, dark mystery.

EXPANDING THE CHURCH DOMAIN

There are also federal-aid programs under which funds can be provided for the construction of houses of worship. The Church of Our Merciful Saviour (Episcopal) of Louisville, Kentucky, obtained a loan of $50,000 to be used for construction on the pretext of rehabilitating substandard buildings in an urban-renewal area. The church received a 20-year loan at 3 per cent to construct restrooms and a modern kitchen and parish house. The exterior of the church is being entirely renovated and new classrooms will be added with modern plumbing and electrical wiring throughout. Other churches in the neighborhood have announced that their facilities also need refurbishing and that they will seek similar government subsidies. Broadway Temple A.M.E. Church has filed an application with the F.H.A. for a $50,000 loan under identical terms.

Some churches have received substantial federal aid by securing a rating as a "shrine site," for the renewal and preservation of which government aid is provided.

Donation of U.S. surplus land and buildings to churches has resulted in notable expansion in the church domain. Under this program, a department of the government will declare a certain property excess to its needs. A survey will then be made to see whether any other branch needs the property. If not, the site is declared to be surplus and turned over to the Department of Health, Education, and Welfare for donation to a nonprofit, educational, or welfare use.

The churches have been first in line for these handsome giveaways and have reaped rich dividends. After obtaining 58.6 acres, on which it constructed Evangel College, the Assemblies of God obtained an additional 29.95 acres of government surplus land at the site of the old O'Reilly General Hospital grounds in Springfield, Missouri, in order to expand the campus. In 1964, St. Michael's College of Wincoski, Vermont (Catholic), obtained a donation of 116 acres and 14 buildings at the site of the Ethan Allen Air Force Base. Loyola University (Jesuit) was awarded 60 acres of government land valued at $4.8 million, without charge, at a strategic and valuable location near Chicago.

Another dimension was being added to federal land donations as this work is under preparation. Carroll College (Jesuit) is reportedly the front runner to obtain free of charge the site of the Glasgow Air Force Base in Helena, Montana. Whether or not this grant is finally consummated, there are many precedents for donations of this kind. The new twist is a lease-back arrangement. Carroll would not use the base at all, but would provide tax-exempt church ownership in order to lease it to Avco Corporation. This is euphemistically described as "a new type of imaginative partnership." [5]

STATE AND MUNICIPAL AID

Many states have initiated their own programs of aid to church schools, as we have already seen. They sometimes provide substantial support for the welfare programs of many churches. In New York state, for example, more than 80 per cent of the welfare performed by the Roman Catholic Church is said to be financed by the state. In half the states, the transportation bill for church schools is paid by the taxpayers. In New York, Rhode Island, Mississippi, and Louisiana, textbooks provided by the state for public schools must also be made available for church schools. Pennsylvania provides grants for church schools via an "authority" from a tax on harness racing. Such assistance to church schools releases their own funds for expansion of their denominational facilities and programs.

Municipalities have often granted preferred treatment to churches in the sale of public land. In both New York City and Boston, many sites have been withdrawn from public bidding and sold to a church at a price far below market value. As we have noted, it took a protracted lawsuit to have this practice terminated as unconstitutional in New York.

Many "giveaway sales" in and around Boston are matters of public record. In February, 1957, for example, the city acquired for park purposes 386,921 square feet in West Roxbury, then sold it at a private sale to the archbishop of Boston for a school and monastery of the Christian Brothers. In January, 1963, the Henry Vane public school was sold by the city of Boston for $4,500 to the Catholic archbishop. The Damon public school, likewise, was sold for $3,000 at a private sale in July, 1967. In 1961, the city of Fall River, Massachusetts, sold 37.65 acres of city-owned land to the Boston Catholic Bishop James L. Connolly for $1. And there have been others.

It might be worth noting that most cities in Massachusetts are very heavily Catholic.

EXEMPTION AND SUBSIDIES

It is evident, then, that the government not only provides tax-exemption for the churches, but also subsidies for them through a bewildering variety of agencies and programs, so numerous and complicated that no man knows or can know their scope or number. There is, again, no tax levied against the amounts received in subsidies. Unfortunately, the government does not usually keep separate records of the amounts which go to church institutions and programs. For example, in the Hill-Burton grants for hospital construction, there is nothing, except possibly something in the name of the institution, to indicate whether the one in question is sectarian or secular. In so far as they can be readily traced, public subsidies to the churches in 12 federal categories and by the states and municipalities add up to the totals shown in the following analysis.

It should be noted (1) that of the Hill-Burton grants totalling about $270 million annually, probably at least one-fourth is allocated to sectarian institutions; (2) that under Housing and Urban Redevelopment, huge sums are channelled into church treasuries; and (3) that the Department of Defense, the Atomic Energy Commission, the National Aeronautics and Space Administration (NASA), the Department of Agriculture, an agency for research in bio-medicine, the Federal Office of Education, and the National Science Foundation all have programs which convey federal funds very generously into churches and church-related institutions. All of these agencies and departments are heavily funded; some have billions or even tens of billions of dollars at their disposal, all of which may be scattered abroad, more or less at the whim and discretion of powerful bureaucrats.

If the American taxpayers were to obtain an exact accounting of how all this money is spent, they would indeed be amazed—and perhaps ready to revolt. One thing is certain: the churches are getting subsidies which should make the Founding Fathers turn over in their graves.

BASIS FOR ESTIMATES

Since Senator Ervin, with an excellent staff having access to all available records, could not determine exactly how much money is being funneled by federal agencies into religious entities, it would indeed be presumptuous on our part to say that we can do so. We have, however, searched through a vast conglomeration of reports, releases, pamphlets, statistics, and other publications, in our quest for information. And we believe that we can present summaries which, though neither complete nor precise, will err only by being too conservative.

In the following, we indicate how we arrive at some of the totals we present.

(1) THE HILL-BURTON PROGRAMS

The Hill-Burton Act, passed in 1946, received its initial appropriation of $75 million in 1948. During recent years, huge sums have been allocated under five programs; these have expanded from $209,728,000 in 1962 to $270,000,000 in 1967. A total of $2,190,000,000 was appropriated during the years 1957–1967 inclusive.[6]

There were 8,587 hospitals with 1,876,927 beds in the United States in 1966, of which 1,205 having about 23,400 beds were church-owned or related.[7] Of these, 788 with 153,664 beds are Roman Catholic.[8] Since we know that sectarian, and particularly Catholic, hospitals received at least a full proportion, we may be sure that the sectarian facilities received not less than $37.8 million and the Roman Catholic alone not less than $25.1 million in 1967.

(2) HEALTH SERVICES

The Department of Health, Education, and Welfare alone lists 141 programs for the promotion of health and physical aid which expended $2,084,000,000 in 1967.[9] When other health programs are added to these, we have a total in 1968 of $4,069,000,000. The Ervin Committee in its Report stated that the Church proportion in these allocations was 10% in 1967. It is probably higher now. At all events, we have under this heading not less than $407,000,000 for sectarian institutions.

EDUCATION

In 1967, the federal government disbursed a total of $12,198,000,000 for an infinite variety of educational programs, divided as follows:

(3) ELEMENTARY AND SECONDARY EDUCATION

The Elementary and Secondary Education Act, passed in 1965, now supports 12 programs, which expended $3,084,100,000 in 1967.[10] Since these funds were distributed through the states, we have no breakdown as to the sums given to public, private-secular, and sectarian institutions. In 1966, about 49 million pupils were enrolled in all elementary and secondary schools, of whom about 6,300,000 were in the non-public.[11] Of these, some 5,350,000 [12] were in Catholic, and the remainder were divided almost equally between Protestant and secular schools. Since non-public pupils comprised 13% of the total, of whom 85% were Catholic and 8% Protestant, and since we know that the sectarian schools received proportionally more than others, we find that at least $286 million went to religious institutions, and, of this, 90% or $258 million, was received by Catholic schools. Their actual grants were probably considerably greater.

(4) THE HIGHER EDUCATION FACILITIES ACT

The Higher Education Facilities Act, passed in 1963, now supports 8 programs which expended $3,590,700,000 in 1967.[13] *The World Almanac* of 1969 [14] lists 1,783 colleges and universities, of which 609 are church-related, 382 are private-secular, and 792 are public institutions. According to the 1968 *Statistical Abstract,* the enrollment in public schools of higher learning was 4,178,000 and in private institutions 1,908,000, or 31% in 1966.[15] We know that there were 434,000 students in 305 Catholic colleges and universities in 1968, whose institutions therefore must have received at least 7%, or $251 million. Assuming that other church-related institutions received a comparable total, we find that sectarian schools of higher learning received some $500 million from the federal government.

(5) ADULT VOCATIONAL EDUCATION

In 1967, the federal government disbursed $908,400,000 [16] under 6 programs geared to adult vocational training. We estimate that at least 10% of this, or $91,000,000, went to sectarian institutions.

(6) OTHER EDUCATIONAL PROGRAMS

Through 18 other programs, the federal government spent another $3,871,900,000 for educational projects.[17] This included grants for Indian education, for libraries, community services, college housing, veterans education, and many more. Assuming that at least 10% of this went to sectarian organizations, we have another $387,000,000.

(7) THE ECONOMIC OPPORTUNITY ACT

Senator Ervin's Committee on Constitutional Rights issued a report on August 2, 1967, covering the operations of the O.E.O. in 1966, which stated that 6% of the allocations went to sectarian institutions. Since then O.E.O. funds have increased to $2.06 billion in the 1969 budget and its allocations to churches and other religious organizations have been increased to far higher ratios than in previous years. According to a plethora of available releases, this proportion now seems, in many communities, to have reached 50%. However, computing the ratio at only 20%, we find that the O.E.O. disburses at least $412,000,000 a year to sectarian entities.

(8) HOUSING AND URBAN DEVELOPMENT

In 1967, the Department of Housing and Urban Development disbursed $7,368,000,000.[18] Vast sums went for loans to build church retirement homes, for rental supplements, and to supply church-related institutions with land at enormous losses to the taxpayers. Even if we assume that only 5% of this went to sectarian organizations, this allocation still totalled no less than $368,000,000.

(9) SURPLUS COMMODITIES AND PROPERTY

The government has many programs under Surplus Commodities. For example, we find under Food for Freedom that $1,444,000,000 [19] is being disbursed in 1969; and under School Meals another $448,000,000 was spent in 1967.[20] Since churches, especially the Roman Catholic, receive a very large proportion of this, we believe that for these and other programs under this heading at least $600,000,000 goes to sectarian organizations.

(10) RESEARCH AND DEVELOPMENT PROGRAMS

The Departments of Defense and Agriculture, the National Science Foundation, the Atomic Energy Commission, the National Aeronautics and Space Administration, etc., have combined budgets of about $110 billion a year. All of these have a multiplicity of programs which overlap with others, but all of which include church-related educational institutions. What these total, perhaps no one knows or can know. Assuming that it is about 10%, we have $1,112,200,000.

(11) INTEREST-COST TO THE GOVERNMENT

Since churches and church-related institutions have now borrowed vast sums from the government at 3% less than the money costs the taxpayers, and since they have also received enormous outright grants, these programs have increased the national debt by not less than $8 or $10 billion and have therefore added at least $300 million annually to the interest that must be paid by the federal Treasury.

(12) OTHER FEDERAL AID

The mere cost of administering all the above programs constitutes a very great expense; and there is an endless multiplicity of other programs, so extensive and so complicated that they stagger the imagination. We estimate that these total a minimum of $1,500,000,000.

In the following, we do not make any attempt to give detailed information concerning local subsidies to church groups; but we consider the total of $1 billion very conservative indeed for programs that are burgeoning in various states across the nation.

SUMMARY

(1) The Hill-Burton Programs	$ 37,800,000
(2) Health Services	407,000,000
(3) Elementary and Secondary Education Act	286,000,000
(4) The Higher Education Facilities Act	500,000,000
(5) Adult Vocational Education	91,000,000
(6) Other Educational Programs	387,000,000
(7) The Economic Opportunity Act	412,000,000
(8) Housing and Urban Development[a]	368,000,000
(9) Surplus Commodities and Property	600,000,000
(10) Research and Development	1,112,000,000
(11) Interest-Loss to the Government	300,000,000
(12) Other Federal Aid; Administrative Costs	1,500,000,000
TOTAL	$6,000,800,000
State and Municipal Aid: Textbooks, Transportation, Welfare, Urban Renewal, Aid to Colleges, etc.	1,000,000,000
GRAND TOTAL	$7,000,800,000

[a] This item alone includes certain long-term loans which have, in many cases, proved unrecoverable in part or in full, as with the Christopher Homes in Tucson, Arizona.

By any count, the totals of government money flowing to the churches are impressive. The rationale for this flow is usually that the government is hiring the churches to perform welfare service more cheaply than it could be done in any other way. These infusions of public money, however, do enlarge and buttress the tax-exempt ecclesiastical structure, a power-complex that exists purely for private and sectarian purposes. It enhances that very economic and cultural dimension which in other times has become oppressive. The government subsidy which may appear to be a blessing in a given case

273

becomes, in multiplication, an onerous burden upon the public. We can now clearly observe one unmistakable result: the churches have already commenced to look more to government and less to their members for their financial support. Perhaps this is because they find government more pliable to their demands than their own communicants. We believe this is a shift which will bring no good either to the churches or to the nation. A church that depends for its maintenance on general taxation and on unrelated business income will not long retain the loyalty or the voluntary support of its communicants. When it is no longer necessary for clerics to serve their flocks in order to live in affluence, the fires of religious devotion will soon flicker and burn low; and, in due course, will die like embers on the midnight hearth.

Citations

1. March 17, 1968.
2. *Church and State,* March 1967.
3. *Catholic Standard,* Feb. 17, 1966.
4. Maryland Court of Appeals, 1965, N. 356.
5. Great Falls *Tribune,* July 12, 1968.
6. Cf. *Grants in Aid,* published by U.S. Dept. of Health, Education, and Welfare, 1967 edition, pp. 200–201.
7. *Modern Hospital Directory,* 1966, pp. 1–275, McGraw-Hill.
8. Cf. 1968 *Official Catholic Directory,* Summary.
9. Cf. *Grants in Aid, ib.,* pp. 283–298.
10. Cf. *Statistical Abstract,* 1968, p. 139.
11. *Ib.,* p. 105.
12. Cf. *Official Catholic Directory.*
13. *Statistical Abstract, ib.*
14. Pp. 319–342. Cf. *Comparative Guide to American Colleges,* pp. 819–823.
15. *Statistical Abstract, ib.,* p. 107.
16. *Ib.,* p. 139.
17. *Ib.*
18. *Ib.,* p. 381.
19. *Ib.,* p. 379.
20. *Ib.,* p. 277.

CHAPTER 11

TOWARD A SOLUTION

THE CHANGING CHURCH

One of the encouraging developments is that clergymen themselves, as we have repeatedly noted, have begun to see the dangers inherent in unlimited religious exemptions. The secular community does not fear the spiritual values taught by churches; but almost every one is beginning to realize that of tax-exempt property and wealth—even of that used for purely religious purposes—there can easily be too much. History is studded with situations in which this has been true. Many keen observers believe that we are approaching such a juncture in the United States. As a matter of principle it can be argued that a wealthy church is a contradiction in terms. The question may well be asked whether churches should accumulate wealth at all.

Most people now believe that any amount of commercial wealth—especially if the income from it is untaxed—is too much; all sections of our population are now almost unamimous in declaring that such assets constitute an excrescence.

There is, indeed, a small minority which argues that if the church has commercial tax-exempt revenue, it can render more and better service. But the historic record demonstrates that as a church accumulates vast holdings, it becomes more and more preoccupied with its temporalities—enmeshed in its own interior business—managing investments, counting profits, making reports—until its spiritual objectives are choked in a field of tares and underbrush.

In our judgment, the laws exempting churches from virtually all taxation of every kind have now become archaic and must be changed. The religious exemption was conceived in another era. It originated in a wilderness-situation where the church was a small shack at the crossroads, which ministered, nevertheless, equally to all members of a frontier community. On this, a tax of even a few dollars might have extinguished an operation which the community felt to be essential to its well-being.

We live in a different world. Largely because of their exemptions, especially in an age of very heavy general taxation, they are set far apart from taxpaying entities, and many churches have become vast financial enterprises and corporations with boards of directors managing diverse business interests in no way related to religion. They have achieved powerful economic, even political, dimensions, controlling important segments of the nation's wealth and economy.

THE SUPER-CHURCH

At this point, the ecumenical movement assumes strategic relevance. Since one of its immediate objectives is the merger of the churches, it envisions a vast ecclesiastical empire—a private corporation whose structure, economy, and political power would rival that of the state itself. Its ability to accumulate and expand would be virtually without limit. It would certainly and immediately assume the powers and perquisites of a state within the state. And it would inevitably demand even greater powers, privileges, and subsidies than are presently granted to any church on American soil. We might quickly regress to the conditions of Ancient Egypt and India and to something resembling the Middle Ages in Europe.

Although some of the circumstances may be different, this is essentially the status which various churches have, in fact, achieved in other periods of history, as we have pointed out in a previous chapter. In many times and places, as a result of its material accumulations, its political influence, and its power to resist the leveling effects of equitable taxation, the church has become not merely the rival but even the master of the state. Under such conditions, its officials become an authoritarian theocracy with their own laws, courts, and procedures, sometimes if not always independent of the civil power. Such was the medieval power-structure. The modern state, as we know it, could not emerge until this theocratic polity was demolished. Such a reckoning always included the expropriation of church property, a tremendous wave of irreligion, and, at the very least, the complete outlawry of the unrelated business income of churches. We may say that the untaxed commercial revenues and properties of churches constituted the basic cause of almost every European revolution.

We can observe the early stages of a parallel development in the United States today. Even though many of our churches are small, this must not blind us to the fact that in recent years others have been steadily centralizing the control of their vastly increasing operations. Local parishes are no longer the definitive terms of the church; we must now think of it as consisting of central boards and agencies which direct and manage them. No longer are we dealing with small sanctuaries at the crossroads or in the wildwood, but with a central headquarters merging with others in a dimension of cumulative power. Farsighted churchmen now are beginning to see that if this process is permitted to continue with the strong nourishment of tax-exemptions it could lead to fearful convulsions and to eventual revolution and expropriation.

The proposal that tax-exemption for churches be reconsidered is therefore gaining currency among religious leaders. It is reflected in the determination by some church congregations to pay the tax, or at least a part of what would normally be assessed.

In Belleville, Illinois, the Ministerial Alliance urged that clergymen be "taxed like everyone else." The State's Attorney for St. Clair County, John M. Karns, Jr., took note and requested that while the State constitution exempts certain properties of clergymen from taxation, it did not exempt personal property. The Belleville ministers criticized the County Board of Supervisors and stated flatly: "It is unfair to taxpayers that ministers get away with it."

THE PRESBYTERIANS

In 1952, the United Presbyterian Church, U.S.A., requested its denominational foundation "to make no investment in unrelated business where such income exemptions are allowable." In 1964, the same denomination recommended repeal of the provision of the

Internal Revenue Code which exempts churches from income tax on profits unrelated to the purpose of the church or its organizations; and it urged that "congregations be encouraged to take the initiative in making contributions to local communities, in lieu of taxes, in recognition of services provided by local government."

The Eden Prairie Presbyterian Church in Minnesota sent $100 to the Village Council in lieu of taxes for the year. The Merriam Park Presbyterian Church of St. Paul has been doing the same. The Central Presbyterian Church of Des Moines, Iowa, allocated $4,000 to the city in lieu of property tax. The congregation reckoned that $3,000 would equal the "functional funds" tax levy which supports such "city services as streets, public safety and sanitation." [1] Said Earl Larson, a member of the church's Session: "Our neighbors are paying $17,070 in taxes that they would not be paying if our property were not exempt." The same congregation disposed of the parsonages it had traditionally maintained and announced that its ministers would henceforth be given a "housing allowance" to provide taxable residences. "From now on I can be a full-fledged citizen in a house on which I am paying taxes." So declared the Reverend Arthur H. Cruickshank.

The Meadowville Presbyterian Church of Louisville, Ky., did not tackle the problem of tax-exemption for its sanctuary, but it did ask the Fiscal Court to rescind the exemption on its two parsonages, since it felt that "all other individuals on the property tax rolls are, in effect, subsidizing a religion."

THE UNITARIAN-UNIVERSALISTS

Other denominations have endorsed these statements and practices, particularly the Unitarian-Universalists. A number of their churches have made voluntary payments in lieu of taxes. The Rev. Philip M. Larson, pastor of Channing Memorial Church of Newport, R.I., announced that his governing body had voted unanimously to contribute $100 to the city "in lieu of taxes for services rendered to our church by the city." The Rev. Paul N. Carnes of Buffalo, N.Y., presented the mayor with a check for $100 as a "token contribution to pay for services rendered . . . We are aware," he declared, "of the financial plight of the city. It is our hope that others who benefit from these services will follow suit."

The Unitarian Society of Cleveland has been contributing $1,329 annually to the city in lieu of taxes. The Unitarian Church of Montclair, N.J., has given $1,000 as a protest "against the long-standing tax-exemption of church property," and "in recognition of Montclair's municipal services to the church." The Unitarian Church of Richmond, Virginia, voted to pay the city $300 in lieu of taxes, which would represent 27.9% of full taxation.

A CHURCH BUSINESS PAYS SOMETHING

The Augsburg Publishing House of Minneapolis, Minnesota, which we have already noticed, paid a full property tax until 1965, when it won exemption by court decree on the plea that it is an agency of the Lutheran Church. Since then, the corporation has voted to pay the city $6,700 annually, as a voluntary contribution, described as payment for police and fire protection and other services rendered. However, at full rates, the levy would be $120,000.

CHURCH RESIDENCES

The Rev. Melvin Keaney, pastor of the Immaculate Heart of Mary Church in St. Louis, Missouri, reported to John N. Poelker, City Comptroller, that his parish owned two residential properties rented to its employees. Father Keaney said that he thought the properties should not enjoy exemption. At the request of the Comptroller, the City Assessor, Joseph Sansone, has moved to assess taxes against them.

The Rev. L. Henry Nielsen, pastor of the large Calvary Lutheran Church of Golden Valley in suburban Minneapolis, Minnesota, announced that he had requested the local assessor to place the church parsonage on the tax rolls. Valued at about $30,000, this should produce from $900 to $1,000 in tax-revenue, according to Pastor Nielsen. He noted that another parsonage belonging to the church but occupied by a lay member of its staff, had been on the tax rolls for some time.

The Meadowville Presbyterian Church of Louisville, Ky., asked the Fiscal Court to rescind the exemption on its two parsonages, since it felt that "all other individuals on the property tax rolls are, in effect, subsidizing a religion."

VOLUNTARY INITIATIVE INADEQUATE

Despite the commendable initiative taken by various local congregations and denominational leaders, it appears that such efforts in themselves will not prove effective. Indeed, it must be noted that some church leaders have vigorously opposed any change in current exemptions. When this question was before the Committee revising the Pennsylvania Constitution, for example, the Catholic Conference of that state voiced sharp hostility to the slightest revision. Many Protestant leaders have also defended present immunities on the very ground of separation of church and state and as an indispensable support for the free exercise of religion.

It seems clear that no substantial reform in church tax-exemptions will be forthcoming either from the churches or the clergy. A solid phalanx of precedents extending back into antiquity consistently enforces our religious exemptions. In spite of the significant developments reviewed in Chapter 4, neither can the courts be expected to effect the necessary alterations.

LEGISLATIVE PROPOSALS

It is our belief that the reforms which we have predicted for the future will result from popular demand and must be accomplished through legislative action and constitutional revision. Various proposals are now under consideration. At least a dozen states are currently contemplating new constitutions and in all of them the issue of tax-exemption is assuming increasing importance. Legislative proposals now before Congress could bring basic and far-reaching changes, though, in our opinion, they do not go nearly far enough.

Two bills introduced by Rep. Wilbur D. Mills have as their purpose the imposition of taxes on the unrelated "active" business and the debt-financed income of churches. This would abolish the tax-immunity on revenue from competitive business and from any property acquired by a church with borrowed funds, as in the case of "leasebacks." These proposals, however, would have no effect on investment-income derived from stocks, bonds, mortgages, capital gains, cash accounts, etc. Should these proposals be written into a revised Internal Revenue Code, this would indeed be progress; but, in our opinion, not enough.

In New York City, fundamental changes in regard to real estate tax-exemptions have been proposed by the Citizens Budget Commission, which pointed out that under present statutes the municipality has no discretion in this matter. A religious group, for example, need only show that it falls technically within the scope of the applicable sections of the Real Property Law, and exemption becomes automatic. The Commission proposes lifting the exemption altogether and then returning in the form of a subsidy a payment commensurate with any public service deemed to have been rendered—the theory being that where there is no tangible service to the community, there should be no exemption. By granting a public subsidy in return for public benefit, the municipality would maintain effective control.

The political implications of such a proposal, however, are too obvious to require delineation. To subsidize any church even for welfare or educational service would run into immediate conflict with many state constitutions and statutes which prohibit that very thing. Furthermore, it would open a Pandora's Box for religious favoritism: what would happen when the members of a single church are in political control? The proposal, therefore, can hardly be considered viable, but it does indicate that community planners are wrestling with the problems involved.

WHAT IS THE CHURCH?

Before advancing our own specific suggestions for reform, it seems desirable that we examine the essential nature of the church as a social institution. Can it qualify as a public charity? Or is it essentially private in character? To this question, there is only one reasonable answer: the church is a purely private institution. The very nature of religious faith makes this mandatory wherever and whenever it is to remain free. Churches practice proselytism. All have their specific creeds, teachings, or attitudes, attractive to their own communicants but often undesirable, unacceptable, or even repulsive to others. The basic element in every church is precisely those qualities or doctrines in which it differs from others and thereby sets itself apart. No church constituency can possibly be equated with the general public, unless we are to have a total union of church and state, such as existed during the Middle Ages. Each church is a special and private group in the United States, dedicated to its own sectarian position and therefore intrinsically different from the population as a whole. The distinctively private nature of the churches is emphasized by the fact that

281

they excommunicate or "disfellowship" those who do not accept their sectarian rules and doctrines.

Recognizing the truth of the preceding, the Washington *Post* editorialized in the following manner concerning the federal anti-poverty program: The Church-State problem, it declared, "is not obviated . . . by the stipulation in the programs that projects using church facilities must be open to persons of all faiths, that religious instruction may not be given, and that religious symbols must be covered up. Churches are commonly open to persons of all faiths; that is how they proselyte. And no amount of covering up religious symbols can avoid making the religious institution itself seem the source of benefactions financed out of public funds. For all the good intentions and good will entailed, we believe there is more danger than welfare in this partnership between church and state." [2]

Churches, therefore, may not claim to be institutions directly serving the welfare of the general public until they become as accessible as are public streets and parks. Such a claim must remain purely synthetic as long as they maintain any sectarian stance or engage in proselytism. Churches are essentially different from the Red Cross, the Community Chest, a public library, or an art gallery. The latter have no creed, no sectarian position, no regard to any person's speculative or philosophical persuasions, no large accumulations of property. They serve all persons on precisely the same terms.

It is because churches are private institutions that we have the First Amendment which stipulates that Congress shall make no law respecting an establishment of religion or prohibiting the free exercise thereof. Public agencies are not to get into the religious field. They must neither promote nor impede religion. And why not? Because religion is a private matter, lying in the realm apart from civil or official concerns. In the light of the ban on acts respecting an establishment of religion, one can only view with amazement and revulsion as well as with extreme alarm the many sections of the Internal Revenue Code which apparently do establish religion. We therefore recommend the following specific reforms.

I. STATUTORY REVISIONS IN THE INTERNAL REVENUE CODE

(1) Section 107, which enables "a minister of the gospel" to avoid all income taxes for life, should be repealed.

(2) Section 119, which enables a cleric to enjoy the living standard of a millionaire without tax-liability should be repealed.

(3) Section 502, which enables exempts to set up tax-free "feeder" corporations should be repealed, at least to the extent that this enables religious organizations to create such corporations.

(4) Paragraphs (1) and (4) of subsection (b) of section 503, which permit all religious organizations and any organization "operated, supervised, controlled, or principally supported by a religious organization" to receive unrelated passive business income without tax-liability should be repealed.

(5) From section 511 (a) (2) (A) the following should be deleted: "(other than a church, a convention or association of churches, or a trust described in subsection (b)). . . ." This is the provision which allows all religious organizations to carry on unrelated active business operations without tax-liability.

(6) Section 3401 (a) (9), which states that the employer of any ordained minister or member of a religious order shall not withhold and transmit income taxes or Social Security contributions to the federal Treasury, should be repealed.

(7) The provision in section 1402 (e) which excuses members of religious orders from payments to Social Security should be removed.

(8) Section 6033 (a) (1), which specifically exempts religious organizations described in section 501 (c) (3) and 511 (a) (2) (A), and these alone, from the necessity of filing returns of any kind, should be repealed.

(9) Furthermore, since churches are purely private and exclusive organizations, and since our Constitution expressly prohibits any law which establishes them, there would appear to be a question whether the special inducements offered contributors to "charity" could be extended to churches, were the Supreme Court to interpret the First Amendment properly. The Congress should certainly reconsider the 5-year carryover, established by section 170 (b) (5) (A), at least insofar as this applies to churches. Actually, it is doubtful that any of the provisions of section 170 as these apply to religious organizations are constitutional. We feel also that gifts from foundations when received by churches should be classified as taxable unrelated business income, since grants from foundations should be tax free only to organizations which exist for an entirely public purpose.

(10) The provisions of the Tariff Schedule contained in section 270.25 and 850 to 850.70, which enable churches to import unlimited quantities of duty-free goods should be repealed.

(11) The right of the cleric to act as a "corporation sole" or in the capacity of a "corporation aggregate" should be terminated.

II. DISCLOSURE

Churches should be required to make full disclosure of their finances just as other corporations are required to do. This would include a complete report of condition and financial operations—revenues, expenditures, properties, and resources. These reports should be available to any interested person. Churches should also be required to register their bonds and be subject to all regulations of the SEC in the same way as others are. Any church or "charity" which fails to make complete financial disclosure, at least to its contributors and membership, should lose all forms of tax-exemption, even on its voluntary contributions.

III. TAXATION OF BUSINESS INCOME

All churches, associations of churches, religious orders (sacerdotal or not) should be required to report all unrelated business income, whether active or passive, including grants from foundations, on Form 990 T and pay the tax on such revenue established for corporations in section 11 of the Internal Revenue Code.

IV. TERMINATION OF IMMUNITIES FOR CLERICS AND RELIGIOUS

All priests, ministers, and members of religious orders should be treated by state and federal taxing authorities exactly as if they were laymen.

In a country where religion is not established by the state, why should preferred status be given the clergy? Clergymen should assume their responsibilities as citizens in the same manner as other members of the community, especially at the office of the tax-collector. Excusing a clergyman from income taxation because he is a member of a religious order which imposes an obligation to give all his money to a church, is an example of clerical privilege. Actually, the clergymen who benefit from this exemption are in less need of preferential treatment than are millions of parents of needy children. Celibates have no family obligations, no children to support, and to educate; according to one defensible point of view, they should be taxed more heavily than others.

Again, there is no logic in the exemption covering a clergyman's housing allowance, which can enable him to escape all tax on a magnificent salary. It is true that he and his family require housing, but so do we all. To extend such an exemption to a minister and to him alone should be extremely embarrassing to self-respecting people and should be withdrawn forthwith.

V. LOCAL PROPERTY TAXATION

All land held by churches but not used exclusively for religious purposes should be fully taxed. Any building, for example, in which bingo games are played should be subject to full taxation.

A "fee formula" or a specific service charge (such as is now under consideration in several states) should be devised even for the church sanctuaries and private schools, under which they would pay the municipality at least for a portion of the services rendered them, such as the cost of paving, sidewalks, sewers, flood control, street lighting, fire and police protection, sanitation, etc.

As we have noted, Dr. Eugene Carson Blake proposed that churches pay one per cent of a normal levy the first year, then increase this by one per cent annually until a level of 10% is attained. In Ontario, the Smith Committee recommended that all church property be assessed at full valuations, then be taxed at 5 per cent of the full rate with an additional 5 per cent to be added each year for a period of 7 years. This would bring the assessment to 35 per cent of parity. We submit these two suggestions for serious consideration. Obviously, the "fee formula" cannot be left to voluntary response, since, to be equitable, it must be applied systematically and universally.

VI. TERMINATION OF CHURCH SUBSIDIES

All church subsides, direct or indirect, should be ended forthwith. No institution definitely related to a church should be granted public funds. Churches desiring to operate a sectarian school should be required to meet public academic standards and should never expect to receive any support from the taxpayers, either directly or indirectly.

VII. OTHER REFORMS

In the studies made for this book, we have inevitably turned up many inequities in the tax-structure which do not directly involve the churches. Problems presented by other kinds of exempts do, however, bear on the general problem of tax-exemption in the United States. We therefore offer these broader proposals which we believe the situation demands.

(1) Private groups, professional organizations, and other great exempts like the National Geographic Society and various wealthy corporations of which there are a great many in Washington and in cities throughout the nation, should also reimburse their communities, at least according to a "fee formula" for services rendered. Harvard does this in Cambridge, but refuses to make any contribution to the city of Boston, where it has additional and very extensive properties.

(2) When the federal government establishes industries in local areas, which must then provide all services for them and their personnel, such plants should be charged the full ad valorem tax. In St. Louis and in Ramsey County, Minnesota, for example, the federal government owns and operates huge munitions plants which do not reimburse these communities with so much as a single penny.

(3) The so-called "low-cost" housing projects financed by federal funds should be charged the full ad valorem tax and the national government should pay it. After these white elephants are created, they are simply dumped on local communities, which must then maintain them, usually at enormous deficits underwritten by local taxpayers. In many cities, such projects constitute a large portion of all tax-exempt property, sometimes surpassing the value of the entire public school system. If the federal government deems these projects necessary, it should certainly maintain them and pay the taxes on them. There is precedent for this in the District of Columbia, where the federal government in effect pays taxes for all its property. Such tax payments would be simple equity. The government should pay what it owes to its own citizens and to the local communities which make the affluent federal colossus possible.

WHAT WILL BE DONE?

One fact is certain: the issues relating to taxation and exemptions are now being discussed as never before and the general subject of churches and their unique exemptions and immunities are being subjected to almost universal scrutiny and criticism. In a nationally syndicated article [3] recently published, George W. Cornell, religion writer for AP, declares that "a growing number of budget-pinched cities and states are taking a harder, hungry look at an old American tradition, the tax-exempt status of churches." And he states categorically that the question is no longer " 'Should the churches be taxed?' . . . . the issue has now become 'What kind of taxes should the churches pay?' "

He continues with a thumb-nail sketch of steps that are now under way in many portions of the nation to place religious institutions, foundations, etc., under certain types of taxation.

Who says there is nothing new under the sun?

Some of the above proposals may seem drastic. We are convinced, however, that they are not only realistic, but also essential to the well-being of the churches themselves. A wealthy church is a self-contradiction, for it soon loses its power and effectiveness as a spiritual operation. The rich and subsidized church—needing nothing and nobody—quickly assumes those historic characteristics of religious establishment which caused the Founding Fathers to include the First Amendment in the Constitution. It loses its vital capacity for service and easily becomes an instrument of oppression, as it has done so often under similar circumstances in the past. Certainly, the admonition of Jesus to the rich young man still has relevance for all churches: "Go, sell what you possess and give it to the poor, and you will have treasure in heaven; and come, follow me." [4]

And did not He who called himself the Son of Man scourge the money-changers from the Temple because they had transformed it "into a den of thieves"? [5] How would he react to the billionaire church corporation of today, immersed to the eyeballs in leasebacks, mortgages, securities, housing projects, bingo games, girdle factories, and stock-market manipulations? Would a simple scourge suffice to cleanse the sanctuaries, or would the flame-throwing steeds of the Apocalypse be called upon to sear the earth and devastate a sinful church?

---

[1] The Des Moines *Register*, Nov. 10, 1963.
[2] The Washington *Post*, Aug. 18, 1965.
[3] Cf. Arizona *Republic*, May 24, 1969.
[4] Matt. 19:21 R.S.V.
[5] Mark 11:17 and Luke 19:46.

APPENDIX I

STATISTICAL TABLES

TABLE I—DEVELOPMENT OF RELIGIOUS ORGANIZATIONS IN THE U.S.A.[1]

Denomination	1660	1740	1820	1860	1900	1950
Anglican-Episcopal	41	246	600	2,145	6,254	7,784
Baptist	4	96	2,700	12,150	49,905	77,090
Congregational	75	423	1,100	2,234	5,604	5,679
Dutch Reformed	13	129	380	1,116	2,296	3,517
Lutheran	4	95	800	2,128	10,287	16,403
Presbyterian	5	150	1,700	6,406	15,452	13,200
Quakers (Friends)			350	728	1,031	654
Unitarian-Universalists			350	928	1,255	758
Methodist			2,700	19,883	53,908	54,000
Disciples of Christ				2,100	10,298	7,769
Christian Scientist					504	3,040
Latter-Day Saints (Mormon)					1,041	2,700
Adventists				136	?	2,712
Assemblies of God						5,950
Brethren						1,029
Jewish		5		30		4,000
Church of God						6,972
Church of God in Christ						3,307
Nazarenes						3,480
Ev. United Brethren						4,323
Church of Christ						14,500
Greek Archdiocese						320
Mennonite						1,211
Pentecostal						3,682
Roman Catholic	12	27	124	2,550	10,339	15,533
TOTALS	154	1,171	10,804	52,532	168,174	259,613

[1] Statistics from the *Historical Atlas of Religion in America*, pp. 160–161, Harper and Row, 1962. The above data was compiled from various federal censuses.

TABLE II—POPULATION AND CHURCH COMMUNICANTS IN THE U.S.A.—1785 to 1964

Year	Population [1]	Communicants	Jewish	Roman Catholic	Protestant, Etc.
1785	3,600,000	1,200,000 [2]	No Data	18,200	1,150,000
1890	62,900,000	20,612,806 [3]	130,496	6,257,871	14,223,439
1906	85,430,000	32,936,445 [4]	101,457 [5]	12,079,142	20,287,742 [6]
1916	101,900,000	41,926,854	357,135	15,721,815	25,847,904
1936	128,180,000	55,807,366 [8]	4,641,184	19,914,937	31,251,245
1964	185,783,493	117,946,002	5,509,000	44,847,381 [9]	68,528,313

[1] For the census counts, cf. the 1963 *Statistical Abstract*, p. 5.
[2] This number based on assumption that 32.85% of the population were church communicants, the proportion given in the 1890 *Abstract of the Census*, p. 259.
[3] Statistics for 1890, from *ib*.
[4] Statistics for 1906 from the 1906 *Census of Religious Bodies*, I 25.
[5] Reports on Jewish synagogues were incomplete in 1906.
[6] This total does not include the Eastern Orthodox or Latter Day Saints congregations, which had a combined total of 387,253 members in 1906.
[7] Statistics for 1916 from the 1916 *Census of Religious Bodies*, I 19–21.
[8] Statistics for 1936 from the 1936 *ib*., I 86–97.
[9] Cf. the *Official Catholic Directory* of 1964, p. 1381.
[10] This includes all denominations except Jewish and Roman Catholic.

TABLE III—RELIGIOUS RATIOS IN THE U.S. POPULATION[1]

Year	All	Protestant	Jewish	Catholic	Unchurched
1785	33.3%	31.1%	No Date	.5%	68.4%
1890	32.8%	22.6%	.2%	10.0%	67.3%
1906	37.4%	23.7%	?	14.1%	62.6%
1916	41.1%	25.3%	.35%	15.4%	58.9%
1936	43.5%	23.6%	3.6%	15.6%	56.5%
1964	63.4%	36.9%	2.9%	23.6%	36.6%
1968	64.3%	37.8%	2.8%	23.8%	35.6%

[1] It should be noted that these statistics, published by the churches, are not wholly reliable, especially for the later decades, since they include children and millions of adults who are not affiliated with any church or ever attend any religious service.

The most important facts here revealed are (1) the extraordinary growth of the Jewish community, concerning which no complete information is available; (2) the sharp decrease and the subsequent expansion of Protestant churches; and (3), most significant of all, the constant, uninterrupted, and enormous growth of the Roman Catholic Church, especially since 1936.

TABLE IV—GROWTH OF THE CATHOLIC CHURCH IN THE U.S.A.[1]

Category	In 1891	1936	1946	1964	1968
Communicants	8,579,966	20,735,189	24,402,124	44,847,371	47,468,333
Priests	8,778	31,108	38,908	57,328	59,863
Brothers			6,721	12,132	12,261
Sisters			139,218	180,015	176,341
Parishes	7,631	12,720	14,523	17,445	18,064
Seminaries	39	197	342	571	561
Seminarians	1,711	22,629	22,950	48,750	39,838
Colleges & Univs.	123	196	211	295	305
Students	?	?	102,665	366,172	433,960
High Schools	624	1,809	2,413	2,458	2,277
Pupils	?	195,821	477,190	1,068,541	1,089,272
Elementary Schools	3,277	7,490	8,036	10,902	10,787
Pupils	665,328	2,212,260	2,141,813	4,566,616	4,165,504
Teaching Religious					104,137
Lay Teachers					90,066
Released Time Pupils			812,998	4,316,931	5,356,340
Total Under Instruction			3,451,735	10,374,336	11,093,024
Hospitals, General			692	803	788
Baptisms			792,987	1,446,301	1,249,965
Converts			87,340	123,986	110,717
Marriages			245,267	329,450	371,155

[1] All statistics in this table are taken from the summaries published in the *Official Catholic Directory*, in each case from that of the year indicated. The most important facts reflected here are (1) the constant growth of Catholic population, marriages, higher education, and the number of pupils attending public schools but receiving sectarian instruction during released time; but (2), since 1964, the increase in lay teachers in Catholic schools; the sharp reduction in seminarians, sisters, baptisms, converts, parochial and diocesan schools, and the number of full-time pupils under Catholic instruction.

TABLE V—RELIGIOUS MEMBERSHIP IN THE 14 CITIES [1]

CITY		All	Prot. Etc.	Catholic	Jewish	Population
Wash.	1906	136,759	92,273	43,788	698	278,718
	1936	271,724	172,684	80,690	18,350	560,000
	1968	276,000	173,100	80,000	22,900	764,000
Balt.	1906	224,968	124,496	100,397	75	508,957
	1936	434,720	172,313	189,407	73,000	848,196
	1968	528,000	281,000	185,000	62,000	915,000
Buff.	1906	196,302	68,289	126,395	618	381,819
	1936	378,425	108,158	248,467	21,000	575,000
	1968	353,000	138,000	200,000	15,000	530,000
Denv.	1906	50,699	32,003	25,003	703	133,859
	1936	142,906	83,148	41,368	18,400	308,472
	1968	298,000	194,000	88,000	16,000	494,000
Rich.	1906	54,506	45,804	8,313	389	85,050
	1936	111,147	93,445	10,202	7,500	188,000
	1968	169,500	141,000	21,000	7,500	220,000
Bos.	1906	376,728	116,057	258,936	1,735	560,892
	1936	520,708	194,196	308,512	18,000	775,000
	1968	335,000	115,000	185,000	35,000	670,000
Prov.	1906	131,214	30,130	100,324	760	175,597
	1936	198,983	41,918	133,265	23,800	253,000
	1968	121,000	41,000	65,000	15,000	208,000
Hart.	1906	43,717	15,978	27,092	647	79,850
	1936	116,961	31,706	61,885	23,360	165,000
	1968	121,000	45,000	32,000	13,500	158,000
St.L.	1906	302,531	91,955	208,775	1,801	575,238
	1936	416,057	158,820	206,237	51,000	818,000
	1968	461,500	247,500	200,000	14,000	675,000
Port.[2]	1906	40,282	22,087	17,781	414	90,426
	1936	98,155	56,750	30,705	10,700	303,000
	1968	400,000	300,000	85,000	15,000	585,000
Pitt.	1906	205,847	83,491	120,232	2,124	321,616
	1936	451,389	160,698	238,691	52,000	670,000
	1968	450,000	200,000	210,000	40,000	600,000
Clev.	1906	146,338	77,769	66,432	2,137	381,768
	1936	518,042	146,203	281,839	90,000	889,000
	1968	592,000	240,000	340,000	12,000	830,000
St. Paul.[3]	1906	103,639	29,085	72,899	655	163,068
	1936	164,581	64,485	86,106	14,000	289,500
	1968	357,000	205,000	140,000	12,000	425,000
Minn.	1906	96,819	49,371	45,642	806	202,718
	1936	206,377	122,938	62,739	20,700	478,000
	1968	285,000	210,000	80,000	12,000	480,000

[1] Population statistics are taken from the *Statistical Abstract*. Data for 1906 communicants from the 1906 *Census of Religious Bodies*, Table 6, Vol. I, pp. 380–407; similar data for 1936 from 1936 *ib.*, Vol. I, Table 31, pp. 442–718.

[2] Statistics for Portland include Multnomah County in 1968 only.

[3] Statistics for St. Paul include Ramsey County for 1968 only.

TABLE VI—RELIGIOUSLY USED EXEMPT REAL ESTATE IN 14 CITIES [1]

CITY		Total	Protestant	Catholic	Jewish
Wash.	1906	$ 10,025,122	$ 8,555,572	$ 1,259,550	$ 210,000
	1936	33,611,530	27,414,495	5,588,058	607,980
	1968	313,610,319	126,673,324	176,816,078	10,120,917
Balt.	1906	15,198,810	12,204,010	2,984,800	10,000
	1936	32,571,060			
	1968	158,977,390	53,099,540	81,633,540	24,244,390
Buff.	1906	11,276,964	6,249,220	4,844,744	183,000
	1936	38,889,616			
	1968	91,941,350	22,321,670	67,201,270	2,327,410
Denv.	1906	3,610,053	2,968,225	517,525	124,300
	1936	9,577,645			
	1968	54,500,000	23,500,000	23,500,000	7,500,000
Rich.	1906	3,078,769	2,307,769	625,000	146,000
	1936	11,335,338			
	1968	77,016,310	67,685,900	8,333,410	997,000
Bost.	1906	27,140,161	19,648,525	6,519,486	587,000
	1936	36,236,884			
	1968	151,302,140	36,742,660	92,672,780	21,886,700
Prov.	1906	4,442,243	3,005,743	1,337,700	94,100
	1936	10,688,367			
	1968	56,603,410	10,495,310	38,857,880	7,250,220
Hart.	1906	3,309,108	2,194,608	984,500	130,000
	1936	10,356,077			
	1968	77,463,650	34,433,580	36,829,940	6,200,130
St. L.	1906	13,751,112	7,068,948	6,072,594	577,500
	1936	31,884,986			
	1968	107,329,410	47,442,650	56,114,840	3,771,920
Port.	1906	2,321,500	1,992,900	139,000	186,500
	1936	7,219,968			
	1968	141,340,950	82,773,500	54,125,060	4,442,390
Pitt.	1906	22,444,929	15,566,625	6,016,204	802,000
	1936	42,778,762			
	1968	125,659,490	38,061,832	71,710,514	15,997,144

TABLE VI—*Continued*

Cleve.	1906	10,877,070	8,120,020	2,278,550	427,000
	1936	32,228,396			
	1968	128,675,190	46,457,830	74,429,480	7,787,880
St.					
Paul	1906	3,404,700	2,258,600	1,067,000	79,000
	1936	11,199,488			
	1968	44,009,474	20,962,234	22,110,880	936,360
Minn.	1906	5,360,050	4,370,550	846,000	96,000
	1936	19,630,165			
	1968	82,775,321	55,184,450	24,214,401	3,376,470

[1] Note again that Portland includes all of Multnomah Co. and St. Paul all of Ramsey Co. for 1968 only.

Data for 1906 from the 1906 *Census of Religious Bodies,* Vol. I, Table 7, pp. 408–513. Data for 1936, from *ib.* 1936, Vol. I, Table 30, pp. 424–439. Note that in the latter totals are not available for the various denominations in individual cities. Data for 1968 taken from this study. The figures for 1906 and 1936 are those reported by the churches themselves. The figures for 1968 are those found on the assessment rolls, and vary from 12% in St. Paul and 25% in Denver to 100% in Richmond and Portland. By and large, they probably average between 40 and 45%.

It is to be noted that in 1906, the Catholic communion in almost all areas was comparatively very poor, a condition which persisted into the Thirties, but which has now been reversed with a vengeance.

TABLE VII—COMMUNICANTS IN THE 14 CITIES [1]

Year	Population	Communi- cants	Protestants	Catholic	Jewish
1906	3,941,571	2,118,351	847,787	1,222,959	13,081
% Communicants		100	41.5	57.7	.6
Ratio to Population	54.0%		22.3%	31.0%	.33%
1936	7,120,178	4,030,165	1,607,452	1,980,113	441,810
% Communicants		100	40.0	49.1	10.9
Ratio to Population	56.6%		22.4%	27.7%	6.2%
1968	7,774,737	4,731,000	2,625,100	1,934,000	270,900
% Communicants		100	53.4	40.9	5.7
Ratio to Population	60.9%		32.2%	24.8%	3.5%

[1] Data for this table from others in this work.

The most dramatic facts reflected here are (1) the great expansion of the Jewish community between 1906 and 1936 and its subsequent partial removal to suburbia; (2) the sharp reduction in the Catholic ratio; (3) the remarkable increase in Protestant and miscellaneous affiliation; and (4) the actual secularization of the American large city, since a large percentage of those claimed as members are such only nominally. Actually what is here demonstrated is a substantive de-Catholicization of the large American city, which, however, has been accompanied by a considerable expansion of that faith in suburbia.

TABLE VIII—EXPANSION OF CHURCH WEALTH IN THE U.S.[1]

Division	1890	1906	1936	1968
				Actual or
	Reported Values	Reported Values	Reported Values	Replacement Values
Protestant	$551,504,498	$941,738,155	$2,741,307,015	$40,588,000,000
%	81.15	74.91	72.98	39.2
Catholic				
	118,371,366	292,638,787	891,435,725	54,277,500,000
%	17.42	23.25	23.73	53.4
Jewish	9,754,275	23,198,925	123,695,037	7,547,800,000
%	1.43	1.84	3.29	7.4
TOTAL	$679,630,139	$1,257,575,867	$3,756,437,777	$102,413,400,000

[1] Data for 1890 from the 1890 *Abstract of the Census;* that for 1906 and 1936 from the 1906 and 1936 *Census of Religious Bodies.* Data for 1968 from this study. Totals for 1890, 1906, and 1936 include parsonages and sanctuaries only; totals for 1968 include all tax-exempt religiously used property, for which assessments have been adjusted so as to reflect the actual or replacement values.

TABLE IX—ASSESSED AND TRUE VALUES OF PROPERTY IN THE 14 CITIES AND THE NATION

Total Assessments in 14 Cities	$ 28,792,137,011
Total True Valuations in 14 Cities	$ 67,255,000,000
Ratio of Assessments to Valuations	42.8%
Assessments Extrapolated for Nation (x 26)	
Assessed Valuations	$ 748,596,000,000
True Valuations	$1,748,600,000,000

TABLE X [a]

ASSESSMENTS, REPORTED ASSETS, AND OUR VALUATIONS FOR COLLEGES AND UNIVERSITIES [b]

Institution	Assessment	Theoretical Value	Reported Assets	Assessor's Value	Our Value for Extra- polation	Our Ratio
BUFFALO						
Canisius	$ 4,512,370		$ 12,630,295			
D'Youville	3,696,080		9,000,000			
	$ 8,208,450	51%	$ 21,630,295	38%	$ 20,500,000	95%
BALTIMORE [c]						
Mt. St. Agnes	2,187,960		3,044,546			
Loyola	2,262,100		6,791,262			
Notre Dame	3,024,240		12,112,832			
Peabody Inst.	1,980,200		3,000,000			
J. Hopkins	33,660,620		94,858,007			
	$ 43,115,120	67%	$119,806,647	36%	$ 86,230,240	72%
WASHINGTON, D.C.						
Cath. U.	24,513,079		50,000,000			
Trinity	7,032,087		11,489,899			
Washington U.	22,068,886		56,000,000			
American U.	16,300,675		29,413,324			
Dumbarton	2,882,952		4,046,793			
Georgetown	34,678,611		75,000,000			
	$107,476,290	60%	$225,950,016	43%	$214,952,580	95%
DENVER						
Regis	1,190,670		6,000,000			
Loretta	2,406,690		12,300,000			

Institution								
U. of Denver [d]	13,355,740	$ 16,953,100	30%	45,000,000	$ 63,300,000	26%	$ 67,812,000	107%
BOSTON								
N-eastern U.	12,845,700			47,172,000				
Simmons	6,539,000			8,620,769				
Suffolk U.	3,241,500			4,580,000				
Emmanuel	8,666,000			12,341,773				
Wheelock	2,400,100			4,136,480				
Emerson	590,000			2,500,000				
Boston U.	35,876,800			150,252,414				
		$ 70,159,100	45%		$229,603,436	31%	$210,477,300	91.5%
RICHMOND [•]								
Vir. Union U.	4,244,050			6,871,750				
State Medical	33,422,440			39,510,300				
U. Richmond	16,931,000			10,300,000				
		$ 54,597,490	100%		$ 56,682,050	96%	$ 54,597,490	96%
HARTFORD								
Trinity	13,410,030		66%	18,600,000		72%	$ 20,115,000	108%
PROVIDENCE								
Providence	8,064,630			17,747,000				
Brown U.	30,774,810 [f]			53,181,000				
		$ 38,839,440	60%		$ 70,928,000	54%	$ 77,678,880	109%
ST. LOUIS								
St. Louis U.	14,150,960			72,133,000				
Washington U.	14,885,420			78,279,324				
		$ 29,036,380	40%		$150,412,324	19.4%	$ 87,109,140	58%

	PITTSBURGH					
Duquesne	12,859,349		28,863,062			
Chatham	4,643,090		7,649,297			
U. Pittsburgh	35,095,905		144,119,008			
Carnegie Inst.	7,045,100		48,035,000			
Mellon Inst.	4,487,190					
	$ 64,130,634	50%	$228,666,367	28%	$192,391,802	84%
	PORTLAND					
Cascade	1,290,960		3,000,000			
Lewis & Clark	6,439,120		12,264,043			
Reed College	6,555,850		9,853,889			
	$ 14,285,930	100%	$ 25,117,932	57%	$ 4,285,930	57%
	CLEVELAND					
WR & Rose Hos.	17,099,160					
Western RU	14,065,530					
Case Tech.	9,723,030		95,068,551			
	40,887,720					
	ST. PAUL					
St. Johns	2,072,050		5,987,752			
	$ 42,959,770	40%	$101,056,303	42%	$158,879,310	127%
	MINNEAPOLIS					
Hamline U.	1,120,180		8,995,047			
Concordia	638,580		6,460,250			
Macalester	1,846,310		19,312,243			
St. Thomas	1,420,480		10,621,623			
St. Catherine	992,910		7,412,896			
	$ 6,018,460	13.3%	$ 52,802,059	11.4%	$ 48,147,680	91%
U. of Minn.	48,109,887		$261,089,676[h]	18.4%	$144,329,661	
TOTALS	$557,300,081	33.3%	$1,625,645,105		$1,367,517,013	55%
Per Cent of Reported Value	34.3				84.2	

ᵃ Since our entire system of projection is based on the ratio between assessed and actual values of real estate, we did considerable research to obtain the data shown in Table X above. We were able to learn the plant values officially reported by colleges and universities in our 14 cities. Since these institutions are numerous and representative, they furnish a yardstick for reliable valuations on exempt property. Our research shows that while some variance exists between our projected bases and those officially reported, this difference demonstrates what we have emphasized throughout—namely, that our valuations on exempts stand at less than parity with the taxable. It is therefore certain that the ratio as well as the total of exempt property in the United States is greater than we show in our extrapolations.

ᵇ Assessments in this table taken directly from tax rolls. Reported Assets are from *American Colleges and Universities,* 10th edition, 1968, published by the American Council of Education, Washington, D.C. Valuations for extrapolations obtained by methods explained previously.

ᶜ Mr. Downs declared that exempts were probably underassessed by 30% in comparison with taxable, a fact borne out by these statistics.

ᵈ If the assets of the Colorado Seminary of a commercial nature could be separated, we would find considerably lower ratios.

ᵉ Note the extreme accuracy of the Richmond assessor.

ᶠ An undetermined portion of this assessment consists of commercial investments, which are not included under book value. If these were omitted, the 54% might well drop to about 40%. The ratio for Providence College alone is 44%. And this, of course, is only book, not actual value.

ᵍ We note that these items are assessed at only 57% of value. We believe that all Portland property is assessed considerably below replacement or actual value, exempt and taxable alike.

ʰ This indicates how drastically Minneapolis exempts are underassessed —to which we called attention in our analysis of the city. The theoretical 33.3% is actually only 18.4% in the case of the great University.

The foregoing statistics demonstrate that our totals for exempt are at least 15.8% below parity and that 19% would have to be added to their total in order to obtain a correct correlation with the taxable. In other words, $108,196,640,000 should be added to the $569,456,000,000 shown in our extrapolation to create a total of $677,652,640,000. This would increase the ratio of exempt to all property at the present time from 32.6% to 36.4%. The exempt property in the United States, therefore, now is equal to 58% of the taxable.

TABLE XI—REPRESENTATIVE CITY OR COUNTY OPERATIONAL BUDGETS

WASHINGTON, D.C.:

Total Budget			$456,150,000
From Real Estate	$101,000,000	21.1%	
From Other Sources	355,150,000	78.9%	
Personal Property		$ 8,900,000	
Sales, Gross Receipts, and Earnings Tax		91,450,000	
Income Taxes		69,000,000	
Miscellaneous		11,750,000	
Fees, Etc.		25,750,000	
Federal Grants		148,100,000	

RICHMOND, VIRGINIA:

Total Budget			$ 66,825,173
Real Estate Tax	$ 18,148,600	27.2%	
Other Sources	48,676,573	72.8%	

Income		Expenditures	
State and Federal Grants	$11,593,620	Schools	$15,903,586
License Taxes	5,826,000	Welfare	13,335,700
Sales Tax	6,921,900	Debt Service	9,374,930
Government Operations	6,100,680	Public Safety	8,279,600
Utilities	4,153,190	Public Works	5,620,300
Utility Tax	3,943,600	Retirement	3,302,000
Personal Property Tax	2,711,000	Parks, Etc.	2,275,900
Water Tax	1,560,000	General Services	1,503,800
Fines, Etc.	1,066,300	Public Health	1,167,700
Other	2,552,140	Courts	1,383,420
		Other	4,216,630
	$46,428,430		$66,363,173
Balance Carried Over	2,248,143	Reserve	461,607
Total	48,676,573		$66,825,173

BALTIMORE, Maryland:

Total Budget			$327,003,456
Real Estate Property Tax	$106,592,670	32.6%	
Other Sources	220,410,786	67.4%	

Additional Sources			
Delinquent Taxes	$ 2,300,000	State and Shared Taxes	$13,935,000
Personal Property Tax	30,542,000	Licenses, Permits	4,505,000
Sales and Use Tax	12,205,000	Fines, Etc.	1,895,000

Income Tax	27,980,000	Investments	3,105,000
Miscellaneous	691,000	Federal Grants	6,351,000
Sub-Total	$ 73,718,000	State Grants	74,857,000
Second Sub-Total	146,692,786	Service Charges	8,670,000
Property Tax	106,592,670	Public Enterprise	24,994,000
Budget	$327,003,456	Other	8,380,786
		Sub-Total	$146,692,786

BUFFALO-ERIE COUNTY,		
N.Y.: Total Budget *		$211,023,498
City-Co. Property Tax Paid		
in Buffalo	$ 80,100,000	39.5%
Other Sources of Income	130,923,498	60.8%
Portion Paid To Buffalo		$ 54,390,000
Other Buffalo Income		77,557,000
For Schools:		
State Aid	$ 37,574,907	
Federal Aid	172,800	
Co. Sales Tax	4,800,000	
Other	2,700,780	
	$ 45,248,487	
Sources of County Income		
Real Estate Tax		28,959,389
Other Sources		50,117,109
Non-Property Tax	$ 3,143,395	
State Aid	17,644,302	
Federal Aid	15,107,109	
Special Activities	7,706,523	
Other	6,515,780	
Total Budget		$211,023,498

DENVER, Colorado: City-		
County Operational Budget		$168,253,860
Real Estate Tax	$ 69,276,836	41.2%
Other Sources	98,947,024	58.8%

Expenditures		Additional Sources of Income	
General Budget	$ 97,523,800	Personal Property and	
Public Welfare,		Utility Taxes	$ 25,220,630
Pensions, Etc.	7,475,200	Other City-Co. Taxes	23,728,144
Moffat Tunnel	509,400	Auto Taxes	1,680,100
Schools	62,745,460	Occupation Tax	10,100,100
Total	$168,253,860	Sales Tax	12,495,600
		Franchise Tax	3,271,000
		Business and Licenses	2,814,800
		Fines and Forfeits	2,820,000

From Government	3,604,475	
Charges for Services	7,403,200	
Other, Miscellaneous	7,709,489	
	$100,847,438	

MINNEAPOLIS, Minn.: City-County Operational Budget $129,600,000

From Property Tax	$100,855,617	77.6%
From Other Sources	28,745,377	22.4%

Expenditures		Sources of City Income	
City Budget	$63,755,158	Ad Valorem Tax	$35,009,781
Schools	38,499,227	Service Charges	9,956,402
County Budget	23,129,672	Special Assessments	4,737,403
Other	1,134,161	Fed.-State-Co. Grants	3,737,403
City Budget Expenditures		State Payments for	
Public Safety	15,110,600	Exempt Property	3,226,223
Debt Service	10,722,415	Local Share of 3%	
Pensions	8,035,189	Excise	2,625,789
Streets and Lighting	6,988,355	Miscellaneous Taxes	2,475,659
Health and Welfare	6,870,542	Other	3,464,018
General Government	5,040,706		
Parks and Recreation	4,067,900		
Libraries	3,021,591		
Improvements	2,401,330		
Sanitation	1,496,530		

MULTNOMAH COUNTY:

City-Co. Operational Budget [b] $138,187,571

From Real Estate Tax	$ 75,199,239	54.5%
From Other Sources	62,988,332	45.5%

The Other Income		Expenditures	
Personal Property Tax	$15,512,340	Schools	$89,954,026
Utilities Tax	9,903,546	Health and Hospitals	6,904,421
Vehicle Fees	4,153,524	General Government	6,291,874
Hospital	1,627,047	Roads and Bridges	4,925,993
Public Service Corps.	9,699,620	Public Safety and	
Cash Carryover	9,441,389	Correction	4,403,968
Other	12,650,866	Library and Co.	
		School Support	3,600,670
		Courts	1,580,425
		Public Welfare	3,362,584
		Recreation	1,162,631
		Sewage	576,604
		Debt Service	7,843,830
		Other	6,113,549

301

[a] In this table we include half the Erie Co. budget as a portion of the cost of city-county government in Buffalo because about one-half the population of the County is within the city itself.

[b] The extremely high rate of expenditure for schools; the very low ratio for welfare, courts, and police; and the fact that virtually no grants are received from the state or the federal governments are the outstanding features of these statistics. We must remember also that there is no sales or use tax, no gross earnings or occupation taxes, and no merchants or manufacturers tax in Oregon. The per capita real estate tax of $134 is virtually the only tax paid by Oregonians, in addition to a modest income tax which is paid to the State and by which it operates most of the services in which it participates and which are certainly equal to those in other states, or actually superior to them.

Note the large carry-over from the previous year; and the fact that the expenditures called for in the budget are $1,456,996 less than the Operational Budget.

302

APPENDIX II

CHURCHES AND THE INTERNAL REVENUE CODE

THE LAW AND THE REGULATIONS

The Internal Revenue Code has many sections and provisions which deal with some phase of church activity. And we should bear in mind that in this crucial area the Regulations issued by the Treasury Department or the Internal Revenue Service—which have the force of law—are often fully as significant as the law itself. It is also notable that in most instances state authorities taxing income follow the models set up by the national government.

THE EXEMPT CHARITIES

Sections 501–514 describe, limit, and elaborate the organizations which may qualify for exemptions and immunities.

Section 501 (a) reads: "An organization described in subsection (c) or (d) or Section 401 (a) shall be exempt from taxation under this title unless such exemption is denied under section 502, 503, or 504." [*]

Under Section 501 (c) we find 17 categories of organizations which enjoy tax-exemption on certain types but not all categories of income. Those listed under paragraph 3 include community chests, trusts and foundations, and entities established for a religious, charitable, scientific, literary, or educational purpose "no part of the net earnings of which inures to the benefit of any private shareholder or

---

[*] Section 501 (d) covers the business operations of certain apostolic (communal) organizations, such as the Shakers. Sections 502, 503, and 504 spell out various restrictions upon income-exemptions, which we note elsewhere in this chapter. Section 401 (a) deals with qualified pension, profit-sharing, and stock-bonus plans.

303

individual, no substantial part of the activities of which is carrying on propaganda, or otherwise attempting to influence legislation, and which does not participate in, or intervene in (including the publishing or distributing of statements), any political campaign on behalf of any candidate for public office."

This means that all organizations listed under 501 (c) (3) are exempt from taxation on certain forms of income provided they do not engage in any of the activities enumerated.

The Cumulative List of 170 (c) organizations published by the Internal Revenue Service now contains more than 150,000 names, some of which, in a single line, cover thousands of entities. For example, Baptist Churches and the Institutions Thereof probably includes well over 100,000 units. Sheldon Cohen, Commissioner of Internal Revenue under Lyndon B. Johnson, estimated that there are more than 1,500,000 170 (c) exempts, of which nearly one-fourth are religious. All of these enjoy double immunity, for their income is exempt from taxation and donors to them may deduct gifts and bequests from otherwise taxable income and estates.

FEEDER CORPORATIONS

Section 501 (c) (1) exempts instrumentalities of government from taxation. The subsection which follows is important for it does the same for "Corporations organized for the exclusive purpose of holding title to property, collecting income therefrom, and turning over the entire amount thereof, less expenses, to an organization which itself is exempt under this section."

This means that any entity listed among the 17 categories under 501 (c) may create a tax-exempt corporation, described more fully in Section 502 as "FEEDER ORGANIZATIONS." An organization operated for the primary purpose of carrying on a trade or a business for profit shall not be exempt under section 501 on the ground that all of its profits are payable to one or more organizations exempt under section 501 from taxation. For purposes of this section, the term "trade or business" shall not include the rental by an organization of the real property (including personal property leased with the real property)."

Here we encounter for the first time a distinction between what is known as "passive" and "active" income. The effect of section 502 is that any 501 (c) organization can set up a subsidiary or "feeder corporation" which may itself be immune to taxation on revenue derived from rentals, and from capital gains in the sale of real estate. If, however, this corporation were to engage in trade or manufacture, i.e., in competitive enterprise, such as production, sales, or service, such operations would be classified as "active" business, and liable to the ordinary corporation tax. The same applies to the active unrelated business income of the great majority of exempts, except churches.

Any entity described in Section 501 (c) (3) may, then, set up a subsidiary corporation which, in turn, may own and operate a real estate cartel, buy and sell property, lease hotels or motels, acquire or construct shopping centers, etc.—all without federal taxation, but under certain restrictions outlined in section 514: leases must not exceed 5 years; the properties must be free from debt; the parent-charity must be the sole owner; and all net income must accrue to it.

The Mormon Church, or a subsidiary thereof, owns a corporation known as Zion Securities, which deals extensively in real estate; it also owns the Utah Hotel Corporation under a similar arrangement which, in turn, owns the Utah Hotel and Motel. We believe that both of these can qualify as tax-exempt "feeder corporations." The Church certainly owns or controls them; all income certainly accrues to it; leases probably never exceed 5 years. If the properties are free from encumbrance, all conditions necessary to qualify as tax-free corporations have been fully met.

REVOCATION OF EXEMPTION

Section 503 (a) (1) (A) provides that exemption is to be revoked for any 501 (c) organization if it engages in a prohibited action or in any transaction which (*ib.* (a) (2)) has "the purpose of divesting corpus or income . . . . from its exempt purposes, and such transaction involved a substantial part of the corpus or income. . . ."

It is well to note that the Code relies heavily on such terms as "substantial," "propaganda," "attempting to influence," etc. Since no definitions or limitations are supplied, government officials are endowed with wide discretionary powers. The result is that an individual church may lose its exemption simply for opposing or supporting a political issue, but could make millions from a competitive business with complete impunity. In practice, a large denomination may spend fortunes for openly political purposes, since the IRS might be motivated to declare or assume that this was not a substantial portion of its overall activity, or did not constitute propaganda.

RESTRICTIONS ON EXEMPTS

Section 503 (c) enumerates a series of actions which 501 (c) (3) or (17)* or 401 (a) organizations may not perform: (1) lend corpus without good security or reasonable interest; (2) pay excessive compensation; (3) render service on a preferential basis; (4) pay excessive prices for securities; (5) sell for less than value; or (5) engage in activity profitable to the creator, his relatives, or substantial contributors.

Section 503 (b), however, specifically exempts from these restrictions the following 501 (c) organizations: (1) all religious entities; (2) any recognized non-profit educational institution; (3) every instrumentality of government; (4) any agency operated, supervised, or controlled by a religious organization; and (5) any qualifying medical facility. This means that any of the organizations here listed may prosecute any of the activities for which they were created and granted exemption without any government supervision, restriction, tax-liability, or disclosure.

Section 504 provides that exemption be revoked for misuse of funds.

EXEMPTIONS, DEDUCTIONS, AND EXCLUSIONS

There are no sections numbered 505–510. Sections 511 and 512, however, are of crucial import, for they distinguish again and more fully between "passive" and "active" business income; and here we find the precise immunities of various 501 (c) (3) organizations. Section 511 (a) (1) states: "There is hereby imposed for each taxable year on the unrelated business income (as defined in section 512) of every organization described in paragraph (2), a normal tax and a surtax computed as provided in section 11." Section 512 (a) explains that "The term 'unrelated business taxable income' means the gross income derived by any organization from any unrelated trade or business . . . . regularly carried on by it . . ." Such busi-

---

* This refers to trusts formed to pay supplemental unemployment compensation.

ness is defined in section 513 (a) in reference to "any organization subject to the tax imposed by section 511" as being "any trade or business the conduct of which is not substantially related . . . . to the exercise or performance by such organization of the charitable, educational, or other purpose or function constituting the basis for its exemption under section 501 (c) (3). . . . ."

This certainly seems to say that any income received by a church (except voluntary contributions from its membership or the public) which results from any except religious activity, such as preaching the gospel, constitutes taxable unrelated business income, subject to the corporation tax established in section 511.

But wait! Under section 512 (b) we find "Exemptions, Additions, and Limitations," which cause the following to be non-taxable: (1) dividends, interest, and annuities; (2) royalties; (3) rents accruing from real and personal property; (4) business leases; and (5) gains from the sale of property, except items which normally constitute a store inventory. All these forms of revenue—known as passive income—are therefore exempt from taxation when received by any 501 (c) (3) organization. We note also that these are the forms of income always exempt from Social Security taxation.

THE UNIQUE POSITION OF CHURCHES

At this point we are confronted by the all-important section 511 (a) (2) which reads:

"ORGANIZATIONS SUBJECT TO TAX.—

"(A) ORGANIZATIONS DESCRIBED IN SECTION 501 (c) (2), (3), (5), (6), (14) (B) or (C), and (17), and SECTION 401 (a).—The taxes imposed by paragraph (1) [a] shall apply in the case of any organization (other than a church, a convention or association of churches, or a trust described in subsection (b)) [b] which is exempt, except as provided in this part, from taxation under this subtitle by reason of section 401 (a) or of paragraph (3), (5), (6), (14) (B) or (C), or (17) of section 501 (c). Such taxes shall also apply in the case of a corporation described in section 501 (c) (2) if the income is payable to an organization which, itself is subject to the taxes

---

[a] This is active, unrelated (competitive) business income.
[b] As described in Subchapter I, section 641, dealing with certain Estates, Trusts, and Beneficiaries.

imposed by paragraph (1) or to a church or to a convention or association of churches.ᶜ

"(B) STATE COLLEGES AND UNIVERSITIES.—The taxes imposed by paragraph (1) shall apply in the case of any college or university which is an agency or instrumentality of any government or any political subdivision thereof. . . . ."

The meaning of this is that the corporation tax will be imposed on the unrelated active business income only of those organizations listed in paragraphs (2), (3), (6), (14) (B) and (C) and (17) of section 501 (c). The inference is that those listed under (1), (4), (7)–(13), (15), and (16) may engage in unrelated business without tax-liability. We should note, however, that 501 (c) (1) organizations are government agencies; and that the others are mutual benefit charities which are strictly limited in their activities and which, therefore, play a very circumscribed role in our economy. We note also that "feeder corporations" will be taxed on active unrelated business income, even when their profits are paid to a church or to an association of churches. Such restrictions, however, would not apply to income from the sales or operation of real estate. Subparagraph (B) states specifically that government owned colleges and universities may not engage in unrelated active business without tax-liability.

The following facts, therefore, emerge: (1) that the great majority of tax-exempts consist of 501 (c) (3) organizations—possibly as many as 80 or 90%; (2) that these are the wealthy corporations which are now amassing huge amounts of property and income; and (3) that, among these, churches and associations of churches, and they alone, are singled out for total immunity. These, therefore, comprise the only important category of private corporations which may engage in any and every kind of competitive business with complete freedom from taxation.

Section 6033 (a) (1) is almost equally important for churches, especially the theocratic and authoritarian; for this confers complete immunity to disclosure upon them. They may, therefore, engage in all kinds of competitive business without informing any one concerning their financial operations or manipulations. Paragraphs 2–6, which follow, provide the same freedom for several other 501 (c) (3) organizations, including recognized charities, qualifying educational

---

ᶜ This refers, of course, not to the income of feeder corporations from the operation of real estate, but to active unrelated business, which is therefore practically prohibited for these subsidiary corporations.

308

institutions, religiously controlled or supervised corporations, and associations which exist to prevent cruelty to animals and children. The same immunity is extended also to fraternal orders or societies and to agencies owned and operated outright by the federal government. This umbrella, however, does not extend to REA co-ops or to the Salt River Project of Arizona since these are not owned directly by the federal government.

It should again be emphasized that churches and associations of churches comprise the only large or important group of corporations that are immune to disclosure as well as to taxation on unrelated (active-competitive) business income. Some are free from disclosure and taxation on related business income; others, such as non-sacerdotal religious orders, are free from taxation and disclosure on unrelated passive business income; still others are subject to disclosure but not to taxation on certain types of investment income. CHURCHES, HOWEVER, ENJOY TOTAL IMMUNITY. And this elevates them into a unique position in American life.

In practice, all this means, for example, that a hospital may engage in the active business for which it was organized without taxation or disclosure; but, should it manufacture and sell surgical supplies, this business would be subject to disclosure on Form 990 T and to the taxation provided in section 11 of the Internal Revenue Code. The Salt River Project or an REA co-op may sell power, and remain free from taxation and disclosure; but should either of them manufacture and sell stoves or refrigerators, disclosure and corporation taxes would be required. The Amana Society, however, since it qualifies as a church, is permitted to manufacture and sell refrigeration equipment with total immunity.

Government corporations, such as the TVA, are endowed with the same advantages.

THE EXTENSION OF THE LAW

The Treasury Regulations go far beyond the words which comprise the statute. According to these—which have the effect of law—sacerdotal orders, like the Benedictines, the Franciscans, and the Jesuits (and perhaps even their individual members) are treated as if they too were churches); but non-sacerdotal orders, like the Trappists, the Christian Brothers, or the Little Sisters of the Poor, are not.

309

ADDITIONAL PREFERENCES

We should note also that under section 270.25 of the federal Tariff Schedules, Bibles are admitted free; and under sections 850 to 850.70, a great many items used exclusively in Eastern Orthodox and Roman Catholic churches are likewise exempt. These include books, religious paintings, sketches, engravings, woodcuts, music, stained glass windows, insignia indicating ecclesiastical rank and office, emblems worn in processions, religious vestments to be held for resale, any article destined for use by a religious, educational, or charitable institution, and such church appurtenances as altars, pulpits, and statuary carved from marble or granite. Under President Kennedy, these tariff regulations were amended to extend all these immunities to church-related organizations.

EXPLANATION AND COMMENTARY

Since the Internal Revenue Code is so complex, it might be well to offer further elaboration and some specific examples of how it operates in regard to various individuals and organizations. In this, we seek simply to state what the laws are, and not how the IRS enforces them. For in some cases, it has ignored its duties by failing to carry out the provisions of the statute, particularly in regard to various non-sacerdotal religious orders, which have been, and continue to be, treated as if they were churches, entitled to total immunity under the Code. If and when a religious order is finally subjected to taxation, this occurs only because of a specific suit and after long-drawn-out litigation.

FOUNDATIONS

Foundations, or charitable trusts, are among the exempts listed under section 501 (c) (3) of the Code. All current revenue is to be disbursed to other exempts. A foundation may not engage in active business, although it may own controlling interest in corporations that do so. It is subject to the restrictions enumerated earlier in this chapter. Although bequests of any size, when left to a foundation, are exempt from estate-taxation, the donor can deduct no more than 20% of current adjusted gross income for a foundation-gift, nor does the 5-year carry-over apply to such a donation.

A TYPICAL 501 (c) ORGANIZATION

There are many thousands of secular, non-profit entities which qualify for exemption under 501 (c). In addition to voluntary contributions, any of these may, as we have indicated, receive passive income in the form of interest, dividends, rentals, lease payments, royalties, and capital gains without tax-liability. However, they are required to report such income on Form 900 A;[a] and should they engage in active business or trade, any revenue or profit from this would be reportable on Form 990 T and taxable under section 11, like any private corporation-for-profit.[b]

For example, let us say that some individuals organize a non-profit corporation to prepare and disseminate educational or scientific material dealing with conservation, historical sites, religious history, or the philosophy of humanism. This corporation may receive voluntary contributions and may invest its funds in securities, a hotel, or a shopping center; and any revenues received from such sources, although reportable, would be exempt from taxation, so long as they are used to accomplish the purpose for which exemption is granted.

However, should this entity operate the hotel it owns, or should it run a drug store in its shopping center, any profit derived from those enterprises would be active, unrelated taxable business income, subject to the corporation tax.

NON-SACERDOTAL RELIGIOUS ORDERS

The Roman Catholic Church has several hundred orders of brothers and nuns called "the religious," who have taken the vows of chastity, obedience, and poverty, but have not been ordained to the priesthood—i.e., they cannot administer the sacraments of marriage, baptism, confession, extreme unction, etc. Since they have taken the vow of poverty, they can neither retain personal income nor possess private property. They simply perform the tasks assigned them by their superiors, and receive maintenance in return. Any possessions they had upon the completion of their vows were given the order; any income they receive later is simply turned over in the same way.

Such religious may receive earned incomes in the form of wages or salaries; but, since this is signed over to the order, the IRS declares

---

[a] This requirement is established in section 6033 (a).
[b] This is established in section 511 (a).

311

that this income is not taxable. Nuns teaching in captive public schools and religious chaplains serving in the armed forces, therefore, contribute nothing to Social Security; nor do they pay any income taxes.

We note again that the religious receive their maintenance; but nothing is said concerning the level at which this may be supplied. Obviously, no one can be maintained for the standard deduction of $600 a year; yet, even if the cost is $10,000, this is never treated as personal income. A Jesuit priest might enjoy a living standard costing $50,000 a year, and this would still not constitute taxable compensation. However, if an ordinary worker receives so much as a sandwich from his employer, the IRS declares this to be taxable income.

Although individual members of religious orders may not retain income or property in their own right, these restrictions do not apply to the orders, which may own, and derive income from, bonds, savings accounts, royalties, industrial securities, lease-rentals, and capital gains. They may also operate schools and hospitals, also exempt from taxation. Thus, the Sisters of the Poor operate an immense chain of hospitals and possess large portfolios of investment funds, all of which are immune from taxation and disclosure. This again is an extension of the statute by Regulation.

However, should any of these non-sacerdotal orders engage in active trade or business, as in the manufacture and sale of wines or liquors, they would be subject to the normal corporation tax and surtax. This is what happened with the Christian Brothers of Napa, California.

SACERDOTAL ORDERS

A sacerdotal order consists of seminarians and priests ordained— or preparing—to administer the seven sacraments of the Roman Catholic Church. Since the special provisions relating to them are not spelled out or even mentioned in the Internal Revenue Code, they have been established by Regulations, which have granted sacerdotal orders, like the Jesuits, exactly the same standing as is accorded to churches and associations of churches.

An examination of the *Official Catholic Directory* indicates that the priests listed therein are about equally divided between the secular and the religious. If a bishop is a Jesuit or a Franciscan, for instance, he is a sacerdotal religious and any income received by him is simply given to the Order. If he is secular, he is permitted to own property and could conceivably be required to pay income taxes.

A Jesuit could, therefore, be a bank president with a salary of $100,000 and he would not be required to pay any income or Social Security taxes; nor would he be under the necessity of filing any tax-report.

TAX-FREE LIVING

Section 107 of the Internal Revenue Code has a most intriguing provision: "RENTAL VALUE OF PARSONAGES. In the case of a minister of the gospel," we read, "gross income does not include— (1) the rental value of a house furnished to him as part of his compensation; or (2) the rental allowance paid to him as part of his compensation, to the extent used by him to rent or provide a home."

The Treasury rulings interpreting this section are indeed marvelous: for these have established (1) that any portion of a cleric's salary given him as a separate payment to maintain his home need never appear on his income tax return at all, *for it is excludable from gross income.* This means that all deductions to which others are entitled may still be taken by the minister or rabbi from what remains to be reported as adjusted gross income.

But even this is not all; for the Treasury Regulations interpret the words "to the extent used by him to rent or provide a home" to include any expense for towels, soap, rugs, linens, blankets, drapes, furniture, insurance, a fence, yard maintenance, repairs to the house, inside or out, to the roof, the furnace, the refrigeration, the plumbing, or anything else; any vandalism or other damage; the cost of water, gas, electricity, and telephone. In fact, every conceivable expense, except for food and personal servants, may be covered by the excludable check handed by the congregation to the minister.

Even this, however, generous as it is, is only the frosting on the cake; the real sweetmeat consists in the fact that principal payments on a contract or mortgage are also excludable from gross income.

And so while the waitress who sits in the pew must report every dime she receives in tips (section 6053) on pain of the severest penalties, the church she attends may do a multi-million-dollar competitive business without even making a report; and the good reverend preaching the Gospel may enjoy a $20,000 or $30,000 salary

313

without owing a penny of income taxes by the simple expedient of renewing and paying off the mortgage on his mansion at frequent intervals.

SPECIAL RELIGIOUS EXEMPTIONS

Section 3401 (a) under "CHAPTER 24" dealing with the "Collection of Income Tax at Source on Wages" declares that "For purposes of this chapter, the term 'wages' means all remuneration (other than fees paid to a public official) for services performed by an employee for his employer, including the cash value of all remuneration paid in any medium other than cash; except that such term shall not include remuneration paid—"

Here follow 16 paragraphs, among which the 9th reads: "for services performed by a duly ordained, commissioned, or licensed minister of a church in the exercise of his ministry or by a member of a religious order in the exercise of duties required by such order. . . . ."

This means simply that no employer will collect or transmit withholding taxes on any remuneration paid to a cleric or to any religious personnel.

In the 1954 Code, churches were excused from the provisions of the federal unemployment levy under section 3306 (c) (8); but this has now been expunged, since it is superfluous.

Section 1402 (e), which deals with "Ministers, Members of Religious Orders, and Christian Science Practitioners," provided, until Jan. 1, 1968, that any minister who wished to participate in Social Security was required to file a special certificate. If he did not, he was excluded from its benefits. If he did, he had to pay the heavier contributions required from independent businessmen.[a]

On the 1st of January, 1968, however, a new provision went into effect: ministers can now escape Social Security only by filing as conscientious objectors, under the Mennonite section 1402 (h), which was inserted to enable members of this cult to avoid the government program.

However, the rewritten section 1402 (e) specifically exempts members of religious orders; and, since even secular priests in the

---

[a] Under section 1401 (a) and (b), this will rise to 7.8% on a base of $6,600 in a few years, or possibly much more.

Roman Catholic Church are unmarried and may qualify for ample support in their rectories and diocesan palaces without any need for taxable income, we cannot see how the revision of the Code will affect anyone except rabbis and Protestant ministers. And even they may be able to excuse themselves through narrow portals.

SECULAR CELIBATE PRIESTS IN TAX-FREE MANSIONS

Since secular Catholic priests have not taken the vow of poverty, they can amass property, and receive personal income which might be subject to income taxation. There is a dynamic sleeper in the Code, however, which has special reference to their situation. This is "Section 119. Meals or Lodging Furnished for the Convenience of the Employer.

"There shall be excluded from gross income of an employee the value of any meals or lodging furnished him by his employer for the convenience of the employer, but only if—

"(1) in the case of meals, the meals are furnished on the business premises of the employer, or

"(2) in the case of lodging, the employee is required to accept such lodging on the business premises of his employer as a condition of employment."

Since a rectory or diocesan palace is the business premise of the employer, these provisions cover every Catholic priest perfectly. The value of all meals and housing furnished by churches, ecclesiastical organizations, and religious orders are therefore excludable from gross income. Thus, while section 107 enables ecclesiastics to occupy million-dollar mansions (already tax-exempt) without reporting their residential value as income, section 119 renders any cost in their operation or in the preparation of meals similarly excludable, *but only if they are furnished by the employer and prepared by other employees*. These provisions are obviously tailor-made for Roman Catholic priests and leave rabbis and Protestant ministers out in the cold.

It is therefore difficult to see how a celibate prelate would need any taxable income in order to support a life of luxury; for his needs can be met to superfluity from sources not classified as taxable income. The value of a rectory or diocesan palace, as well as the cost of meals and household servants, are excludable from gross income. And since

315

the garb he wears, the cars he has at his disposal, and the cost of travel are all deemed necessary for the cleric in the performance of his professional functions, these too are tax-exempt. He can, therefore, enjoy the living standard of a millionaire without tax-liability.

Furthermore, since gifts are never reportable by the recipient, and since any donor may—under section 2503 (b)—give up to $3,000 a year to another person without reporting it, it is conceivable that a bishop or a cardinal could become a millionaire in his own right without tax-liability.

Finally, since neither the priest nor his church is required to make any reports to the government concerning its finances, and since the church funds and those of the bishop are inextricably intertwined, it seems impossible that these could be segregated. The Catholic bishop is, in fact, the ruler of an independent princedom, subject only to the authority of the Vatican. The Mormon bishop is likewise subject only to the authority of his church.

THE CORPORATION SOLE AND AGGREGATE

What has been said so far by no means exhausts the unique powers and privileges of ecclesiastical functionaries. In nearly half our states what is known as a *corporation sole* is a legal entity, which, though never mentioned in the Internal Revenue Code is a reality of the utmost importance. As such, a bishop, acting as if he were the incarnation of his ecclesiastical organization, is permitted to hold in his own name unlimited assets in the form of real estate, cash, stocks, bonds, mortgages, etc. A special feature of this arrangement is that, since each successor to the office is invested automatically with all these riches, no deeds or other instruments are necessary to effect a transfer of ownership.

What the bishop does with this property, especially the revenue, no one knows but himself and possibly the authorities in Salt Lake City or in Rome. He makes no reports to the priests under him, to the laymen of his congregation, to his fellow-bishops, or to any legal authority. If he actually owns all these assets, he may be a billionaire; if he does not, then the Vatican certainly does, for the laity who have contributed everything have neither any ownership in, nor any control over, this accumulation of material things.

Thus it is that the properties of the Church of Jesus Christ of Latter Day Saints are titled to their presiding prelates; and that the

316

churches, parochial schools, and other real estate belonging to the Roman Catholic Church are titled to their bishops.

Another popular form of theocratic incorporation is known as the *corporation aggregate,* noted in our first chapter. Here the title is nominally vested in a board; but, since the bishop not only presides over it but also appoints the other members, this form is often preferred over the corporation sole. Where no legal provisions for ecclesiastical incorporation exist, as in Virginia, Catholic properties are titled to the bishop in fee simple, who deposits two copies of his will with the appropriate authorities of his church.

DEDUCTIONS AND CONTRIBUTIONS

The provisions of section 170 are only slightly less crucial than those of sections 501–514, because they deal with deductions granted donors who contribute to 501 (c) organizations, and particularly those described in paragraph (3). The General Rule is that "There shall be allowed as a deduction any charitable contributions . . . payment of which is made within the taxable year." Section 170 (b) (1) (A) and (B) provides that taxpayers may deduct 20% from adjusted gross income for contributions to any 501 (c) organization and 30% [a] for certain qualifying organizations.[b]

THE 5-YEAR CARRY-OVER

On January 1, 1964, a new paragraph, wonderfully advantageous for certain 501 (c) organizations, was added to the Code. This is section 170 (b) (5) (A), which permits individuals who make contributions which qualify for the 30% deduction to carry over any excess beyond this limitation in equal amounts each year for not more than 5 additional years. Such contributions must be made [c] (1) to an instrumentality of government; (2) to a 501 (c) (3) organization; (3) to an association of war veterans; (4) to a fraternal society; or (5) to a non-profit cemetery.

This means that a man with adjusted gross income of $30,000 may present his church, college, or other qualifying charity with an item of property appraised at $54,000 and take deductions of $9,000 in each

---

[a] Cf. section 170 (b) (5) (A).
[b] As specified in *ib.* 170 (b) (1) (A).
[c] Cf. *ib.* 170 (c) (1).

317

of 6 successive years. Thus it becomes vastly more advantageous for donors to present large gifts to their favorite charities.

By making a full carry-over contribution for several years in succession, a man can qualify for the "Unlimited Charitable Deduction."

THE UNLIMITED DEDUCTION

Section 170 (b) (1) (B) is followed by subparagraph (C) which establishes what is known as the Unlimited Charitable Deduction, under which any taxpayer who has contributed 90% of his taxable income during 8 of the 10 preceding years to charity may deduct an unlimited proportion of his income during subsequent years, even when the contribution is to his own controlled foundation. Note that this ratio refers neither to gross nor to adjusted, but only to taxable, income, which is often far smaller. Since many wealthy men are able, by utilizing the loopholes in the Code, to reduce their taxable income to a very small amount, relatively small contributions are often sufficient to confer upon them the right to use the Unlimited Deduction to build up their own foundations.

RICHES FROM GIVING

Sections 642 (c) and 643 (a) (3) provide that a donor may give highly appreciated stocks or other assets of any kind to his church or other qualifying charity and be credited with deductions at full present market or appraised valuations without paying any capital gains tax. Section 651 provides that a donor may give an income-producing asset under the terms described in section 170 (b) (5) and 170 (c) and 642 (c) and still receive all revenues produced by it for life, after which these will accrue to the charity. Such an asset, of course, would also be excludable from an estate for the purpose of computing estate- or inheritance-taxation.

A wealthy man may, therefore, give industrial stocks which cost him $10,000 but are now worth $100,000 to his church; he receives the full 30% deduction from his adjusted gross income; the revenue from this is then paid to him for life, and, at his death, is excludable from his taxable estate.

By this device, churches and other exempts have been enriched by billions; and individual donors have actually been able to increase their wealth by millions of dollars over what they would have retained or left to their heirs had they given nothing at all.

TAX-EXEMPT GIFTS AND BEQUESTS

Section 2522 provides that gifts in any amount to organizations which qualify the donor for the 30% charitable deduction are exempt from gift-taxation, which may reach 57¾% (section 2502 (a)). Section 2055 provides that in computing taxable estates, any portion willed to one of these entities is likewise excludable.

CHURCHES IN BUSINESS

We have already emphasized that churches, associations or conventions of churches, and sacerdotal orders are granted powers and immunities under the Internal Revenue Code which give them unequal status on the American scene. They are permitted to operate as self-contained empires above and beyond the law, totally without restriction, and accountable to no one. They can own and operate hotels, race tracks, steel mills, canneries, newspapers, publishing houses, luxury retirement homes, shopping centers, or any other kind of business enterprise whatsoever, not only without taxation, but also without disclosure, particularly to their own contributing memberships.

Let us then enumerate briefly some of the popular methods by which churches are now penetrating and infiltrating the world of business, *en masse*.

LIQUOR AND GAMBLING

In the 1954 Code, churches were explicitly excused from paying taxes on profits derived from bingo and other wagering, under section 4211 (a), or for admissions to athletic events, under section 4233 (a) (1). These sections have now been deleted, since they are superfluous under section 511 (a) (2) (A) and the all-inclusive exclusion of section 6033 (a) (1), which eliminate the need for any reports by churches concerning any kind of business activity. Many Roman Catholic churches operate full-scale gambling casinos on their premises and derive huge profits from the sale of alcoholic beverages.

THE PURCHASE AND LEASEBACK

One of the more popular devices by which exempts, and particularly churches, may cooperate with businessmen for their mutual enrichment through tax-avoidance, is known as the purchase-and-leaseback. A man or a corporation has, let us say, operated a hotel, a shopping center, or other facility for ten years, or until most of the depreciation has been exhausted; a church (or other non-profit entity) then purchases it for, say, $1 million of borrowed money and leases it back to the operator at a rental which exceeds the payments necessary to liquidate the mortgage. The original owner pays the taxes, insurance, and all other upkeep. By this maneuver, in effect, he transforms even the land he has sold into a depreciable asset; and he has $1 million (less a capital gains tax) for new investment. In 20 years, the church obtains, without lifting a finger, $200,000 of current profit plus a capital gain of $1 million. The particular advantage enjoyed by a church over most other charities is that it need not divulge such transactions to any one. The cooperating parties to these leasebacks may well avoid more in taxes in 20 years than the property is worth.

We describe a number of such arrangements in Chapter 8. Known instances are numerous and increasing. For example, the Southern Baptist Convention purchased the Burlington Mills of North Carolina and leased them back to the previous owner for 20 years. In 1964, the Roman Catholic diocese of Austin, Texas, acquired a chain of 22 Massachusetts nursing homes and immediately leased them back to the former owner, Geriatics Management, Inc. We know of a great many such transactions, but these are undoubtedly only a small proportion of the total already consummated.

BUSINESS FRONTS

An even more lucrative possibility may be realized by a church or an organization created on the pretense of being one which may lend some money at exorbitant interest to establish a business, which thereafter in perpetuity pays not only *this* tribute to the church but also 30% of its adjusted gross income—all deductible by the business and non-reportable by the recipient. In this manner, the fact of substantive church-ownership may be effectively and permanently concealed.

For example, in a certain western state it was widely rumored and generally believed that a powerful church in the area furnished the original capital to establish a cement block company, operated by two partners, who were the owners of record. With the cooperation of the Church hierarchy, the assets and revenues of the company grew into a multi-million-dollar enterprise. The business could pay heavy interest on the loan continuously and, in addition, contribute 30% of adjusted gross income as a deductible gift from the partners to the Church each year. The partners thus avoided most of their own income taxation.

The same church has substantive ownership of a California horse-breeding ranch which, a few years ago, produced a thoroughbred which won the Kentucky Derby. Thirty per cent of all net earnings became tax-deductible contributions to the Church.

It is rumored—but cannot easily be documented—that the same Church actually controls chains of super markets and drug stores, a huge savings and loan association, and various other businesses under similar arrangements.

We know that the American wing of the Jesuit order owns at least 28 universities and extensive investments in radio, T-V, and in rich wineries and distilleries. The extent of their portfolio cannot be determined exactly, but it must be fantastic.

According to an article published in 1958 by the powerful German periodical, *Der Spiegel,* this order has wide-ranging investments in many of the largest corporations in the United States, particularly oil and aircraft manufacturing, with totals running into the billions. According to the author, A. P. Giannini was simply acting as an agent for the Jesuits when he organized the Bank of Italy (now the Bank of America), a financial colossus still controlled by the Order. If this is true, then this institution is probably the largest religious business front in the world.

THE CHURCH AS A TAX-UMBRELLA

Let us examine another device for tax-avoidance now becoming exceedingly popular and available only to religious organizations and those who work hand-in-glove with them. A businessman with a manufacturing or mercantile establishment which operates with leased equipment or an inventory purchased on credit—and therefore virtually without equity—sells this enterprise with no down payment to a religious entity for $200,000. He is now the manager of a business with a net income of $20,000 a year, which he turns over to the purchaser, which then simply returns it. This money is no longer earned income but a capital gain, which is immune to Social Security taxation and only half of which need be reported under adjusted gross income. He deducts $3,000 as exemptions for the members of his family; another $2,000 as taxes, interest on his house-mortgage, and for other obligations; miscellaneous deductions total $1,500; finally, in appreciation, he makes a $1,000 deductible contribution to the church. The remaining $2,500, when reported as joint income with his wife, creates a tax-liability of about $370.

Had he continued as before, his income and SS taxes would be nearly $5,000 a year; now, he can invest his additional income in tax-free securities, and, in 20 years, create an estate of perhaps $200,000 more than he would otherwise have been able to accumulate. In the meantime, the "church" obtains $20,000 in contributions —all tax-exempt. And, at the end of 10 years, the "manager" can buy back the business at any pre-arranged price. Since the church invests no money in the purchase of such an enterprise, there is no limit to the number it can acquire. For precise descriptions of how this is done, note our discussions in chapters 4 and 8 concerning the Stratford Retreat House, which is a classic example.

THE UNPARALLELED COMMERCIAL ADVANTAGES

These and other bizarre business transactions, available to churches and sacerdotal orders, are, of course, only a small fraction of those commercial enterprises by which religion is reaping the harvests of Mammon. Thousands of these are prospering and growing because their owners are immune to taxation and disclosure.

The preferences, advantages, immunities, and exemptions now accorded various religious personnel and their organizations under our Internal Revenue Code may not yet place them quite in the same category with the hierarchy of the Holy Roman Empire; but they are certainly sufficient to make of them a uniquely privileged class.

And we might add that even these advantages seem insignificant compared to the enormous sums the federal government is now channeling into ecclesiastical organizations by back-door methods in spite of the Constitutional provision which prohibits such grants.

And should certain powerful religious groups obtain the funds for which they are now clamoring to support and expand their sectarian education and indoctrination, the time will soon be upon us when these American clerics will have outdistanced all their predecessors in the advantages, immunities, preferences, political influence, and economic power conferred upon them illegally by our government at the expense of the general public.

ADDENDUM—THE TAX REFORM BILL OF 1969

The Tax Reform Bill of 1969, passed by the House on August 7 and transmitted to the Senate for consideration, contains the following alterations: (1) the right of churches and conventions and associations of churches to operate untaxed and unreported unrelated business has been deleted from section 511 (a) (2) (A); (2) however, they are granted a 5-year moratorium for divestiture and may continue to operate existing businesses as usual until 1976; (3) furthermore, no audits are ever to be made of church records and it is clearly implied that no church will be required to make any report concerning unrelated business even after the moratorium expires; (4) it is very significant that no one in the IRS below the status of District Director may even question a church because of its violations of the Code, and we know from observation that the Service has shown little interest in or concern over the unlawful activities of church-related organizations; (5) although many other 501 (c) organizations, such as fraternal societies, social clubs, and many types of membership organizations will be taxed even on passive investment income, churches are specifically exempted from this requirement; and (6) only that portion of any real estate or other income-producing property still financed by borrowed money will be subject to taxation. Since the net income from real estate is very small while heavy interest payments are being made, the tax during this period will be negligible; and, as the mortgage is liquidated from depreciation, the levy will be reduced proportionately as church equity and revenue increase. Finally, churches are even to be granted a 15 year moratorium from taxation on leaseback operations.

All this constitutes perhaps 10% or 15% of what we advocate in this book. It is obviously far less than the people of this country have rightly expected. It is an emasculation of real reform. We hope that the Senate will at least reduce the moratorium to one year, require all churches to report fully all unrelated business activity just as individuals and other corporations must, and give any IRS agent the right to audit church reports. Churches should also be taxed on investment income, like clubs, fraternities, and other membership organizations.

Yet what has been done is at least a miniscule beginning—one which would never have occurred, except for the labors of Americans United for Separation of Church and State.

INDEX

325

Ariz. Prot. Council of Churches, grants to, 261
Ariz. State U., scandal at, 255–256
Arrington, W. Russell, 57
Aryans, 16
Assessments on private home in Buffalo, 90
A. T. & T., 230
Athens, ancient, no taxes in, 18
Atlanta, x, 117
Atomic Energy Commission, grants of, 268
Augsburg Publishing House, 77, 179, 213, 279
Austria, 22, 31

Baker, Earl, Assessor, Salt Lake Co., 208
Baltimore, x, 53; (note) 53; (note) 66; (note) 90; analysis of, 100–108; semi-southern background of, 100; riots in, 101; fire in, 101; religious history of, 101; 184; budget of, 299–300
Baltimore and Ohio RR., 103
Bank of America, 233
Baptist Convention of Texas, 251–252
Baptist Foundation of America, 249
Baptist Joint Committee, declaration of, 49
Baptist publishing enterprise, 73
Baptists, 29
Barlow, Joel, 128
Barnes, Wilson, Judge, ruling of, in Murray case, 66–68
Beacon Press, 213
Beatitudes, the, retirement home in Phoenix, Ariz., 225
Bell Tel. Co. of Ill., 55
Belleville, Ill., Ministerial Alliance, 277
Bemis Bags, 217

Benedictines, 41, 241, 309
Bernardin, Bishop Joseph L., 194
Bethel Af. Meth. Epis. Ch., 224
Bethel Baptist Church, Housing Corporation of, in D. of C., 201
Betts, the Rev. Darby, 225, 226
Bezy, Father Gregory, 241
Bigotry in American colonies, 27–28
Billy Graham Christian Crusade Complex, 179
Biltmore Hotel of Dayton, 217
Bingo, Church income from, 197
Birmingham, 117
Blake, Eugene Carson, 45, 46–47, 49, 61
Bonneville Dam, 146
Borden Co., the, 217
Boston, taxes in, x, 116; analysis of, 120–127; heavy taxes in, 127, 161
Boston College High School, 126
Boston College, the Jesuit, 121
Boston, the House of the Archbishop in, 126
Boulder Presbytery, camp of, 215
Bowers, Elaine, viii
Boyer, Harry, of AFL-CIO, 58
Boys Town of Nebraska, 235
Brahmanas, Brahmanism, influence of upon Catholic Ch., 17–18
Breasted, James Henry, 14
Bridgeport Brass Co., 239
Brigham Young Un., 204
British Isles, 22
Broadman Press, 213
Broadway Temple, AME., 266
Brothers of Christian Instruction, denied exemption, 74–75
Brown, Father Henry, 194
Brown, Joe, realtor, gift of, to church, 219
Brown University, 134, 135

Channing, William Ellery, 120
Chapultepec, Palace of, 24
Chavenelle, Gilbert, City Manager of Dubuque, statement of, 54
Cheops and Khafre, pyramids of, 13
Chicago, 239, 260
Chiniquy, Father, 30
Christ Church Cathedral in St. Louis, 142
Christ of the Gospels, the, in Graeco-Roman world, 18–19
Christian Beacon, The, 219
Christian Brothers, the, 41; case of, 69–71; largest producer of wines, brandies, 69; paid tax, 70; sued for refund, 70; forced to pay full tax, 70–71; Judge Halbert's decision concerning, 71, 268, 309, 312
Christian Gospel, the, espoused church-state separation, 18
Christian Scientists, position of, on taxation, 49; in W. Philadelphia, 75; in Germantown, 75
Christianity, the religions antedating, 13
Christianity Today, 199, 216–217
Christians, dissident, persecuted, 20
Christopher Homes, the K. of C., 239–240; (note) 273
Christ's Church of the Golden Rule, communal policies of, 254–255
Christ's Episcopal Church in Cleveland, wealth of, 214
Church, a, definition of, 281–282
Church affiliation, ratio of, in U.S., 184
Church business, typical, unrelated, 43–44
Church commercial property in D. of C., estimate of value of, 202–203

Church income from voluntary contributions, estimate of, 198; by principal divisions, 198; passive and active business defined, 210; unrelated business of, growing, 210–211
Church of Jesus Christ of Latter-Day Saints; see Latter-Day Saints
Church of Lady of Guadalupe, 25
Church of Our Merciful Saviour, the, obtained loan for repairs, 266
Church retirement homes, discussion concerning, 222–225
Church subsidies, termination of, 285
Church, the, as a tax-umbrella, 321–322; purchase by, of business without investment, 321–322; how this operates in typical case, 321–322
Church, the changing American, 275–277
Church Triumphant, The, 17
Church Wealth and Business Income, ix, 62, 109, 183, 188
Church wealth, property, and income, growth of, 35–36; division of, 35–37; ancient and modern growth of, 37–38; never ceases to expand, 45–46, 244–245; dangers of, 275; exemption of, archaic, 276; expansion of, in U.S., 294
Churches, in 14 cities, 185; unique position of, under Internal Revenue Code, 307–309
The Churchman, The, vi
Chyet, Rabbi Stanley C., 51
Cincinnati, x
Cistercian monks, business of, 240; produce White Monk Foods, 241
Cities, major, problem of taxation

328

333

ance business of, 236, 239–240; and Yankee Stadium, 239; portfolio of, 239

Know-Nothing Party, position of, 30, 101

Kshatriyas, duties of, 16

KSXX, radio station in Salt Lake City, 208

Kunes, Kenneth R., Assessor in Phoenix, 59; statement of, 256

La Foret, summer camp of, 215

Lafayette Hotel in Buffalo, 86

Land, public, sold on preference basis, 267–268

Larson, Earl, statement of, 278

Larson, Rev. Philip M., 278

Latter-Day Saints, Church of Jesus Christ of (Mormon), in Phoenix, 59; suit of (note) 59; cannery in Portland, 148; included, 192; operates businesses in concealment, 195; to build temple in Washington, 199; complex of, 203–209; history of (note) 206–207; skyscraper of, in N.Y., 213–214; Institute of, at ASU, 255–256; manipulations of, 256; corporations of, 305; form of church ownership in, 315–316

Lawrence, David L., Catholic governor of Pennsylvania, 58

Leaseback operation, the, 216–217

Legislators, fear of churches among, 56

L'Enfant, Major Pierre, 91

Lepetit Company of Milan, 227–228

L'Espresso, statement of, concerning Vatican wealth, 229

Letters to the Editor, 55

Levites and priests, Jewish, 15

Licinius, execution of, 19

Life magazine, 265

Lincoln Memorial, 91

Lincoln-Westmoreland Housing Corporation, 201

Lindbergh, Charles, 138

Lindsey, Judge Ben, 109

Lindsey, Mayor, of New York, 83

Lindstrom, Ernest, Representative, of Minnesota, 57, 179–180

Linse, Eugene W., 251

L'Instituto Farmacologico Serona, manufacturer of Pill, 227–228

Liquor and gambling business by churches, 319

Listerine Co., interest of Catholic Church in, sold, 238

Little Sisters of the Poor, 309

Loew's State Theatre of Boston, 239

Loma Linda Food Co., 217

Lord Baltimore, a converted Episcopalian, 29, 100

Loretto Heights College, 261

Los Angeles, x

Louick, Maurice, 52

Louis XV, King of France, 138

Lowe, Julian, president of LDS stake, 199

Lowell, Dr. C. Stanley, 72

Loyola Un. of Los Angeles, commercial businesses of, 238

Lutherans, Lutheranism, Luther, 21, 22, 29; in Ramsey Co., 167, 168; in new world, 166

Lutheran Brotherhood, insurance business of, 236

Lutheran Church, the American, policy statement of, 47

Lutheran schools in Toledo, 263

Lutzen, Battle of, 22

Mack Trucks, 217

Madison, Founding Father, 28

Madonna Hall, in Cleveland, 160, 164

334

Madonna Towers of Rochester, Minn., owned by Oblate Fathers, 79, 179

Mahoney, Borden V., Assessor in Hartford, 128

Manatee Circuit Court, appeal from, 78

Manchester Guardian, the, viii

Manichaean heresy, 20

Marcionites, 20

Marden, Richard C., urged taxation, 58

Marist College of Poughkeepsie, 264

Marist Fathers, business of, 241

Marquette Un., grants to, 264

Martin's Carriage House, 201

Maryland, 29

Maryland Court of Appeals, 67, 265

Maryland Tax Court, 76

Marymount College, 265

Masonic Lodge (ritual), 160

Mass. Order of Foresters, 236

Mather, John and Cotton, 120

Maximilian, Archduke of Austria, 24

Mazzini, 23

McCabe, Charles, statements of, concerning Rev. Hensley, 250–251

McIntire, Dr. Carl, and ICCC, holdings of, 219

McKeag, George W., statement of, 48

Medders, Ernest, bilked Poor Sisters of St. Francis, 252–253

Meddles, Owen, 249

Mellon, fortune of, 151

Mellon Institute, the, 156

Memphis, 117

Mercyhurst College, 263

Merriam Park Presb. Church of St. Paul, 167, 278

Methodist Church, Board of Christian Concerns of, 48; publishing enterprise of, in Nashville, 73; bookstore of, in Portland, 76; apartments owned by, 202, 214

Medieval Church, power structure of, 276

Mexican-Americans in Denver, 109

Mexico, 45, 47

Michaux, Elder Solomon Lightfoot, 201

Mid-City Baptist Church of New Orleans, 247

Mills, Wilbur, 48, 219, 280

Milwaukee Sentinel, The, 238

Ministers and rabbis, immunities of, 42, 103, 314

Minneapolis, 166; analysis of, 174–180, 187; budget of, 301

Minnesota, the State House Tax Subcommittee, report of, 53; Council of Churches of, 49, 179; Supreme Court, decision of, 79

Missouri and Mississippi Rivers, 137

Mitchell, L. B., Chief Deputy, Bd. of Revision and Tax Assessments, Cleveland, 159, 160

Mitchell-Lama Act, 85, 166

Mobile, 117

Moe, Gordon E., Assessor in Minneapolis, 175

Monongahela River, 151

Montana Constitution, provisions of (note), 55; (note), 74

Montgomery Co., Ohio, 53

Moretti, Professor Luigi, Vatican troubleshooter, 200

Mormons; see Latter-Day Saints

Most Precious Blood, Church of, raided by police, 197

Mott, Calif. State Parks Director William Penn, 248

Mt. Airy Baptist Church, high-rise apartment complex of, 201

Mt. Alverno Convent, 78

Mt. Olivet Lutheran Church in Minneapolis, 179

Mt. Olivet Methodist Church of Arlington, 219

Mt. St. Joseph Academy, in Buffalo, 86

Multnomah Co., budget of, 301

Murphy, Justice William, statement of, in re Madonna Towers, 79

Muskingum Presbytery of Ohio, 214

Mussolini paid Vatican $90 million and entered into concordat with it, 24

Mutual Protective Insurance Co. of Omaha (Cath.), 236

Napoleon III, 24

Nashville, x, 117; Protestant publishing business in, 73; sought to tax church property, 73; new attempts in, under way, 73

Nassau Plastics and Wire Co., 220

Natchez-Hattiesburg diocese, antipoverty funds for, 260

NASA, grants of, 268

National Association of Evangelical Churches, 49

National Council of Churches, skyscraper owned by, 218

National Council of Churches and U.S. Catholic Conference, joint statement of, in re taxation of unrelated business church income, 49–50

National Defense Education Act, 259

National Federation of Priests Councils, 194

National Geographic Soc., 91, 96, 286

National Register, estimate of, in re value of Catholic schools, 34, 110; business of, 237; tax-exemptions of, 237

National Science Foundation, 268

Negroes in cities, 84, 92, 100–101, 109, 116, 120, 123, 128, 138, 148, 152, 159, 167, 175, 184

Netterville, William M., 249

New Amsterdam, 1st name of Hartford, 128

New Haven Railway, 239

New Jersey, revenue problems of, 58; League of Municipalities in, 59; church income from bingo in, 197

New Mexico Council of Churches, grants to, 261

New Orleans, 138

New Testament Scripture, 18

New Thought groups, 192

New York, constitution of, 75; ruling of Supreme Court of, 86, 263; Catholic archdiocese in, 193; Stock Exchange, 213; welfare program in, 267

Newton Asphalt Co., 202

Niagara Circle in Buffalo, 86

Niagara Falls, 83

Nichols, Dr. Roy, statement of, 51

Nicholson, Judge Dana, ruling of, 77

Nielsen, Rev. L. Henry, 279

Ninth Amendment, 72

Northern Kingdom of Israel, 15

Northwestern University, 55, 109

Notre Dame of Maryland, 265, 266

Nunlist, Edward, Executive Director, Board of Property Assessments in Pittsburgh, 152

Nursing homes acquired by Catholic diocese of Austin, Texas, 223

Oberhansley, Rex, Utah legislator, 208

Oblate Fathers, owners of Madonna Towers, 179; litigation of, concerning taxation on Towers, 179–180; required to pay tax by Minn. Supreme Court; business of, 242

Obregon, assassinated by Catholic fanatic, 24

Oddfellow Lodge (ritual), 160

Office of Economic Opportunity, funds distributed by, 260–262, 271, 272

Office of Education, grants of, 265, 268

Official Catholic Directory, 84, 101, 121, 126, 128, 138, 148, 164, 184, 312

O'Hair, Madalyn Murray, 66–68

O'Hayes, Budget Director Frederick, of N.Y., 54

Ohio River, 151

Old South Church, 123

Old Stone Presbyterian Church of Cleveland, 163

Olson, Earl E., Assistant Historian of LDS Church, 195

Ontario Study, The, 59–61

Oral Roberts University, 265

Orders, R. C. religious, 231–234

Oregon, Oregonians, legislature of, considered bill to tax churches, 59; ruling of Supreme Court in, 76; tax-conscious and democratic, 146; voted to outlaw parochial schools, 147

Oregon *Journal*, 149

Opus Dei, businesses of, 235

Orsinger, Victor J., bilked Society of the Divine Saviour, 253–254

Ormsby, Msgr. J. Stanley, 194

Osiris, 13; priests of, 14–15

Otis, James, 120

Our Lady of Rosary Church, in Buffalo, 194; of the Rockies Camp, 215; of the Snows, business of, 241–242

Outcastes, 16

Pagan temples razed, 20

Papacy, 24

Parker, Theodore, 120

Parochial schools, federal subsidies to, 263–264

Parsonages, as thing concerning, in IR Code, 42; tax policies of states toward, 75–76

Patristic literature, 20

Paul, St., teaching of, 19

Paulians, 20

Paulician heresy, 21

Pauly, Mr. Luke, Assessor in Buffalo, concern of, 84, 86

Pavlak, Gerald, 194

Peachtree Hotel given Baptists, 217

Peden Corp., 248

Pennsylvania, church tax-exemptions in, 58; Supreme Court of, ruling, 75; subsidies in, to church schools, 267

Pepsi Cola plant, 55

Perry, Dr. Woodrow, 51

Persians, 16

Peterson, Leonard L., Principal Clerk in Office of Assessor in St. Paul, 166

Pharaoh, 14

Philadelphia, 54, 261

Phoenix, x

Pikes Peak, 108

Pilgrim's Inn, 242

Pine Crest camp, 215

Pirates, the Pittsburgh, 153

Pittsburgh, x; (note) 52; analysis of, 151–158, 161, 167, 187, 215, 224

Plymouth Rock, 28

Poe, Edgar Allan, 116
Poland, Poles, 21, 31, 84, 128, 152
Police, N.Y., raided Church of the Most Precious Blood, 197
Poor Sisters of St. Francis Seraph, bilked by Medders, 252–253; wealth of, 252; grants to, by government, 253
Pope Pius, vi, 23; Innocent III, 21; Paul, 194; bequest to, 197
Population and church communicants in U.S., 289
Porter, Adele, viii, 259
Portland, x; taxes Methodist book store, 76, 123, 187, 189; analysis of, 146–151
Portugal, no revolution in, 25
Post, the Washington, story in, 201, 205; editorial in, 282; the Denver, story in, 227–228
Potomac Plaza in Washington, 99, 200
Powers, Assessor Ronald V., 242
Presbyterians, 29; Ministers Fund, 236; *Life,* statement of, 235; the United, Church, 277–278; the Meadowville of Louisville, 279
Press, the Pittsburgh, 153
Priests, celibate, tax-free mansions and income of, 315–316
Printing Industries Assn. of San Diego, 218
Property assessments, in 4 cities, 181; changes in, 182; compared to tax-budgets, 190; of churches, 285
Protestant denominations, 28, 29; growth of, 31; membership and bodies of, 32–33; New York Study of, 50; financial reports of, 196
Protestant Episcopal Church, 212
Protestant upheaval in Washington, 92

Protestantism, Minneapolis, pre-eminence of, 178–179
Protestants, ratio and properties of, 192
Providence, x; (note) 90; analysis of, 132–137, 161
Provincial Council, the Second Catholic, 31
Public schools in Mass. virtually donated to R. C. Church, 268
Pupils in Catholic schools, 185
Purchase-and-Leaseback, the, 43, 319–320
Puritan Church of Peoria, Ill., 250
Puritanism, the Boston, 120

Quakers persecuted in Virginia, 27, 29
Quebec Act, provisions of, 30

REA co-op, 309
Reader's Digest, viii
Real Form Girdle Co., owned by the Cathedral of Tomorrow, 220
Redemptorist Fathers, bequest to, 197
Reed, Louis, statement of, 234
Reform, crying need for, 256
Reformation, purpose of, 21–22
Reformed Church of America, 212
Reforms, in property taxation, suggested, 285–286
Regis College, 261
Register, Norman, 74
Regulations, the Administrative, of the IRS, 303, 309–310
Rehoboam, revolt against, 15
Reincarnation, doctrine of, 17
Religious and racial composition of 14 cities, 184
Religious exemptions, special, in IRC, 314–315
Religious membership in 14 cities, 291

338

St. Michaels College, 267

St. Paul, x; analysis of, 165–174, 175, 179

St. Paul's Episcopal Church in Washington, 202; in Richmond, 214; retirement home of, in San Diego, 223–224; Towers, 225, 226

St. Peters Fishing Lures, 241

Salisbury, Franklin, viii

Salt Lake City, x, 203, 316

Salt Lake Co., exempt property in, 208–209

Salt River Project, 309

Samaria, 15

San Antonio, Texas, 76

San Diego, x

San Francisco, 108, 146

San Pasquel Academy of San Diego, 217–218

Sansone, Joseph, St. Louis Assessor, 279

Santa Maria Camp, 215

Savannah, x, 117

Saxton, John, 238

Schiotz, Dr. Frederick, 48

School District of Abington vs. Schemp, 67

Schumacher, William R., a Catholic layman, statement of, 51

Seattle, x, 205

Securities and Exchange Commission, 247–248, 254

Sedita, Mayor, of Buffalo, 83

Separated Brethren, 19

Serbia, Serbians, 152, 159

Seventh-Day Adventist Church, business complex to be built by, 200–201, 217

Seversmith vs. Machiz, case of, 71–72

Shaker Savings Assn., 214

Shale oil industry, 109

Sheen, Bishop Fulton J., 50

Sheraton Hotel of New Haven, 239

Sherman, Francis H., 56–57

Shrine of the Immaculate Conception, 97

Shriver, R. Sargent, statement of, 260

Sibley Hospital, 201

Siegienski, Msgr. Joseph, 53

Sister Kenny Foundation, 178

Sisters of the Blessed Sacrament, grant to, 260

Sisters of Bon Secour, 89; (note), 89

Sisters of Mercy, 201–202

Sisters of St. Francis, 77–78

Sisters of St. Vincent de Paul, 197

Sisters of the Poor, 312

Slovakians, 159

Smith, Ernest D., Maine legislator, 56

Smith, Gerald G. LDS stake president, 213

Smith, Joseph Fielding, letter to, 195

Smith, Percy L., Office Manager, Assessor in Richmond, 56, 117

Social Security, 42

Società General Immobiliare, a church holding company, 72; not taxed, 72, 99, 227; builder of Watergate Towne, 200

Societies and associations, Catholic, 235

Society for Propagation of the Faith, 196; of the Divine Saviour, 201; bilked, 253–254

Son of Man, reaction of, 287

South America, 24, 25

South Georgia (Meth.) Conference, 217

South Park Baptist Church of Houston, 75–76

Southern Baptist Convention, Study